KEY TO THE HANDBOOK

D1452488

THE MACMILLAN

HANDBOOK OF ENGLISH

THE MACMILLAN
HANDBOOK OF
ENGLISH Seventh Edition

Robert F. Willson, Jr.
University of Missouri–Kansas City

John M. Kierzek
Late of Oregon State University

W. Walker Gibson
University of Massachusetts

Macmillan Publishing Co., Inc.
NEW YORK

Macmillan Publishing Co., Inc.
866 Third Avenue, New York, New York 10022

Collier Macmillan Canada, Inc.

Library of Congress Cataloging in Publication Data

Willson, Robert Frank (date)
  The Macmillan Handbook of English.
  Sixth ed. (1977) by John M. Kierzek.
  Bibliography: p.
  Includes index.
  1. English language—Rhetoric.   2. English
language—Grammar, 1950–   . I. Kierzek, John M.,
1891–   . II. Gibson, Walker. III. Kierzek,
John M., 1891–   . Macmillan handbook of
English. IV. Title.
PE1408.W6144 1982   808'.042   81–6016
ISBN 0–02–428140–9   AACR2

ACKNOWLEDGMENTS

The American Heritage Dictionary of the English Language, entry for the word *cool.* © 1980 by Houghton Mifflin Company. Reprinted by permission from *The American Heritage Dictionary of the English Language.*

The Atlantic Monthly, book review for *Soldiers of the Night* by David Schoenbrun. Copyright © 1980, by The Atlantic Monthly Company, Boston, Mass. Reprinted with permission.

Cheryl Boes, "Skewed Language." Used by permission of the author.

Jennifer Borron, "Words, Words, Words: Shakespeare's Contribution to Our Language." Used by permission of the author.

Audrey C. Foote, "Notes on the Distaff Side." Used by permission of the author. Copyright ©

1976, by The Atlantic Monthly Company, Boston, Mass. Reprinted with permission.

Alice Griffin, *Rebels and Lovers: Shakespeare's Young Heroes and Heroines.* Reprinted by permission of New York University Press from *Rebels and Lovers: Shakespeare's Young Heroes and Heroines* by Alice Griffin. Copyright © 1976 by New York University.

John Gunther, *Inside Russia Today.* Harper & Brothers, 1958. Used by permission of Harper & Row, Publishers, Inc.

Nancy Hale, "The Two-Way Imagination." Reprinted from *The Saturday Evening Post.* © 1961 The Curtis Publishing Company.

Ernest Hemingway, "Big Two-Hearted River, Part 1." From Ernest Hemingway, *In Our Time.* Copyright 1925, 1930 by Charles Scribner's Sons;

ACKNOWLEDGMENTS

copyright renewed 1953, 1958 by Ernest Hemingway (New York: Charles Scribner's Sons, 1930). Reprinted with the permission of Charles Scribner's Sons.

Herbert Hoover, *The Memoirs of Herbert Hoover: Years of Adventure.* Copyright 1951 by Herbert Hoover. Herbert Hoover Presidential Library Foundation, Leesburg, Virginia.

Alfred Kazin, from *A Walker in the City,* copyright 1951, 1979, by Alfred Kazin. Reprinted by permission of Harcourt Brace Jovanovich, Inc.

Joseph Wood Krutch, *The Great Chain of Life.* From *The Great Chain of Life* by Joseph Wood Krutch. Copyright © 1956 by Joseph Wood Krutch. Reprinted by permission of Houghton Mifflin Company.

Allan Nevins and Henry Steele Commager, *A Pocket History of the United States.* Copyright © 1951, 1956, 1966 by Allan Nevins and Henry Steele Commager. Reprinted by permission of Pocket Books, a Simon & Schuster division of Gulf & Western Corporation.

The New Yorker, review of movie "The Eyes of Laura Mars," May 5, 1980. Reprinted by permission; © 1980 The New Yorker Magazine, Inc.

Norman Podhoretz, "My Negro Problem—and Ours." Reprinted by permission of Farrar, Straus and Giroux, Inc. Excerpt from *Doings and Undoings* by Norman Podhoretz. Copyright © 1953, 1954, 1955, 1956, 1957, 1958, 1959, 1962, 1963, 1964 by Norman Podhoretz.

Random House Dictionary of the English Language, entry for the word *crowd.* Reprinted by permission of Random House, Inc., from *Random House Dictionary of the English Language.* Copyright 1947, copyright © 1966, 1973.

Bertrand Russell, *Education and the Good Life.* Copyright 1926 by Horace Liveright, Inc. Copyright renewed 1954 by Bertrand Russell.

Terry Sickel, "Bigot." Used by permission of the author.

Vilhjalmur Stefansson, from *Hunters of the Great North,* copyright 1922, 1950 by Vilhjalmur Stefansson. Reprinted by permission of Harcourt Brace Jovanovich, Inc.

Virginia Stoker, "Law and Disorder." Used by permission of the author.

Harold S. Ulen and Guy Larcom, Jr., *The Complete Swimmer,* 1949. Reprinted by permission of Macmillan Publishing Co., Inc.

Webster's New Collegiate Dictionary, entries for the words *formicary, formidable,* and *stiff.* By permission. From *Webster's New Collegiate Dictionary* © 1981 by G. & C. Merriam Company, publishers of the Merriam-Webster dictionaries.

Webster's New World Dictionary, entry for the word *pull.* With permission. From *Webster's New World Dictionary,* Second College Edition. Copyright © 1980 by Simon & Schuster, Inc.

William Carlos Williams, "To Waken an Old Lady." From *Collected Earlier Poems of William Carlos Williams.* Copyright 1938 by New Directions Publishing Corporation. Reprinted by permission of New Directions.

Richard Wright, "The Ethics of Living Jim Crow" from *Uncle Tom's Children,* copyright 1937. Used by permission of Harper & Row, Publishers, Inc., New York, New York.

Printing: 1 2 3 4 5 6 7 8   Year: 2 3 4 5 6 7 8 9

Preface

The seventh edition of *The Macmillan Handbook of English* marks a departure from the format of previous editions. Although the book remains a combined rhetoric and handbook dedicated to the propagation of precise, effective writing, the rhetoric section has been redesigned to move students from study of words and phrases, sentences, and paragraphs to composition of the whole essay. The introductory chapter of the rhetoric, "The Task of Writing," has changed focus accordingly, covering such essential matters as organization, tone, precision, and clarity, as well as addressing the important questions of gender and pronoun choice. Many outdated illustrations of formal and informal usage, most of which were taken from speeches rather than essays, have been replaced with more current examples of writing.

Other illustrative material has been added to subsequent chapters. I have introduced a short discussion of the history of the language to give students some notion of the development and sources of English words and phrases. Exercises in sentence combining have been added to the section on subordination in Chapter 3, "The Sentence," in the rhetoric. Chapter 5 now provides a thorough list of subjects for writing, along with class-tested suggestions for treating these subjects. Students may also trace the evolution of an entire essay from prewriting to proofreading. For the first time the rhetoric includes a chapter on writing themes about literature and film; this chapter offers definitions of important literary terms, suggested critical approaches, and a list of books for further study. The research paper chapter remains essentially the same, except for the substitution of a new, informative sample paper on Shakespeare's contribution to our language.

Section II, "A Handbook of Writing and Revision," now deals exclusively with specific writing, spelling, and mechanical problems and their correction. Material treating paragraph development has been incorporated into Chapter 4, "The Paragraph," in the rhetoric. New exercises designed to give students more practice in correcting errors have been added to the various subsections. The "Guide to Usage" has been updated to include and comment on the latest abuses of the language; the chapter on letter form and the résumé has been removed to an appendix.

I believe the seventh edition of *The Macmillan Handbook of English* is a fuller, more coherent and useful text than past editions. It could not have been revised without the help of many composition instructors who took the time to provide me with constructive and clearly stated suggestions. I would particularly like to thank Ms. Pat Brayman and Mr. Ted Otteson of the University of Missouri–Kansas City English Department for their sound ideas and assistance. To my editor, Anthony English, goes deep appreciation for his careful review of the manuscript and his many sound and witty revisions. Ms. Helen Bennett of the University of Missouri–Kansas City General Library gave expert assistance in locating reference books and journals; to her I extend heartfelt thanks.

Robert F. Willson, Jr.

Contents

CONTENTS

Chapter 4
The Paragraph

132

Chapter 5
Problems of Subject and Focus

161

xi

Chapter 6
Problems of Composing

Chapter 7
Writing Themes About Literature and Film

Chapter 8
The Research Paper

CONTENTS

SECTION II
A HANDBOOK OF WRITING AND REVISION   297

Chapter 9
Grammar and Usage   299

CONTENTS

Chapter 10
Mechanics

Chapter 11
Punctuation

CONTENTS

xvii

A RHETORIC

FOR

WRITING

1 | *The Task*

of Writing

INTRODUCTION

For most of us the direction to write about anything instills panic and incurable writer's cramp. Perhaps our fears are traceable to the realization that expressing ourselves on paper means putting our personalities or "souls" on the line for others to criticize. We would rather hide behind a comfortable mask than speak up and have others point their accusing fingers at us. In many situations, after all, the quiet, pensive person receives considerable credit for *appearing* to be wise. Joan Didion, a professional writer, describes the harsh demands of her craft:

> In many ways writing is the act of saying *I,* of imposing oneself upon other people, of saying *listen to me, see it my way, change your mind.* It's an aggressive, even a hostile act. You can disguise its aggressiveness all you want . . . but there's no getting around the fact that setting words on paper is the tactic of a secret bully, an invasion, an imposition of the writer's sensibility on the reader's most private space.
>
> —"Why I Write"

Ms. Didion's statement dramatizes especially well the dilemma of the student writer called upon by his or her instructor to write a thousand-word theme calling for reform of television programming. The student may have an opinion or several opinions, but most students are not secret bullies and tend to shy away from people who are.

They are particularly wary about invading someone else's private space, and certainly do not want anyone invading theirs. Yet the ability to express oneself clearly and persuasively in written form not only guarantees the award of high grades in English courses but means probable success in the business and professional worlds. Remaining behind that comfortable mask surely has more disadvantages than putting on the guise of a bully for the writing occasion.

Yet there are ways of invading your reader's space without necessarily playing the bully or endangering anyone's fragile personality. Writing is a craft, comparable to dancing or playing a musical instrument. It involves making something or performing something rather than revealing your inner being to strangers. Your opinions and beliefs are important components of any writing you may do, but a fair reader will judge those opinions more on how capably they are defended or illustrated than on whether they are proper opinions. Defense or argumentation might be called a tool needed to construct your report or essay; learning how to use language for this purpose, moreover, is easier than learning how to read a musical scale. Realizing this fact will help to demystify and depersonalize writing so that you can adopt more readily the assertive stance Ms. Didion talks about. The first section of this *Handbook* is designed as a rhetoric that provides long-recognized tools to construct the kind of expository writing that will fit your purposes in almost any situation.

Although the word *rhetoric* has been used lately to describe false or phony statements by political speakers ("That's a lot of rhetoric!"), the term's original meaning—the art of spoken or written discourse—is the one we wish to stress here. The rhetorical section of this book is designed to familiarize you with such terms as *style, tone, diction,* and *structure* and to show how these elements may be used in your own writing. Of special value are the excerpts from essays and books by professional writers like Ms. Didion; these samples illustrate just how skillfully someone can apply the elements of rhetoric.

Both professional essays and those written for English

courses are composed in a form called the *expository essay.* *Expository* refers to the act of presenting or explaining facts and ideas. Outlining the steps in changing a tire or criticizing the latest trend in movies requires the writer to use the techniques of exposition. The word *essay* comes from the Old French *essai,* which meant "an attempt or trying out," in the sense of a trial balloon. Knowing the derivation of this word will help you remember that your composition, report, or term paper will not be accepted as a work chiseled in stone but as a personal effort to convince your reader that the position taken is sound. Such writing is not creative in the sense of a poem, play, or piece of fiction, which, by the way, is more likely to reveal private feelings or biases. Yet the expository essay can and should be creative within the bounds established by its main or controlling idea. We will talk more about main and controlling ideas later.

GOOD EXPOSITORY WRITING: SOME HINTS AND A SAMPLE

There are many opinions about what constitutes good expository writing. Business leaders are likely to value facts and brevity; their time for reading is limited and they look for the bottom line. Readers of book reviews may also value brevity, but they expect in addition some critical evaluation or comparison of the reviewed book with another like it. Obviously you should not try to tailor your style to each new audience being addressed. It is, however, a sound idea to keep your audience in mind in conducting an argument, selecting details, and adopting a particular tone. In most cases you will be writing for instructors who give their definition of good writing in the form of a grade. *That* particular audience is well worth knowing and understanding!

Some generally agreed-upon qualities of good expository writing can be listed here. These characteristics are not exclusive, however. Effective writing often seems to have about it an indefinable property that emerges from the writer's ability to interest, entertain, or persuade. We assert this qualification because we do not want to imply that a successful essay will automatically take shape, like French bread or chocolate cake, from a recipe. Following the recipe for good writing will help to develop readable essays, but it will not guarantee that all of you will become William Buckleys or Mary McCarthys after a few hours of baking.

Precision and Clarity

Precision and clarity are inevitably linked because precise description of something normally makes it clear to the reader. Much of writing, after all, involves describing an event, object, idea, or opinion for someone who has only your words and imagination to go on. Wherever possible, for instance, use *concrete* instead of *general* or *abstract* words. In describing an event like an accident try to make the incident as vivid as possible: "The green, late-model Cadillac rammed the right-rear fender of the yellow Volkswagen, crumpling the fender like a collapsed accordion." How much more picturesque that sentence is than the following one: "This big car ran into a little one and wrecked it." The example is extreme but it illustrates the value of concrete details in achieving clarity and precision. The same approach should be used in essays that attempt to persuade, instruct, or entertain; often such essays require description to achieve their ends as well.

Lack of clarity may also result from errors in pronoun choice, misplaced modifiers, unparallel structure, and so forth. (These errors are discussed in the *Handbook* section.) In order to insure that you are making sense, it is probably a good idea to read your essay into a tape recorder and play it back several times. Words read aloud can be more readily visualized and assimilated; any weak links or confusing instructions should soon make themselves evident. Ideally you should enlist a friend or spouse as your guinea pig, although some sort of bribe (doing the same for

6

them?) may be required. Ask for brutal truth: Is my argument clear? Have I used words in their correct senses? Is the whole essay coherent? If the answers are NO to any of these questions, take the required time to rewrite and rearrange. Precision and clarity are the primary requirements of effective writing, and weaknesses here are most vulnerable to attack from casual readers and instructors.

Honesty

One mistake beginning writers often make is to try to impress their readers by using big words they do not understand or by adopting the third-person pronoun *one* in order to sound more impersonal and formal. This tendency is part of the masking impulse we discussed at the beginning of this chapter. The writer attempts to hide behind a mask of false authority rather than striving to find his or her own voice. Here is an example of such artificial language quoted by Edwin Newman in *A Civil Tongue:*

A young man writes to a Maine newspaper about an older man who "became an experiencing person in my life, lending an aura to my developing personality of absolute rapport and communicatory relevance."

As Newman points out, a "civil tongue" would have said that the older man was sympathetic and understanding. Unfortunately, as Newman's book makes painfully clear, our language is being abused, even damaged, by writers and speakers who have forgotten the sound of the human voice. They seek instead to impress their audiences with professional jargon and legal- or governmentese. The evidence is convincing that recognized expository writers use precise, uninflated Anglo-Saxon—not multisyllabic—words in their essays. With these words, effective writers also create metaphors or pictures that allow the reader

7

to visualize difficult concepts or emotional states. The goal of such word choices is more honest and direct communication, the kind of writing that impresses the reader with the sincerity of the writer. Write as much as possible in your own voice or manner; sharp-eyed readers will quickly detect any attempt to inflate opinions with the hot air of artificial language.

Intention

Another essential quality of effective writing is the writer's awareness of intention or purpose. Rhetoric prescribes four widely accepted purposes or aims of the essay: *exposition, argumentation, narration,* and *description.* Writers who seek to inform or explain will present facts and ideas to their readers. Most of the writing done for an English class will, as we have said, fall into the category of exposition. Essays that define political systems like socialism, outline the steps required to make a film, or compare the main characters in *Crime and Punishment* and *Great Expectations* have the specific purpose of informing and explaining. Writers who seek to convince or persuade their readers will enlist the aid of techniques used in argumentation. Such essays usually entail the testing out of a theory or thesis. Declarations that the draft should be restored or that laws against the use of marijuana must be rescinded call for support by persuasive arguments that depend more on logic and fact than on emotional appeals to like-minded people. Thinking of your audience as a jury instructed to decide only on the basis of the evidence presented will help in determining the course of your argumentative essay. Narrative essays represent action or events in chronological order and require the writer to entertain his or her audience. Short stories or novels take this form, as do essays in which the writer is asked to narrate a memorable trip or stimulating moment. Many expository and argumentative essays use narrative effectively: a criticism of airport security, for example, can best be buttressed by narrating a personal incident involving check-in or boarding procedures. Description may also be used in expository or argumentative essays to paint a detailed picture of some scene or person. Considerable meaning can be conveyed by juxtaposing (e.g., setting side by side) brushstrokes in a word picture. William Styron, in an essay about Potter's Field, the paupers' burial island near New York City, achieves an ironic comment on class differences by underscoring the discrepancy between Manhattan's skyscrapers and the obscured concrete grave markers of the poor:

> The towers of Manhattan are faint and blue in the distance, rising like minarets or monoliths; . . . . Here in the field weeds and brown, unsightly vegetation grow in thick clusters, tangled together over the numbered concrete markers. There are no proper gravestones in the meadow.
>
> —WILLIAM STYRON, "Potter's Field"

English instructors have been known to assign short exercises that require the detailed description of a leaf or of the classroom itself. Students should be advised of this possibility and begin building up their powers of observation.

By deciding in advance what your primary purpose is (often this decision is made for you by an instructor), you will know the appropriate tools of rhetoric to select for the job. This knowledge will also help to balance concerns about your audience, since a firm sense of objective can often overcome the reader's biases about word choice, organization, and tone.

Organization

Most of us must be prodded to arrange the clutter of impressions in our minds; the act of organization requires about the same degree of energy as cleaning our rooms. Discarded shirts and shoes seem to pile up, along with the dust, with a relentless force we are hard pressed to control. Jumbled opinions, ideas, beliefs, emotions—these, too, call for ordering if we are to write with skill and precision.

No doubt you have experienced the sense of dismay with which ideas tumble out of your head when someone mentions topics like abortion, defense spending, crime and punishment, or current movies. Although it may not be necessary to outline statements in a heated discussion with a friend, organizing arguments beforehand is of tremendous help when serious writing begins. If, for example, your task is to convince the reader that a certain new movie is worth seeing, decide what three or four main reasons—the exciting plot, the inspired acting, the skillful directing—you believe are most noteworthy. Then proceed to arrange these points, adding sound examples or illustrations, in a sequence of increasing importance that will build a sense of expectation into the essay. Was the inspired direction the most arresting quality? Did the acting save the film from an otherwise weak plot? Moving from *least* significant to *most* significant quality is an almost sure-fire method of giving your essay the climactic feel of a good play—or a good movie. Whether you use this method of organization or others that we will outline later, selection and decision making are essential; if everything about a certain movie seems to you equally fascinating, it will be difficult to prove to your reader that you are a dependable guide. A key question to ask is: Why did this movie impress me *more* than others I have seen lately? The answer should spur the act of ordering that will result in a readable, effective essay.

More about the prewriting activity will be presented in the next chapter, "The Process of Planning and Writing."

Tone

Speaking of movies, we have all become familiar with cliché lines that screenwriters turn to in certain dramatic situations. One favorite line is "I don't like the *tone* of your voice," or the standard variation, "Don't use that

10

tone with me!" In this sense we understand *tone* to mean a certain inflection of voice by which we express anger, humor, irony, or disgust. Tone in writing has a somewhat more specialized meaning: the attitude of the writer toward the subject or reader. A good writer consciously works to establish a tone that best suits the subject and purpose of the essay. In most writing situations, especially those involving exposition or analysis, the writer will strive for a neutral tone aimed at convincing the reader that the argument or analysis set forward is reasoned and objective. TV newscasters are supposed to acquire a neutral tone of voice for objectivity's sake.

Note the tone of wisdom and good will in the following excerpt:

> It is human nature to wonder about the future and to imagine what the world will be like fifty or a hundred years hence. Our dreams and aspirations for the future, however, need not be idle fantasies; they can, and often do, serve as an impetus for new inquiries and new discoveries.
> —MICHAEL DEBAKEY, "The Medical Prognosis: Favorable, Treatable, Curable"

This modified tone should probably be the one to strive for in your classroom writing, since for the beginning writer the temptation to shout opinions instead of reasoning them through with the reader is great indeed. (Read some letters to the editor of your daily newspaper for samples of the strident tone we are talking about.)

Some subjects, however, do call for greater passion or humor than others. Here are two selections whose tones should be immediately identifiable. Can you explain why the writers chose to put on these particular masks?

> How many innocent must suffer to punish the guilty or right ancient wrongs? How many jobs equal one cancer death? Is disclosure of sexual or fiscal impropriety justified when the result is destruction of an otherwise admirable career? Is "covert activ-

11

ity" less or more moral than welfare? Is bribery never, ever justified?

—DAVID B. WILSON, "Is Candor Always Advisable?"

Whether big money can by itself stave off the onrush of another generation of illiterates, only the Lord knows. It would take all that plus a miracle, and thus far Jimmy Carter has not demonstrated a propensity for creating miracles. Even though his initials are the same as His.

—GOODMAN ACE, "The Wincers"

No matter what tone you adopt in any essay, try to maintain it throughout. An occasional humorous or ironic comment in an otherwise serious essay will contribute variety in an admittedly regularized, sometimes tedious process. If, however, there are too many attempts at wit or informal joke-telling, the reader is likely to become impatient with the voice he or she hears.

SPEAKING AND WRITING

As the discussion of tone illustrates, it is important to cite differences between speaking and writing. To many beginners the task of writing seems elementary because they assume they need only transfer their style of speaking to the page. They notice no distinction between their performance in conversation and their performance in composition—it is all a matter of "communication." Yet beginners soon learn, usually from the comments of their English instructors, that there are major differences between talking and writing, and that beginners had better discover quickly what the differences are. The root of the differences is that we get away with errors, inconsistencies, and assumptions in speech that are not tolerated in expository writing. They are not tolerated in writing because they hinder understanding.

Perhaps the primary distinction between speech and

writing is that speech depends on sound, whereas writing depends on sight and on those strange processes of the mind that translate written symbols into sound and meaning. Readers read what *they* interpret, not what someone else says to them. There are other differences important to the linguist, of course, but the main distinction is that speech benefits from the help of certain visual and audial aids writing does not have. In speech we add to and qualify our meaning by physical gestures: by movement of the hands, shrugs, and facial expressions such as smiles, frowns, or even the lifted eyebrow. Our resources of sound are many—intonation, the rise and fall of the voice, the changes in pitch. We can vary the intensity or the volume of sound; we can, on occasion, whisper, shout, mumble, or even growl. All these add meaning; they are strengths written language does not have.

On the other hand, spoken language has obvious weaknesses. That collection of fleeting, ephemeral noises we call human speech is gone a moment after it is uttered. Often it is gone even before it has been heard accurately— a wonderful phenomenon for those of us with hot tempers who tend to revile the parentage of strapping truck drivers when they blow us off the road. Perhaps our words linger for a while in someone's memory, especially if they are spoken lovingly or disparagingly, but the speech itself cannot be called back to life. It may be caught and preserved on tape or on a phonograph record, but most of what has been thus saved was first worked over and shaped and set down in writing before it was recited. It is only partly spoken English, often self-consciously delivered. Written English has a longer life, a greater permanence; it will exist, in Shakespeare's words, "So long as men can breathe or eyes can see." Writing is also the more accurate communication because it can be reread, examined, and studied. Because it is enduring and susceptible to critical review, it demands greater care in its composition. As a writer you assume a responsibility to build your sentences, to select and arrange your words, and to use or modify the rhetorical and stylistic devices that other writers have created and developed.

STANDARD ENGLISH: FORMAL AND INFORMAL

Formal Varieties

The language that we call *formal*—for want of a term with less unfortunate connotations—is far from being by definition cold, reserved, or stodgy. It has warmth, strength, beauty, and an infinite range and variety. It is not confined to a few scientific and scholarly treatises. The great body of our literature, from Shakespeare and Bacon down to the latest book on the international monetary crisis, is written in formal English. It is the language striven for by authors of most books of history, sociology, political science, botany, chemistry—many of the textbooks that you use in college. It is the language of the professions, such as law, medicine, teaching. It is the language of all serious essays, of a good part of all novels and poems. Most business letters are written in formal English. As a matter of fact, a good share of the nation's private and public daily work is carried on with the help of formal English.

There are some generally agreed-on guidelines for formal writing that should be followed by anyone required to write, for example, a business letter, letter of application, graduate thesis, or formal speech.

1. Slang or colloquial diction should not be used. Expressions such as "cool dude" or "Dig it!" imply a forced familiarity with the reader that cannot exist in formal writing.
2. An objective tone characterizes formal writing because the writer is usually striving for a mood of rationality or straightforwardness.
3. Third-person pronouns (especially the neutral pronoun *one*), rather than the informal *you*, are found in formal essays and books. (Note that we address

14

the reader as *you* in this textbook, a sign that we aim at a less formal relationship with the reader than might exist in textbooks on other subjects.) A typical formal sentence might read, "*One* may find many examples of corruption in public office should *he* take the time to investigate." The pronoun *he* does not have any particular gender connotations; it is simply used to agree with the singular *one*. The pronoun *I* is also generally not found in formal essays, although many writers today do not follow the rule closely.

4. Contractions are not found in formal writing: "Drivers *should not* drink" instead of "Drivers *shouldn't* drink." It is also standard practice to write out numbers: *fifty* instead of 50.

The following quotations are written according to the rules of formal English. The writers distance themselves from their audiences but by no means assume a condescending pose.

One cannot be too optimistic. No single world-minded institution, no matter how affluent or prestigious, is likely to successfully change the character of its educational experience without also risking a large exodus of its students. But with a sufficient critical mass of prestigious institutions committed to a more realistic rendering of our global circumstances, some significant breakthroughs are in fact possible. It will take the bold resolve of many institutions to overcome the country's present myopia. It will take uncommon effort to prepare this generation of young Americans for a world which they cannot in fact now discern in their classrooms.

—GEORGE W. BONHAM, "The Future Forsaken"

[Note the speech-making style of the last two sentences in particular. Formal usage often characterizes the great political speeches of men like Winston Churchill and Abraham Lincoln. In writing, this form of delivery is especially effective in closing paragraphs about subjects of some magnitude: war, poverty, moral crisis, and so forth.]

We are likely to call Jonson's method "classical," Shakespeare's "romantic." If we are careful enough not to make the

15

terms imply too much, they have a certain convenience. But Jonson is classical only in a general sense of strong consciousness of form; the particular form he achieves is distinctly his own. And Shakespeare has likewise a stronger sense of form than has generally been allowed him. Moreover, it is a mistake to see these two as heirs to separable traditions. One cannot simply equate impulse and variety, for instance, with the medieval heritage, and formal restraint with the classical; the relations are far more complicated.

—MADELEINE DORAN, *Endeavors of Art*

[Ms. Doran uses *we* here in the formal sense of a community of educated scholars or readers who are familiar not only with the works of Jonson and Shakespeare but with commentary on them. Note also the long sentences punctuated by semicolons, another prominent feature of the academic formal style.]

It may prove difficult to find examples of pure formal style in most works. For instance, many stylists who otherwise observe the guidelines of formal prose will sometimes use the personal pronoun *I* instead of *one*. The important thing to remember, however, is that formal English essays are marked by appropriate diction, orderly structure, and a neutral tone. The expression and communication of ideas are part of a planned process, not a spontaneous outpouring. Ideas are grouped and arranged in some logical sequence. There is a serious attempt to show the interrelationship between ideas. As a consequence, paragraphs tend to be more fully developed than in the informal varieties of English; the complexity of a sentence is usually proportionate to the maturity of its thought.

Informal Varieties

The essential unity of standard English is much more important than the differences among its varieties. (Nonstandard English is generally understood to refer to words and meanings that are dialectic or illiterate. Slang words are examples of nonstandard usage.) A professional essayist does not stop writing formal English and begin writing informal English as if stepping through a door from one room to another, after having changed into something more comfortable. Informal English prose generally has a serious intent, but it is written for common readers who are expected to enjoy their reading in a relaxed mood. Wit and humor arc major ingredients of informal essays; they perform the function of a good joke at an after-dinner talk: relaxing an expectant and well-fed audience. Informal essayists likewise select everyday words whose general meanings are widely understood. In most informal writing, the actual extent of the informality consists in no more than the attitude of the writer toward the material and the reader. (Remember our definition of *tone.*) You may find in such essays the same discriminating taste in choice of words, the same respect for present-day standards in grammatical correctness and usage, and the same mature structure as in the best formal writing. The only difference is that the writers frankly and freely interpret their subjects through their own personalities or through their own likes and prejudices. The personal pronoun *I* regularly appears in informal essays, contractions are allowed, and colloquial words or idioms often surprise by their appropriateness.

The following selections show the range of styles that can be found in informal writing. Note too the strong substructure of organization beneath the apparently relaxed, conversational manner.

The construction of the Gateway Arch was a project that never had my approval. When it was completed, in 1965—a six-hundred-thirty-four foot arch next to downtown St. Louis to commemorate the westward expansion of the United States—I made no secret of my resentment. I pointed out to anyone who would listen what seemed to be a rather significant flaw in the reasoning of those who had persuaded the federal government to spend some thirty million dollars on a monument identifying St. Louis as the Gateway to the West—the fact that the Gateway to the West happened to be Kansas City. I suppose the people who thought a gateway arch might look nice on the west bank of the Mississippi at St. Louis considered the fact that they were more than two-hundred miles from the true gateway a trifling

17

detail—something that could be planned around without much difficulty, the way a Corps of Engineers dam-and-reservoir project sometimes plans around the absence of a river—but it was no small matter to me. By chance, I was born in Kansas City, and I grew up secure in the knowledge that I was living in the Gateway to the West, not to speak of the Heart of America.

—CALVIN TRILLIN, "Regional Thoughts from Atop the Gateway Arch"

[Trillin's tone could well be described as complaining, the result of rivalry between two Missouri cities. Yet the surface of complaint is underpinned by a logical argument, developed later in the essay, that many pioneers headed west from Kansas City. Note the relaxed use of dashes to subordinate useful information and the insertion of the word *nice* for satiric purposes.]

I sometimes wonder—this may be regarded as a digression—whether there is not another accomplishment players must have if they are to last in the major leagues. This is the ability to spit with good velocity when the television camera is on them. It seems clear that a method of communication has been worked out between the television crews and the players. This is not necessary when a player is close enough to see the red light that means the camera is transmitting a picture on the air, but when he isn't, I suppose his instructions come from somebody in the television crew, perhaps by Navy semaphore flags. As soon as he gets the message, he shifts his tobacco or chewing gum and lets go.

—EDWIN NEWMAN, *A Civil Tongue*

[The mock-serious tone only thinly hides Newman's distaste with this habit among baseball players. Carefully selected diction is the key to achieving the lightly satiric objective here. Note the phrase "good velocity," which is usually applied by players and announcers alike to a pitcher's fastball. "Lets go" in the last sentence serves a similar purpose.]

What was I looking for? I knew the intelligence establishment was overgrown and overblown. I knew it tapped phones, read mail, engaged in dirty tricks; that it mixed in the internal affairs of other nations, propped up "friendly" governments and tried to "destabilize" others. I knew that for a generation or more Congress had preferred to look the other way rather than exercise the appropriate and necessary control, and I knew the dangers to democracy when police power is allowed to range unchecked.

> —SHANA ALEXANDER, "The Assassination of President Kennedy"

[The tone of this excerpt is serious and straightforward. Ms. Alexander's use of repetition, normally a feature of formal writing, is especially effective here in suggesting that the personal pronoun *I* could represent her reader too. Note the ironic criticism achieved by placing *friendly* and *destabilize* in quotation marks.]

A more intimate kind of informal writing echoes the style of everyday conversation. Many "how-to" or "do-it-yourself" books and manuals are written in this manner. The writer wants to achieve a friendly, chatty relationship with the reader and so may season his prose with colloquialisms and well-known figures of speech. Although normally reserved for personal letter writing, conversational prose can prove useful in reproducing dialogue for narrated incidents used in expository or descriptive essays.

The following piece of advice comes from a writer who sets out to instruct job-seekers in the do's and don't's of interviewing. Notice the somewhat breezy manner:

> If you slouch over him [the recruiter], sidewinderlike, he is not going to be impressed. He'll figure you would probably slouch through your workdays. He wants you to come at him with lots of good things going for you. If you watch the recruiter's eyes, you can see the inspection. He glances quickly at shoes, coat, shirt; dress, blouse, hose—the whole works.
> —KIRBY W. STANAT, "Want a Job?"

[The tone of voice here is an almost exact reproduction of informal conversation. Note the use of verbs and verb phrases like "figure" and "come at him" to achieve this mood. Is *sidewinderlike* a word?]

19

Formal or Informal?—The Student's Choice

A logical question at this point would be, "What level of usage should I adopt in my classroom writing assignments?" That decision—and many others—may in fact be made for you by your instructor. Follow his or her directions. An informal style like that of Trillin or Alexander is obviously appropriate for essays describing childhood accidents or family trips; in other words, it works best for the writer who is asked to recount personal experiences. Argumentative essays, on the other hand, call for a more formal approach in which analysis is conducted in an objective manner. The third-person pronoun may not be necessary in such essays, but formal diction and organization are. Remember that a formal stylist does not automatically employ big or bookish words and a cold, distant tone. Too much intimacy is likewise out of place. Aim for consistency whatever your—or your instructor's—choice of style.

GENDER AND PRONOUN CHOICE

We have heard and read a great deal lately about the intrusion of political issues in the Olympic Games. It has been said that boycotts or demonstrations by the players transform amateur sports fields into arenas where governments compete for international attention. This argument ignores the truth that the games have always been political, the Berlin event of 1936 being a singular example. There is also some question about the purely amateur nature of the competition, since some countries openly pay athletes to do nothing but run, jump, or swim. Nonetheless, the controversy has received considerable media attention, thus guaranteeing that many people will pay some heed to it.

A similar phenomenon can be observed in the world of language, especially in America. The women's movement has attacked traditional usage as sexist, perpetuating a system of economic and social repression. Words such

20

as *workman, spokesman,* and *chairman* have been cited by language watchers who claim that use of the generic *man* implies that only men hold these particular jobs in our society. The suggested modifications have sometimes proved successful, even inspired: *worker, drafter,* and the like, make clear that most jobs do not need a gender suffix. Other changes—*chairperson, spokesperson, anchorperson*—lack imagination but are now widely used and accepted. Fortunately many titles—*president, senator, doctor, professor*—stand secure, and the positions to which they refer now include growing numbers of women. Since there will be many situations in which the gender question will arise, especially in the use of pronouns, it is important to be aware of the accepted alternatives to exclusive use of the generic *man* and the masculine pronoun.

Traditionally, one of the masculine pronouns, *he, his, him,* has been written to refer to nouns that give no indication of gender. The pronoun *he,* as we have already shown, is normally selected in formal sentences to agree with the antecedent *one: "One* never knows just how *he* will behave until the situation arises." Practice seems slow to change in formal writing, although some practitioners attempt to avoid the gender problem by repeating *one* instead of *he.* In other less formal writing situations it is now widely recognized as correct to acknowledge both genders in the pronoun.

Every *doctor* must follow *his or her* conscience in this matter.

The *senator* who forgets this lesson may quickly lose *his or her* seat.

Any *worker* would be foolish to permit such behavior toward *him or her.*

This alternative may at first sound awkward, but by following the practice of acknowledging both genders, you are in fact letting your reader know that you are aware of the existence of both male and female doctors, lawyers, and secretaries. (By the way, the shorthand device *he/she* should never be used to substitute for *he or she.* It has no

21

equivalent in speech and is sure to alienate readers concerned with precision.)

It sometimes proves cumbersome to repeat the *he or she* formula in long sentences: "The typical consumer buys ten cars in *his or her* lifetime; *he or she* eats six tons of food; seven hundred suits or dresses grace *his or her* body . . . ." *Plural constructions* are often the best way out of this maze: "Typical *consumers* buy ten cars in a lifetime; *they* eat six tons of food; seven hundred suits or dresses grace *their* bodies . . . ." Using the plural pronoun also helps to break the habit of beginning sentences with dictatorial-sounding generalizations: "*Every* pilot should thoroughly check out his or her plane before take-off." Note how the following plurals help to create a somewhat more relaxed tone for what are still generalizations:

Pilots should thoroughly check out *their* planes before take-off.

If instructors expect good work, *they* need to give clear instructions.

Comedians who tell bad jokes should be jailed for *their* excesses.

Most of the writing you do will not call for formal usage, i.e., the *one–he* construction. It is therefore probably a good idea to recognize the gender pronoun and avoid using masculine pronouns unless referring specifically to a man.

The sample essay that follows offers an interesting, provocative view of the political aspects of language as they relate to male–female roles.

THE ESSAY

To write essays you should read essays. Read them on a variety of subjects. Newsmagazines, such as *Time* and *Newsweek,* regularly feature articles on subjects ranging from cancer to culture shock written in a manner designed both to inform and to provoke the reader's thoughts. These essays are addressed to a literate and informed audience; many of the allusions found in them are to the works of literature and art commonly introduced in undergraduate survey courses. Yet the writers of these essays assume no specialized knowledge in their readers, and their work is, as a result, a useful model for students who want to instruct and entertain a wide audience. Although the styles of news-magazine essays are sometimes marred by excessive wit and sarcasm, their arguments are generally tightly constructed, with a clear sense of purpose and an easy movement from the statement of a thesis to its proof. Reading essays like the following with an eye to the logic of the argument, the use of proof, and the form of the conclusion will help you understand the scope—and limitation—of the papers you will probably be called on to write.

NOTES ON THE DISTAFF SIDE

Audrey C. Foote

Once upon a time there lived a kind of creature called a spinster. Within the memory of our oldest inhabitants the word was still quite often heard. The elders recall that it denoted a never-married female person of, as the French say, a certain age.

"Like Gloria Steinem?" my daughter asks.

Not exactly. No, it was then generally used for a withered crone with skinny shanks, a tart tongue, and persnickety mannerisms. Recently the term has come to be considered inhumane like its grosser synonym *old maid*. *Old maid* hardly exists anymore except as the name of a simple card game, and *spinster* is quite moribund, dying of atrophy or maybe murdered as an act of common verbal decency. My ten-year-old son, when queried, had no idea of its traditional meaning. "A worker?" he guessed.

Yet the condition of unmarried mature woman, voluntary or no, continues to exist, even flourish, and to present a challenge to the much-vaunted resourcefulness of our language. For nothing has really emerged in *spinster*'s place to apply to such an individual. *Maiden lady* has a poor image, prissy, sniffy, rabbity. Its components are as archaic as the whole; for almost any grown woman now, *maiden* is probably inaccurate, certainly impertinent. As for *lady,* who would be so gauche as to use that anymore? Egalitarian chic tolerates it only ironically, or in the compound *cleaning lady;* it's as if the humbleness of the profession acts as antidote to the pretention. What else is there? Surely not the awful neologism *bachelor girl,* with its sad suggestion of stockings draped in the shower or an icebox full of yogurt and diet cola, and its pathetic grab at the tawdry glamour of supposed male license. Anyway, the use of *girl* for any female past puberty is guaranteed these days to raise the hackles of those people formerly known as girls. This is a famous pitfall for older adults, even ones who consider themselves quite liberated; it took me a while to realize, when my daughter who is in college spoke of "the women at Wellesley," that she was *not* referring to the faculty.

The most fashionable current alternative is probably *single,* now barbarously used as a noun, as in Maxwell's Plum. That does indeed have one signal charm: it applies equally to either or any sex. However, it too is saddled with a disastrous modifier, *swinging,* and its sleazy snigger. There may be other terms— quaint regionalisms, brutal argot, sociological jargon—waiting in the wings to be beckoned onstage by Webster's fourth international edition—hardly a happy thought. But there does seem to be no turning back. To the extent that it still has any meaning at all, *spinster* is so glued in a matrix of drab associations, so freighted with dreary connotations, that it is probably well beyond all hope of rehabilitation. And yet, the fact is, there was a time, long, *long* ago, when it was a perfectly honorable and very useful title.

Spinster, according to dictionaries, originally and sensibly meant nothing more than a woman who spins. By Elizabethan times it was restricted to refer to an unmarried woman of "gentle" birth. In the seventeenth century it lost this aura of aristocracy and designated any unmarried woman. Finally, perhaps in the patriarchal prime of the Victorian period, it acquired its classic—to us—significance: unattractive, elderly, unmarried female. Poor degenerate word! Era by era it has been stripped linguistically of 1) occupation, 2) husband, 3) social status, 4) youth and beauty—and now of any viable meaning whatever.

This decline should not be surprising since a similar insidious process seems to have taken place with almost every title that ever had the slightest taint of female dominance or even independence. (One of the few good things to be said of aristocratic societies is the fact that rank outweighed gender. Thus a few women—well born, well endowed, or just downright deter-

24

mined—were able to aspire to the highest positions. In an egalitarian world, all women are supposed to be equal, at least to each other if not quite equal to men. So women have more often been ruling monarchs than presidents.)

Among the devolutions of female titles, one example is the word *governess*. It once meant, literally, a woman who governs, but it came to designate, usually, a "career" of last resort for the shabby genteel and barely competent. *Secretary* has become bifurcated; when applied to a man, it is often followed by "of State" or appears on a company letterhead just below Chairman of the Board. Of a woman it means she can type, though recent Washington scandals have put even that modest skill in question. *Dame* (derived from the Latin *domina*, like *dominant* and, naturally, *domineering*) also once meant a woman leader. Now it's about as elegant as *broad*. And *madam*, once honorific, is now used, in English at least, mainly of managers of whorehouses.

There is nothing new about all this, it's only too familiar, and it might be attributed to our democratic disdain for all such hierarchic titles. But, significantly, this deterioration is true only of women's titles, not of men's. Are there any Jewish princes? Are lesbians called kings? Is a pimp ever called a monsieur?

Perhaps the unkindest cut of all is the fact that most of these debased terms have somehow acquired wounding sexual meanings, meanings that mock either abstinence or excess and acknowledge no ground between. *Spinster* and, to a large extent, *governess* bear the burden of implied frigidity or frustration. *Madam* and, to a lesser extent, *mistress* connote not only loose living but often a venal profiteering in sex.

The word *mistress* is a particularly pungent example of distortion. *Mistress* once meant (and this is still the first meaning in that chivalric source, the *Oxford English Dictionary*) merely one who rules, who has others in her employ. Later it was applied to any proper housewife; then it came to be used, metaphorically and microcosmically, to mean the ruler of a somewhat dwindled and undependable estate, a man's heart. From this still quite chaste compliment, it declined further to be an only relatively polite term for—as the *Oxford Dictionary* daintily phrases it—"a woman who illicitly occupies the place of wife." All this seems to have happened rather fast and with a certain amount of overlap, sometimes catching the innocent in a verbal time warp. I was told of a proud old woman (of the ilk once called *lady*) who condescended with noblesse oblige and calf's foot jelly to appear at the hospital bedside of her disreputable gardener. A nurse accosted her. "Only family are admitted. Are you the wife?" The old gorgon drew herself up and answered with hauteur, "Certainly not! I am his mistress!" But even the decadent connotation, which did at least have some remnants of seedy romance, has become sociologically obsolete now that expenses are shared as well as beds, and neither love nor money stays in one place very long.

As most women are very well aware, a similar rule applies when the names of animals are used for people. While usually such names are derogatory (and beastly unfair that is too!) to both sexes, they are invariably even more so for women. Dog—bitch (or slut, which also once meant simply a female dog) ox—cow, gander—goose, fox—vixen. It isn't much, admittedly, but one can at least say, "He's a gay dog" or "strong as an ox" or "smart as a fox." But do we ever hear "cheerful bitch," kind as a cow," or "clever as a vixen"?

And so it seems inevitable that from the moment it was decided that a spinster must be a woman, the word was doomed. Whatever evidence there is, and there's plenty, to suggest that in some time or some place it is the husband who sweeps the floor and the wife who tills the fields, the one skill or occupation that has been almost uniquely feminine is spinning (quite unlike knitting, which was originally a male accomplishment). This seems to have been established as early as the fall of the first fig leaf. An ancient verse begins: "When Adam delved / and Eve span . . . ." Chaucer's medieval Wife of Bath, fat and gat-toothed but apparently irresistible (she boasted of five husbands, no spinster she!), remarked wryly that God gave women "deceit, weeping and spinning."

This fact that *spinster* is associated with an activity practiced by women could be enough to explain its low repute, just as *secretary* and *librarian* lost status when they came to be women's occupations. But *spinster* is a very special case since it is the only one of these words deriving from a specific skill which has come to mean something entirely different—a single woman. There is clearly something more involved here than mere misogynistic condescension as reflected in the change in the other titles. I suspect it has to do with male mistrust of the unmarried woman, fused with primitive superstition concerning the mysterious power of a woman who spins.

Dr. Samuel Johnson, though an eighteenth-century male chauvinist notorious for his sneer that a woman preacher is like a dog walking on its hind legs, once remarked, "The prejudice and pride of man has long supposed the sword and spindle made for different hands." The sword and spindle—a provocative conjunction suggesting that the spindle is the female weapon. In *The Erotic World of Faery,* Maureen Duffy, in good Freudian tradition, bluntly states that the spindle is a substitute penis. It's not necessary to be so anatomical, but the spindle does seem to represent power which is linked in some way with the bearer's sexuality. What psychology proposes, anthropology endorses. For among those cultures and peoples for whom we have yet to find a better word than *primitive,* spinning and its equipment have always been suspected to be a source, or at least a symbol, of female power. And this feminine force has usually been regarded as a kind of black magic, dangerous to male dominance.

Fearful of such strength, and thinking that it derived from— or was implemented by—spinning, men in primitive cultures have hedged it about with taboos. Too useful to be forbidden, spinning did have to be controlled. Sir James Frazer in *The Golden Bough* gives lots of examples from obscure tribes with names as exotic as their behavior. Sanctions are enforced against spinning, or even holding a spindle, at all occasions critical for men: childbirth, hunting, mealtime, seed sowing, and councils. Mostly Frazer explains these taboos by the idea that the twisting action of the spindle is supposed, by sympathetic magic, to entangle— nets, guts, wheat, tongues, and even wits. Twisting and entangling; such is the devious and sneaky way that women's wiles are thought to work against men.

Mythology, folklore, and fairy tales place a similar emphasis on this triad of women, spinning, and power. The most explicit splice of women, spinning, and power appears in the Greek concept of the three female spinners called the Fates. Even Zeus, king of the gods, was subject to them. And by means of spinning they held control over the duration—the *span*—of every human existence. Clothos spun the thread of life. Lachesis measured it, and Atropos with her scissors (castrating shears, perhaps?) cut it off.

In fairy tales the feminine force associated with spinning is usually malignant. "Sleeping Beauty" tells of the encounter between a princess and a witch. (And aren't princesses in fairy tales man's ideal of *good* women, pretty and submissive, prizes

27

for a hero's triumphs, while witches are bad women who wield mysterious force?) The princess finds the witch spinning in a tower, pricks her hand on the spindle, and falls under an evil spell. She is revived at last only by gallant male intervention.

Women have not all been above cultivating the myth of their magical powers, in the hope of securing from it influence or at least protection. Mostly this has been a fatal miscalculation; the reputation for such power has done a great deal of harm. It has subjected girls and women to all kinds of taboos. Despite the reverence the Greeks accorded their goddesses, they kept their wives and daughters pretty well locked up. And in real life those women thought to be witches couldn't save themselves from being burned at the stake.

Most women, as if aware of the consequences, have renounced all claim to such impotent power. Of course there are and always have been some women who have employed—and now promote in best sellers—a watered-down kind of magic. They instruct in mere manipulative charm—those petty, pretty devices formerly of the harem, now of the Total and Fascinating Pussycats. But this kind of power—which in fact is nothing of the kind—is only a sort of game, graceful or grotesque depending on the wit of the woman, which men can afford to indulge or even enjoy. It too doesn't provide any true security or autonomy. Nevertheless, in the search for the kind of strength that leads to equality, the art of spinning may still have something to offer. We can think of it, not as a sign of female magic, but as a symbol of the very prosaic but invaluable possession of a marketable skill. It can stand for a means of economic independence and even for freedom of choice whether or not to be a *spinster*.

Discussion and Evaluation

Ms. Foote's essay appears on the surface to be an attempt to find a fitting modern word for a single woman, in other words, an attempt at exposition. But as the clever title hints (*distaff* refers to both a part of the spinning wheel and woman's work), she is engaged in more than just linguistic goldmining. Her *argument* or *thesis* is that male dominance of woman can be illustrated by the denigrating terms used to describe her and her work. She also offers a *solution* or *answer* to the problem she outlines by urging women readers to accept spinning as a symbol of economic independence that can come from possessing a marketable skill. Her argument persuades because she develops it through *specific examples* and *illustrations.* Note, for example, her explication of animal terms applied to women in paragraph 12. Her *tone* is serious without being ponderous; she interjects witty comments—"Are there any Jewish princes?"— and humorous anecdotes (see the disreputable gardener and his mistress in paragraph 11) to keep the pace lively. We know she is serious about her purpose but not wholly serious about herself. A preachy tone would surely turn off both male and female readers. The essay reveals many of the techniques of *exposition*—defining words, tracing etymologies—but the aim is to convince, as in an *argumentative* essay, that in the game of sexual politics the title *spinster* has power. *Narration* and *description* also play their parts in the essay, demonstrating that the potent essayist may employ all forms of writing to create his or her final product.

This essay ranges throughout the various levels of *usage.* The *diction* or *word selection,* especially as illustrated by such words as *moribund* (paragraph 3) and *pungent* (paragraph 11), is typical of formal essays; many sentences exhibit classical *balance,* employing the semicolon to join two independent clauses (or complete sentences). The objective *voice* of formal writing is found here, with Ms. Foote rarely electing the personal pronoun *I.* Yet the argument is certainly filtered through her personality: responses by her children appear in paragraphs 2 and 3; exclamations like "Poor degenerate word!" bear the stamp of personal irony; and parenthetical remarks (see paragraphs 7 and 11) pronounce Ms. Foote's opinions, not proved fact. While recognizing that informal usage defines the general character of the essay, we are also aware of *colloquial* words—*grosser* (paragraph 3), *sniffy, rabbity* (paragraph 4)—that are justified by the sheer force of their descriptiveness. Many instructors would probably object—and with sound reasons—to the radical mixture of formal and colloquial diction. But this habit is increasingly found among professional writers and it can result in livelier, more readable prose than might be the case with strict adherence to the rules.

The major strength of this essay is the carefully *researched subject*. "Notes" in the title suggests a somewhat loose approach listing dictionary entries and giving the impression that the writer has no pressing *purpose* in mind. Yet as the essay progresses from its fairy tale opening to the myth concerning the Greek Fates, the reader begins to realize that not only does no satisfactory title exist for a single woman, many of those that do exist and have been indicative of prominent places for women in society—*madam, governess* (paragraph 10); *mistress* (paragraph 11)—are now debased. Then, at the close of paragraph 14, Ms. Foote moves beyond her etymological exercise to a larger, more speculative argument that the role of the spinster has become associated in men's minds with the mysterious functions of the Fates, who spin out, measure, and then cut short their lives. Psychological complexity now replaces dictionary definition; the essay leaps from exposition to argument. The secure underpinning for this jump, which is admittedly sudden and dangerous, is the undeniable evidence of debasement found in labels for women like *spinster*. By establishing herself as an *authority* on the subject, Ms. Foote has already won half the battle of persuading her readers, many of whom are men.

"Notes on the Distaff Side" represents the Mount Everest of essay writing to beginners. Its lively diction, vivid word pictures (see in particular the opening sentence of paragraph 10), witty comments, clear sense of purpose and varied style—all these rocks of writing technique reach up to a considerable height. Although all of you will not reach the professional pinnacle represented by "Notes," you will be successful in working many of its characteristics into your own style. That accomplishment should help to make the adventure worthwhile, even if it also requires attention to detail and the hard work of reading and research. Writing is one of those skills, like mountain climbing, that improves with practice.

The next chapters, on words, sentences, and paragraphs, will familiarize you with the basic tools and techniques of composing. Once you have mastered these, you will be ready to begin the process of planning and writing effective essays.

EXERCISES

EXERCISE 1, CLARITY AND PRECISION. *Translate these unclear and garbled sentences into clear, concise informal English.*

1. Owing to the failure to finalize the meeting, we were required to relocate in a different time frame.
2. Emilia arrives after Desdemona has received fatal abuse at the hands of Othello.
3. The whole poem evolves only about him.
4. Once the chairperson has prioritized this year's goals, the entire committee can begin to interface.
5. Seeking input about educational philosophy is essential to viable interaction between experiencing parents and teachers.
6. We must access the TV program at the optimum time.
7. As the motorized vehicle continued along its prescribed route it impacted the two-wheeled vehicle at an intersection.
8. After our last telephonic communication I was of the opinion that we had reached a mutual commitment on the program.
9. The bullies were told to cease and desist from their assault and battery against my friend and companion Eric.
10. The two leaders dialogued about the meaningful role each would play in the evolution of a peaceful world order.

EXERCISE 2, FORMAL, INFORMAL, AND COLLOQUIAL USAGE. *Identify the level of usage in each of the following sentences. Indicate the words or phrases that prove your claim. Change any colloquial or formal sentences to informal sentences by making the appropriate changes in diction, punctuation, and so forth.*

1. We cannot fail to comprehend the significance of the context.
2. I bombed out on the exam today.
3. We shouldn't have tried to jump that electrified fence.
4. One feels apprehensive about the future military growth in our democratic society.
5. Got wheels, man?
6. Their claim of superiority is exaggerated; our team will vanquish them handily.
7. I was nervous about the upcoming talk with the dean.
8. Even though I hit the sheets before the witching hour, I felt wasted the next day.
9. We shall nominate a candidate with exceptional intelligence, proven experience, and the will to prevail.
10. She's positive that Mike is wired pretty good today.

EXERCISE 3, GENDER. *Rewrite the following sentences, eliminating references to gender or using pronouns that acknowledge both genders.*

1. A student needs to be sure of his objectives in order to succeed.
2. Man will halt his aggression when he finds the path to peace.
3. Jane is the spokesman for the local sportswriters.
4. A chairman should listen closely to the complaints of his faculty.
5. Anyone who knows his math can solve that problem easily.
6. She is one of the best lady lawyers in the country.
7. The ticket-buyer should mail in his money and form as soon as possible.
8. If the jaguar is frightened he will attack with blinding speed.
9. One must be careful to record his impressions before the deadline.
10. Salesmen are rarely courteous to customers returning merchandise.

EXERCISE 4, TONE. *Describe the dominant tone (i.e., the attitude of the writer toward the subject or audience) in each of the following excerpts. Determine as well the level of usage—formal, informal, colloquial—in each sentence.*

1. You must never forget that the peaceful, happy church is the true community of faith. It makes life more pleasant for the pastor, it attracts new members, and it has a much higher stewardship (financial) potential than the quarrelsome congregation. One of the main goals of your pastoral administration, then, is to achieve and preserve a state of tranquility in your church. Since Christians, from the early days of the faith, have shown a regrettable tendency to fuss and fight among themselves, this is no simple problem. However, a clever, tactful, courteous, thick-skinned minister can calm the most cantankerous of congregations. Here are a few hints to help you in this enterprise of Christian love.

   —CHARLES MERRILL SMITH, "Advice to a Young Clergyman"

2. Now that I am entering early middle age, I hear many women complaining of husbands and ex-husbands who are attracted to younger females. This strikes the older woman as unfair, of course. But I remember a time when I thought all boys around my age and grade were creeps and bores. I wanted to go out with an older man: a senior or, miraculously, a college man. I had a certain contempt for my coevals, not realizing that the freshman in college I thought so desirable, was some older girl's creep. Some women never lose that contempt for men of their own age. That isn't fair either and may be one reason why some sensible men of middle years find solace in young women.

   —ANN ROIPHE, "Confessions of a Female Chauvinist Sow"

3. Those who insist that they are signs of a severe social disease can be dismissed as starry-eyed moralists, sentimentalists and understandably without influence or power. As a matter of fact, the few serious moral critics of our society do not have constituents. Intellectually and temperamentally they cannot appeal to the masses. Neither can they expect support from radicals of the right or the left because they tend to be as

much concerned with methods as they are with ends; they cannot accept moral ends through immoral means.

—KENNETH B. CLARK, "The American Dilemma"

4. He had a dash about him and a vivaciousness, to say nothing of his courage, which could not help but attract the attention of his superiors, and he received choice assignments for such a very young officer. He had a superb confidence that fortune was always working for him; "Custer's luck," he called this continual smile of the gods, and for a number of years it appeared that he was right and that it actually existed. As it turned out, "Custer's luck" was not an inexhaustible commodity.

—RALPH K. ANDRIST, "General George Armstrong Custer"

5. For those who study the great art of lying in bed there is one emphatic caution to be added. Even for those who can do their work in bed (like journalists), still more for those whose work cannot be done in bed (as for example, the professional harpooners of whales), it is obvious that the indulgence must be very occasional. But that is not the caution I mean. The caution is this: if you do lie in bed, be sure you do it without any reason or justification at all. I do not speak, of course, of the seriously sick. But if a healthy man lies in bed, let him do it without a rag of excuse; then he will get up a healthy man. If he does it for some secondary hygienic reason, if he has some scientific explanation, he may get up a hypochondriac.

—G. K. CHESTERTON, "On Lying in Bed"

6. I say we had best look our times and lands searchingly in the face, like a physician diagnosing some deep disease. Never was there, perhaps, more hollowness at heart than at present, and here in the United States. Genuine belief seems to have left us. The underlying principles of the States are not honestly believed in (for all this hectic glow, and these melodramatic screamings), nor is humanity itself believed in. What penetrating eye does not everywhere see through the mask? The spectacle is appalling. We live in an atmosphere of hypocrisy throughout. The men believe not in the women, nor the women in the men.

—WALT WHITMAN, "Democratic Vistas"

7. The white youth of today are coming to see, intuitively, that to escape the onus of the history their fathers made they must face and admit the moral truth concerning the works of their fathers. That such venerated figures as George Washington and Thomas Jefferson owned hundreds of black slaves, that all of the Presidents up to Lincoln presided over a slave state, and that every President since Lincoln connived politically and cynically with the issues affecting the human rights and general welfare of the broad masses of the American people—these facts weigh heavily upon the hearts of these young people.
—ELDRIDGE CLEAVER, *Soul on Ice*

EXERCISE 5, WRITING EFFECTIVE PARAGRAPHS. *Compose a paragraph of about 75–80 words in which you attack the present state of popular music. Adopt an angry tone as you address an audience of classmates. Then rewrite the paragraph in a more objective or neutral tone for an audience of adults. Remember to adopt the level of usage that best suits the subject and audience.*

SUGGESTED FURTHER READING

The following books dealing with some of the matters discussed in this chapter—the levels and varieties of English usage, the sources of its vocabulary, the relation of spoken to written English—will be found in almost every college library.

ADAMS, J. DONALD. *The Magic and Mystery of Words.* New York: Holt, Rinehart and Winston, 1963.

BLOOMFIELD, MORTON W., and LEONARD NEWMARK. *A Linguistic Introduction to the History of English.* New York: Alfred A. Knopf, 1963.

BRYANT, MARGARET M. *Modern English and Its Heritage.* 2nd ed. New York: Macmillan Publishing Co., Inc., 1962.

CARROLL, JOHN B. *The Study of Language.* Cambridge: Harvard University Press, 1958.

COPPERUD, ROY H. *American Usage: The Consensus.* New York: Van Nostrand Reinhold, 1970.

EVANS, BERGEN, and CORNELIA EVANS. *A Dictionary of Contemporary American Usage.* New York: Random House, 1957.

FOLLETT, WILSON. *Modern American Usage: A Guide.* New York: Hill and Wang, 1966.

FOWLER, H. W. *A Dictionary of Modern English Usage,* 2nd ed. Oxford: Clarendon Press, 1965.

GIBSON, WALKER, Editor. *The Limits of Language.* New York: Hill and Wang, 1962.

JESPERSEN, OTTO. *Growth and Structure of the English Language,* 9th ed. New York: Doubleday and Co., 1955.

NEWMAN, EDWIN. *Strictly Speaking: Will America Be the Death of English?* Indianapolis: Bobbs-Merrill, 1974.

PYLES, THOMAS. *Words and Ways of American English.* New York: Random House, 1952.

ROBERTSON, STUART. *The Development of Modern English.* New York: Random House, 1952.

2 | *Words and Phrases*

ENGLISH WORDS AND OUR LANGUAGE'S HISTORY

Although it is not crucial to good writing to know the detailed history of our language, some knowledge of that history can help any writer develop an enriched sense of the range and variety of words in English. Unabridged dictionaries generally list about 200,000 words, an inventory so large that it qualifies English as the General Motors of languages. None of us will ever learn the origins of all these words, let alone their meanings. Our purpose in this section is simply to describe the three main periods of English and to discuss the various "model" changes that have occurred on the linguistic production line.

Old English (OE) or Anglo-Saxon (AS)—449–1066 A.D.

The English language belongs to a family of languages called Indo-European. This large group of languages is supposed to have originated in Central East Europe in about 3500 B.C. Although no one has ever heard or read an Indo-European word, historians of the language have long recognized evidence that it did exist. Armenian, Hellenic (Greek), and Italic (Latin) are members of the Indo-European family; one branch, Germanic, is the direct parent of Anglo-Saxon or Old English. There were inhabitants of Britain before the Angles and Saxons invaded the country, and their language too was a part of the Indo-European family. Britain had also been conquered and ruled by Romans from 55 B.C. on, but neither the early Briton nor

37

Roman tongue left any significant trace on our present-day language.

Sailing from the mainland of Europe in 449 A.D., the Angles, Saxons, and Jutes came to help the Britons defeat northern enemies, the Picts and Irish, who had invaded their country. The European allies helped King Vortigern to win victory, but they overstayed their welcome, essentially controlling the country until 1066 A.D., when William of Normandy defeated Saxon King Harold at the Battle of Hastings. During this 600-year period, England became civilized and largely Christianized. The political map divided the country into four kingdoms—Northumbria, Mercia, Wessex, and Kent—and each of these cultures exerted its influence on the country at various times. Nearly sixty thousand words made up the language during this period, with some influx of Danish words resulting from sporadic invasions and conquests by the Vikings. Like Anglo-Saxon, Danish borrowings were simple and descriptive of family life and daily work: *give, hit, sister, low.*

Anglo-Saxon was an *inflected language,* that is, words changed form, usually by the addition of prefixes or suffixes, to express grammatical or syntactical relations. The OE verb *gefrūon* means "have heard," with the *ge-* prefix signaling the past tense. (German is a modern inflected language.) Modern English, however, is an *uninflected language,* that is, the position of the word in the sentence determines meaning, function, and so forth. We know *sail* is the verb in the following sentence because it comes after the subject and before the object: "They sailed to Sicily." The movement away from inflected to uninflected form was a gradual one and no doubt allowed for a greater influx of words from other languages. During the Anglo-Saxon period, however, the language spoken and written in England looked more like modern German than English.

Middle English—1066–1500 A.D.

When William the Conqueror defeated King Harold at Hastings, he began almost immediately to establish the language and culture of Norman France in the English court. But the people of Britain still spoke Anglo-Saxon in their daily commerce, while the Catholic Church continued to use Latin as its official language. By the middle of the fourteenth century, English was the accepted language of the ruling classes, the legal system, and the Church. In fact, the dominant dialect became the East Midland dialect of London, which has persisted to this day. Geoffrey Chaucer, the famous English poet, wrote his *Canterbury Tales* in the East Midland dialect.

While Norman French did not take over from Anglo-Saxon the position of universal language in England, it did contribute many social, political, and economic words to our language. *Parliament, crown, sovereign, jury, plaintiff, castle, grocer,* and *chamber* are all Norman words. We should realize, however, that Norman words did not automatically replace Anglo-Saxon ones. In many instances pairs of words, one from each language, have survived and may be used synonymously: *work* (OE) and *labor* (OF), *cow* (OE) and *beef* (OF), *deer* (OE) and *venison* (OF), *room* (OE) and *chamber* (OF). Note that in most instances the Norman word sounds more formal than the Old English one.

Norman words made their steady way into English not only because they were used by court, legal, and literary figures, but also because Norman French was uninflected. The English that was evolving from Anglo-Saxon in the fourteenth century was also becoming less inflected or "synthetic." This change meant that English was able to grow, adding new words from European cultures and societies. The result was Middle English, the language perfected by such writers as William Langland and Geoffrey Chaucer.

By the end of the fourteenth century, Middle English had acquired a distinctly modern look and sound. Except for the somewhat strange spellings, the following passage from the Bible, translated by John Wycliffe in 1380 A.D., should be easily comprehended after one careful reading.

And eft Jhesus bigan to teche at the see; and myche puple was gaderid to him, so that he wente into a boot, and sat in

the see, and al the puple was aboute the see on the loond.
And he taughte hem in parablis many thingis.

In this excerpt you can see that Middle English writing,
like Anglo-Saxon, functions largely through coordinate
clauses, that is, independent clauses joined by *and.* Modern
English, on the other hand, has developed the subordinate
clause as a means of indicating relations and shades of
meaning. Note also that the ME plural pronoun was *hem*
instead of *them.*

Modern English—1500–Present

Two significant events ushered in the Modern English
period: William Caxton's establishment of a printing press
in 1476 A.D., and the continental Renaissance contribution
of many Greek and Latin words. By printing a large number
of books in London English, Caxton helped to set the
dialect of that region as the national standard. His transla-
tions in particular regulated usage as he selected words
that could be understood by the largest body of readers.
During the early 1500's many Latin and Greek words appeared in literature and government documents as humanist scholars like William Lyly and John Colet fostered an
interest in works from the classical world. While there was
a reaction against such Latinate words as *laureate, impedi-
ment,* and *prolixity,* the Elizabethan age (1558–1603) marked
a stage of rapid growth in English vocabulary. With the
performing and publishing of Shakespeare's plays and the
appearance of the King James Bible (1611 A.D.), Modern
English was recognized as one of the richest, most diverse
languages. The King James Bible was particularly important in preventing the language from becoming too heavily
Latinate and pedantic. Translators, many of whom were
in fact scholars, sought to use language that was simple
and dignified.

40

OUR CHANGING LANGUAGE

Three major influences on the course of the English language since 1500 are worth noting. First, dictionaries, grammars, and printing houses, the earliest of which appeared in the eighteenth century, have instituted standards of correctness in spelling, pronunciation, and meaning that had not until then existed. (Shakespeare, like most of his contemporaries, spelled his last name in several different ways.) Second, the introduction of universal education, especially in this country, has contributed to the growth of awareness about standards of usage in writing, reading, and speaking. Third, the speech heard on television, on radio, and in the movies has strongly influenced usage throughout England and America, all but obliterating regional differences. Asking for a *bag* in a grocery store anywhere in America is likely to produce a brown paper container, even though in that particular region a *bag* is called a *sack* or *poke*. Although the changes that have resulted from these influences may at times perplex us (every TV anchorperson now seems to say *hopefully* instead of *it is hoped*), we cannot forget that weeds as well as flowers are bound to grow in the garden of a living language. Trying to impose strict laws on usage and on the importing of foreign words, as has in fact been tried in France, would lead to a stultified, probably pedantic language—if such lawmaking could work. It is reassuring to note as well that although certain nonwords like *input* and *prioritize* do from time to time creep into the garden, other growths like "Far out!" and *rehab* die from neglect.

Although the spoken language is subject to fads and rages, written English requires us to compose in a language that will be understood by the widest possible audience. One of the reasons we have such a rich vocabulary is that writers have kept alive words and images that might otherwise fade from conversation. By following the practice of these writers you will be helping to enrich a language that has already proved indispensable to people throughout the world. By studying the history of our language, moreover, in particular the original meanings of words and phrases, your own writing will begin to reflect the versatility and simplicity that are the strengths of Standard written English.

USING THE DICTIONARY

If a word always stood for only one thing or only one idea, communication would be simple indeed. But words have a way of acquiring many meanings through their use by different people at different times under different conditions. Our review of the history of the English language shows just how fluid and adaptable a living language can be. Some of the most common words, such as *get, give, hard, take, run, read, stand, shoot,* have dozens of meanings each. As an illustration of the complexity and multiplicity of meanings that a word can acquire, consider the first in the list—*get.*

He got a reward. I'll get home early. Did you get him on the phone? Can you get *Dallas* on your TV set? Go get your coat. Can you get him to eat? Get going. Get the supplies to them. He got six months for that. He's got the habit. Drugs will get him. Did you get the wig she was wearing? You'll get caught in the storm. Get it?

We speak of the *denotation,* or the exact, literal meaning of a word, and of the *connotation,* or associated meaning of a word. To be more exact we have to point out that literal meanings and associated meanings blend and merge, change with time and circumstance, and to some extent differ with every different person using these words. Consider a very common noun—*dog.* How did so many opposite associated meanings attach themselves to this poor animal?

42

Faithful as a dog. The bill collector dogged him. They showed dogged courage. He's a lucky dog. He's going to the dogs. It's a dog's life. It's dog eat dog with him.

Many words—and very important ones too—seem to live perpetually in a fog, because there is nothing tangible or visible for which they stand: nothing at which you can point your finger and say, "This is it. This is what I mean." When you say *dog* or *chair* or *book,* you can, if it is important enough, find some dog or chair or book to point to and say, "This is it." But when words stand for ideas, such as *temperance* or *democracy* or *security,* the problem is much harder. All you can do is qualify and define, or point to a person who is temperate, a state that is democratic, a social system that provides security. Such vagueness is not a very satisfactory condition for speakers and writers, but it is the best we have. When we do not choose our words carefully, when we do not define, or point to examples, we may be talking about one thing and our listeners or readers may be thinking another. And that is a worse condition.

To make the art of exact communication by words even more difficult, some people seem to use words in devious ways. Words have always been used by some people to conceal meaning, not to reveal it. Think of the way some politicians or their spokesmen distort meaning by using euphemisms: *inoperative,* we quickly learned, meant an outright lie when it was used by press secretaries and others during the Watergate scandal of the early nineteen seventies. With other people, abstract words have only one real meaning—the meaning *they* have assigned. A difference of opinion over what a word means, however, does not always imply dishonesty or evil intent. Profoundly honest people may differ in their understanding of words, depending on differences in their background, their training, and their temperament. In the mind, the meaning of a word can change under the stress of emotion, or even under the stress of political campaigns and elections. Such words as *socialism, capitalism, extremism, recession,* and *bureaucracy* mean one thing to members of a political party when it is in office and another thing when it is out of office.

A dictionary lists the words of a language, in alphabetical order, and gives information about their meaning, their spelling, their use, their pronunciation, and their history; the degree of completeness of this information depends on the size and purpose of the dictionary. The information found in a dictionary is based on an extensive study of the language in action; for every word listed, a great mass of information has been collected, classified, filed, and studied by a trained staff and, where necessary, by consultants from special fields in which the word is used. All information in a reliable dictionary is based on a study of usage. *A dictionary reflects usage; it does not prescribe it.* It is an authority only insofar as it accurately reflects usage.

The various dictionaries of the English language fall into the following classes:

1. The monumentally complete ones, in which a word gets full historical treatment, with quotations illustrating its use from the time of its birth to the date of completion of the dictionary:

The New English Dictionary, in 10 vols. and a supplement, 1888–1928, reissued in corrected edition as *Oxford English Dictionary,* 12 vols., 1933 (also known as *N.E.D., O.E.D.,* the *Oxford,* and *Murray's*). *The Compact Edition,* 2 vols. 1971. In the *N.E.D.* there are 1,827,306 quotations of usage.

2. The one-volume unabridged dictionaries, which you find in schoolrooms and libraries for reference use. They are usually kept up to date by spot revisions and by "New Word Sections." The *New International,* however, has been entirely rewritten.

Webster's Third New International Dictionary. Springfield, Mass.: G. & C. Merriam Company, 1971.
Funk & Wagnalls New Standard Dictionary of the English Language. New York: Funk & Wagnalls Company, 1963, 1966.
The Random House Dictionary of the English Language. New York: Random House, 1966, 1967.

44

3. The one-volume, desk-size dictionaries, one of which almost every college student buys as a part of his working equipment. Each one of these listed here is well worth the cost; the choice is usually governed by the recommendation of the student's English instructor.

Webster's New World Dictionary, 2nd College Edition. Cleveland and New York: The World Publishing Company, 1976.
Webster's New Collegiate Dictionary. Springfield, Mass.: G. & C. Merriam Company, 1975, 1977.
The American College Dictionary. New York: Random House, 1973.
The American Heritage Dictionary of the English Language. New York and Boston: American Heritage and Houghton Mifflin, 1973.

The following kinds of information may be secured from a desk dictionary:

1. The Meaning of a Word. As you can see by examining the various excerpts from dictionaries that are reprinted here, a dictionary uses several methods of clarifying the meaning of a word. First, it uses *phrases of definition,* and it often follows the definition with illustrative examples. Second, it uses *synonyms,* either immediately after the defining phrase or in a group below where the synonyms are compared and contrasted. Then, at times, it may present a special list of *idiomatic phrases* using the word. The dictionary also classifies the different meanings a word may have, numbers them, and, if a word has special technical uses, labels these uses and explains them. Some dictionaries list the oldest meanings first; others begin with the most commonly used meanings. It is important to know which method your dictionary uses. You should read *all* the definitions of a word before deciding to use the word in a certain sentence.

In the selection from *Webster's New World Dictionary,* note that the most recent, the most commonly used sense of the word is given first. The thirteen different uses of *pull* as a transitive verb *(vt.)* are given in order, numbered, and, where necessary labeled, as: 6. [Colloq.]; 7. [Colloq.];

45

9. [Dial.]. The definitions of *pull* as an intransitive verb and as a noun follow.[1]

pull (pool) *vt.* [ME. *pullen* < OE. *pullian*, to pluck, snatch with the fingers: ? akin to MLowG. *pull*, a husk, shell] 1. to exert force or influence on so as to cause to move toward or after the source of the force; drag, tug, draw, attract, etc. 2. *a)* to draw out; pluck out; extract [to *pull* a tooth] *b)* to pick or uproot [to *pull* carrots] 3. to draw apart; rip; tear [to *pull* a seam] ☆4. to stretch (taffy, etc.) back and forth repeatedly 5. to stretch or strain to the point of injury [to *pull* a muscle] ☆6. [Colloq.] to put into effect; carry out; perform [to *pull* a raid] 7. [Colloq.] to hold back; restrain [to *pull* one's punches] 8. [Colloq.] ☆*a)* to take (a gun, knife, etc.) from concealment so as to threaten *b)* to take or force off or out; remove [to *pull* a wheel from a car] 9. [Dial.] to draw the entrails from (a fowl) 10. *Baseball, Golf* to hit (the ball) and make it curve to the left or, if left-handed, to the right 11. *Horse Racing* to rein in or restrain (a horse) so as to keep it from winning 12. *Printing* to take (a proof) on a hand press 13. *Rowing* *a)* to work (an oar) by drawing it toward one *b)* to transport by rowing *c)* to be rowed normally by [a boat that *pulls* four oars] —*vi.* 1. to exert force in or for dragging, tugging, or attracting something 2. to take a deep draft of a drink or puff at a cigarette, etc. 3. to be capable of being pulled 4. to move or drive a vehicle (*away, ahead, around, out,* etc.) —*n.* 1. the act, force, or result of pulling; specif., *a)* a dragging, tugging, attracting, etc. *b)* the act or an instance of rowing *c)* a drink *d)* a puff at a cigarette, etc. *e)* a difficult, continuous effort, as in climbing *f)* the force needed to move a weight, trigger, etc., measured in pounds *g)* *Baseball, Golf* the act or an instance of pulling a ball 2. something to be pulled, as the handle of a drawer, etc. ☆3. [Colloq.] *a)* influence or special advantage *b)* drawing power; appeal —**pull apart** to find fault with; criticize —**pull down** 1. to tear down, demolish, or overthrow 2. to degrade; humble ☆3. to reduce 4. [Colloq.] to get (a specified wage, grade, etc.) —☆**pull for** [Colloq.] to cheer on, or hope for the success of —**pull in** 1. to arrive 2. to draw in or hold back 3. [Slang] to arrest and take to police headquarters —**pull off** [Colloq.] to bring about, accomplish, or perform —**pull oneself together** to collect one's faculties; regain one's poise, courage, etc. —**pull out** ☆1. to depart ☆2. to withdraw or retreat ☆3. to escape from a contract, responsibility, etc. 4. *Aeron.* to level out from a dive or landing approach —**pull over** to drive (a vehicle) to or toward the curb —**pull through** [Colloq.] to get through or over (an illness, difficulty, etc.) —**pull up** 1. to uproot 2. to bring or come to a stop 3. *a)* to drive (a vehicle) to a specified place *b)* to make (an aircraft) nose up sharply 4. to check or rebuke —**pull′er** *n.*
SYN.—pull is the broad, general term of this list, as defined in sense 1 of the *vt.* above; **draw** suggests a smoother, more even motion than **pull** [he *drew* his sword from its scabbard]; **drag** implies the slow pulling of something heavy, connoting great resistance in the thing pulled [he *dragged* the desk across the floor]; **tug** suggests strenuous, persistent effort in pulling but does not necessarily connote success in moving the object [he *tugged* at the rope to no avail]; **haul** implies sustained effort in transporting something heavy, often mechanically [to *haul* furniture in a truck]; **tow** implies pulling by means of a rope or cable [to *tow* a stalled automobile] —**ANT. push, shove**

46

Notice here and in the excerpt from *The Random House Dictionary of the English Language*[2] how carefully the various synonyms are illustrated and distinguished. These illustrations and discriminated synonyms are a valuable help to finding and using the exact word.

---

crowd[1] (kroud), *n.* **1.** a large number of persons gathered closely together; throng: *a crowd of angry people.* **2.** any large number of persons. **3.** the common people; the masses: *The crowd needs leadership.* **4.** any group or set of persons: *They cater to a society crowd.* **5.** a large number of things gathered or considered together. **6.** *Sociol.* a temporary gathering of people responding to common stimuli and engaged in any of various forms of collective behavior. **7.** audience; attendance: *Opening night drew a good crowd.* —*v.i.* **8.** to gather in large numbers; throng; swarm. **9.** to press forward; advance by pushing. —*v.t.* **10.** to push; shove. **11.** to press closely together; force into a confined space; cram: *to crowd clothes into a suitcase.* **12.** to fill to excess; fill by pressing or thronging into. **13.** *Informal.* to place under pressure or stress by constant solicitation: *to crowd a debtor for payment; to crowd someone with embarrassing questions.* **14. crowd on sail,** *Naut.* to carry a press of sail. [ME *crowd(en)*, OE *crūden* to press, hurry; c. MD *crūden* to push (D *kruien*)]
—**Syn. 1.** horde, herd. CROWD, MULTITUDE, SWARM, THRONG are terms referring to large numbers of people. CROWD suggests a jostling, uncomfortable, and possibly disorderly company: *A crowd gathered to listen to the speech.* MULTITUDE emphasizes the great number of persons or things but suggests that there is space enough for all: *a multitude of people at the market on Saturdays.* SWARM as used of people is usually contemptuous, suggesting a moving, restless, often noisy, crowd: *A swarm of dirty children played in the street.* THRONG suggests a company that presses together or forward, often with some common aim: *The throng pushed forward to see the cause of the excitement.* **3.** proletariat, plebeians, people, populace. **8.** assemble, herd. **9.** shove, press. **11.** pack, squeeze, cramp.

---

2. The Spelling of a Word. If your instructor has marked *rythem* as misspelled, you may have trouble finding the correct spelling, *rhythm,* in the dictionary. The difficulty, however, is rare; ignorance of the first letter or two in a word is much less common than vagueness about those at about the middle or at the end. In by far the greater number of instances, the dictionary is the quickest and surest check for the spelling of a word. Some words have variant spellings. Where these are indicated, you will be

---

[2] Reprinted by permission of Random House, Inc., from *The American College Dictionary.* Copyright 1947, copyright © 1966, 1973.

safe in using the first one listed. In the following unit are some of the ways in which variant spellings are listed in dictionaries.

THE AMERICAN COL-LEGE DICTIONARY

color: Also, *Brit.,* **colour**
theater: Also, *esp. Brit.,* **the-atre**
check, n: Also, *Brit.,* **cheque**

STANDARD COLLEGE DICTIONARY

color: Also *Brit.* **colour**
theater: Also *esp. Brit.* **theatre**

glamour: Also *U.S.* **glamor**

WEBSTER'S NEW WORLD DICTIONARY

aesthete: Also spelled **es-thete**
connection: connexion, British spelling

WEBSTER'S NEW COLLEGIATE DICTION-ARY

pyjamas: *chiefly Brit. var of* **pajamas**
theater *or* **theatre**

3. The Pronunciation of a Word. The pronunciation of a word is usually indicated by respelling it with diacritical marks and symbols or respelling it in some form of a phonetic alphabet. The method used is explained in detail at the front of every dictionary. A study of these explanations is worthwhile. A brief summary of the symbols used is given at the foot of every page or every two pages facing each other in the dictionary proper. Where two or more pronunciations are current, the dictionary will give both. Check the respelling, the variant accent, the pronunciation symbols, and the stress or accent points in the following from the *New Collegiate*.[3]

---

for·mi·ca·ry \'fòr-mə-ˌker-ē\ *n, pl* **-car·ies** [ML *formicarium,* fr. L *formica*] : an ant nest
for·mi·da·ble \'fòr-məd-ə-bəl *also* fòr-'mid- *or* fər-'mid-\ *adj* [ME, fr. L *formidabilis,* fr. *formidare* to fear, fr. *formido* fear; akin to Gk *mormō* she-monster] **1** : causing fear, dread, or apprehension <a ~ prospect> **2** : having qualities that discourage approach or attack **3** : tending to inspire awe or wonder — **for·mi·da·bil·i·ty** \ˌfòr-məd-ə-'bil-ət-ē; fòr-ˌmid-, fər-ˌ\ *n* — **for·mi·da·ble·ness** \'fòr-məd-ə-bəl-nəs; fòr-'mid-, fər-'\ *n* — **for·mi·da·bly** \-blē\ *adv*

---

[3] By permission. From *Webster's New Collegiate Dictionary,* © 1981 by G. & C. Merriam Co., Publishers of the Merriam-Webster Dictionaries.

48

Pronunciation symbols and the indication of accents may vary between dictionaries. Observe these symbols carefully in the dictionary you own and use.

4. Labels: Subject, Geographical, Usage. Every dictionary uses geographical and subject labels to show that a word in the sense indicated is characteristic of a region or language or that it has a special meaning in connection with a certain subject. To understand this more clearly, you might check the labels used with the following words: *pone, jollity, Erse, tot, trauma, suture, kirk, syne, cannikin.* You will find some of these words with a subject label in one dictionary and no label in another. A similar lack of agreement exists in connection with usage labels. *Webster's New World Dictionary* uses the following where in the judgment of its editors these labels are called for: *colloquial, slang, obsolete, archaic, poetic, dialect, British. Webster's New Collegiate* uses "status labels" instead of "usage labels." These are *obsolete, archaic, slang, substandard, nonstandard, dialect.* The "regional labels"—*dial Brit, New Eng, chiefly Scot,* and other similar ones— are classified under status labels. The *Standard College Dictionary* uses "restrictive labels," as follows: *illit., slang, dial., informal,* and other labels indicting regional or national divisions, such as *Southern U.S., Brit., Scot. The American College Dictionary* lists the following usage labels: *archaic, colloq., humorous, obs., slang, poetic, obsolesc., rare, Scot., Scot and N. Eng., South African, U.S.* Note that neither the *New Collegiate* nor the *Standard* uses *colloq.* All of the four still use *slang* as a label. Note the various usage labels in the following two excerpts, the first shown being from *The American Heritage Dictionary.*[4]

[4] ©1980, Houghton Mifflin Company. Reprinted by permission from *The American Heritage Dictionary of the English Language.*

---

cool (kōōl) *adj.* **cooler, coolest. 1.** Moderately cold; neither warm nor very cold. **2.** Reducing discomfort in hot weather; allowing a feeling of coolness: *a cool blouse.* **3.** Not excited; calm; controlled. **4.** Showing dislike, disdain, or indifference; unenthusiastic; not cordial: *a cool greeting.* **5.** Calmly audacious or bold; impudent. **6.** Designating or characteristic of colors, such as blue and green, that produce the impression of coolness. **7.** *Slang.* Having a quiet, indifferent, and aloof attitude. **8.** *Slang.* Excellent; first-rate; superior. **9.** *Informal.* Without exaggeration; entire; full: *He lost a cool million.* —*v.* **cooled, cooling, cools.** —*tr.* **1.** To make less warm. **2.** To make less ardent, intense, or zealous. —*intr.* **1.** To become less warm. **2.** To become calm. —**cool it.** *Slang.* To calm down, slow down, or relax. —**cool one's heels.** *Informal.* To be kept waiting for a long time. —*n.* **1.** Anything that is cool or moderately cold: *the cool of early morning.* **2.** The state or quality of being cool. **3.** *Slang.* Composure: *recover one's cool.* [Middle English *col*, Old English *cōl*. See **gel-³** in Appendix.*] —**cool′ly** *adv.* —**cool′ness** *n.*

Synonyms: *cool, composed, collected, unruffled, nonchalant, imperturbable, detached.* These adjectives apply to persons to indicate calmness, especially in time of stress. *Cool* has the widest application. Usually it implies merely a high degree of self-control, though it may also indicate aloofness. *Composed* and *collected* more strongly imply conscious display of self-discipline and absence of agitation. *Composed* also often suggests serenity or sedateness, and *collected,* mental concentration. *Unruffled* emphasizes calmness in the face of severe provocation that may have produced agitation in others present. *Nonchalant* describes a casual exterior manner that suggests, sometimes misleadingly, a lack of interest or concern. *Imperturbable* stresses unshakable calmness considered usually as an inherent trait rather than as a product of self-discipline. *Detached* implies aloofness and either lack of active concern or resistance to emotional involvement.

Now look for various usage labels in the excerpts from dictionaries reproduced on pages 46–47 (*Webster's New World* and the *Random House*), and then examine carefully the selection below, which is quoted from *Webster's New Collegiate Dictionary.*[5]

5. Derivation of a Word. As you know, our words have

---

¹stiff \'stif\ *adj* [ME *stif,* fr. OE *stif;* akin to MD *stijf* stiff, L *stipare* to press together, Gk *steibein* to tread on] **1 a :** not easily bent **:** RIGID **b :** lacking in suppleness <~ muscles> **c :** impeded in movement — used of a mechanism **d :** DRUNK **e :** incapable of normal alert response <scared ~> **2 a :** FIRM, RESOLUTE **b :** STUBBORN, UNYIELDING **c :** PROUD **d** (1) **:** marked by reserve or decorum (2) **:** lacking in ease or grace **:** STILTED **3 :** hard fought **:** PUGNACIOUS, SHARP **4 a** (1) **:** exerting great force <a ~ wind> (2) **:** FORCEFUL, VIGOROUS <a ~ dose> **5 :** of a dense or glutinous consistency **:** THICK **6 a :** HARSH, SEVERE <a ~ penalty> **b :** ARDUOUS, RUGGED <~ terrain> **7 :** not easily heeled over by an external force (as the wind) <a ~ ship> **8 :** EXPENSIVE, STEEP <paid a ~ price> — **stiff·ly** *adv*
syn STIFF, RIGID, INFLEXIBLE, TENSE, STARK *shared meaning element* **:** difficult or impossible to bend or enliven *ant* relaxed, supple
²stiff *adv* **:** in a stiff manner **:** STIFFLY
³stiff *n* **1 :** CORPSE **2 a :** BUM, TRAMP **b :** HAND, LABORER
stiff–arm \'stif-,ärm\ *vb or n* **:** STRAIGHT-ARM

---

[5] By permission. From *Webster's New Collegiate Dictionary,* © 1981 by G. & C. Merriam Co., Publishers of the Merriam-Webster Dictionaries.

come from many languages, and some have undergone many changes in form and meaning. A daisy, for instance, was a "day's eye," a nasturtium was a "nose twister," our common dandelion was once a "lion's tooth." And would you believe that our word *emerald* had an ancestor that in Latin was once *smaragdus* and in Greek *smaragdos*? The Roman Emperor Nero once used a polished *smaragdus* as a lens in front of his near-sighted eye. So you see that the derivations of words are interesting in themselves, and they might enrich your understanding of words.

The following words have unusually interesting origins: *bedlam, boycott, broker, calico, curfew, dollar, exhume, lunacy, panic, sandwich, sinister, saxophone, tawdry, thug, vandal.*

6. Grammatical Information. A desk-sized dictionary gives adequate information about plurals of nouns and the principal parts of verbs. Inflectional forms are usually given only when they are irregular or when they present difficulties of spelling or pronunciation. For example, no plurals are given for *book, chair, handkerchief* because it is assumed that these nouns, and all others like them, form their plurals in the regular way. But after *index* you find two plurals: *indexes, indices;* after *deer* you find the information that the plural is also *deer* (occasionally *deers*); after *ox* you find the plural is *oxen* (rarely *ox*). Similarly, no principal parts are given after regular verbs, especially when no special problems are involved: see *talk, walk*. But note that *study* is followed by *studied, studying* to show what happens to the ending in the formation of the past tense and the present participle and gerund. Then look up the verb *lie,* which has two main meanings, and note that the principal parts are necessary to distinguish between the two meanings: *lie* [recline], *lay, lain, lying; lie* [prevaricate], *lied, lying.* The last example also illustrates that when the past tense and the past participle have the same form, it is given only once:

lie: He *lied.* I had *lied* about it. [lie, lied, lying]
bring: He *brought* it. I had *brought* it with me. [bring, brought, bringing]

51

ring: He *rang* the bell. I had *rung* it a minute earlier. [ring, rang, rung, ringing]

7. Idiomatic Phrases. Many of the simple, everyday verbs of the language, through many years of various uses and associations, have acquired special meanings in phrases that we call *idioms*. Notice the quotation from *Webster's New World Dictionary*, page 46, to understand what is meant by an idiom: *pull apart* [to criticize], *pull down* [to degrade, to humble], *pull for* [to cheer on], *pull off* [to accomplish], *pull oneself together* [to regain poise], *pull over* [to drive to the curb], *pull through* [to get over an illness], *pull up* [to uproot, to come to a stop]. Anyone can see that these are not literal meanings of the verb. Here are a few more examples of idioms, from various dictionaries: *give ground, take stock, take the floor, have it in for, have it out, run out of, do away with, do for, put one down, shoot the breeze.* See [§ 23] for a fuller discussion of idiomatic speech.

8. Synonyms and Antonyms. Pairs of words that have exactly the same meaning—literal and associated—are not too common in the English language, but words may have approximately the same meaning, or approximately the same meaning in certain uses. Examine the excerpts from dictionaries listed here and study the synonyms under *cool, crowd, pull, stiff*. Note that synonyms are used in illustrative phrases and then sometimes in a separate list where they are compared and contrasted. Antonyms are listed less commonly than synonyms.

EXERCISES

EXERCISE 1, DEFINITIONS. *Look up the meanings of each of the following words. List at least two very different meanings for each.*

intern	aggravate	irony	criticize
propaganda	fellow	nice	curious

EXERCISE 2, SPELLING. *Look up each of the following words. Decide whether both spellings are used in your locality or whether one is more common than the other.*

adviser, advisor	glamorize, glamourize	sulfur, sulphur
although, altho	night, nite	theater, theatre

EXERCISE 3, PRONUNCIATION. *Look up the pronunciation of the following words. Notice where the accent is placed in each word. Where more than one pronunciation is listed, try pronouncing the word in each way. Which form do you use in your own conversation?*

acumen	data	Don Quixote	inquiry
adult	decade	exquisite	irreparable
aspirant	decadence	finance	lamentable
combatant	despicable	formidable	perseverance
culinary	Don Juan	gondola	superfluous

EXERCISE 4, STATUS OR USAGE LABELS. *What usage or status label—if any—follows each of the following words?*

alarum	coulee	heap	loser
belike	enthuse	hokum	petrol
bozo	goober	joker	scam

EXERCISE 5, DERIVATION. *From what language did each of the following words come?*

banjo	lava	prairie	rodeo
chinook	mosquito	rebus	sapphire
ersatz	pongee	riata	soprano

EXERCISE 6, IDIOMATIC PREPOSITIONS. *Supply the idiomatic prepositions as required in the following sentences.*

1. Since I was so concerned (   ) my business at that time, she was concerned (   ) my health.
2. At that period we differed (   ) almost everything.
3. She especially differed (   ) me about money matters.

4. Finally we separated (   ) one another.
5. Neither of us, however, proved to be capable (   )
   living alone.

CONCRETENESS

*In general, a concrete word with a clear image has more effect
than an abstract one, a specific word evokes more response than a
general one, and a homely word makes more friends than a bookish
or pretentious one.*

A concrete noun, such as *bridge, wall, needle, cloud, smoke,
shoe,* or *apple,* names something that can be perceived
through any of the senses. In other words, it names something you can touch, see, hear, taste, smell, or feel. *Abstract*
words name ideas, or qualities, as *beauty, cleverness, elitism,
truth, loyalty,* or *doubt.* Now of course you can seldom give
a concrete equivalent of an abstract word, but you can—
and should—spell out your concept of the abstraction you
use. To say "My father is both stubborn and easygoing"
is not enough if you want to present him dramatically;
bring him out on the stage for us to see, and show him
in the middle of an argument.

General words name classes or groups; *specific* words name
the individual objects, actions, or qualities that compose
the group. The terms are to some extent relative: *furniture*
is a class of things; *chair* is more specific than *furniture,*
more general than *armchair* or *rocking chair.*

Weapon is a general noun. When, for example, you write,
"Mrs. Hanks assaulted her husband with a deadly weapon,"
what control do you have over what goes on in your reader's mind? What picture do your words call up? Did she
stab him with a steak knife, club him with a baseball bat,
slash him with a safety razor blade that she had slipped
out of the medicine chest, or shoot him with a .22 caliber
pistol? You say the police found an ornament that she
had dropped in the scuffle. It was probably a piece of jewelry—which is more specific than *ornament*—but it would

have been more specific and more effective to say "a jade green earring."

The verb *move* is general; *stride, amble, creep, glide, jog* are all more specific ways of moving. The adjective *large* is general; when you try to make it more specific, you discover that different varieties of largeness are associated with different nouns. For instance, *bulky, towering, brawny, fat, spacious, hulking* are applicable to which of these—a building, a man, a room, a tree?

Homely words are those associated with the objects and activities of everyday living; *bookish* or *pretentious* words are those associated with excessive literary formality.

The following pairs of words and expressions will help to make the distinctions clearer:

ABSTRACT WORDS

the faithfulness of an animal; the harmony of music; a misfortune of battle; extreme intoxication.

CONCRETE WORDS

She served him like a dog; my mother hummed a ballad; a shell fragment ripped open his right arm; he was lit up like a Christmas tree.

GENERAL WORDS

Furniture, clothing, cutlery, kitchen utensil, a crime, an industrial worker, a flower, an animal.

SPECIFIC WORDS

Sofa, raincoat, a carving knife, a frying pan, burglary, a welder, a rose, a lion.

BOOKISH OR PRETENTIOUS WORDS

Frigidity, inebriated, suspend, incarcerated, the matutinal meal, to delve, intestinal fortitude.

HOMELY WORDS

Coldness, drunk, hang, jailed, breakfast, to dig, courage.

These are by no means scientific classifications applicable to all words in the language. We are merely picking out handfuls of words as samples and saying in effect: "Look at these. This type of word seems to do something more to your imagination and comprehension than that one." Abstract and general words are not bad words; they are necessary for the expression of abstract qualities and general ideas. Bookish words are natural in certain scholarly, formal contexts. But in the writing of the average student, abstract and general words are used too often where concrete and specific words would do a better job. Remember, disagreement over the meaning of an abstract term is frequent.

The following examples should help to make the idea clearer. You may assume that the "General and Ineffective" examples are not topic, or thesis, sentences.

GENERAL AND INEFFECTIVE WRITING

In order to make washing clothes in public more pleasant, we need larger buildings and some means to pass the time.

CONCRETE AND SPECIFIC WRITING

We should build Laundromats the way the Romans built public baths. There should be a central, preferably vaulted, hall full of washers and dryers and ironing boards. Other halls should be equipped as nurseries, gymnasiums, and pool halls. There should be bingo on Tuesday and visits by political candidates on Thursdays. Perhaps even fish fries on Saturdays. Urban visionaries constantly suggest turning old railroad stations and warehouses into boutique complexes. Why not Laundromats instead?

—JANE O'REILLY, "Meet Me at the Rinse Cycle"

GENERAL AND INEFFECTIVE WRITING

President Carter's aides are best described as infantile types with little sense of public decorum.

CONCRETE AND SPECIFIC WRITING

There is a very definite style among some younger Carter staffers. They are overgrown fraternity and sorority boys and girls. Now in their late twenties and early thirties, they still seek the comfort and solace of the local neighborhood bars; they go there to "get crazy" or "get wasted," put beanies with airplane propellers on their heads, watch TV, pick up dates, and drink beer with tequila chasers.

—SALLY QUINN, "The Carter Style— Beanies, Beer, and Jesus"

GENERAL AND INEFFECTIVE WRITING

Fourteenth century doctors used many strange methods to treat symptoms of the Black Death.

CONCRETE AND SPECIFIC WRITING

When it came to the plague, sufferers were treated by various measures designed to draw poison or infection from the body: by bleeding, purging with laxatives or enemas, lancing or cauterizing the buboes, or application of hot plasters. None of this was of much use. Medicines ranged from pills of powdered stag's horn or myrrh and saffron to potions of potable gold. Compounds of rare spices and powdered pearls or emeralds were prescribed, possibly on the theory, not unknown to modern medicine, that a patient's sense of therapeutic value is in proportion to the expense.

BARBARA W. TUCHMAN, *A Distant Mirror*

GENERAL AND INEFFECTIVE WRITING

He searched the body carefully and found some interesting objects.

CONCRETE AND SPECIFIC WRITING

He dropped to his knees and turned the body over and fumbled with the shirt cuffs. The man wore a watch, but the band was plastic and the watch itself was covered with a waterproof case. He searched the pockets for a coin, a jack-knife blade, a lighter. He tore open the man's shirt, hoping to find a medallion or dog tags, and there, dangling from a slender chain, was a gold-plated razor blade, one of the ritual tools of the cocaine fraternity. He unfastened the chain and held the razor to the sun.

—PETER BENCHLEY, *The Island*

57

EXERCISES

EXERCISE 1, GENERAL AND SPECIFIC WORDS. *Find several specific words for each of the following general words.*

jewelry	animal	to move	road	to laugh
flower	ship	to speak	grass	to dance
entertainment	car	to sing	bird	to hit

EXERCISE 2, ABSTRACT AND CONCRETE WORDS. *Construct sentences in which you give concrete examples of each of the following abstract terms.*

unselfishness	ignorance	fear
efficiency	stubbornness	laziness

EXERCISE 3, REVISING WITH SPECIFIC AND CONCRETE WORDS. *Rewrite the following sentences, making them more specific and concrete.*

1. On the porch a row of elderly women sat and rocked and watched the new guests come in.
2. An irritated and impatient policeman was trying to give directions to a driver.
3. The sounds at midnight are interesting to hear.
4. A little boy was happily playing in the alley.
5. The man leaned against the wall and fell asleep.

DICTION

Selecting the right word for the right situation is an important key to good writing. Words that work together are like parts of a jigsaw puzzle snapped snugly into place to form a beautiful picture. Forcing parts to fit when they refuse will create a distorted picture; words that do not fit will only confuse your reader. The art of choosing and arranging words in writing is called *diction,* and we will devote a few pages to matters that bear directly on this art. Further suggestions for improving word choice can be found in § 21–25 of the "Handbook" section.

Informal and Colloquial Words

Words labeled "Informal" or "Colloquial" in the dictionary should not be used in formal essay writing. They may be used in dialogue or when quoting someone, but they do not belong in the body of your papers. Words that are not labeled in the dictionary represent general English usage and should be used in your essays and examinations. Remember too not to use contractions; write out all contracted forms.

COLLOQUIAL OR INFORMAL WRITING

The prof didn't hand back our exams today. We lived it up the whole night, but by six I was tapped out.

GENERAL WRITING

The professor did not hand back our examinations today. We had an exciting time for part of the night, but by six A.M. I was ready for bed.

Slang

As a general rule, it is best not to use slang in the essays you write for your English class. Attitudes are changing toward the labeling and use of slang words; some articles written for magazines such as *Saturday Review* and *The New Yorker* do reveal instances of slang from time to time. Here is an example from an essay written by Thomas Griffith for *The Atlantic Monthly:* "In all this marketing and money-making, the poor *chump* of a fan is the last to be considered." Words like *chump, yahoo, schlemiel,* and *creep* have a vivid, descriptive quality that cannot be denied. Words like *cool, farout, lousy,* and *scummy,* however, do not have the same pictorial impact and are not generally found in published writing, except in dialogue.

EXERCISE. *Try to find more descriptive words or phrases for those in italics. You may rewrite the sentences in any way that you believe makes them better.*

1. Robert Redford is a *boss dude* who gives off *good vibes.*
2. Little Ronnie's behavior has been *yucky.*
3. The music at last night's concert was *farout.*
4. The way he answered the phone showed that he was a *total jerk.*
5. When are you going to stop wearing such *scummy-looking threads?*

Regionalisms

Many words or phrases are native to a particular region of the country. They are natural and handy when inhabitants of that region are talking to one another. In writing anything other than personal letters, however, you should avoid these localisms, mainly because there is a possibility your reader will not understand them. You can probably find a reasonable substitution in the dictionary.

LOCALISMS

He was *rarin' to* run for President. She put the groceries into a *poke.* The pigs seem *hale* today.

GENERAL WORDS

He was *eager* to run for President. She put the groceries into a *bag.* The pigs seem *healthy* today.

Nonstandard Words

Nonstandard or illiterate words should not be used in your essays, except when quoting an uneducated speaker. Since dictionaries do not list many examples of nonstandard usages—it is difficult to keep up—you will have to depend on your own good judgment to keep these out of your papers.

DICTION

ILLITERATE WRITING

They ain't no way I'm *gonna* do it. *Youse* haven't *went* to the show yet? *Me* and Frank *learn* each other.

STANDARD WRITING

I am not going to do it. You haven't gone to the show yet? Frank and I teach each other.

Technical, Scientific Words

Your reader (often your instructor) is not likely to be familiar with technical or scientific terms for everyday objects. Use general words wherever possible, except in an essay that is intended for an audience of specialists. Do not try to impress your readers with specialized jargon; unless you explain that *heliotrope* refers to any plant that turns toward the sun, do not use it.

TECHNICAL

His sentences exhibit the notable *taint of periphrasis.* John had a *pericardial episode.* From time to time it is healthful to pause and encounter the *flora and fauna* of the region.

GENERAL

His sentences say things in a roundabout way. John had a heart attack. Stop and smell the roses.

Ornate and Archaic Words

In the movie *My Little Chickadee* W. C. Fields tells Mae West that her name (Floribel) is "a euphonious appellation." Fields had a penchant for such florid expressions, most of which only served to puff up otherwise mundane statements. ("Euphonious appellation" translates as "pleasant-sounding name.") Avoid such overwriting in your essays. Remember that the strength of our language lies in the many concrete, one-syllable words that gracefully convey sound and sense when joined together.

Archaic or out-of-date words may also often be found

in overwritten passages. Your dictionary labels such words to help you in making decisions about their use. Remember that age does not automatically lend character to words and phrases.

FLORID OR ARCHAIC WRITING

We found that all the company was *forspent* after its long *sojourn*. The *puerile pleasures* of youth must inevitably give way to the *privations* of one's *majority*.

GENERAL WRITING

Everyone was *tired* after the long *trip*. *Childhood pleasures* must eventually give way to *adult hardships*.

More examples of current usage can be found in the "Guide to Usage," pp. 522–546. If you are doubtful about the appropriateness of any word or phrase, consult your dictionary.

EXERCISE, DICTION. *Following is a selection of letters to the editor about a variety of subjects. Read them carefully, keeping an eye on word choice: colloquialisms, slang, regionalisms, ornateness, general vs. concrete words, and so forth. Make corrections as you see fit, giving reasons for your decision. How does your correction improve the sentence?*

I just returned from a second visit to the giant redwoods of Muir Forest.

I am reminded of Governor Reagan's comment to some conservationists a few years ago: "If you have seen one redwood tree, you have seen them all." One might as well say: "If you have loved one woman, you have loved them all."

To limit oneself to the pleasure of seeing one tree one time not only means missing the thrill of seeing many trees many times but also missing the forest.

DR. HUGH W. SPEER

Merriam

The article in *The Star*, Aug. 31, saying that so many unwed teen-age mothers now keep their babies was most interesting.

A very real and tragic aspect of this problem is the economic and emotional harm done to the teen-mom's parents. The teen-mom is not equipped or prepared in maturity, finances or inclination to provide the baby with needed hour in, hour out, day in, day out care.

As a consequence, the care—and cost—falls all too frequently on the teen-mom's own parents, parents who in age and disposition have looked forward to a bit of middle age or later leisure to themselves without the burden of raising another crop of kids.

The teen-mom cools her conscience by "keeping" her baby. But in fact she unloads the baby on her own mom and is off, free of responsibility, to return to school, play, or to do it all over again. Of course, frequently with public funds being drawn upon.

The child suffers emotionally in whatever upbringing results.

Far better to have a strong, on-going sealed-records adoption program.

LYELL H. CARVER

Bartlesville, Okla.

The overwhelmingly important issue of every presidential campaign since Truman-Dewey in 1948 has been the same: Which candidate is less likely to get the world into World War III and a nuclear holocaust?

There really isn't much to be said for Jimmy Carter this year except that he does have 3½ years of experience in the presidency and he hasn't gotten us into the Big One yet.

Reagan, on the other hand, is a big spender for military hardware, has a hair-trigger demeanor when it comes to Russia and China and, as recent remarks in the campaign have verified, ain't too smart.

Anderson is a pretty unknown quantity, really, but he certainly seems smarter than the other two and doesn't sound like anyone who would push the button first and ask questions later in the bunker. Still, he can't win.

All of which leads me to just one absolute as election day nears: The best chance we have of even having an election in 1984 is to vote for poor, old Billy Carter's brother. We can survive his indecisiveness and smile, probably, a lot sooner than we can survive an aging ex-movie star who still thinks in terms of fast-draw shootouts in the middle of Main Street against the bad guys.

AUBREY ANDERSON

Kansas City

The days now number over 300. More than 300 times the sun has risen and set on carbon copy days for the hostages in Iran. These days have flipped over like loose-leaf pages on a secretary's desk calendar, days which show no appreciable progress and hold no guarantees. We can't say that we are now one-fourth, one-half or three-fourths of the way to our goal.

Many of us hurt for the hostages. We turn over in our minds how deplorable it is to hold human beings like dogs on leashes, to keep them from sunlight, fresh air and freedom of movement.

But as day after day slips past, we think of the hostages less frequently. Those of us who are religious remember them as we pray, often with a brief footnote: Oh yes, Lord, remember the hostages. Then we proceed to pray for the annoyances that clutter our lives like hay fever and the economy.

Sometimes it's easier to forget. In the beginning of the captivity we felt strongly indignant. We were verbal in expressing our disgust at the injustice of holding our fellow Americans. We hoped that in a few days, or weeks, all of them would fly home and we could watch joyous reunions on the 10 o'clock news. Then we could sigh, feel good and say, "Wasn't that satisfying?" A happily-ever-after conclusion.

But that hasn't happened. It now seems easier to push the hostages back into a corner of our consciousness and feel only a little bit bad every day. We wonder what complex problems will confront them when they are freed. We feel uncomfortable, perhaps even guilty, to be so free when they are not. We rationalize our guilt. After all, it is not within our power to alter their circumstances.

We are in a sense powerless. The only power we do hold is that of caring. We can care a great deal. We can pray, we can write letters in the hope that a single letter will reach a single hostage and he or she will know that the greater family of Americans does care about them and their plight.

I hope there will yet be a happy ending in the form of a reacquaintance with freedom for each hostage. Although they would face difficulties resulting from their captivity, we wish for each of them the opportunity to overcome the difficulties;

64

the chance to readjust and share again precious liberties that those of us on this side of the crisis take for granted.

Let's not slip into the nonchalant attitude we held toward Vietnam. Instead, let's keep the needs of these fellow citizens in the forefront of our thoughts. If the only thing we have to offer them is a deep sense of caring, perhaps it is better than offering them nothing at all.

MARILYN J. SHANK

Independence

3 *The Sentence*

WHAT IS GRAMMAR?

Grammar is the systematic description of language as it is, or was, spoken. Definitions of grammar, however, need not be so succinct. The editors of *Webster's Third New International Dictionary*, who try to phrase their definitions for the layman as well as for the scientist, define grammar as "a branch of linguistic study that deals with the classes of words, their inflections or other means of indicating relation to each other, and their functions and relations in the sentence as employed according to established usage and that is sometimes extended to include related matter such as phonology, prosody, language history, orthography, orthoepy, etymology, or semantics."[1]

The subject of this book is the grammar of contemporary American English, and a genuinely scientific or linguistic approach to it would develop a *descriptive grammar*, a grammar in which there were no rules handed down but, instead, generalizations derived by observing at large how all persons speak and write American English.

Distinction Between Grammar and Usage

Unfortunately, a strictly descriptive approach to our language poses a problem. The scientific grammarian recognizes no such thing as good grammar or bad grammar, for the way each individual speaks and writes is *a* valid grammar, following patterns acquired or established dur-

---

[1] *Webster's Third New International Dictionary*, p. 986.

ing a lifetime. To acknowledge only that everyone has a grammar, however, is to ignore the practical consideration that a grammar must be reasonably understandable to at least two people if language is to serve its function, which is to let Ferdinand tell Isabella that he is unexpectedly called to a business meeting in Las Vegas, that he has lost the car keys, or that the laundromat won't take Canadian quarters. If we concede that grammar is not only a unique and variable phenomenon but a potential and desirable common medium, we open the door to the *prescriptive grammarian*, the grammarian ready to say, "The grammar I choose shall be the common one." Oppressive as that declaration sounds, two facts support it: it has a practical foundation and a well-established reputation. Many people do think there is a right and a wrong way to put words together. As long as that belief survives, and it shows little sign of going away, there is reason for learning what people think is correct. The problem is that the term *grammar* can cover both the scientific analysis of language as it comes spontaneously off a multitude of speakers' tongues and the concept of a proper and an improper speech. Only the second meaning involves the speaker's judgment, the conscious selection of one phrasing over another in response to some external measure of propriety, such as occasion, subject, audience, argument, or simply the opinion of society. The linguist dealing with issues of grammatical judgment uses the term *usage* to avoid confusing the imposed conventions of language with the grammar of unpremeditated utterance. For our purposes, however, the distinction is unnecessary. Correct usage, like any other form of functioning language, has its grammar too. A handbook having as its objective the improvement of its readers' use of language must make judgments, make comparisons, and point out appropriate and effective language patterns in terms of the standards of its day. When we speak of grammar in this book, we mean the descriptive grammar of usage as defined by the speech and, especially, by the writings of men and women whose sensitivity to the precise, effective use of language has earned them faithful

67

audiences and enduring respect. They at once follow and lead the conventions of correct usage.

It is important to remember that correct usage can be led. No grammar known has proved unchangeable, like the law of gravity, and good grammar is constantly in the process of modification. That is why we map even its cultivated landscape descriptively, in terms of what is actually happening.

Is a Knowledge of Grammar Helpful?

Many students, at some time or other, question the value of a knowledge of grammar as an aid to better writing. What part of grammar is useful? What part is useless? The answer must be different for every different person. Many people write well and speak well without knowing much about grammar, but for those who by reading this book admit their capacity for self-improvement, grammar is both a convenient chest of tools and a practical code of communication. Like a chest of tools it enables the student to build effective sentences and to repair faulty ones. It is a code or a technical vocabulary, understood by both teacher and learner, necessary in learning and teaching.

How, for instance, can a student correct the eccentricities of such a sentence as, "This is strictly between he and I," if he knows nothing about pronouns, about prepositions, or about the conventional uses of the objective case? How can a teacher explain the punctuation of phrases and clauses in a series if the student does not know what phrases and clauses are? When a person says, "I done pretty good in the test today," he expresses his thought with absolute clearness—but clearness is not enough. How can this speaker learn to make the statement in a more generally acceptable form, and how can a teacher help him learn it, if he does not have some understanding of verb forms in current usage? Or the accepted use of adjectives and adverbs? A knowledge of grammatical terms will at least provide a common ground of explanation between student and instructor, and a mutual understanding of the technical vocabulary involved is the first requisite in the explanation of any procedure.

THE PARTS OF SPEECH OR WORD CLASSES

Words are classified according to their *function* or *use in the sentence* into what are called parts of speech. Notice that in this system of classification it is the *use in the sentence* that always determines the part of speech of a word in a given situation. Many words, especially those that have been in the language for a long time, have acquired several uses, just as they have acquired many meanings. In your desk dictionary, look up a few simple, everyday words that occur to you as you glance about the room: *glass, floor, wall.* You immediately think of such uses as *the glass in the window, you live in a glass house, we glassed in our porch,* and you see the word *glass* used as a noun, as an adjective, and as a verb. Now make the same test for *floor* and *wall.*

The parts of speech are *nouns, pronouns, verbs, adverbs, adjectives, prepositions, conjunctions,* and *interjections.*

The Noun

A *noun,* also called a *substantive,* is a word that names something. It may name a person, a thing, a place, an animal, a plant, an idea, a quality, a substance, a state, an action. Use each of the following properly in sentences and try to determine under which classification each noun falls: *man, lion, city, oak, book, liquids, beauty, affection, flight, stupor, relativity.* When a noun names a person, a place, an object, it is called a *concrete noun;* when it names a quality, an idea, a mental concept, it is called an *abstract noun.* Concrete nouns name physical, visible, tangible objects; abstract nouns name things that do not have a physical substance. For the practical value of this information, see §§ 21, 24, 26. A proper noun is the official name of some individual person, place, or object; a common noun names any one of a class or kind. In English, proper nouns are capitalized; common nouns are not. See § 8.

NOUNS

The underground *spaces* seem to attract every *eccentric passion.* A small and ancient *man* with a *Bible,* an American *flag* and a *megaphone* haunts the *subways* of *Manhattan. He* opens the *Bible* and quotes from it in a strong but old and monotonous *voice.* He uses the *megaphone* at *express stops,* where the *noise* is too great for his *voice* to be heard ordinarily, and calls for *redemption.*
—TOM WOLFE, "The Subway"

The *knowledge* he has acquired with *age* is not the *knowledge* of *formulas,* or *forms* of *words,* but of *people, places, actions*—a knowledge not gained by *words* but by *touch, sight, sound, victories, failures, sleeplessness, devotion, love*—the human *experiences* and *emotions* of this *earth* and of oneself and other *men;* and perhaps, too, a little *faith,* and a little *reverence* for the *things* you cannot see.
—ADLAI STEVENSON, speech at Princeton

The Verb

A *verb* is a word (or group of words) that expresses action, occurrence, being, or mode of being. See § 3 and § 6.

VERBS

The high grey-flannel fog of winter *closed off* the Salinas Valley from the sky and from all the rest of the world. On every side it *sat* like a lid on the mountains and *made* of the great valley a closed pot. On the broad, level land floor the gang plows *bit* deep and *left* the black earth shining like metal where the shares *had cut.* On the foothill ranches across the Salinas River, the yellow stubble fields *seemed to be bathed* in pale cold sunshine, but there *was* no sunshine in the valley now in December. The thick willow scrub along the river *flamed* with sharp and positive yellow leaves.

It *was* a time of quiet and of waiting. The air *was* cold and tender. A light wind *blew up* from the southwest so that the farmers *were* mildly hopeful of a good rain before long; but fog and rain *do not go together.*
—JOHN STEINBECK, "The Chrysanthemums"

70

The Pronoun

A *pronoun* is usually defined as a word that takes the place of a noun. And, like a noun, it can be called a *substantive*. This brief definition, useful enough as a practical shortcut, must be modified by pointing out that certain pronouns, such as *none, nobody, anything,* and the impersonal *it,* do not take the place of any noun but are words more or less arbitrarily classified by grammarians and lexicographers as pronouns. Pronouns are further classified as personal, demonstrative, relative, interrogative, and indefinite. See §4. The following table indicates how certain words usually function in these classes. It must be understood, however, that some of these words may also be used as other parts of speech.

PERSONAL
I, you, he, she, it, they, we, thee, thou

DEMONSTRATIVE
this, that, these, those

RELATIVE
who, which, what, that, whoever, whatever, whichever

INTERROGATIVE
who, which, what

INDEFINITE
one, none, some, any, anyone, anybody, someone, each, somebody, nobody, everyone, everybody, either, neither, both

The Adjective

An *adjective* is a word that modifies (describes or limits) a noun or pronoun. It may denote quality, quantity, number, or extent. The articles *a, an, the,* and the possessive forms of nouns and pronouns, when used to modify nouns,

71

are here considered in the classification of adjectives. Pronouns have two forms of the possessive: the first form (*my, our, your, her, his, its, their*) when placed before a noun functions as an adjective; the second form (*mine, ours, yours, his, hers, theirs*) functions as a pronoun.

ADJECTIVES

It was *an eloquent, sharp, ugly, earthly* countenance. *His* hands were *small* and *prehensile,* with fingers knotted like *a* cord; and they were continually flickering in front of him in *violent* and *expressive* pantomime.

—R. L. STEVENSON

The place through which he made *his* way at leisure was one of *those* receptacles for *old* and *curious* things which seem to crouch in *odd* corners of *this* town, and to hide *their musty* treasures from *the public* eye in jealousy and distress.

—CHARLES DICKENS

One of *our* men saw *your* horse throw you and break through *the* fence. They left *their* work, at *my* suggestion, and ran to see if you needed help.

PRONOUNS

That horse of *mine* is a problem. May I borrow one of *yours* to get me back to the ranch?

The Adverb

An *adverb* is a word that modifies a verb, an adjective, or another adverb. Less commonly an adverb modifies a preposition, a phrase, a clause, or a whole sentence. Adverbs express the following relations in a sentence: time, place, manner, degree, frequency, affirmation or negation. See also §5.

TIME

It will rain *tomorrow.* The guests will *soon* be here. They are *now* arriving.

PLACE

Come *in*. Leave your umbrellas *outside*. Place them *here*, please.

MANNER

She expresses herself clearly. Her sister sings *beautifully*. She learns *quickly*.

DEGREE

You are *very* kind. This is *too* good. It is *entirely too* expensive.

FREQUENCY

She is *always* pleasant. She called *twice*. It rains *often*. It *never* snows.

AFFIRMATION OR NEGATION

Do *not* go there. *Certainly*, he will return. *Yes*, he was there. *No*, you can *not* see him. *Perhaps* he will call you. *Undoubtedly* he is busy.

The Preposition

A *preposition* is a word used to show the relation between a substantive (noun or pronoun), called the object of the preposition, and some other word in the sentence. A preposition thus introduces a group of words called a phrase, which may be used as an adjective, as an adverb, or, less frequently, as a noun. Many prepositions are single, short words:

at the game, *by* the house, *in* the room, *for* payment, *from* home, *off* duty, *on* land, *above* the clouds, *after* the concert, *around* her neck, *before* dawn, *behind* his back, *between* dances, *below* the covering, *over* the top, *through* the skin, *until* daybreak

There are also a number of so-called group prepositions, the use of which you can readily see:

by means of, in front of, on account of, in place of, with respect to, according to, because of, in addition to, in spite of.

73

The Conjunction

A *conjunction* is a word that connects words, phrases, or clauses. Conjunctions are either coordinating or subordinating. Adverbs used as connectives, either coordinating or subordinating, are called *conjunctive adverbs.*

The words commonly used as coordinating conjunctions are *and, but, for, or, nor, yet, both—and, not only—but also, either—or, neither—nor.* In contemporary usage, *so* is used as a coordinating conjunction in loose, informal writing and in speech, but its use should be avoided in most serious writing except in direct quotations.

Some of the words used as subordinating conjunctions are *if, although, though, that, because, since, so that, in order that, as, unless, before, than, where, when.*

Correlative conjunctions (conjunctions used in pairs) are *both—and, not only—but also, either—or, neither—nor.*

Some words commonly functioning as adverbs may be used as conjunctions: *how, why, where, before, after.* Such connectives as *however, therefore, nevertheless, hence,* and *accordingly* are often classified as conjunctive adverbs. In modern prose they are commonly used as transitional expressions. There is no profit in worrying over the question of whether they are transitions or conjunctive adverbs; the only important fact here is that in modern writing these expressions, with the exception of *hence, thus,* and *still,* are usually not placed at the beginnings of clauses in compound sentences. They function more accurately when they are set within the clauses. See § 14 for a discussion of the punctuation that should be used with these transitional expressions.

The Interjection

An *interjection* is a word or group of words used as an exclamation expressing sudden or strong feeling. Note that an exclamation point is not the inevitable punctuation of an interjection. For most interjections, especially the mild ones, a comma or a period is sufficient. Examples are *Ah, Oh, How* . . . .

THE VERBALS

The *verbals*—gerunds, participles, and infinitives—are mutations. They are derived from verbs and have some of the forms and functions of verbs, but they serve primarily as other parts of speech. Verbals may have tense forms, they may take complements, and they may be modified by adverbs. In these contexts they are like verbs. Their primary function, however, is as nouns, adjectives, and adverbs.

The Gerund

A *gerund* is a verbal used as a noun.

The man began *shouting* incoherently. [Note that *shouting* is the object of the verb *began*. It is modified by the adverb *incoherently*.]

Writing a poem is not easy. [*Writing* is the subject of the verb *is,* and has *poem* as its object.]

His eligibility for office was established by his *having been* so successful as governor. [Note the form of the gerund. Note also that it takes the adjective *successful* as its complement.]

The Participle

A *participle* is a verbal used as an adjective. It is, of course, also used as a part of a verb phrase, as in "He *was reading* a book." It may appear in a few uses with an adverbial sense, as in "They came *bringing* gifts" or "The boys ran off, *shouting* protests." Our main concern, however, is with the adjective use of the participle: "*driving* rhythm; *framed* picture." Note also such sentences as "He *was asking* you a question" and "Teasing her was *asking* for trouble," in

75

which *asking* is a part of the verb phrase in the first combination and a gerund in the second.

The *overworked* men again faced the *howling* wind. *Gripping* the rope, they slowly pulled the *mired* truck past the *waiting* soldiers. They noted a staff car *turning* in their direction. *Having saved* the truck, they relaxed for a moment. [Note here the tense forms and the positions of the participles.]

The Infinitive

An *infinitive* is a verbal that may be used as a noun, an adjective, or an adverb. The infinitive may be recognized by its sign *to*. Occasionally the sign is omitted.

Mary did not want *to drive* her car. [Used as a noun object of the verb *did want*. Note that it takes an object.]

Mary hoped *to be taken* home. [Note the passive form.]

We did not dare *refuse* her request. [Note the omission of the sign *to*.]

She had no car *to drive*. [Used as an adjective to modify *car*]

She was happy *to come* with us. [In adverbial sense, modifies *happy*]

To *watch* her happiness was a pleasure. [In noun sense, as subject of verb *was*]

In such use the infinitive can replace or be replaced by its participle, as, "*Watching* her happiness was a pleasure." Note, however, that the meaning changes slightly.

EXERCISES

EXERCISE 1, PARTS OF SPEECH AND VERBALS. *Identify the parts of speech and the verbals in the following selections:*

Both the American and the Japanese arrangement of the arc of life, however, have in point of fact secured in each country the individual's energetic participation in his culture during the prime of life. To secure this end in the United States, we rely on increasing his freedom of choice during this period. The Japanese rely on maximizing the restraints upon him. The fact that a man is at this time at the peak of his physical strength and at the peak of his earning powers does not make him master of his own life. They have great confidence that restraint is good mental training *(shuyo)* and produces results not attained by freedom. But the Japanese increase of restraints upon the man or woman during their most active producing periods by no means indicates that these restraints cover the whole of life. Childhood and old age are "free areas."

—RUTH BENEDICT, "Bring Up Children"

It is little wonder that human beings have so much trouble saying what they feel, when they are told that there is a specialized vocabulary for saying what they think. The language of simplicity and spontaneity is forced to retreat behind the barricades of an official prose developed by a few experts who believe that jargon is the most precise means of communication. The results would be comic, if they were not so poisonous; unfortunately, there is an attitude toward the use of language that is impervious to human need and drives some people back into silence when they realize the folly of risking human words on insensitive ears.

—LAWRENCE LANGER, "The Human Use of Language"

EXERCISE 2, VERBALS. *Identify the verbals in the following sentences. The verbals are gerunds, participles, and infinitives.*

1. Attending a boat christening is fun; I usually like to go.
2. Being a devoted bowler, John has his average to consider.
3. Lorna, a tired and harried stockbroker, tries to avoid being involved in charity telethons.
4. Arriving late, still absorbed in his chess game, Carl tries to be courteous to a roomful of relatives without revealing that he is unable to recall a single name.
5. Having finished milking the elk, Nanook retreats to his igloo.

6. One day Jean took my protesting brother to church to watch two strangers being married.
7. The night being hot and muggy, we sat there sweltering as we listened to the concert.
8. Wishing to avoid an argument, the officer pretended to be enjoying himself as Tommy kicked his shins.
9. Sitting in the next row were two old and respected friends dressed in gorilla suits.
10. Having bowed politely, the butler began to study the expressions on the faces of the assembled guests.

THE ELEMENTS OF THE SIMPLE SENTENCE

Defined in terms of form or pattern, a *sentence* is a basic unit of language, a communication in words, having as its core at least one independent finite verb with its subject. In addition to being a basic unit, the sentence is a natural one. It nearly always contains two pieces of information the listener as a user of language is conditioned to expect from it: who or what is involved, and what does he, she, or it do or feel. When it leaves out one or the other component, the sentence, if it is still a sentence, is responsible for justifying the sense of insufficiency it creates. Because examples without both parts are uncommon, we speak of sentences in general as complete units, capable of standing alone without the support of supplementary comment.

On the basis of the types of clauses, coordinate and subordinate, that enter into their structure, sentences are classified as simple, complex, and compound.

The following sentence diagrams are included to help you identify the main parts of a sentence. In a *simple sentence* the parts are referred to as *subject* and *verb,* and the diagram divides them in the following way:

A sentence containing a *direct object* looks like this in diagram form:

$$\text{S} \mid \text{V} \mid \text{O}$$

Addition of an *indirect object* is signified in the following way:

Subjective and *objective complements* are identified by slanted lines:

$$\text{S} \mid \text{V} \setminus \text{SC}$$

$$\text{S} \mid \text{V} \ / \ \text{OC}$$

Articles, adjectives, prepositions, and other *modifiers* are indicated by slanted lines below the main line:

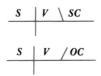

Whenever a *phrase* is *subject* or *object* in the sentence, it is represented by the following symbol:

$$\text{S} \mid \text{V} \mid \bigwedge$$

Subject and Verb: The Independent Clause

The *simple sentence* contains a single independent clause. In it, the subject, the verb, or both may be made up of two or more things or actions. A multiple subject or verb is a *compound* one.

79

The *independent clause* is a basic unit of grammar that will occur again, and what it is should be understood now to avoid confusion later. An independent clause, which may be a sentence in its own right, as the definition of a simple sentence implies, is a group of words containing a subject and a verb, and perhaps a modifier, that relies on no external information for meaning. The independent clause is complete, just as the average sentence is complete, which is why the independent clause constitutes the basic form of sentence. The examples below are both sentences *and* independent clauses.

```
    S          V
People  are  working.
```

people	are working

```
   S       S    V
Boys  and  girls  play.
```

Boys
girls   play

```
   S       S     V        V
Boys  and  girls  laugh  and  shout.
```

Boys   laugh
girls   shout

Complements

Some verbs express a general action, and the sentences they help to form have a sense of completeness. Other verbs, however, require a third element—in addition to subject and verb—to form a complete expression. That element is called a *complement* (related to *completion*). There

80

are three main types of complements: *direct objects, indirect objects,* and *subjective complements.* Less common are the *objective complement* and the *retained object.*

The Direct Object. The *direct object* of a verb denotes that which is immediately acted upon or receives the direct action of the verb.

```
S      V       O
```
Mary bought a record.

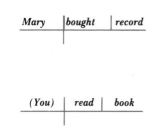

```
V       O
```
Read this book.

```
V  S  V  O
```
Did you hear him?

The Indirect Object. The *indirect object* names, without the use of a preposition, the one to whom or for whom the action involving a direct object is done.

Marilyn told *me* a story.

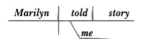

He taught *us* a lesson.
I gave the *dog* a bath.

Note that when *to* or *for* is expressed, the substantive following becomes the object of a preposition, as in "Marilyn told a story to me," "Dr. Jones taught mathematics to us," "She gave a dollar to the man."

The Subjective Complement. The *subjective complement* refers to the subject and describes or limits it. It is often called a *predicate substantive* if it is a noun or pronoun, and

81

a *predicate adjective* if it is an adjective. See also § 5 in the "Handbook" section.

Tom is a *major* now. [Predicate substantive]

Tom	is \ major

It looks *good* to me. [Predicate adjective]

It	looks \ good

A common error committed by beginning writers is the misuse of adverbs for subjective complements. In the sentence above, "It looks *well* to me" would be incorrect—and sound pretentious as well. Verbs such as *seem, become, go, remain,* and *prove* often invite the misuse of an adverb complement. Verbs of the senses—*feel, look, smell, sound, taste*—also require adjective subjective complements.

He felt *bad* about it. [not *badly*]

It tastes *sour* to me. [not *sourly*]

The air smells *foul* tonight. [not *foully*]

The Objective Complement. The *objective complement,* used with verbs such as *elect, choose, make, call, appoint,* and the like, refers to the direct object.

They made her their *chairperson.*

They	made / chairperson	her

They called him *crazy.*

The Retained Object. The *retained object* is used with a verb in the passive voice.

82

They were given *food.*

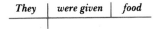

He was taught a good *lesson.*

A simple sentence may have adjectives, adverbs, and phrases as modifiers. Do not be confused by the number of these modifiers. Diagramming the sentence will help you to show it is still a simple sentence.

The little boy gave his mother a red rose.

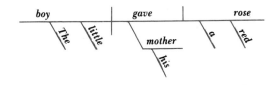

Phrases

In its general, loose sense, a *phrase* is any group of words. Thus we say that a man "phrases his thoughts" when he puts them into words, or that a woman expresses her ideas in "well-balanced phrases" when her sentences are well built and rhythmical. The word *phrase* in its general sense has its legitimate place in the language. In the study of grammar, however, the word refers to one of three kinds: the verb phrase, the prepositional phrase, or the verbal phrase.

The verb phrase, which is not discussed in this chapter, is actually a verb consisting of more than one word, such as *have been persuaded, has loved, will be honored.*

The Prepositional Phrase. A *prepositional phrase* consists of a preposition, its object, and modifiers of the phrase or any of its parts.

A prepositional phrase may be used as an adjective.

83

A graduate *with a knowledge of mathematics* and a desire *for advancement* should find a job *in one of the new industries*. [Note that the first phrase modifies *graduate*, the second modifies *knowledge*, the third modifies *desire*, the fourth modifies *job*, and the fifth *one*. Note also that the second phrase is a part of the first and the fifth is a part of the fourth.]

He must have studied several subjects *of no particular value*. [The phrase, a modifier of *subjects*, has within it two modifiers. *Must have studied* is an example of a verb phrase.]

The father *of the child* [adjective] watched *from the window* [adverb].

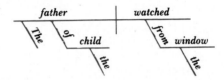

A prepositional phrase may be used as an adverb.

Slowly he walked *toward the door*. [The phrase functions as an adverb of place or direction, modifying the verb *walked*.]

She sat *on a stool* and selected a cherry *from the basket*.

If you are angry *at your best friend*, you must be careful *with your speech*. [Here the phrases function as adverbs modifying adjectives.]

Under the bridge two hikers had built a fire.

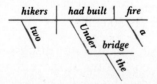

A prepositional phrase may be used as a noun. This use is quite rare.

The best time for study is *in the morning*. *On the mantel* would be a good place for it. [The first phrase is used as a noun subjective complement; the second is used as the subject of the verb *would be.*] *For me to criticize his work* would be presumptuous. [With *for*]

The best time *for study* is *in the morning.* [As adjective and as noun]

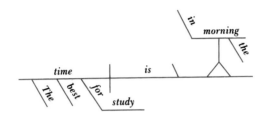

The Verbal Phrase. A *verbal phrase* consists of a participle, a gerund, or an infinitive and its complements and modifiers.

The Participial Phrase. A participial phrase consists of a participle, its complement, if it has one, and any modifiers of the phrase or any of its parts. It is generally used as an adjective. A thorough understanding of the uses of participial phrases is of practical value to any writer because their misuse results in a stylistic fault known as the *dangling modifier.* For a discussion of dangling modifiers, see § 28 in the "Handbook" section.

The car *now turning the corner* belongs to my father. [The phrase modifies *car*. The participle is modified by the adverb *now,* and it has for its object the noun *corner.*]

The letter, *stamped and sealed,* lay on the table. *Distracted by the sudden noise,* the speaker hesitated and then stopped in mid-sentence. [Note the possible positions of the participle in relation to the word it modifies.]

Having given him the required amount, I left the store. [Notice that within the participial phrase there is another participle, *required,* modifying *amount.*]

85

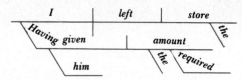

The Absolute Phrase. The absolute phrase is made up of a noun or pronoun (a substantive) followed by a participle. The substantive has no grammatical relation to any word in the sentence outside the phrase; it stands as an independent element. An absolute phrase cannot become a dangler. Note the following examples carefully.

Our assignment having been finished, we asked for our pay. [*Having been finished* modifies *assignment.*]

If the same thought is expressed as a participial phrase, "*Having finished our assignment,* we asked for our pay," it is no longer grammatically independent of the rest of the sentence. In that case the assignment has to have been finished *by* somebody or something that the remainder of the sentence is required to furnish, whereas in the absolute phrase it is simply given as finished by a person or persons unknown.

The class having been dismissed, the instructor wearily picked up his books. We walked toward the north, *each taking one side of the ridge.* [The substantive is *each.*]

The Gerund Phrase. A gerund phrase consists of a gerund, its complement, if it has one, and any modifiers of the phrase or any of its parts. A gerund phrase is always used as a noun; it may therefore function as the subject of a verb, as a complement, or as the object of a preposition.

Arguing with him does little good. *Piloting a speed boat* requires great skill. [In both sentences the gerund phrase is used as a subject. By this time you should be able to identify the modifiers and the complements.]

Willard enjoyed *watching television.* [Direct object].

86

You can get the address by *stopping at our house.* [Object of preposition]

I would call that *violating the spirit of our agreement.* [The phrase is used as an objective complement referring to *that.*]

Hearing that song brings back sad memories to me. [Subject of verb]

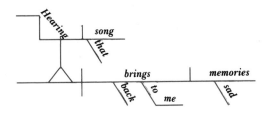

Mary objected to *my telling the story.* [Object of preposition]

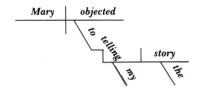

The Infinitive Phrase. An infinitive phrase, like other verbal phrases, may have a complement and modifiers. In addition it may have what is called the *assumed subject* of the infinitive. The assumed subject of an infinitive is in the objective case. An infinitive phrase may be used as an adverb, an adjective, or a noun.

We stood up *to see better.* [Modifies the verb]

We are happy *to have you back with us.* [Modifies an adjective]

Whether to believe him or to call Taylor was a real problem for me. [A noun, used as the subject of the sentence]

We knew him *to be the worst troublemaker in school.* [Notice that the infinitive *to be* has *him* as its assumed subject. "We knew him; he was the worst troublemaker in school" puts an actual subject in place of the assumed one, and, incidentally, takes the sentence out of the *simple* class.]

87

My orders were *to deliver the guns.* [Noun used as subjective complement]

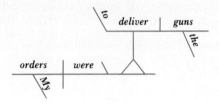

I am happy *to see you again.*

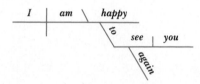

She wanted me *to drive the car.*

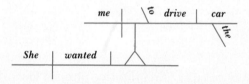

EXERCISES

EXERCISE 1, PARTICIPLES. *Pick out the participles in the following sentences and tell what word each participle modifies.*

1. The doctor's Porsche is a complicated machine.
2. Compressed to a minimum, my study is the size of a telephone booth.
3. In spite of its reduced area, it contains thousands of socks that don't match.
4. In it are over seven miles of extension cord winding back and forth.
5. Only a genius could design this amazing mess.

6. The designer was faced with several puzzling limitations, like walls and doors.
7. Every bit of needed clothing had to be identified with color-coding.
8. Having succeeded in solving one problem, he soon faced another.
9. The completed arrangement of furniture meant finding room for a bed.
10. In addition this seemingly snarled and confused location had to allow for the presence of the designer.

EXERCISE 2, PARTICIPLES AND GERUNDS. *Pick out each gerund and participle in the following sentences and tell how each is used.*

1. Most students entering college enjoy being welcomed to a new experience.
2. Having been duly warned and advised, they return to their normal routines.
3. Some students, impressed and perhaps disturbed by the advice, resolve to become devoted scholars.
4. Urged on by curiosity, some begin exploring their new and exciting surroundings.
5. Finding old friends and making new contacts are in themselves rewarding experiences.
6. There are always a few lost, unhappy souls who, unable to make new friends, amuse themselves sadly by browsing in the library.
7. Some even think of writing home to surprised and pleased parents, thereby revealing their homesickness without actually admitting it.
8. The happiest are the extroverts, adjusted to life anywhere, taking life day by day as it comes and not worrying much about it.
9. Classes soon start, and then loneliness is forgotten in the excitement of meeting new professors, buying books, and getting a routine of studying established.
10. College life becomes a challenging adventure, demanding much from each student and giving much in return.

EXERCISE 3, PHRASES. *In the following sentences pick out each phrase and tell whether it is prepositional, participial, gerund, or infinitive.*

1. My brother urged me not to miss the concert.
2. I telephoned Margie early in the afternoon.
3. Thanking me warmly, Margie agreed to come with me.
4. Getting two tickets was the problem of the moment.
5. Knowing the condition of my bank account, I decided to get help from my friends.
6. A friend in need seems to be the only kind of friend that I have.
7. I found everyone in great need of financial help.
8. In despair I decided to test my brother's fraternal loyalty.
9. He had a long sermon to give me, but in the end he agreed to help me.
10. Looking very pretty, Margie added beauty to an evening of exciting music.

THE ELEMENTS OF THE COMPOUND SENTENCE

A *compound sentence,* as the name indicates, is made by compounding or joining two or more simple sentences. The parts are of equal or *coordinate* grammatical weight. Each has its own subject and verb. Such joining may involve the use of conjunctions and proper punctuation. See § § 13 and 14 in the "Handbook" section. The examples used here are shorter than the typical compound sentence.

She should not take risks; she has three small children.
I warned her, but she was persistent.

The walk was slippery, and she fell and hurt herself badly.

Note that the parts of a compound sentence must relate to each other. Do not make two independent sentences into a compound one. Similarly, writing is smoother if two related thoughts are compounded rather than given as two separate sentences.

THE ELEMENTS OF THE COMPLEX SENTENCE

We have seen that simple sentences are units structurally and grammatically complete, and that compound sentences can be broken up into such complete and independent units. A thought expressed in a simple sentence is thereby given primary rank or importance. Ideas expressed in the coordinate units of a compound sentence have equal weight. It is of course quite possible for communication to function, as it were, on a single plane without degrees of structural emphasis. Modern English, however, has developed a system whereby many differences in the relationship of one idea to another, or of one fact to another, can be expressed by differences in grammatical structure. It has developed and perfected the dependent clause and the complex sentence.

Clauses

In the many possible variations of the useful complex sentence, the notion that main clauses are for big ideas and subordinate clauses are for lesser ideas is often completely lost. Perhaps it is better to think of a complex sentence only in grammatical terms—main or coordinate clauses are at the top level structurally; dependent clauses are dependent structurally. In the following examples pick out what you think is the important idea in each sentence and then decide whether it is in the grammatically independent clause.

He had a feeling that his number was up, that he would die on the beach.

It seems that the entire invasion fleet was heading for the wrong beach.

It should be added that a sudden and unexpected last-minute order from Hitler kept the Germans from moving up their panzer divisions.

A *complex sentence* has at least one main clause, grammatically independent and able to stand alone, and one or more dependent clauses.

Like the independent clause, the *dependent clause* will appear in numerous grammatical and mechanical situations, and knowing one when it appears is important to forming and punctuating sentences correctly. A dependent clause must hang on to an independent clause to have meaning. The clause *the cheaper of the two dishwashers ranked higher in the performance ratings* leaves no one in doubt as to what is involved or what it did. By themselves, the words *which we did not buy* don't even make a splash in the imagination as they fall. A combination works: *The cheaper of the two dishwashers, which we did not buy, ranked higher in the performance ratings.* Because *which we did not buy* only adds to a thought instead of constituting one, its position in the expression of the thought is *subordinate,* of lesser importance; the thought it is added to is a *main* clause. The subordinate or dependent clause may function as a noun, an adjective (as in the example), or an adverb.

A dependent clause is often joined to the main clause by a relative pronoun, *who, which, that,* or by one of the numerous subordinating conjunctions, such as *after, although, as, because, before, if, since, unless, when, where, why,* but sometimes the sign of dependence or subordination is omitted, as in the following examples:

The progress [*that*] *they made in college* depended on the friends [*whom*] *they had found.*

I realized [*that*] *he had not understood the error* [*that*] *I had pointed out to him.*

The boy [*whom*] *he referred to* was the one who had begged, "Say [*that*] *it isn't so, Mister!*"

The Noun Clause. A dependent clause may be used as a noun.

AS SUBJECT OF A VERB
What he says means little to me.

AS OBJECT OF A VERB
She thought *that she would go to Paris.*

AS SUBJECTIVE COMPLEMENT
Her explanation was *that she was bored with life.*

AS OBJECT OF A VERBAL
Be sure to accept *whatever she offers you.*

AS OBJECT OF A PREPOSITION
It depends upon *how many can play Saturday.*

AS AN APPOSITIVE
His first argument, *that women are inferior to men,* was easily proved false.

EXAMPLES
What he told the officers was never revealed. [Noun clause used as subject]

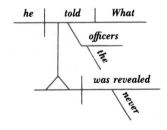

The teacher said *that the answer was correct.* [Noun clause used as object]

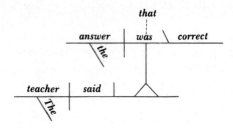

Give it to *whoever calls for it.* [Noun clause used as object of a preposition]

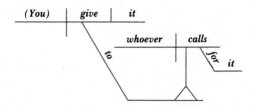

The Adjective Clause. A dependent clause may be used as an adjective. Adjective clauses are either restrictive or nonrestrictive. An important thing to remember in this connection is that restrictive clauses are *not* set off by commas. See § 13 in the "Handbook" section.

RESTRICTIVE

We needed a car *that was rugged and light.*

Do you know anyone *who has two tickets to sell?*

A teacher *who speaks poor English* is badly handicapped.

Try to remember the exact time *when you saw the accident.*

Isn't this the shop *where you found your bargains?*

NONRESTRICTIVE

I have been reading *Jaws, which was written by Peter Benchley.*

We camped that night near Maupin, *where we found some moss agates.*

94

My father, *who is a lapidary,* was delighted with the find.

I am rooming with John Cooper, *who is now a sophomore.*

A restrictive clause helps to identify the word it modifies. It points it out. It says, "That particular person or thing and no other." In the second group of sentences, no identification is added. The person or thing is already identified, sometimes by name, sometimes by other means.

Note that if you are looking for structural signals to recognize clauses, the words *where, when,* and *why* may introduce adjective clauses. Think of them in terms of "place where," "time when," and "reason why," and you will not be confused. These three words, however, have other uses too. See the examples given below.

ADJECTIVE CLAUSES

We found no reason *why he should be held.*

He was seen near the place *where the crime had been committed.*

It was the hour *when thieves and tired students prowl.*

This is the boy *who brought the papers.* [Adjective clause modifying *boy*]

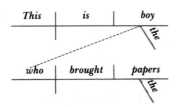

In the examples below the words introduce clauses that are not adjectival.

ADVERBIAL CLAUSES

You will begin writing *when I give the signal.* [Modifies the verb]

Put it back *where you found it.* [Modifies the verb]

NOUN CLAUSES

We never did know *where he found it.* [Object of *did know*]

Why he went home is a mystery to me. [Subject of verb *is*]

The Adverbial Clause. A dependent clause may be used as an adverb to show time, place, cause, condition, concession, comparison, manner, purpose, or result.

TIME

You must sit still *while the orchestra plays.*

Parents may come in *before the main doors are opened.*

He played professional football *until he was injured.*

After you finish your test, hand in your papers to me.

PLACE

I will go *where they send me.*

He hid *where no one thought to look.*

CAUSE

He grows roses *because he loves flowers.*

Since no one volunteered, James finished the work himself.

I can't go with you, *as that would be breaking my promise.*

CONDITION

If I were he I should invest in tax-exempt bonds.

Children will not be admitted *unless they are accompanied by their parents.*

In case you have no parents, any adult will do.

CONCESSION

I agreed to go with him *although I was very tired.*

No matter what he says, I will not be angry.

96

THE ELEMENTS OF THE COMPLEX SENTENCE

COMPARISON

He is as dependable *as the rising sun.*

Jack is older *than I am.*

MANNER

Marion looks *as if she were ready for bed.*

He speaks *as a tactful man should speak.*

PURPOSE

They came to America *in order that they might find religious freedom.*

RESULT

The night was so stormy *that we could not see the highway.*

ADDITIONAL EXAMPLES

Carol is happier *than I am.* [An adverbial clause of comparison]

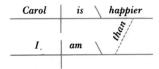

The whistle blew *before the ball was fumbled.* [An adverbial clause of time, modifying the verb *blew*]

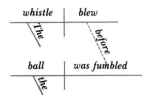

We found no reason why he should be held *until he is arraigned.* [An adverbial clause modifying an adjective clause]

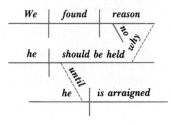

97

EXERCISES

EXERCISE 1, NOUN CLAUSES. *In the following sentences pick out each noun clause and tell whether it is used as the subject of a verb, as the complement of a verb or verbal, or as the object of a preposition.*

1. At noon they told me that I was selected to be the first to jump.
2. Why they handled the selection in such a way puzzled me at the time.
3. I forgot to tell them what my target was.
4. My assistant and I joked about what we had planned to do that night.
5. Then I remembered that my wife must be informed.
6. The starter wanted to show me what I should do with the timing watch.
7. Of course I realized that he was joking.
8. I had expected severe anxiety after the final count and the start.
9. That there was little nausea came as a pleasant surprise.
10. I announced that everything was going according to schedule.

EXERCISE 2, ADJECTIVE CLAUSES. *Pick out the adjective clauses in the following sentences and tell what word each clause modifies. Be able to tell which clauses are restrictive and which are nonrestrictive.*

1. I have been reading books that tell about human rights.
2. One writer asserts there is no such thing as a natural right.
3. His contention, which I agree with, is that all rights are made by human beings.
4. I asked him where we got the rights that are mentioned in the Declaration of Independence.
5. The author I speak of is a man whom my father knew at Wisconsin.
6. He rubbed his chin with a gesture that indicated he was thinking deeply.

7. I understood the reason why he was careful about his choice of words.
8. "The rights you mention," he said, "are rights that people had to fight for."
9. We talked about the reasons why Jefferson called them unalienable.
10. It is a pleasure to know people with whom you can discuss ideas.

EXERCISE 3, ADVERBIAL CLAUSES. *Pick out the adverbial clauses in the following sentences.*

1. The rain that had been threatening us all day came before we had finished our work.
2. We were working where the rocks had to be blasted out.
3. Because the traffic was heavy, we kept one lane of the road open.
4. Before each blast was set off, two girls waved the traffic to a halt.
5. Ashley, who was more experienced than I, told me what to do.
6. Although we had never had an accident, we worked under constant tension.
7. When the highway was clear, I pressed the handle down, and a long strip of roadway shuddered as if it were writhing in agony.
8. While the traffic waited, the bulldozers quickly shoved loose rocks off the open lane so that the cars and trucks could proceed again.
9. I think that some of the drivers were as relieved as we were.
10. While we were clearing off the rocks, the downpour came; soon the cut was so muddy that we had to stop work for the day.

THE PROBLEM OF SENTENCE EFFECTIVENESS

Effective use of language is not always a correct use of language. "I git thar fustest with the mostest men" is a famous formula for winning battles from the lips of Confederate General Nathan Bedford Forrest. It is not correct according to the standards set by the educated speaker, the experienced, careful worker with words; but it is more effective, in the right place, than "I arrive on the scene first with the greater number of troops." Indeed, one might suspect the leader who used the alternative of being a desk-bound campaigner.

Is effectiveness, then, independent of correctness? Absolutely not. Those few happy accidents in which ignorance has stumbled upon a successful phrasing are too rare to count on as a principle to follow. Correctness comes first. When it is well in hand, experiments within its bounds can be made for that desirable state of correctness, effectiveness. Only when correctness is understood beyond the possibility of error can it be abused and misused for the sake of incorrect effectiveness, and even then it will always risk looking just sloppy.

Correctness is important because it is universally functional. A misspelled word in a business letter or a misused verb in an interview can brand an otherwise able teacher or professional person as careless and perhaps unreliable in his or her own field. Bad spelling and bad grammar show; educated people notice them immediately. Crudity in vocabulary or usage makes many persons wince. In your college courses, many an otherwise excellent answer, test paper, or report may get a lower grade because of slips in spelling or grammar. Outside college, in industry, in business, in the professions, these mistakes can be even more damaging. It is no mystery, then, why we stress correctness in our language studies.

To be realistic about effectiveness, as distinguished from correctness, let us admit freely, before we go into this matter of improving something that is adequate, that for most routine occasions "correct" writing is good enough. We are here concerned with the student who is not satisfied with merely "correct" writing, the student who is disturbed that although he writes correctly and honestly, he is yet

100

ineffective. Some of the qualities of effective communication are stressed elsewhere in this book. It is well to review them here briefly before we continue discussing sentence patterns. Diction is important. The words a writer uses should be exact, fresh, alive. Picture-making words are better than vague, general words. A fresh perspective can flavor a style. Humor can lighten and liven it. Even such devices as spacing on the page and use of properly opaque paper are important.

We are dealing here primarily with the grouping or arrangement of words in sentences—not exclusively, of course, because no skillful juggling of poorly chosen words can make effective sentences. First, let us examine sentence unity.

SENTENCE UNITY

The problem of unity in a sentence is primarily one of "not enough" or "too much."

Not Enough in the Sentence

The completeness or unity of a sentence is based, in one sense, on its structure. As we shall see later, it is also based on its thought or content. The sentence, however, is not a formula or an unchangeable pattern. On the contrary, it is a unit of such variety and flexibility that no rule, only the good sense of the writer, can decide when "not enough" becomes "complete," and when "complete" becomes "too much."

Often there is "not enough" in a sentence when the writer fails to describe, narrate, or explain exactly what is happening. In such weak sentences there are either too few details or the wrong ones. Like a jury trying to make a decision about the accused, readers do not have enough evidence about the crime. Here is the opening paragraph of a student essay written about a first accident:

101

Not being careful can lead to a lot of trouble, especially in driving a car. One of the most terrifying experiences in driving a car is having an accident. This happened to me last summer.

The first sentence may be sound advice, but its tone could easily turn readers away, since it is the kind of advice—"Be careful when crossing the street"—that we tend to tune out. The second sentence is a better opening for the essay, yet it is unconvincing without some feel for the experience itself. Consider this alternative: "The chilling sound of screeching brakes, the medicinal odor of seeping anti-freeze, the jolt of an opening parachute—these are the nauseating sensations of an automobile accident." Although we may not want to be at the scene, the writer has placed us there by means of skillful description. It may then be right to go on to say something about how the victim thought such an experience could never happen to him. Isn't this a feeling that could be shared by most readers? The third sentence might then begin, "Last summer I discovered not only that such a frightening thing could happen, but also that I could do little to prevent it." In the present state of his first paragraph, the writer does not really have much of an accident to tell about. More details about the surprise and disorientation involved in the experience would transform these "not enough" sentences into "complete" ones.

Obviously, a sentence is "not enough" when it is not grammatically complete; that is, when it does not have an expressed or implied subject and verb or a required object. For a discussion of sentence fragments see § 1 of "A Handbook of Writing and Revision."

Too Much in the Sentence

A sentence may have "too much" in several ways. First, two unrelated ideas of the same weight and importance may be thrown together to make a compound sentence. The proper cure for this sort of fault is subordination. Second, a sentence may appear bulging and baggy from having too many related minor details thrown into it. Finally, a sentence may lack unity because the writer tossed into it some unrelated minor detail that popped into his mind while he was writing.

UNRELATED DETAILS

The library, old and dusty and well lit with bright new fixtures, was a melancholy place to work. ["Melancholy" seems related to "old and dusty" but not clearly to the new lighting.]

UNIFIED

The library, though well lit with new fixtures, was old and dusty and a melancholy place to work.

UNRELATED DETAILS

After the Communists took control in Vietnam, freedom of the press, which is guaranteed by a Constitutional amendment in the United States, was suppressed by the new regime. [If the sentence is about Vietnam, the reference to the United States is merely thrown in. If it is part of a contrast between the two governments, it might be acceptable.]

UNIFIED

After the Communists took control in Vietnam, freedom of the press was suppressed by the new regime.

UNRELATED DETAILS

The good sense of the director, who is a corpulent individual, is respected by all who know him. [His good sense has nothing to do with his shape.]

UNIFIED

The good sense of the director is respected by all who know him.

Overloading a sentence with details can obscure its unity and destroy its clearness and order. If the details are important, they should be told in separate sentences where they can be given proper value. If they are unimportant, they may be omitted.

CONFUSED

Military training teaches a person to stand up straight and walk with his head up; this helps in future life because it becomes a habit and so many people have the bad habit of walking stooped and this leads to poor health and poor appearance.

Military science teaches also common courtesies, not only to your superior officers but to everyone to whom courtesy is due; for instance when you enter offices, or the courtesies you should use when you are using firearms while hunting or shooting in the presence of another person.

The remedy for sentences like these is a return to the first principles of thought communication: say one thing at a time; say it as simply and clearly as possible; say it so that it cannot be misunderstood.

What does the reconstruction suggest the writer meant to say in these sentences?

REVISED

Military training teaches a person to stand erect and to walk with his head up. [That is enough for one sentence.] Good posture [Is that what the writer meant by "this" and "it"?] becomes habitual. It leads directly to better health and better appearance.

Military science also teaches common courtesy, not only to officers superior in rank but to everyone. [Are there some persons to whom "courtesy is not due"?] For instance, it teaches one how to enter an office, or how to handle firearms with safety to others. [These two examples are so badly chosen that no sentence can make them apt or congruous.]

USES OF SUBORDINATION: SENTENCE COMBINING

The phrase *sentence combining* is now popular among teachers and theorists of composition. Its popularity can be traced to the ease with which the phrase is used to illustrate the more traditional concepts of coordination and subordination. By means of artful combining, the beginning writer can achieve greater sentence variety, placing main ideas in main clauses and subordinating ideas in dependent clauses and phrases.

Many student writers find subordination difficult because from their earliest days of speaking they have fallen into the habit of coordinating ideas by use of the conjunction *and.* Think of how many times you have heard reports like this one: "We drove to the river and brought out the cooler and it started to rain and we played volleyball . . . ." In that fast-moving convoy of facts there is no distinction among the various details; all of the events appear to have happened consecutively and to have had the same impact on the speaker. But because rain fell, the picnic and the volleyball game obviously had to be postponed, unless the picknickers ate and played in the rain. They may have done just that, but the reader cannot tell from the account. The order and significance of events may be clarified by the artful use of subordination: "After we arrived at the river and unloaded the cooler, the rains came, delaying lunch and the volleyball game for about an hour." Now we have a clear picture of the episode, with the rain falling where it ought to fall.

Excessive use of coordination or of short declarative sentences can also cause problems of emphasis. Unclear or shifted emphasis in a sentence will make your reader wonder whether you are a trustworthy guide for the journey. Practice will help you find your way along the trail. Let us try arranging the details in the following sentences to illustrate the importance of proper emphasis.

My car is light blue.

My car is a '79 Ford.

My car has an automatic transmission.

My car was in an accident last Thursday.

A standard rewriting might read: "My car, a light blue, '79 Ford with an automatic transmission, was in an accident last Thursday." The main idea is that the car was in an accident. Although no one would write the improbable sentence that follows, it demonstrates how important the decision about the main idea is: "My car, a light blue '79 Ford involved in an accident last Thursday, has an automatic transmission." Unless this writer is trying hard to be satiric, he or she has subordinated the main piece of information and given independence to a trivial detail. Any sane reader would want out of this essay at the first stop sign.

It is possible to emphasize equally important details through subordination. You may write "My car, a '79 Ford, is sleek and fast" or "My car, sleek and fast, is a '79 Ford." The decision is yours and depends on the sentence's purpose in context. Either of these alternatives would be better than separate declarative sentences or a coordinate sentence (i.e., two independent clauses joined by *and*). If you are unsure of how to locate the sentence's main clause, simply look for the subject, verb, and object or complement.

EXERCISES

EXERCISE, SENTENCE COMBINING. *The following sets of sentences can be rewritten as one sentence by using the techniques of subordination. In each rewrite you should compose a complex sentence with a major clause and subordinate clauses or phrases.*

1. The little boy was lost in the woods.
   He wandered away from home on Friday.
   He slept on the cold ground all night.
   He was found early Saturday morning.
   He was dirty and shivering but alive.
2. Tony has a powerful serve.
   I usually can't return it.
   My only hope of beating him is to tire him out.
   I hit many drop shots and lobs.
3. His cigarette was lighted.
   It dropped behind the cushions.
   The sofa burst into flames.
   No one escaped alive.
4. She knows what is required to be a good doctor.
   Physicians have to be intelligent.

106

> They must work long hours.
> They have to be humane and sensitive.
> 5. The movie was a flop.
> It was too long.
> The dialogue was stilted and unrealistic.
> There was no action to speak of.

More exercises in sentence combining are available in the Workbook. Practice will help you become adept at achieving sentence variety and at providing emphasis in the sentence.

Accuracy and Variety

Combining sentences is an important act in developing style in your writing. For this reason you should also be aware of the ways in which clauses and phrases can be arranged to arrive at greater accuracy and variety. Here are some examples of sentence elements that will help you in becoming a successful sentence combiner.

The Dependent Clause. By this time you should be familiar with the various types of dependent clauses and with the structural signals that show their dependence. In the following examples, does the revision improve the accuracy of expression, give unity to sentences, or relieve the monotony of too many clauses on the same level?

A. I well remember a strange conversation I had with a man once. This man was a friend of mine. He and I had served together in the Marines.
B. I well remember a strange conversation I once had with a friend of mine, with whom I had served in the Marines.

A. Do not be in too much of a hurry to join an organization. Study its membership before you join.
B. Before you join an organization, investigate its membership.

A. Space suits are personalized garments. You must make many alterations on one of them. Otherwise it will not fit properly. In this respect it is like a bridal gown.
B. Because space suits are personalized garments, you need to

107

make more alterations on one of them to make it fit properly than you do on a bridal gown.

—WALTER M. SCHIRRA, JR., *We Seven*

The Useful Participial Phrase. The substance of a coordinate clause may be better expressed in a *participial phrase*.

COORDINATE

My decision to enter college came suddenly, and I soon faced several obstacles.

PARTICIPIAL

Having made a sudden decision to enter college, I soon faced several obstacles.

But the participial phrase, useful as it is, contains several built-in dangers: it can become a dangler (see §28); its overuse can produce a stiff, awkward style; and, if the wrong detail is subordinated, it can distort rather than clarify meaning. With these cautions in mind, study and analyze the following examples:

A. A law school or a medical school can be an essential part of a great university. Each school must be properly staffed and directed.
B. A law school or a medical school, if properly staffed and directed, can be an essential part of a great university. [Past participles]
A. I could not overcome my difficulty. I could not understand it.
B. Unable to understand my difficulty, I could not overcome it. ["Being" is understood before *Unable*.]
A. There was one problem not solved by the Commission. This was how to widen the highway without moving the historic church.
B. The problem left unsolved by the Commission was how to widen the highway without moving the historic church.

Gerund and Infinitive Phrases. Gerund and infinitive phrases may be used on occasion to gain economy and compactness in writing.

A. For three days he punished me. He refused to eat my desserts.
B. For three days he punished me by refusing to eat my desserts.

A. Their working hours were shortened. This resulted in more spare time for recreation and enjoyment.
B. Shortening their hours of work resulted in more time available for recreation and enjoyment. [Note how the vague *this* has been avoided.]

A. The housewife has children whom she must clothe. She must take care of them and worry about them. The married professional woman has all these duties and, in addition, must face the sometimes harsh demands of her job.
B. The housewife has children to clothe, to care for, to worry about; the married professional woman has all these duties and, in addition, must face the sometimes harsh demands of her job.

Conciseness: The Prepositional Phrase. A prepositional phrase may be used to express a detail more accurately and more concisely than a clause or a sentence.

A. We wrote our exams at separate tables. There was a proctor in front of us. Another one stood behind us.
B. We wrote our exams at separate tables, with one proctor in front of us and another behind us.

A. The professor repeated his instructions. It was to help those who came late.
B. For the benefit of the latecomers, the professor repeated his instructions.

A. The examination was over. Then the students got together and compared their answers.
B. After the examination the students got together to compare answers.

A. I turned in my exam. I did not stop to go over my answers.
B. I turned in my exam without a second glance at my answers.

Notice that in the first of the preceding examples traits of informal conversation—shortened sentences, unsubordinated thoughts—stand out.

Compactness and Economy: The Single Word. A minor detail worth only a single word instead of a whole sentence or a clause is better expressed in a single word.

109

A. There were two new girls, and they both wore green double-knit dresses that had short sleeves.
B. The two new girls both wore short-sleeved dresses of green double-knit.
A. The house was old. The lawn around it was enclosed by yew hedges. These hedges were neatly clipped.
B. The lawn around the old house was shut in by neatly clipped yew hedges.

Uses of the Appositive. Like clauses, phrases, and verbals, the appositive (i.e., a word or phrase in apposition restating another word or phrase in terms that expand or define it) may be used to express details the writer wishes to subordinate. Consider this piece of autobiographical writing:

A. I was born in Middleville, Ohio. It's a small town. Most of the people in it are farmers. They raise cows for milk and a lot of apples. Still, it's the county seat of Whiteside County.

Obviously this is a wordy passage, marred by many faults in addition to a lack of subordination. It can be improved by the use of appositives:

B. I was born in Middleville, Ohio, a small dairy and apple-farming community and the seat of Whiteside County.

The following groups of sentences will further illustrate the resources of the appositive:

A. Lutetium was discovered in 1905. It is a chemical element. It is one of the rare-earth elements. The name comes from *Lutetia.* In ancient days Paris was called that.
B. Lutetium, a chemical element, member of the rare-earth group, was discovered in 1905; its name was derived from *Lutetia,* the ancient name of Paris.
A. The custom of kissing under the mistletoe was once an old Druid religious ceremony. It is now a pleasant part of our Christmas.

110

B. The custom of kissing under the mistletoe, once an old Druid religious ceremony, is now a pleasant part of our Christmas.

A. Tony is a friendly sort of person, and he hasn't made an enemy in his life.

B. Tony, a friendly sort of person, has not made an enemy in his life.

To sum up the subject of subordination, two parallel versions of one more paragraph are given below. The sentences in the second version use dependent clauses or phrases to give a more effective allocation of meaning and emphasis. As a result, the writing in the second paragraph should seem more mature, more sophisticated, more accurate in conveying different shades of meaning, and more pleasing in style.

VERSION A

A great deal of traditional cultural education was foolish. That must be admitted. Boys spent many years acquiring Latin or Greek. At the end they could not read a Greek or Latin author. Neither did they want to. Of course this was not true in a small percentage of cases. Modern languages and history are preferable to Latin and Greek. This is in every way true. They are more useful, and they give much more culture, and it all takes less time. An Italian of the fifteenth century had to learn Latin and Greek. Everything worth reading was in those languages or in his own. These languages were indispensable keys to culture. Since that time great literatures have grown up in various modern languages. Development of civilization has been very rapid. A knowledge of antiquity has become less useful. A knowledge of modern nations and their comparatively recent history has become more useful in understanding our problems. The traditional schoolmaster's point of view was admirable at the time of the Revival of Learning. Now it is unduly narrow. It ignores what has been done since the fifteenth century. History and modern languages are not the only things contributing to culture. Science contribues too. But science must be properly taught. Education should have other aims than direct utility. It is possible to maintain this viewpoint. It is not necessary to defend the traditional curriculum. Utility and culture are not incom-

111

patible. They only seem to be. But they must be understood broadly.

It must be admitted that a great deal of the traditional education was foolish. Boys spent many years acquiring Latin and Greek grammar, without being, at the end, either capable or desirous (except in a small percentage of cases) of reading a Greek or Latin author. Modern languages and history are preferable, from every point of view, to Latin and Greek. They are not only more useful, but they give much more culture in much less time. For an Italian of the fifteenth century, since practically everything worth reading, if not in his own language, was in Greek or Latin, these languages were the indispensable keys to culture. But since that time great literatures have grown up in various modern languages, and the development of civilization has been so rapid that the knowledge of antiquity has become much less useful in understanding our problems than knowledge of modern nations and their comparatively recent history. The traditional schoolmaster's point of view, which was admirable at the time of the Revival of Learning, became gradually unduly narrow, since it ignored what the world has done since the fifteenth century. And not only history and modern languages, but science also, when properly taught, contributes to culture. It is therefore possible to maintain that education should have other aims than direct utility, without defending the traditional curriculum. Utility and culture, when both are conceived broadly, are found to be less incompatible than they appear to the fanatical advocates of either.

—BERTRAND RUSSELL, *In Praise of Idleness and Other Essays*

LONG AND SHORT SENTENCES

Has the length of sentences much to do with effectiveness, as it has with style? Turn back to the last two selections, which you have just studied for subordination. Version A contains twenty-eight short sentences; version B has only ten sentences, most of them fairly long. Both selections say essentially the same thing—but the first seems aimless, undeveloped, and at times misplaced in emphasis.

Before we arrive at any hasty decision that a paragraph of long, complex sentences is more effective than a paragraph of short, simple ones, we should compare the ways in which two men, both good writers, chose to report similar moods of contentedness. The first man wrote his piece in very short sentences.

Across the open mouth of the tent Nick fixed cheese cloth to keep out mosquitoes. He crawled inside under the mosquito bar with various things from the pack to put at the head of the bed under the slant of the canvas. Inside the tent the light came through the brown canvas. It smelled pleasantly of canvas. Already there was something mysterious and homelike. Nick was happy as he crawled inside the tent. He had not been unhappy all day. This was different though. Now things were done. There had been this to do. Now it was done. It had been a hard trip. He was very tired. That was done. He had made his camp. He was settled. Nothing could touch him. It was a good place to camp. He was there, in the good place. He was in his home where he had made it. Now he was hungry.

He came out, crawling under the cheese cloth. It was quite dark outside. It was lighter in the tent.

Nick went over to the pack and found, with his fingers, a long nail in a paper sack of nails, in the bottom of the pack. He drove it into the pine tree, holding it close and hitting it gently with the flat of the ax. He hung the pack up on the nail. All his supplies were in the pack. They were off the ground and sheltered now.

Nick was hungry. He did not believe he had ever been hungrier. He opened and emptied a can of pork and beans and a can of spaghetti into the frying pan.

"I've got a right to eat this kind of stuff, if I'm willing to carry it," Nick said. His voice sounded strange in the darkening woods. He did not speak again.

—ERNEST HEMINGWAY, *In Our Time*

And now notice how differently another man says almost the same thing, "This is the place I had searched for, where for the moment I was happy and at peace."

Beyond Blake Avenue was the pool parlor outside which we waited all through the tense September afternoons of the

113

World's Series to hear the latest scores called off the ticker tape—
and where as we waited, banging a ball against the bottom of
the wall and drinking water out of empty coke bottles, I breathed
the chalk off the cues and listened to the clocks ringing in the
fire station across the street. There was an old warehouse next
to the pool parlor; the oil on the barrels and the iron staves
had the same rusty smell. A block away was the park, thick with
the dusty gravel I liked to hear my shoes crunch in as I ran
round and round the track; then a great open pavilion, the inside
mysteriously dark, chill even in summer; there I would wait in
the sweaty coolness before pushing on to the wading ring where
they put up a shower on the hottest days.

Beyond the park the "fields" began, all those still unused
lots where we could still play hard ball in perfect peace—first
shooing away the goats and then tearing away goldenrod before
laying our bases. The smell and touch of those "fields," with
their wild compost under the billboards of weeds, goldenrod,
bricks, goat droppings, rusty cans, empty beer bottles, fresh new
lumber, and damp cement, lives in my mind as Brownsville's
great open door, the wastes that took us through the west. I
used to go round them in summer with my cousins selling near-
beer to the carpenters, but always in a daze, would stare so
long at the fibrous stalks of the goldenrod as I felt their harshness
in my hand that I would forget to make a sale, and usually go
off sick on the beer I drank up myself. Beyond! Beyond! Only
to see something new, to get away from each day's narrow battle-
ground between the grocery and the back wall of the drugstore!
Even the other end of our block, when you got to Mrs. Rosenwas-
ser's house and the monuments works, was dear to me for the
contrast. On summer nights, when we played Indian trail, running away from each other on prearranged signals, the greatest
moment came when I could plunge into the darkness down the
block for myself and hide behind the slabs in the monuments
works. I remember the air whistling around me as I ran, the
panicky thud of my bones in my sneakers, and then the slabs
rising in the light from the street lamps as I sped past the little
candy store and crept under the fence.

—Alfred Kazin, "The Block and Beyond"

We may notice that out of the thirty-five sentences in
the Hemingway selection, twenty-seven are fewer than ten
words long. Hemingway was obviously striving to give the

effect of random thoughts and impressions going through the mind of his character, who at the end of a long day of tramping was relaxed and happy and not disposed toward much thinking. In the Kazin selection, which is taken from a personal reminiscence and not a novel, all of the sentences are twenty words long or longer. Only the exclamations "Beyond! Beyond!" break this pattern—and do so with dramatic effect. There is a complex mood here, as the image of children playing in a wading ring contrasts with the symbolically foreboding image of a single child hiding behind a grave marker. Both writers, however, are trying to convey a feeling of homelike pleasure and mystery about the scenes they describe.

VARIATIONS IN ORDER

Sentences should fit the thoughts they contain, or, as in the Hemingway selection just analyzed, the mood they are creating. Most sentences, without any conscious effort on the writer's part, fall into an instinctive pattern, subject—verb—complement. This natural pattern is not sacred; it can be changed to make a statement more exact or more attractive by inverting the elements or shifting the modifiers, but it should be left alone unless there is something to be gained by tampering. The following pairs of sentences illustrate changes of emphasis created by varying the word order.

A. They elected him their president. [Now change the basic S—V—C order.]
B. Him they elected their president. [What word is emphasized here?]
A. All six hundred rode into the valley of death. [Normal order]
B. All into the valley of death rode the six hundred. [Note the change of emphasis because of the inversion.]
—ALFRED LORD TENNYSON

It is relatively easy to throw modifiers around *(the cry was loud—loud was the cry)* or to shift from the active to

115

passive voice *(Susan hit me—I was hit by Susan)*, but an alternative order should not hinder the linking of one sentence to another. The following paragraph shows how well variety and coherence can be achieved when the writer keeps clearly in mind the central idea of the paragraph.

When one considers the different rates at which people read, it's miraculous that films can ever solve the problem of a pace at which audiences can "read" a film together. A hack director solves the problem of pacing by making only a few points and making those so emphatically that the audience can hardly help getting them (this is why many of the movies from the studio-system days are unspeakably insulting); the tendency of a clever, careless director is to go too fast, assuming that he's made everything clear when he hasn't, and leaving the audience behind. When a film has as much novelistic detail as this one, the problem might seem to be almost insuperable. Yet, full as it is, *The Godfather* goes by evenly, so we don't feel rushed, or restless, either; there's classic grandeur to the narrative flow. But Coppola's attitudes are specifically modern—more so than in many films with a more jagged surface. Renoir's openness is an expression of an almost pagan love of people and landscape; his style is an embrace. Coppola's openness is a reflection of an exploratory sense of complexity; he doesn't feel the need to comment on what he shows us, and he doesn't want to reduce the meanings in a shot by pushing us this way or that. The assumption behind this film is that complexity will engage the audience.
—PAULENE KAEL, *Deeper Into Movies*

LOOSE AND PERIODIC SENTENCES

A *periodic sentence* is a complex sentence in which the main clause comes at the end, as "Just as the technicians were locking the hatch in place, one of the bolts broke." A *loose sentence* is a complex sentence in which the main clause comes first, followed by dependent clauses and other modifying elements, as "I realized that I had discussed the wrong topic only after I had handed in my paper." Short sentences are often periodic; long sentences tend to be loose. Since the mind grasps the thought of a short sentence, or even of a moderately long one, quickly, it is only in long sentences that periodic structure has any noticeable psychological effect.

The periodic sentence builds suspense. It tends to hold up the meaning until the end, to force the reader to consider first the various details on which the main thought is based. It makes him or her wait. Overused periodic structure is a little like an aged drunk holding your lapel and breathing into your face to tell his life story.

Notice in the following paragraph how a skillful writer combines the two types of complex sentences. In writing, the occasional conscious change from a loose to a periodic sentence, like tightening the belt, helps keep things from dragging.

For the kind of courage which does not consist in repression, a number of factors must be combined. [Periodic] To begin with the humblest: health and vitality are very helpful, though not indispensable. [Loose] Practice and skill in dangerous situations are very desirable. [Simple: periodic effect] But when we come to consider, not courage in this and that respect, but universal courage, something more fundamental is wanted. [Periodic] What is wanted is a combination of self-respect with an impersonal outlook on life. [Periodic] To begin with self-respect, some men live from within, while others are mere mirrors of what is felt and said by their neighbors. [Loose] The latter can never have true courage; they must have admiration and are haunted by the fear of losing it. [Loose] The teaching of "humility" which used to be thought desirable was the means of producing a perverted form of this same vice. [Periodic] "Humility" suppressed self-respect but not the desire for the respect of others; it merely made nominal self-abasement the means of acquiring credit. [Loose] Thus it produced hypocrisy and falsification of instinct. [Simple: periodic effect] Children were taught unreasoning submission and proceeded to exact it when they grew up; it was said that only those who have learned how to obey know how to command. [Loose] What I suggest is that no one should learn to obey and no one should attempt to command. [Loose] I do not mean, of course, that there should be no leaders in cooperative enterprises; but their authority should be like that of a captain of a football team, which is suffered voluntarily in

117

order to achieve a common purpose. [Loose] Our purposes should be our own, not the result of external authority; and our purposes should never be forcibly imposed upon others. [Loose] This is what I mean when I say no one should command and no one should obey. [Loose]

—BERTRAND RUSSELL, *Education and the Good Life*

PARALLEL STRUCTURE AND BALANCE

One of the rhetorical devices available to writers is known as the *balanced* or *parallel* construction. At its elementary level, the device is a thoroughly practical means of writing a graceful sentence by making a noun parallel with another noun, a gerund with another gerund, a phrase with another phrase, a clause with another clause.

SCATTERED

Choose a house that is spacious, with a good exposure to the sun and that people like to look at. [An adjective, a phrase, a clause]

PARALLEL

Choose a house that is spacious, sunny, and attractive. [Three adjectives]

SCATTERED

I was glad to be there for the lecture and seeing how the models work. [A noun and a phrase]

PARALLEL

I was glad to be there for the lecture and the demonstration of models. [Two nouns]

SCATTERED

I have only one suggestion to make: cultivate friends who you think are loyal, have a cheerful disposition, and who are ambitious. [An adjective, a verb, and an adjective]

118

I have only one suggestion to make: cultivate friends who you think are loyal, cheerful, and ambitious. [Three adjectives]

For a discussion of the "false parallel," see §31.

Forced into service when it is not required to give wandering sentences focus, parallel structure becomes a conspicuous art. Carried too far it becomes a mannerism. Used judiciously, however, to fit thought and occasion, it will seldom reach the point of affectation. In his essay on studies, Francis Bacon deftly balances phrase with phrase without excess.

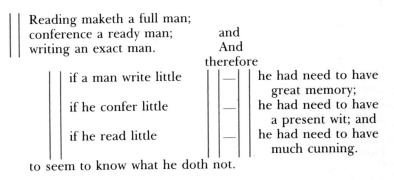

Reading maketh a full man;
conference a ready man;   and
writing an exact man.   And
                                 therefore

if a man write little   —   he had need to have
                                great memory;

if he confer little   —   he had need to have
                                a present wit; and

if he read little   —   he had need to have
                                much cunning.

to seem to know what he doth not.

As Bacon's contemporaries not only tolerated but admired rhetorical mannerisms, we should, perhaps, marvel at Bacon's restraint rather than at his elaboration. You can find other examples of skillful parallelism in the work of present-day writers. Here is an example of balance in the closing paragraph of an essay about tourists. Notice how effective the three-part sentence structure proves to be in a concluding paragraph.

As soon as the last boat has gone, down comes the curtain. The "gondoliers" shed their white linen jackets and silly straw hats and go back to Burano, taking Eric, highly dissatisfied with his earnings and saying if this goes on he will die of hunger. The sweet old women let the smiles fade from their faces, put

119

away their lace-making pillows, and turn to ordinary activities of village life such as drowning kittens. The father of the clover babies creeps about on his knees finding four-leafed clovers for the next day. The evening reproaches ring out, the moon comes up, the flapping *Daily Mails* blow into the lagoon. Torcello is itself again.

—NANCY MITFORD, "Tourists"

Antithesis

Antithesis is another effective way of achieving balance in sentences. The device is a favorite of political speakers like Churchill and, more recently, President John F. Kennedy: "Ask not what your country can do for you; ask what you can do for your country"; "Those who make peaceful revolution impossible will make violent revolution inevitable." The second example vividly illustrates how balance is achieved by opposing "peaceful" to "violent," and "impossible" to "inevitable." As with parallel structure, antithesis can be carried too far by the beginning writer striving to sound like a great orator. Remember that both devices tend to be more appropriate to speech-making than to the essays you are likely to write.

In the following selection, notice the varied and pleasing rhythm of loose and periodic sentences throughout, the frequent use of balance, and here and there the effective development of climax. Notice too how the argument, like the style in which it is presented, is both compelling and balanced.

As I see it, the United States is the first nation—though so complex and unclassifiable an entity almost resists definition as a single unit—to suffer/enjoy the death throes of the Renaissance. How could it be otherwise, since our nation is sensitive, energetic, swarming with life, and, beyond any other developed nation in the world, the most obsessed with its own history and its own destiny? Approaching a kind of manic stage, in which suppressed voices are at last being heard, in which *no extreme viewpoint is any longer "extreme,"* the United States is preparing itself for a transformation of "being" similar to that experienced

120

by individuals as they approach the end of one segment of their lives and must rapidly, and perhaps desperately, sum up everything that has gone before.

It is easy to misread the immediate crises, to be frightened by the spontaneous eruptions into consciousness of disparate groups (blacks, women, youth, "the backlash of the middle class"); it is possible to overlook how the collective voices of many of our best poets and writers serve to dramatize and exorcize current American nightmares. Though some of our most brilliant creative artists are obsessed with disintegration and with the isolated ego, it is clear by now that they are all, with varying degrees of terror, saying the same thing—that we are helpless, unconnected with any social or cultural unit, unable to direct the flow of history, that we cannot effectively communicate. The effect is almost that of a single voice, as if a communal psychoanalytic process were taking place. But there does come a time in an individual writer's experience when he realizes, perhaps against his will, that his voice is one of many, his fiction one of many fictions, and that all serious fictions are half-conscious dramatizations of what is going on in the world.

Here is a simple test to indicate whether you are ready for the new vision of man or whether you will fear and resist it: Imagine you are high in the air, looking down on a crowded street scene from a height so great that you cannot make out individual faces but can see only shapes, scurrying figures rather like insects. Your imagination projects you suddenly down into that mass. You respond with what emotion—dread or joy?

In many of us the Renaissance ideal is still powerful, its voice tyrannical. It declares: *I* will, *I* want, *I* demand, *I* think, *I* am. This voice tells us that we are not quite omnipotent but must act as if we were, pushing out into a world of other people or of nature that will necessarily resist us, that will try to destroy us, and that we must conquer. *I will exist* has meant only *I will impose my will on others.* To that end man has developed his intellect and has extended his physical strength by any means possible because, indeed, at one time the world did have to be conquered. The Renaissance leapt ahead into its own necessary future, into the development and near perfection of machines. Machines are not evil, or even "unnatural," but simply extensions of the human brain. The designs of our machines are no less the product of our creative imaginations than are works of art, though it might be difficult for most people—especially artists—to acknowledge this. But a great deal that is difficult, even outrageous, will have to be acknowledged.

If technology appears to have dehumanized civilization, this is a temporary failing or error—for the purpose of technology is the furthering of the "human," the bringing to perfection of all the staggering potentialities in each individual, which are nearly always lost, layered over with biological or social or cultural crusts. Anyone who imagines that a glorious pastoral world has been lost, through machines, identifies himself as a child of the city, perhaps a second- or third-generation child of the city. An individual who has lived close to nature, on a farm, for instance, knows that "natural" man was never *in* nature; he had to fight nature, at the cost of his own spontaneity and, indeed, his humanity. It is only through the conscious control of the "machine" (i.e., through man's brain) that man can transcend the miserable struggle with nature, whether in the form of sudden devastating hailstorms that annihilate an entire crop, or minute deadly bacteria in the bloodstream, or simply the commonplace (but potentially tragic) condition of poor eyesight. It is only through the machine that man can become more human, more spiritual. Understandably, only a handful of Americans have realized this obvious fact, since technology seems at present to be villainous. Had our earliest ancestors been gifted with a box of matches, their first actions would probably have been destructive—or self-destructive. But we know how beneficial fire has been to civilization.

—JOYCE CAROL OATES, "New Heaven and Earth"

REPETITION, SOUND, AND RHYTHM

Balance, parallel structure, and apposition are, in a sense, forms of repetition—repetitions primarily of phrasing or structure rather than of words, although within balanced phrases words may be repeated. Note this repetition in the quotation from Bacon on page 119:

a full man	write little	he had need to have great memory
a ready man	confer little	he had need to have a present wit
an exact man	read little	he had need to have much cunning

Then in the selection just quoted note the repetition of structure:

its own history	its own destiny
his voice is one of many	his fiction one of many fictions
it is easy to misread	it is possible to overlook
more human	more spiritual

that will necessarily resist/ that will try to destroy/ that we must conquer.

Single words may be repeated for emphasis or for a smoother rhythmic flow of sounds, quite apart from a balance of structural units, as you will notice in the following:

as you *love* your *country,* I *love* my *country.* . . .
—ADLAI STEVENSON

Before *parents* can be *parents* they must have lived a good part of their lives.
—CARL VAN DOREN

we shall fight in France, *we shall fight* on the seas and oceans, *we shall fight* with *growing* confidence and *growing* strength in the air . . . *we shall fight* on the landing grounds. . . .
—WINSTON CHURCHILL

Euphony

Good prose should be easy to read aloud. Pleasing audible effects depend partly on an avoidance of harsh sounds or combinations of letters difficult to pronounce and partly on combinations of sounds, stresses, and variations in pitch that appeal to our sense of hearing. *Cacophony* is the name for jarring and harsh sounds. Many tongue twisters are familiar examples of cacophony.

She sells sea shells. . . .
The Leith police dismisseth us.

Euphony is the word that describes pleasing sounds. Some of the pleasure we get from good prose comes from various patterns of stresses called *rhythm.* Occasionally—and

123

largely by accident—prose rhythms approach the regular metric forms of verse, but any conscious effort to arrange prose accents in poetic forms is usually out of place. The rhythms of prose are irregular—and yet one feels that in rhythmic prose there is an appropriate music. Read the following passage aloud, always remembering that the syllables stressed may be stressed in many different degrees:

Thus from the grim gray of their skies they had alchemied gold, and from their hunger, glorious food, and from the raw bleakness of their lives and weathers they had drawn magic. And what was good among them had been won sternly, sparely, bitterly, from all that was ugly, dull, and painful in their lives, and, when it came, was more rare and beautiful than anything on earth.

—THOMAS WOLFE, *Of Time and the River*

The final selection in this chapter was written several years ago, but it has lost none of its freshness and power. It is a description of the sorry performance of William Jennings Bryan at the famous trial of John T. Scopes, the Tennessee school teacher who attempted to teach Darwin's theory of evolution. The prose rhythms in it cannot be felt through silent reading. It should be read aloud.

Thus he fought his last fight, thirsting savagely for blood. All sense departed from him. He bit right and left, like a dog with rabies. He descended to demagogy so dreadful that his very associates at the trial table blushed. His one yearning was to keep his yokels heated up—to lead his forlorn mob of imbeciles against the foe. That foe, alas, refused to be alarmed. It insisted upon seeing the whole battle as a comedy. Even Darrow, who knew better, occasionally yielded to the prevailing spirit. One day he lured poor Bryan into the folly I have mentioned: his astounding argument against the notion that man is a mammal. I am glad I heard it, for otherwise I'd never believe it. There stood the man who had been thrice a candidate for the Presidency of the Republic—there he stood in the glare of the world, uttering stuff that a boy of eight would laugh at. The artful Darrow led him on: he repeated it, ranted for it, bellowed it in his cracked voice. So he was prepared for the final slaughter. He came into life a hero, a Galahad, in bright and shining armor. He was passing out a poor mountebank.—H. L. MENCKEN, "In Memoriam: W. J. B."

EXERCISES

EXERCISE, SENTENCES IN ORDER. *One of the best ways to test the logic of paragraph development is to reorder sentences that have been jumbled. You are forced, in a sense, to rethink the argument for the writer, testing whether or not transition between points can be observed.*

Here are five sample paragraphs in which the sentences have been deliberately jumbled. Rearrange them so that each paragraph achieves coherence and order.

1. (1) Then in 1972, a group of dissatisfied students, dubbing themselves "the dirty 13," charged that the traditional courses compromised the school's philosophy. (2) In the school's earliest years, focal problem learning was only one item on a schedule that also included required lecture and laboratory attendance. (3) Last year, almost half of all CHM students opted for this alternative. (4) In response, administrators offered the alternate Track II in which all structured courses could be waived: Progress would be evaluated by faculty observation and exams.

   [From "Grass Roots Doctors," by Elizabeth Ehrlich, *Change*, October 1978, p. 17.]

2. (1) Clearly the connections between the classroom and the world have to be made. (2) Reading Coffin's book may be a reminder to some, and an awakening to others. (3) The question remains—how? (4) Armstrong concludes that societal "roles" are too strong for the education of individuals to make much of a difference. (5) Coffin thinks that dropping students into the ghetto for a while might help to stir their social consciences. (6) He feels we ought to try changing the law.

   [From "A Good Man Was Hard to Find," by Joyce Bermel, *Change*, October 1978, p. 60.]

3. (1) A good example of David's moral support occurred during the shooting of the last scene of the film. (2) Moreover, he was an enormous source of moral support in any occasional

conflicts with Corman over various scenes in the movie. (3) Frankenstein, having killed the despotic ruler, has installed himself as President and decreed a series of political reforms, among them the abolition of the annual Death Race. (4) "The country," he says, "no longer requires a gratuitous display of violence to prove to the world that its virility is intact." (5) It was David who constantly encouraged me to have the courage of my convictions.

> [From "Another Evening with David Carradine," by Paul Bartel, *Take One*, July 1978, p. 17.]

4. (1) He died as the train was pulling into Kansas City. (2) He made a few halfhearted attempts to stop drinking, but none took. (3) In the fall of 1943 he was playing a club date in Los Angeles and caught the flu. (4) He went to a party at the Zanzibar Room in Hollywood and got on the Sante Fe Chief the next day heading for New York. (5) His doctors told him to slow down, but as his manager, Ed Kirkeby, said, "He really just didn't know how." (6) His weight, always a problem, ballooned up to nearly 300 pounds, and his ankles became so swollen it was difficult for him to walk.

> [From "Fats Is Misbehavin' Again," by Peter Andrews, *Horizon*, September 1978, p. 92.]

5. (1) Great towering trees, beautiful and exotic plantings are all arranged around and in exhibits containing animals and reptiles in their natural habitats. (2) The Detroit Zoo was the first barless zoo in America, and with the exception of the snow leopard exhibit and the maternity dens at the polar bear exhibit, all newly constructed exhibits adhere to the barless theme. (3) Today, the Detroit Zoological Park is the last outpost in the metropolitan area where young and old can experience a sanctuary-like atmosphere. (4) Our 600 mammals, 700 reptiles and 1,000 birds are on display in 40 exhibits.

> [From "Michigan's Top Zoo Celebrates a Birthday," by Robert Willson, *Michigan Living Motor News*, August 1978, p. 22.]

TECHNIQUES FOR SENTENCE BUILDING

The ten samples that follow were taken from a variety of sources: books, articles, student essays, radio and TV programs, speeches. They represent a somewhat limited range of errors or lapses, but the comments on how they might be improved bring in strategies that could be followed in other sentence correcting exercises. For further examples of awkward or weak sentence patterns, and suggested corrections, see the *"Handbook"* section.

1. "Anyone who watches evening network TV receives a heavy diet of violence."

The writer has tried to strengthen his opening sentence with a metaphor. Although the idea of comparing consumption of TV with food intake is not a novel one, the appropriateness of the metaphor should be obvious. We nibble on sitcoms while munching potato chips; both are certainly mindless activities. The section to be strengthened here concerns the verb *receives.* Note that this verb is too vague: One can receive a package and a blow to the head—both very different receptions. It could be argued that the passive voice also has legitimacy, because the TV audience for any program would hardly be called active. Still, to give the metaphor greater weight and logic, would not the verb *consumes* be better? If the passive is more desirable, why not *is fed* in place of *receive?*

A suggestion: Work to achieve complete consistency in the use of metaphors. Make both verbs and nouns work for you.

2. "The Pope apparently died of a heart attack."

Here the writer's attention has shorted out. He has not seen the inadvertently humorous situation created by the misplacement of the modifier *apparently.* The sentence should be rewritten, "The Pope died of an apparent heart attack." This blooper was delivered on the evening news, a good occasion to hear such mistakes, since the writers of news stories are often required to read them as well.

A hint: Place modifiers next to the words they modify. Whenever you use such adjectives or adverbs, take a look at the words that come before and after them.

127

3. "A campaign was started in 1972 by the PTA and other supportive members to receive aid from the government."

Here you can see the disadvantages of using the passive voice to describe some event. The reader must wait until he has passed the verb phrase *was started* in order to find out who began the campaign. A revision that answers this question and gives directness would read: "In 1972 the PTA and other supportive members [Who are these: Does the writer really mean to say *supporters?*] started a campaign to receive aid from the government." Notice that the passive nature of the sentence is reinforced by the verb *receive;* campaigns are designed to "win" something, not "receive" it.

A reminder: Give your readers as much specific detail as possible. The following questions are left unanswered here: Who are the supporters? What agency in the federal government grants such aid? How much money was sought?

4. "To someone with no ability to scrutinize what he or she does in terms of greater goals, early ratification can be, and usually is, stultifying."
—DAVID MAMET, "Learn to Love the Theater"

Although public speakers sometimes can be forgiven excesses or confused phrasing in a moment of inspiration, this address maker seems not to have thought through what he intended to say. *Someone* is too general a pronoun; the speech is about acting, so *an actor* would be better. And what does "scrutinize what he or she does in terms of greater goals" really mean? It is likely that the speaker really means to warn the beginning actor against believing favorable reviews and to urge the value of long-range planning. *In terms of* qualifies as the culprit phrase here: It is too indefinite. Another trouble spot is "early ratification can be, and usually is, stultifying." If something usually is true, it is better simply to say so, without unduly interrupting the flow of the sentence. A suggested revision reads: "To an actor incapable of self-evaluation and unsure of his career goals, early ratification usually is stultifying."

5. "He is and always has been, an aggressive-type hitter."

Too many writers these days tack on *type* to adjectives that should stand alone. "It is a fast-type car," I heard a student say the other day. The "and always has been" interrupter functions to underscore the longstanding aggressiveness of the hitter. But is it necessary? Doesn't the sentence, like the batter's swing, gain power from simplicity and directness? "He's an aggressive hitter" has the sharpness of a line-drive double to the wall.

A suggestion: Don't try to build sentences by adding the flab of superfluous or redundant words.

6. "It is interesting to note the fact that many men find no satisfaction in their careers."

The fact that sentences are good examples of verbal cluttering. Unless you refer to specific facts in a report or analysis—"There are several facts that support this conclusion"—it is best to avoid using the construction. Here the problem is compounded by the introductory pronoun subject and verb *It is*. The pronoun refers to no clearly distinguishable noun; it simply signals the arrival of the subject *many men*. Depending on the context (let us say this sentence is part of an analysis of a report on male career planning), the sentence can be cleaned up to read, "Many men find no satisfaction in their careers."

7. "The defensive players began digging themselves in a hole when they made some mental errors in the first half, and they were buried later in the game when the corner backs failed to cover receivers going for long passes."

The sentence attempts an analysis of reasons for losing a football game. There is nothing wrong with the diction or the punctuation; the writer even succeeds in developing

129

a metaphor to describe the team's collapse. To achieve greater impact, however, the writer should have taken advantage of punctuation designed to provide variety and economy. By substituting a semicolon for the comma and conjunction, the sentence also becomes better balanced. Many sentences that follow the pattern of two independent clauses joined by *and* could be made more direct and economical by this method.

A reminder: Be sure that the second half of the sentence is in fact an independent clause. If it is a dependent clause or participial phrase, a comma must be used.

8. "They come from all sides of the political spectrum, they're as honest as the day is long, and most work as hard as dogs."

This writer attempts a heartfelt description of his congressional colleagues. While we cannot doubt his sincerity, we can ask some questions about his knowledge of physics. A color spectrum or band is divided by shades of color; to say that a spectrum has sides is to distort the metaphor. The writer's colleagues may "range from one end to the other" of the spectrum, but they probably will not be found on its sides. More important, the expression *political spectrum* has become a cliché, and although it may not be as worn out as *honest as the day is long* or *work as hard as dogs,* it should be avoided in serious writing. Although it is not always easy to know when you are falling into a cliché, test yourself by asking whether or not the comparison (clichés often emerge in comparisons: *smooth as silk, slimy as a snake,* and so on) is yours or one you have heard spoken frequently. The answer should give some idea about the originality of your statement.

9. "My decision to buy a car came suddenly, and I ran into many problems with financing."

One of the most difficult things for beginning writers to do is to subordinate their ideas in sentences. Often it is simply easier to write two sentences: "I ran into Paul at the game. We decided to eat together afterward." But the events are really connected in the writer's mind and in time. "After Paul and I met at the game, we went out to eat." In the preceding example the writer has tried to make the two clauses coordinate, joining them with a comma and *and.* Here a participle helps in subordinating one part of the sentence to the other: "Having decided suddenly to buy a car, I ran into many problems with financing." This arrangement focuses your reader's attention on a process with stages rather than on two separate events.

A reminder: Whenever you find yourself overusing a coordinate conjunction to join two independent clauses, see whether or not subordination can be achieved by use of a participle.

10. "At least an hour was spent examining the evidence, and the police finally concluded that the accident was my fault."

At first glance this sentence appears to require subordination: ". . . examining the evidence, the police finally concluded that. . . ." In fact, the sentence suffers from a lack of detail, thereby sounding more like a report filled out on a form than a vivid representation of what actually happened. What evidence was examined? How many and what kind of police (i.e., patrolmen, detectives) were involved? Did the police interview the other driver? What was the weather like during this period? What was the *writer* feeling during this ordeal? Not that all of these questions can—or should—be answered in one sentence. But the impact of the sentence on the reader can be heightened by a skillful selection of concrete details. In this sentence, the writer clearly believes he was not at fault. Has he convinced you?

A suggestion: Read some of your favorite fiction with an eye on how the novelist sets certain scenes.

4 *The Paragraph*

WHAT IS A PARAGRAPH?

One beauty of our native tongue is that English can always borrow from another language when it is at a loss for words. *Paragraph,* for example, is derived from two Greek words, *para,* "beside," and *graphein,* "to write." It was at one time a mark, usually ¶, written in the margin of a manuscript beside the place where a unit or subdivision of the text was to begin. The conventional signal now used to indicate a new paragraph is of course indention—that is, beginning a line a little to the right of the margin. (In some situations paragraphing is indicated instead by a skipped line and a new sentence beginning at the left-hand margin.) However it is marked, paragraphing can be considered a form of punctuation. It suggests that readers are to make a major pause in their progress—as much as several seconds if they are reading aloud—and that they are to prepare for a new unit of discourse following, in some reasonable order, the one they have just finished.

The function of this punctuated, or paragraphed, unit varies with different kinds of prose. In dialogue, the paragraph often marks off a single speech of a character. In description it may divide the details of a scene or object being presented. Paragraphs may be organized in a simple sequence of time, as when one writes instructions on the operation of a machine. They may mark off units into which a subject has been divided, a familiar textbook formula (three causes of a war, four classes of a society). In discussions of facts and ideas—usually spoken of as exposition— a common paragraph unit comprises a step in a logical argument. Since it is exposition or persuasion that most concerns students, we give our attention primarily to such paragraphs. If we speak of a paragraph of exposition, for the moment at least, as a related group of sentences calculated to advance an argument, with or without a summarizing or topic sentence, we probably come close to describing the actual practice of writers.

Writers who begin a sentence with a dependent clause —for instance, "When I saw him on the street yesterday . . ."—have a pretty good idea what their main clause is going to say. "When I saw him on the street yesterday, he looked perfectly well." Similarly, experienced writers, composing an introductory sentence in a paragraph, have a fair idea of how that sentence is going to relate to the major point of the paragraph—a point they may be preparing to state in what is called a *topic sentence* later on. In terms of larger structures yet, practiced writers are aware of what a particular paragraph is going to contribute to the whole point of a developing article, or even a book. Writers should be ready constantly to change schemes, for they learn as they compose. But enormous quantities of waste motion are saved if they maintain a maximum awareness of the various relationships between a particular unit being written and all the other units of which it is to become a working part.

For beginning writers, simultaneous coordination of all these relationships comes hard, and planning paragraphs by outline as they plan whole essays is advisable, at least in the early attempts. The topic sentence of a paragraph is that sentence that states the subject of the paragraph, suggests the attitude taken toward the subject in the paragraph, and, usually, anticipates the paragraph's conclusion. Experimental drafting of a few topic sentences can be helpful, even when the writer knows that the topic sentence may have to be rewritten and that it need not be the opening sentence. (The topic sentence of this paragraph is the last one.) Any procedure, in fact, that helps students recognize a number of possible relations between the component sentences of the paragraph is useful.

The most familiar diagnosis of poor paragraphs in exposition is that they lack organization. By this one means:

1. *Lack of coherence*—that is, unrelated statements are made; relations between statements are not clearly shown.
2. *Lack of unity*—that is, digressions from the main thought or the topical idea are made; irrelevant details are included.

As we have already hinted, it is fruitless to consider paragraphs in isolation from the larger units of which they are a part. Perhaps the fairest way to approach the paragraph as a single piece is to concentrate on introductions, the first paragraphs in expository essays. You can study an introductory paragraph without the sense that you have missed what went before it, for there is nothing before it except the title. What we shall do here, therefore, in the next few sections of this chapter, is to consider in some detail several introductory paragraphs of the sort found in essay collections. In each case, the writer is *introducing* his reader to the exposition that is to follow. This work on the paragraph can be related to the section "Beginnings and Endings" in Section I, Chapter 6, where larger problems of organization are considered.

KINDS OF INTRODUCTORY PARAGRAPHS

Coherence in Paragraphs

We have said that writers in their first paragraphs are introducing the reader to their exposition, but introducing can be done in so many different ways that the statement is not very helpful without some elaboration. There are at least three common and useful ways a paragraph can introduce a piece of expository prose.

First, the paragraph can contain a statement of a thesis to be argued. This is an obvious and sensible mode of beginning, as if to say, "Here is what I am going to show you." Often such a paragraph will include a reference to general opinion on the subject and how the writer's treatment will differ.

Second, the paragraph may tell a story, or begin to tell one, even though it will be clear that the whole essay is not fiction at all. The story will then be used as an example or a piece of evidence to support a thesis being argued.

Third, the paragraph may concentrate on a single key term to be defined, as a way of launching the demonstration to come.

In addition to setting the stage for what is to follow, an introductory paragraph introduces something of immense importance to the whole: the writer. Or, perhaps we should specify, that particular self he or she wishes to put forward for the particular circumstances and purposes of the writing. The way sentences in a paragraph relate to each other to introduce an argument, then, must be appreciated not only as a strategy in logic but as the image of a personality that assumes a definite relation (or *tone*) toward us. While writers are exposing *arguments*, they are dramatizing through language a *person* speaking formally, informally, intimately, or distantly, as the case may be. The composition of a well-organized paragraph requires paying as much attention to tone as to the logical arrangement of ideas. In the good writer, the argument and the voice presenting it are fused.

The Paragraph as a Statement of a Thesis to Be Argued

In expository writing it is of course common practice to state at the outset the thesis or argument that the writer proposes to advance in his essay. For one thing, this is simple politeness to the reader. Often the statement is preceded or immediately followed by a reference to general prevailing opinion on the subject, or to a condition that needs correcting, or to past treatments of it by other writers. The reader is to assume that prevailing opinion and past treatments are to be qualified, or perhaps demol-

135

ished utterly, by the new treatment the author is putting forward. If some condition needs correcting, the author may begin by suggesting that action is needed now. This approach can, however, come dangerously close to a formula. The student using this approach, therefore, should take note of the various ways in which professional writers modify the formula.

Here is an uncomplicated piece of prose from a popular American magazine, *The Atlantic Monthly;* watch the formula at work.

[1] So poorly defined is the frontier between fact and fiction these days that on both sides of the border smuggling has become a major industry. [2] Journalists, particularly the flashier ones, prosper by employing fiction techniques in their reporting; a fact is never allowed to speak for itself. [3] On the other side, novelists who embroider upon public events are spared the trouble of having to invent either scene or character. [4] In the prevailing confusion, isn't it about time to draw a clearer boundary?

—THOMAS GRIFFITH, "Too Good to Be True"

[1] The first sentence states the condition that the writer feels needs correcting. This thesis statement is given weight by the use of the metaphor of border crossing. The tone here is informal yet concerned.

[2] The group on one side of the border—journalists—is described as "smuggling" fiction techniques to embroider facts. Note the modifier *flashier.*

[3] *On the other side* links this sentence with the preceding one, identifying novelists as smugglers of events and characters from real life. The phrase *spared the trouble* is a form of ironic understatement; the writer is in effect saying they are lazy.

[4] *Clearer boundary* keeps alive the border metaphor in this sentence, which issues a call to action. *Prevailing confusion* stands as the writer's assessment of this semi-serious dilemma. Do you see any possibility of resolving it?

As you see, the writer has taken pains to connect his sentences to one another by the use of transitional phrases and by seeing to it that succeeding sentences enlarge upon or define references in previous sentences. Sentence 4, for example, not only links up with sentence 3—"In the prevailing confusion"—but also specifically recalls the border metaphor introduced in sentence 1. Throughout, the

136

use of this metaphor helps Griffith to maintain a lightly ironic tone, concerned about the blurring of fact and fiction but not ready to go on a hunger strike about it. The question in sentence 4 is put seriously and based on the thesis statement in the opening sentence; we legitimately expect the writer to address the question he has raised even if his ironic tone suggests he is not sure of finding an answer.

The next passage, from the same magazine, begins with a paragraph citing prevailing opinion on the subject and stating how the author disagrees with it. Read it the first time quickly to get a sense of the person speaking here.

[1] The conflict of the generations is neither a new nor a particularly American story, but it is perhaps exacerbated by the self-consciousness and the partial segregation of teenage culture, to such an extent that both old and young are exceptionally vulnerable to their mutual criticisms. [2] I do not care to add to the complacency of my agemates who, from their clubs, pulpits, and other rostrums, attack the alleged "softness" of the young, whom they have themselves brought up, while failing to see the difficulties young people face today precisely because the manifest hardships with which earlier Americans coped have been, for millions, attenuated. [3] These hardships cannot be artificially restored, at least for people over twelve; however, I believe that college students are now beginning to find new ways to become active politically, and hence responsible humanly.

—DAVID RIESMAN, "Where Is the College Generation Headed?"

[1] The first sentence connects what is to follow with an ageless problem—the conflict of the generations—and suggests a modern climate of opinion in which the assumptions the author is about to attack can flourish.

[2] Here the author, aware of the climate of opinion he described in his first sentence, explicitly separates himself from those holding the prevailing view of teen-age "softness." He does so because he recognized (first sentence) how vulnerable the young are to such attacks. Note the subtle but clear relation between the two sentences.

[3] *These hardships* repeats an important word from the preceding sentence. Then the key clause of the whole article follows, introduced by the connective *however*. In spite of their loss of traditional hardships, young people are learning to act responsibly.

The difference in tone between the two paragraphs, which should be obvious on a first quick reading, may be explained by a number of differences in their rhetorics, at least some of which we can mention here. For one thing, note the length of the sentences: Whereas Thomas Griffith, in a paragraph of just over eighty words, writes four sentences, David Riesman, in a considerably longer paragraph, writes only three. Riesman's vocabulary is also sophisticated; some of his words *(exacerbated, attenuated)* may have sent you to the dictionary. Riesman expects a good deal of his readers. He addresses them formally, he does not avoid complex ways of talking, and he does not make things any easier by introducing appealing metaphors or an ironic tone, as Griffith does. The relations between Riesman's sentences are not immediately obvious. There are no in-jokes about novelists or anything else, and indeed we may feel some alienation in this speaker's crack about his age-mates in their pulpits and rostrums. How can we account for such difference in rhetoric and tone? We cannot assume that the two writers are addressing different audiences, for both these articles appeared in different issues of the same magazine. Nor is the difference primarily that they are dealing with different subjects, although this no doubt has something to do with it. Rather, the answer is to be found in the individual decision of each writer to project a different speaking personality. Each man's precise motives for making such a decision are elusive—Griffith does write a regular column called "A Party of One"; Riesman is an occasional contributor—and would probably be as difficult to discover entirely as the motives for most human behavior.

We have now examined two expository paragraphs employing variations of the thesis-to-be-argued formula. Each paragraph is constructed of sentences knit together with transitional devices, some more obvious than others, but all at least competently handled. The tone of each selection is different, but note that the writer's choice of tone is not necessarily a function of his subject.

The Paragraph of Anecdote as Evidence for a Thesis

We begin this section with an article that takes a stand on the abuses of language. See how the argument is begun with a seemingly innocent observation by Jacques Barzun.

[1] Like five million other people I spend part of each day in a New York bus, and some of that time my eyes rest on the sign:

PLEASE REFRAIN FROM
CONVERSATION WITH OPERATOR
WHILE BUS IS IN MOTION

[2] After some years of dumb staring, it has come over me that this foreign-language text means, "Please do not talk to the driver between stops." [3] But this knowledge does not make me sure that I shall ever understand that other sign, found in every shop, which reads: "Illumination is required to be extinguished before these premises are closed to business." [4] Before it, I find I have only one thought: "WHOM is speaking?"

—JACQUES BARZUN, "How to Suffocate the English Language"

[1] A disarming opener: note how the author specifically makes himself no better than anyone else. We are to sense the humor of this pretentious sign even before he labels it with *this foreign-language text.*

[2] Three linked phrases: *part of each day, some of that time, after some years.*

[3] *This knowledge* refers to *it has come over me.*

That other sign, yet similar, of course, in its stuffiness.

[4] *Before it:* note the transitional phrase, with its reference to the *other sign.*
The author's joke on grammar at the end implies that his reader shares his immediate recognition of absurdly ungrammatical forms.

The next sentence of this article, beginning its second paragraph, opens with the phrase "These public displays of literary ineptitude . . . ." The anecdote of seeing the sign on the bus, it is clear, is to be taken as one piece of evidence for a larger fact. The sign about illumination is another piece of evidence. This technique is a form of what is called the *inductive approach*, starting with a specific occasion or instance and moving to a generalization. (See

139

Chapter 6, "Problems of Composing.") One advantage to using a personal anecdote as evidence is that the reader momentarily enjoys the comfortable feeling of being told a story. It provides a pleasant avenue into what may turn out to be a tough neighborhood before the trip is over, and it distracts the reader from questioning the truth of the evidence. If a generalization begins the discussion there is every likelihood the reader will stop to say "I can think of exceptions." And if the writer immediately provokes the reader's antagonism, the rest of the argument will have an uphill fight. In a story narration such as this one, however, the speaker's relation to his reader is easy and good-humored; he is having fun with his subject.

In another example of personal anecdote as an introductory device, we confront a speaker who is puzzled by a common belief about the qualifications of job applicants. What begins as a somewhat humorous curiosity in the writer's mind quickly becomes a fact of business life which leads him to some careful self-examination. Notice how dramatically the tone shifts, in the second paragraph, from lighthearted bafflement to sober exposition of fact.

[1] I used to think it curious, if not a bit sad, as I began to notice that the only men who stated their height on résumés I'd receive were those six feet or taller. Why, I puzzled, would these résumé writers think anyone could possibly care how tall an editor is—unless the dejected fellows were scraping the barrel of their assets for something to say about themselves.

[2] One day I realized they weren't as off-base as I had thought. I chanced upon a sociological study, which found that when the starting salaries of graduates of the same business college were compared, the taller men's

[1] Note the off-handed way in which the fact of the applicants' size was communicated to the author. Colloquialisms like *a bit sad* and *scraping the barrel* also convey the author's mood of bemused condescension about the matter. Though not a specific incident, this generalized anecdote accomplishes the task of involving the reader in the writer's puzzlement.

[2] With *One day* we shift to a serious discussion while retaining something of the colloquial flavor with *off-base,* a baseball metaphor that nicely characterizes the gamesmanship of the applicants. By citing the two sociological studies, the author has appealed to au-

140

salaries were significantly higher. In addition, another social psychology experiment had 140 recruiters make a hypothetical choice between two equally qualified applicants, one man six feet, one inch, and the other five feet, nine inches. Only one percent chose the short man.

—LEONARD H. GROSS, "Short, Dark, and Almost Handsome"

thority and has impressed us with "scientific" findings. The final, short sentence, with its revealing fact, gives a dramatic close to the paragraph.

The third paragraph of this essay begins "These revelations stirred up some suppressed anxieties . . . ," thereby applying the anecdote to the feelings of the author himself on the subject of height. We read on: "Being somewhat undersized all through childhood, I worried if I'd reach that critical five feet eight that enabled you to be a cop or a fireman (these occupations being symbols for the worrisome question—'Will I be a Real Man?')." Note the reference to general opinion, so familiar in our earlier examples, an opinion from which the writer will explicitly diverge: "Height can only be a factor insofar as it represents 'Authority' and transmits a strong and dependable image, . . ." Now we know that we are to take the anecdote as a piece of evidence for a much more serious concept, namely the role of height in determining success for men in our society. But the writer does not entirely lose his good-natured storytelling manner, as his humorous but sensible observation at the close of the third paragraph proves: ". . . a hose will smother more flames than the foot of a fireman even as big as Wilt Chamberlain ever could."

The Paragraph as a Definition of a Term

The point of a piece of exposition often depends on one or two significant words. Many of the significant words have been so mauled by excessive handling that they are invoked less for their meaning than for their easy capacity

141

to adapt to a variety of meanings without retaining the shape of any. *Liberal, idea, tolerance* are three of them. Anyone writing an essay making important use of such terms must anticipate a reader's very proper question: What do you mean by that? In the following three opening paragraphs, definition of one of these terms is the central problem the paragraph must solve, or at least face. Within this definition of common function, however, the paragraphs again differ markedly in tone.

[1] Any education that matters is *liberal*. [2] All the saving truths and healing graces that distinguish a good education from a bad one or a full education from a half-empty one are contained in that word. [3] Whatever ups and downs the term "liberal" suffers in the political vocabulary, it soars above all controversy in the educational world. [4] In the blackest pit of pedagogy the squirming victim has only to ask, "What's liberal about this?" to shame his persecutors. [5] In times past a liberal education set off a free man from a slave or a gentleman from laborers and artisans. [6] It now distinguishes whatever nourishes the mind and spirit from the training which is merely practical or professional or from the trivialities which are no training at all. [7] Such an education involves a combination of knowledge, skills, and standards.

— ALAN SIMPSON, "The Marks of an Educated Man"

[1] Strong, terse statement, italicizing the crucial term.
[2] Links: repetition of *education* and the final phrase, *that word,* which refers to the italicized term.

[4] *Pedagogy* is a linking echo of *education.*
Note again the repetitions of *liberal,* the key word.
[5] The phrase *liberal education* combines the two.

[5, 6] Sentences 5 and 6 are linked and balanced by the references to time in each: *in times past* and *now.*
This is the crucial sentence of the definition.
[7] *Such an education*—i.e., a liberal one—again reinforces the links between the sentences.

The writer is now ready to proceed with his discussion of "knowledge, skills, and standards." He has set up a

142

working definition of *liberal,* however general it may be, and he has set it apart from its political connotations. The tone is serious, and the reader, although he is expected to share the values of education here referred to, is certainly not left with the impression that the speaker knows him intimately. This is formal discourse.

We now look at another problem with a word, the word *idea.* Here is a distinguished composer beginning an essay on the creative process in the writing of music.

[1] The word "idea" is a very vague term for what we really mean when we talk of the composer's creative imagination. [2] The German word *Einfall* is the perfect expression needed in our situation. [3] *Einfall,* from the verb *einfallen,* to drop in, describes beautifully the strange spontaneity that we associate with artistic ideas in general and with musical creation in particular. [4] Something—you know not what—drops into your mind—you know not whence—and there it grows—you know not how—into some form—you know not why. [5] This seems to be the general opinion, and we cannot blame the layman if he is unable to find rational explanations for so strange an occurrence.

—PAUL HINDEMITH, "How Music Happens"

[1] The speaker concedes immediately that he has a problem of definition.

[2] *Word* is repeated; *in our situation* refers also, more generally, to the first sentence.

[3] *Einfall* repeated; *describes beautifully* refers to *is the perfect expression* in the sentence preceding.

[4] This unorthodox punctuation is Hindemith's attempt to express in words *the strange spontaneity* he mentioned in the previous sentence.
[5] *This* refers, perhaps a little vaguely, to the thought processes just described.

Hindemith's tone is a good deal lighter and friendlier than that in the previous passage, partly because of his clever mimicking of popular responses to the word *idea* in musical creation. (All those dashes!) Notice that the writer expresses some charity for those who know less than he does—"we cannot blame the layman." He is a little more human, a little less formidable, than the preceding writer.

You will recognize the reference to "general opinion" in the final sentence, an opinion with which Hindemith is about to disagree in the rest of his article, at least to the extent of describing a composer's process of creating music in something like rational terms. The paragraph of definition, in this case, not only deals with a term, but in doing so also uses the first technique described in this chapter, the argument in contrast to prevailing opinion. Methods, it is important to make clear, are often successfully combined, as in the example just given. Our process of critical analysis is based on a completed process, and in practice the writer does not ask beforehand, "Now which of three, or six, or fifteen techniques should I use in this paragraph?" The practical question is much harder: "How can I so organize this paragraph that the reader will respond exactly as I want?" Knowing the categories of critical analysis will not, alone, solve all paragraphing problems—reading will discover plenty of excellent introductory paragraphs that seem to fit none of the categories—but it will help the inexperienced writer, who must sometimes choose an opening self-consciously and deliberately, as when answering an examination question.

Of the three elusive words mentioned, *tolerance* gives off the deepest sound and seems to defy all but the most piously respectable approach. Must the appropriate tone for defining it be impersonal or strictly formal? Not necessarily. We must not press too hard our notions of appropriateness, for, as already noted, subject matter and tone are not the same thing. It does not follow that because a topic is supposed to be serious, we must necessarily speak of it seriously. *Consistency* in the way we speak of it is another matter; "the departed" at the beginning should not turn up as "the stiff" near the end, unless the best we can afford is cheap humor. The quality of tone is the writer's own decision, and in the case of some great writers, as the following passage should show, the decision can be surprising.

144

[1] Can you define tolerance? [2] I can't, any more than I could define love or faith, or fate, or any other abstraction. [3] My mind slips about, tries a definition, finds it won't quite work, drops it, tries another, and so on. [4] And people whose minds are better than my own seem to be in the same plight here. [5] They propound definitions, they defend them stoutly and philosophically, but sooner or later the definition crumbles under the onslaught of some other philosopher, and the world is left where it was. [6] Well, not quite where it was. [7] Despite the failure, two valuable things have occurred. [8] Firstly, the human mind has been exercising itself, and my goodness, how desirable that is! [9] It has been trying to discover something, and it has become stronger and more agile in consequence, even though nothing has been discovered. [10] And, secondly, the abstract subjects on which it has exercised itself have gained in prestige. [11] Tolerance is important, no one can deny that, and if it is talked about so that people dispute what it is, or isn't, its importance should be maintained or increased.

—E. M. FORSTER, "Toward a Definition of Tolerance"

[1] Definition problem immediately stated, and the reader directly involved *(you)*.
[2] The speaker, with his informal contractions *(can't)*, cheerfully admits his own limitations.
Links: *define*, sentence 1; *define*, 2; *definition*, 3; *definitions*, 5.
[4] *And* connects the writer's mind with everyone else's.
[5] This sentence echoes, in more elegant language, the way in which the speaker described his own train of thought in sentence 3.

[6] *Well:* highly informal. *Where it was:* another linkage by repetition.
[7] The *failure* summarizes what has been described so far.
[8, 9, 10] Familiar logical organization: *firstly, secondly.* (*First* and *second* are now the preferred adverbial forms.) The speaker is jocular, of course, about minds exercising themselves, implying it does not happen very often!

[10] *Gained in prestige* links with *important* and *importance* in the final sentence.
[11] *Tolerance* returns us neatly to the first sentence.

ADEQUATE PARAGRAPH DEVELOPMENT

Rarely do college students write paragraphs that are too long; the chief difficulty is finding enough to say so that their paragraphs will not resemble a series of slightly expanded sentences.

If three or four paragraphs appear on every page of a theme, the paragraphs are probably too short. A five-hundred-word essay split into ten or twelve paragraphs contains paragraphs that are too short. The paragraphs of a newspaper story are short, it is true; so are the paragraphs of a business letter. But we are not speaking of those special types of writing when we say "expository" writing. In expository writing it is customary to develop ideas more fully or to group ideas into larger units than in news stories or in letters. In expository writing a series of very short paragraphs is an indication of malnutrition; paragraphs need to be fed details to make them effective.

UNDEVELOPED PARAGRAPH

Advertisements in magazines and on television these days are a lot better than they are given credit for. Some of them are quite funny. I think advertising is more interesting than a lot of other things going on nowadays. [This is vague, repetitious, undeveloped. Note especially some of the undefined words and phrases: *a lot better* (how are they better?), *more interesting* (in what way?), *a lot of other things* (what sort of things?).]

REWRITTEN PARAGRAPH

The growth of humor in the writing of advertisements is a pleasant phenomenon of recent years. In magazines and on television many writers of ads have been exploiting a sense of the absurd, almost as if they were making fun of themselves. A well-known airline has produced commercials featuring Peter Sellers, in various continental guises, as a barker for the company's sophisticated service. Sellers' exaggeratedly condescending tone made you laugh at the same time you were seduced by the snob appeal of his message. In a somewhat different approach one desperate American car-maker has modified an old folk tale in its magazine and TV ads. These commercials depict a long line of hum-drum cars following its unique and racy coupe to the dealership of "P. Piper." Altogether this kind of fun-making is a healthy development in a profession that often appears to take salesmanship all too solemnly.

146

ADEQUATE PARAGRAPH DEVELOPMENT

UNDEVELOPED PARAGRAPH

I like to travel all right, but it is the people you meet rather than the things you see that I appreciate. When I visit a new place I am really happy to find some new faces and names that I can make friends with. [This paragraph has reduced informality to not much more than chattering. Again it is vague and unconvincing. Note how, in the revision, the writer has exploited the unintended rhyme—new places, new faces—to enliven his first sentence. Then he proceeds with some relatively concrete, memorable examples.]

REWRITTEN PARAGRAPH

When I go traveling, it is new faces, not new places, that I go to see. The Grand Canyon is certainly an awesome sight, but what I remember most vividly from my visit there is the figure of a priest I met in a hotel lobby. Lean, ascetic, with flashing black eyes, he spoke to me of his order and its commitment to teaching. And at Yellowstone Park, where I was duly impressed by Old Faithful, an elderly woman with bright silver hair and the manner of an actress took one look and sniffed. "Another dull show in the provinces," she concluded scornfully. Sightseeing is all very well, but I suspect our own human depths may be more mysterious and fascinating than any canyon. Thoreau put it better, at a time when maps still contained large, unexplored blank spaces. "What does Africa, what does the West stand for?" he asked. "Is not our own interior white on the chart?"

Some sketchy paragraphs are the result of a failure to think in larger units. The writer fails to decide on the central idea, and then does not see that those miniature paragraphs are merely parts of the topic idea.

SKETCHY PARAGRAPHS

Dad and Mother marveled at the way my sister Lois and I got along; they still do in fact. They are proud of the family unity we show.

When Lois married, I was as thrilled and happy as she, I am sure. I think I knew better than anyone else what a wonderful wife she would be. Her marriage is an example to me.

Although my sister never attended college, she has encouraged

147

me greatly. I am working to live up to the high standards she set for me, and I am constantly hoping that some day I can in some way repay her.

[Try combining under a topic sentence like this: *My sister Lois has been a companion and an example to me.*]

The buzzard usually glides over wooded areas in search of food because a domestic animal is more likely to meet a mishap in the forest than out in a plain pasture. Also one will find buzzards around the sloughs in the summer because the water is drying up and the buzzard will feed on the dead fish.

The buzzard lives in a nest on top of high cliffs and in tree tops.

It is against the law to shoot buzzards because they scavenge the animals that have died in the woods through accident.

[Try combining these three paragraphs under a topic sentence that makes a statement about the feeding and nesting habits of buzzards.]

I suppose any mother is happy and proud when her daughters surprise her by cooking a meal. I know that my mother always is. This is one way in which we like to make her happy.

Mother always remembers kindness, whether it be in thoughts or actions, and always forgets the unkindness of others. She appreciates having us cook for her.

[Try constructing a topic sentence about Mother's appreciation of a kind act.]

The tendency of beginners is to write in generalizations and abstractions: "The closing hour at the cafe is always a scene of great confusion." What actually is going on? Why not make us see—hear and smell, too—the various details of that confusion? Just what did you see that justified your conclusion that the closing hour at the cafe is a scene of confusion? In criticism, the statement "I like this poem" is of course practically meaningless. Why do you like it? Because it irritates you? or because it soothes you? In presentation of character—"My father is an honest man." How is he honest? What does he do that shows honesty? Drag

148

him out on the stage and let us watch him being honest. In discussions of college problems—"Dormitory rules are more liberal, and thus more demanding, than parental rules"—give us examples, many of them. Let us see college men and women in situations that require choice; let us see how they behave and what they think in relation to questions of social morality. Give us action and proof. Give us the evidence that you have observed.

Here are some examples to show how details can be used.

BEFORE

Holding a little boy by the hand, a fat old woman waddled slowly up the staircase.

AFTER

Her carpet slippers flapping against the stone steps, the huge woman made her way laboriously up the staircase. Her dark shapelessness almost hid the little boy beside her, whose thin white arm stretched taut as she pulled him along.

BEFORE

The closing hour at the cafe where I work is always a scene of great confusion. The juke-box is playing, the customers are shouting their orders, everyone is impatient and in a hurry.

AFTER

The raucous blast of a Beatles number from the jukebox and the bellows of customers impatient for their final orders of ham-burgers and french fries turn closing hour at the cafe where I work into a fair approximation of the last moments aboard the *Titanic.*

Notice that the writer's "scene of great confusion" has now become more vivid for the reader through the addition of a few concrete details. Remember that concrete writing does not call for overwhelming the reader with descriptive minutiae. It ought to be the art of making each statement specific and unmistakably pertinent.

149

PROBLEMS OF INTERNAL ORGANIZATION

Most paragraphs, wherever they may appear, are built around a *central theme* or *idea*, which is often expressed in a single *topic sentence.* And most paragraphs are made up of sentences connected by transitional devices that can be identified. We will now take a look at some additional techniques for organizing, or unifying, or holding together expository paragraphs.

In the following paragraph, notice how all the details have been chosen to relate to the initial topic sentence and its key phrase, "old dark house." This is a simple approach that consists of seeing to it that all the items of a list belong in that list, but it is not as easy as it looks.

The Haunting is set in that pleasantly familiar "old dark house" that is itself an evil presence, and is usually inhabited by ghosts or evil people. In our childhood imaginings, the unknowable things that have happened in old houses, and the whispers that someone may have died in them, make them mysterious, "dirty"; only the new house that has known no life or death is safe and clean. But so many stories have used the sinister dark house from-which-no-one-can-escape and its murky gardens for our ritual entertainment that we learn to experience the terrors as pleasurable excitations and reassuring reminders of how frightened we used to be before we learned our way around. In film, as in story, the ambience is fear; the film specialty is gathering a group who are trapped and helpless. (Although the women are more easily frightened, the men are also powerless. Their superior strength doesn't count for much against unseen menaces: this may explain why the genre was often used for a male comedian—like Bob Hope in *The Ghost Breakers.* Russ Tamblyn serves a similar but feeble cowardly-comic function in *The Haunting.*) The action is confined to the house and grounds (the maze); the town is usually far away, just far enough away so that "nobody will hear you if you scream."

—PAULINE KAEL, "Zeitgeist and Poltergeist; or, Are Movies Going to Pieces?"

150

Still another technique of unifying a paragraph is to build all or most of the sentences around a comparison or a contrast. Comparison requires finding similarities in two things. Usually the more familiar thing or idea is used to explain the less familiar one: to explain the game of squash show how it is similar to tennis, the more familiar game. In what ways is piloting a plane like driving a car? How are Canadians like their continental neighbors in the United States? Contrast, on the other hand, is telling what a thing is not like. How does college life as you see it now differ from college life as you thought it would be? How does the Western way of living differ from the Oriental way? How does capitalism differ from communism? How does propaganda differ from news? These are typical subjects that invite treatment by contrast, not in paragraphs alone but also in entire essays or articles.

A white-collar employee of an American corporation visiting a Soviet institution of comparable rank will be in for some surprises. [Topic sentence] For one thing the offices of the establishment will be secondary to the plant, instead of vice versa which is usually the case in the United States. Also the visitor will note that a considerable number of executive officers in a Russian industrial organization, even engineers, are women. On a superficial level other points can be mentioned. First, there is little of the personal byplay and banter that accompany much American business endeavor and office routine; no coffee break, for example. Bosses are aloof. Second, lunch takes place in a cafeteria on the premises, maintained by the establishment; no corner drugstore, bar, or hotdog stand. Third, nobody has to catch the 5:25; commuting, if any, is by bus. Another point is that jobs are different in function. No Soviet plant has a public relations department or advertising department, office for employer-employee relationships, or even a sales manager and staff. Salesmanship, the first of all occupations in America, does not exist in our sense at all.

—JOHN GUNTHER, *Inside Russia Today*

The following, with its touches of grim humor that so few people associate with the author, may inspire you to compare and contrast your chosen occupation with others:

151

The great liability of the engineer compared to men of other professions is that his works are out in the open where all can see them. [Topic sentence] His acts, step by step, are in hard substance. He cannot bury his mistakes in a grave like the doctors. He cannot argue them into thin air or blame the judge like the lawyers. He cannot, like the architects, cover his failures with trees and vines. He cannot, like the politicians, screen his shortcomings by blaming his opponents and hope that the people will forget. [Note how the use of phrases, "like the architects" and "like the politicians," breaks the monotony of each repetition.] The engineer simply cannot deny that he did it. If his works do not work, he is damned. That is the phantasmagoria that haunts his nights and dogs his days. He comes from the job at the end of the day resolved to calculate it again. He wakes in the night in a cold sweat and puts something on paper that looks silly in the morning. All day he shivers at the thought of the bugs which will inevitably appear to jolt its smooth consummation.

On the other hand, unlike the doctor his is not a life among the weak. Unlike the soldier, destruction is not his purpose. Unlike the lawyer, quarrels are not his daily bread. To the engineer falls the job of clothing the bare bones of science with life, comfort, and hope. No doubt as years go by people forget which engineer did it, even if they ever knew. Or some politician puts his name on it. Or they credit it to some promoter who used other people's money with which to finance it. But the engineer himself looks back at the unending stream of goodness which flows from his successes with satisfactions that few professions may know. And the verdict of his fellow professionals is all the accolade he wants.

—HERBERT HOOVER, *The Memoirs of Herbert Hoover: Years of Adventure*

Specific transitional words and phrases in the preceding paragraphs help relate the component sentences to each other. We have been using such terms as *echo, refer,* and *link* to signify these relations. We can now summarize these connecting expressions as follows:

1. *Conjunctions and transitional adverbs,* which include words and phrases such as *and, but, yet, however, therefore, consequently, moreover, accordingly, at the same time, as a result, for example, on the other hand, finally.*

2. *Pronouns,* such as *this, that, these, those, his, her,* and

152

its, which refer to an antecedent in a previous sentence. It is extremely important that the young writer make sure references of pronouns are clear. See 26 in the "Handbook."

3. *Repetition of key words,* of which examples, particularly clear in paragraphs of definition, appear in earlier pages of this chapter.

4. *Parallel structure,* through which the reader is led back to sentences phrased in similar forms.

For a close study of connectives, transitions, and internal organization, follow the themes and variations, almost like musical motifs, in the following passage:

[1] The first sentences of this book were written nearly two years ago. [2] *Outside my window* on *that* spring *morning,* as on *this,* a *bird sang.* [3] *Outside a million windows, a million birds had sung as morning swept around the globe.* [4] Few men and few women were so glad that a new day had dawned as *these birds* seem to be.

[2] Introduces key words. Pronouns *that* and *this.*

[3] Repeats *Outside . . . window, bird,* and *morning; sung* echoes *sang.*

[4] Pronoun *these.* Repeats *birds.*

[5] Because my *window* looks out on a southern landscape, my *bird* is a cardinal, with feathers as bright as his half-whistled song. [6] Farther *north* in the United States he would be a *robin,* more likely than not—less colorful and somewhat less melodious but seemingly no less pleased with the world and his place in it. [7] Like *us,* robins have *their* problems but *they* seem better able to take *them* in *their* stride. [8] *We* are likely to awake with an "Oh, dear!" on our lips; *they* with "What fun!" in their beaks. [9] Mr. Sandburg's peddler was remarkable because he seemed so *terribly glad* to be selling fish. [10] Most robins

[5] Again repeats *window.* Repeats *bird.*

[6] Contrasts *north* with *southern* in sentence 5. Introduces key word.

[7] Repeats *robin.* *Their* contrasts with *us.* Pronouns.

[8] *We* ties in with *us.*

[9, 10] Repeated phrase, *terribly glad.*

seem *terribly glad* to be eating worms.

[11] For some time I have been thinking that I wanted to write a book about the *characteristics* and *activities* of living things. [12] During the week or two just before, I had been wondering with what activity or characteristic I should begin. [13] Reproduction, growing up, and getting a living are all, so I said to *myself,* fundamental *activities.* [14] Combativeness in the face of rivals, solicitude for the young, courage when danger must be met, patience when hardships must be endured, are all typical *characteristics.* [15] But *my cardinal* proposed a different solution. [16] Is any *characteristic* more striking than the joy of life instead?

—JOSEPH WOOD KRUTCH, *The Great Chain of Life*

[11] Introduces two key words— *characteristics* and *activities.*

[12] Repeats key words.

[13] Pronoun refers to *I* (i.e., "I should begin . . .) Repeats key word.

[14] Repeats key word.

[15] *My cardinal* refers to *cardinal* in sentence 5.
[16] Repeats key word.

ORGANIZING PARAGRAPHS IN SEQUENCES

To understand how paragraphs are related to one another is to begin to see how a whole essay is organized. A paragraph that reflects a list of items to be considered is one obvious illustration. But note that in the following piece of historical writing, the authors have subtly given their third "factor" an added importance by granting it a paragraph to itself.

As late as 1808, when the slave trade was abolished, numerous Southerners thought that slavery would prove but a temporary evil. [Summary of preceding paragraph]
But during the next generation the South was converted into a section which for the most part was grimly united behind slavery. [Topic sentence of the paragraph] How did this come about? Why did the aboli-

154

tionist spirit in the South almost disappear? [Questions to be answered by what follows] For one reason, the spirit of philosophical liberalism which flamed high in Revolutionary days gradually became weaker. [One possible answer] For another reason, a general antagonism between puritanical New England and the slaveholding South became evident; they differed on the War of 1812, the tariff, and other great issues; and the South felt less and less liking for the so-called Northern idea of emancipation. [A second possible answer] But above all, certain new economic factors made slavery more profitable than it had been before 1790. [This third possible answer provides a topic sentence for the whole section to follow, comprising the following two paragraphs.]

One element in the economic change is familiar—the rise of a great cotton-growing industry in the South. [First example of an "economic factor" topic sentence of the first half of the paragraph] This was based in part on the introduction of improved types of cotton, with better fibers [one explanation of the rise of the cotton industry], but in much larger part on Eli Whitney's epochal invention in 1793 of the "gin" for cleaning cotton [second explanation]. Cotton culture rapidly moved westward from the Carolinas and Georgia, spreading over much of the lower South to the Mississippi River and, eventually, on into Texas. *Another factor which placed slavery on a new basis was sugar growing.* [This second "economic factor" provides a topic sentence for the second half of the paragraph.] The rich, hot delta lands of southeastern Louisiana are ideal for sugar cane; and in 1794–1795 an enterprising New Orleans Creole, Étienne Boré, proved that the crop could be highly profitable. He set up machinery and vats, and the crowds which had come from New Orleans to watch the boiling-off broke into cheers when the first sugar crystals showed in the cooling liquid. The cry, "It granulates!" opened a new era in Louisiana. A great boom resulted, so that by 1830 the state was supplying the nation with about half its whole sugar supply. This required slaves, who were brought in, in thousands, from the Eastern seaboard.

Finally, tobacco culture also spread westward and took slavery with it. [Third "economic factor" and topic sentence of this paragraph] Constant cropping had worn out the soil of lowland Virginia, once the greatest tobacco region of the world, and the growers were glad to move into Kentucky and Tennessee, taking their Negroes with them. Thereafter the fast-multiplying slaves of the

155

upper South were largely drained off to the lower South and West. This diffusion of slavery relieved many observers, because it lessened the risk of such a slave insurrection as Nat Turner's Rebellion, a revolt of sixty or seventy Virginia slaves in 1831—which, incidentally, did much to increase Southern fear of emancipationist doctrines.

—ALLAN NEVINS AND HENRY STEELE COMMAGER,
The Pocket History of the United States

Here is a similar technique of dividing one's subject into parts and permitting the paragraph divisions to punctuate these parts.

The Soviet Union's cosmic rocket added a new member, if a miniscule one, to the system of planets revolving around the sun since eons past. Its success is a dramatic step toward sending rockets to seek out secrets of the solar system—and perhaps to explore some of the measureless space beyond. And it has stimulated men further to look up at the "stars that sweep, and turn, and fly," and ponder the nature of the universe. [This statement introduces the next idea, which is the heart of the piece.]

Space, from earthman's point of view, has three main divisions. [Main topic sentence] *The first and smallest is the solar system.* [Topic sentence of first subdivision] The sun, with a diameter of 864,000 miles and its mighty force of gravitation, holds the nine known planets in their elliptical orbits. In addition, the solar system includes thirty-one satellites of the planets (not counting the earth's artificial satellites); thousands of asteroids, which are rather like tiny planets; comets and meteors. As astronomical distances go, the size of the solar system is not astronomical: it is only about 7,350,000,000 miles across. [Particulars and details to clarify the topic sentence]

The next division of space is "our" galaxy: an aggregation of about 100 billion stars. [Topic sentence of second subdivision] Our sun is an average star in this "Milky Way." The nearest star to us after our sun is so distant that it takes light four and one-half years to travel to us. The galaxy itself is so vast that it takes light 100,000 years to travel from one edge of it to the other. Yet ours is a medium-sized galaxy. [Particulars and details]

Beyond our "Milky Way" is the third division of space—all the rest of the universe. [Topic sentence of third subdivision] In the unimag-

156

inable reaches of this really outer space are countless numbers of aggregations of suns. All these galaxies rotate and move in space. The most powerful telescopes can find no end to them. [Again, particulars and details]

— *The New York Times Magazine,* "To the Planets and Beyond"

The next example is from an essay in which the writer describes and illustrates creativity in many kinds of activity. Her major device for linking paragraphs is the repetition of the word *imagination.* See what other ways of making transitions you can identify.

Imagination is a kind of blind spot in the average, nonwriting member of society. Because, of course, everybody has imagination. If you have the thought, "Everyone hates me"; or if you consider it a good idea to see what is the matter with the light fuse by poking your finger into the socket; or if you suppose that you can sail a boat because you have seen other people do it; or if you conclude that a friend has turned against you, when in fact her brusqueness was the result of not thinking about you at all; those are all examples of an undisciplined imagination. It is obvious how dangerous such imaginings can be.

Malicious gossip—which takes the place of creation in noncreative lives—of course draws heavily on the imagination. Fear and superstition have their roots in imagination. The fact is that imagination is antisocial in that it is not in any relation at all to everyday reality. Then what is imagination in relation to?

Probably because of such destructive phantasies as those I listed, imagination hasn't a terribly good reputation in our society. Of course, to say that so-and-so is lacking in imagination is understood as not a compliment. But if I call someone a dreamer; or remark that someone has a head full of fancies; or say to someone, "That's all your imagination"—those are not compliments either. It might be objected that such disparagements only apply to those who might be called the amateur dreamers; that a novelist, for instance, is expected to have a highly active imagination. Yet to say "She certainly has a *lively* imagination" isn't praise either. That old phrase "Nothing but imagination," is one of the commonest, one of the most damning, in use today. I would point out, however, that even the

157

greatest novels are "nothing but" paper, ink, a certain amount of miscellaneous information, and imagination.

The space age opening before our eyes is "nothing but" the end result, scientifically supported, worked out with infinite toil, of man's first mad, unreasonable image of himself flying. When it was first entertained, a good while before Daedalus, that image was about as adapted to reality as if I were to feel the urge to lie, like Ariel, in a cowslip's bell. Yet today we do fly. Science fiction once prophesied, in its apparently wild flights of fancy, many of the aerial feats that have come to pass. Are these the only phantasies which are allowed to come to pass? May not what science fiction calls teleportation also come to pass, along with the contents of that bottle in *Alice in Wonderland* marked DRINK ME, and may it not be possible for some woman in the future to become tiny and find herself curled inside that golden cup?

—NANCY HALE, "The Two-Way Imagination"

In reading the essays of professionals, as well as those written by classmates, it is helpful to develop a sensitivity to various techniques of transition from paragraph to paragraph. "How has the writer connected these parts?" can be your repeated question—and sometimes you will find that both professional and amateur have not connected them as well as they might. Similarly, when writing your own compositions, you can develop a critical awareness of paragraph sequence by giving regular attention to the endings and beginnings of paragraphs. Fairly early in the development of reading skill, and eventually in the development of proficiency in writing, this awareness of how paragraphs can be linked together becomes almost automatic—and an impressive feature of a mature style.

By now you should feel more at home with the elements—words, sentences, paragraphs—that make up whole essays. It is time to try your hand at composing something more ambitious than a nicely turned paragraph. In the next chapter we will begin with some suggestions of workable subjects, then move to a full-scale discussion of the various ways these subjects might be treated.

EXERCISES

Exercise 1, Introductory Paragraphs. *Look through an anthology of modern essays, noting the introductory paragraphs. Find a paragraph stating a thesis to be argued, one telling an anecdote, and one offering a definition. Find one using a combination of these methods. Find one that fits none of these categories. Can you invent a useful fourth category to contain it?*

Exercise 2, Writing Introductory Paragraphs. *Write three possible opening paragraphs for an essay, "The Roles of the Sexes in America Today." Use each of the three approaches outlined in the first part of this chapter.*

Exercise 3, Tone. *Rewrite your three paragraphs, drastically changing the tone (e.g., from serious to humorous, distant to familiar) in each case.*

Exercise 4, Paragraph Variety. *Locate examples of the following:*

1. A paragraph with a topic sentence at the end.
2. A paragraph used as a transition between two topics of an essay.
3. A paragraph with a light tone on a heavy subject.
4. A paragraph within which the tone shifts.
5. A paragraph summarizing a section of an essay or chapter.

Exercise 5, Revising a Paragraph. *In the following passage, revise and combine the sentences, inserting transitions where necessary, in order to produce a logical and readable paragraph:*

Students of the English language have divided its historical growth into three main periods; the Old English Period, from 450 to 1100, was the first one. The Middle English Period lasted from 1100 until 1500. The Modern English Period began in 1500 and lasted up to the present time. The people of England did not stop speaking one kind of language and begin speaking another in any one year. The change was gradual. There were definite historical events occurring at the times mentioned which caused a more rapid change in the language of the people of England. The Angles, Saxons, and Jutes invaded England in 449. The Norman Conquest occurred in 1066. The English Renaissance began about 1500.

5 *Problems of Subject and Focus*

SELECTING A SUBJECT

One of the questions on a history examination reads: "What were the chief military and political arguments against Lincoln's issuing the Emancipation Proclamation in 1862?" A proper answer will take at least a paragraph or two of discussion, a characteristic that designates the question an *essay question*. Like any essay, the answer requires some thought and organization, but one problem is solved by the question itself: there is no doubt what is to be written about. Now, by way of contrast, observe the devious mind of the English instructor: "Write a five-hundred-word theme on the subject of humor." That is not a question but an order; it has no correct answer. Humor is in addition a broad topic that must be narrowed and focused if it is to be covered at all in five hundred words. Deciding where to begin is the preliminary step in any piece of writing, but it is a crucial step when no specific information has been requested.

Preliminary Planning

If the length of a paper is established in advance, it will automatically affect the paper's subject. An eight-hundred-word theme on some new fad, a recent development in science, the author John Jakes, or any other subject is, before all other considerations, an eight-hundred-word

161

theme. The student faced with such a theme and the professional writer paid to supply a six-thousand-word article on the commercial uses of nuclear energy have a common obligation to interest the reader in a limited space. When filling space receives more attention than interesting the reader, the temptation is to think of large subjects that promise to take up room with little effort. Subjects like "Humor," "Games People Play," "Street Crime," "Politics," or "Vacations" are not suitable subjects for short papers; they are warehouses full of random facts, opinions, and impressions.

Replace the problem of filling a blank space with that of engaging a reader's interest, however, and the task changes from a matter of *discovering* what to talk about to one of *selecting* what is most important to say.

An effective piece of writing forces the reader to notice aspects of its subject he or she has not already considered. The more general the treatment of the subject, the greater the probability is that the reader will have heard it or thought it before. When writing about something, therefore, you must be prepared to describe it in detail. Everyone can visualize a forest, but the writer describes the kinds of trees composing it, the colors and shapes of the leaves, the depth of the shade, the thickness of the undergrowth, the positions of the trunks, and the texture of the barks until it is no longer *a* forest but *the* forest. An immense subject, such as American politics, requires proportionately elaborate detail, which means more exposition. A six-thousand-word subject will not fit into an eight-hundred-word theme.

Limiting the Subject: "Prewriting"

How does one know when a subject is the right size? By thinking about it carefully before beginning to write. Let us say an eight-hundred-word theme is set with no more prescriptive reference to subject than that it should be based on an interest or hobby. A quick review of your interests produces the subject of folk music. Since the assignment requires that you inform your readers about something, the techniques of *exposition* are called for. These techniques will allow you to approach the subject in a variety of ways: Your essay might *define* folk music, *compare* or *contrast* it with other kinds of music, *identify* some of the typical instruments, such as the acoustical guitar or banjo, *classify* such styles as bluegrass or blues, or *explain* the folk process itself. Although in the act of writing the essay you may *narrate* the events, let us say, at a folk concert, or *describe* the dress or customs of folk artists, or *argue* for the need to preserve the songs of native singers, your main purpose will be *expository*, that is, to inform your readers about some aspect of a subject they may have heard about but do not fully appreciate or understand.

Now ask what you can tell your readers about folk music that lies *within your experience* and is neither *trite* nor *general.* In response to that tough question, you may decide to focus the essay on a single idea, the relationship between folk and country and western music. Note that this idea, though still broad, yields the advantage of referring to a kind of music that is probably better known to many people than folk music. The next step is to state the main idea in the form of a summarizing sentence. A more conventional term for such a statement is *thesis sentence,* which indicates that the main idea is being presented as something to be proved or demonstrated to the reader. While the essay on folk music may not require an impassioned argument or plea, its thesis should be convincingly enough developed so that the reader believes in the authority of the writer's assertions. Stating a thesis will also help you get away from the simple listing approach—"Another point to mention is . . ."—that too often characterizes weak expository essays. Pursuing a thesis means giving your readers an *expanding* knowledge of the subject, not a shopping list of details arranged in no apparent order.

Let us say that your general purpose in writing the essay on folk music is to illustrate how folk lyrics are more simple and genuine than the lyrics of present-day country songs. Jotting down this purpose will give you the first component

163

of a rough outline that should prove helpful in the actual writing stage. The next step is to devise a sentence that expresses your main idea in specific language: "While folk and country and western song lyrics touch on similar themes of unrequited love and extramarital affairs, folk lyrics tend to be more genuine and sincere." There you have a target to shoot at, a rough plan of operations, and some idea of the ammunition you are going to use. *Comparison* and *contrast* will play an important role in this project. In fact, you can clearly see that a good way to begin such an essay is by pointing out a major difference between folk and country music: Lyrics in folk music were not written down but transmitted orally through the songs. Another contrast can be traced to this same oral tradition, by which many folk songs were brought to this country from England and Scotland. Modern country music is strongly influenced by the writing style of popular music, which tends to be more urban and sophisticated than its folk sources. By listing these contrasting points, you will soon be engaged in the process of giving *concreteness* to your essay. The unavoidable task, given the thesis statement, is to compare two *specific* songs, one folk, the other country, which present a similar theme. Such a comparison will represent the *center* of your essay, the proof that clinches the original claim about folk lyrics. Remember that although other matters—acoustic versus electrified instruments, natural versus slick production values—may interest you, they are not a direct part of the main idea and should be kept out of the body of the essay. Such observations may be inserted by way of parenthetical remarks or footnotes, but only if they illustrate some aspect of the thesis.

Deciding on a good *title* for the paper is the third step in the planning or prewriting stage. Good titles attract interested readers and help to keep writers on the track. They reveal the writer's thoroughness in exploring the subject by telling the reader that an interesting conclusion has been reached. "Folk Music" would not stand as an effective title for our essay; it is too broad and uninteresting. The following title, however, is almost sure to catch a reader's eye: "Folk Versus Country Lyrics: A Loss of Innocence." This title yields information not just about the *subject* but about the *thesis* as well.

The practice, then, of limiting the subject calls for three steps:

1. State your objective or goal as a *main idea.*
2. Write out a summarizing or *thesis sentence.*
3. Devise a suitable *title.*

You will probably change your plan as you proceed, but every writer must do that. It may prove difficult, for example, to find a folk song and a country song that tell a similar story or deal with a similar theme. So long as you keep your main idea and your first general plan, change will improve the final product.

Nature of the Plan or Outline

Every paper written needs a plan, although some plans spend their life cycles in the heads of the writers without every emerging on paper in the form of outlines. Some plans take the form of a series of notes on the back of an old envelope. The experienced writer may plan almost subconsciously; some writers say that they do all their outlining mentally, whereas others say that they write out elaborate outlines on paper. But inexperienced writers have everything to gain by using paper and pencil to record and clarify the planning that goes on in their heads. Even when inspiration is powerful enough and spontaneous enough to leap onto a page without intermediate steps, *an outline of the finished work is an excellent check of organization and logic. If there are flaws in the product of inspiration, an outline may reveal them.*

The Informal Outline. A short paper should have a short outline. A few notes on a piece of scrap paper may suffice. Suppose the urge comes to write a thoughtful little essay on childhood memories. Seize your scrap paper at that moment and begin a list of things you recall from early childhood. Some recollections will be vivid, some won't. Perhaps the difficulty of remembering them at all strikes you. Jot that thought down too. Now sit back and consider what you have, a list of things that must once have impressed you and the thought that they are a good deal less impressive today. Think how the two might fit together. One solution is to begin with the result, the difficulty of remembering. Start your actual paper with a short paragraph developing that subject, lead in your list of memories, and then pause. What you need is a conclusion, although you may have already glimpsed one from reviewing your notes. A speculative paragraph on why these particular recollections should surface while a million other experiences lie undisturbed in the cerebral mud is one acceptable choice for rounding off the topic, but there are others. An appealing short essay can be written in this way and perhaps should always be. Its spontaneity would more than likely be dampened by the imposed order of a full-blown formal outline.

The Process of Synthesis. Making an outline is often spoken of as a process of dividing a subject. It is assumed that the thought mass exists in its entirety in the writer's mind, and in preparing it for the market he methodically slices it up into pieces called topics and subtopics. That may be true for some. For most of us outlining is a process of synthesis, not division. We usually begin with a problem and the necessity of doing something about it. Our first suggestion may be an ill-favored and disreputable little idea. We pull it out and look it over. It seems promising— possibly. But then we look around again—by thinking, by reading, by observing—and pull out other ideas to add to it. We jot down these ideas on paper. Some writers use file cards, which they can later organize in coherent order. Before long, if we are fortunate, we have enough, or perhaps more than enough for our purpose. Then and only then can we begin to select and arrange and divide.

Some of us are gifted with orderly minds that require formal approaches to any activity, in particular, writing. For that reason, we have included specific information here on the steps in putting together a formal outline.

CONVENTIONS OF THE FORMAL OUTLINE

There are a number of conventions governing the formal outline:

1. The parts of the outline, heads and subheads, should be labeled by alternating figures and letters as follows: I, II, III, and so on; A, B, C, and so on; 1, 2, 3, and so on; a, b, c, and so on. Periods, not dashes, should be placed after these figures and letters.

2. No punctuation is needed after the topics in a topic outline. In a sentence outline, each sentence should be punctuated in the conventional manner.

3. The heads in any series should be of equal importance. That is, the heads numbered I, II, III, IV, and so on, should actually be divisions of the whole paper; heads numbered with capital letters should be coordinate divisions of heads numbered with Roman numerals; and so on.

4. Coordinate heads should be expressed in parallel form—that is, in a given series, nouns should be made parallel with nouns, adjectives with adjectives, and so on. But although parallel structure is desirable and logical, clearness and directness should never be sacrificed to gain strict parallelism. There are times when nouns and gerunds can live side by side in a formal outline.

5. In a topic outline, all heads and subheads must be topics. In a sentence outline, all heads and subheads must be sentences. Sentences should not run over from one head to another.

6. Each head and subhead should be as specific as it is possible to make it in an outline. Vague topics and sentences are bad because they tend to hide flaws in the logic or organization of the outline.

7. Using such headings as "I. Introduction," "II. Body," "III. Conclusion" is unnecessary and undesirable. Such divisions do not indicate correctly the structure

167

of most essays or articles. Many papers written by students are too short for a formal introduction or conclusion. In most long papers the conclusion is simply the main topic which the writer wants the reader to hear about last—for reasons explained elsewhere. Separate introductions are used more often than separate conclusions in essays of six thousand words or more, but in the outline it is better to use a topic that tells what is said in the introduction than to use the vague "Introduction" itself.

8. Since an outline represents a grouping of parallel parts, it is illogical to have a single subhead under any head. A single subhead can usually be combined with its head with benefit to the logic and organization of the outline.

Here are two kinds of conventional outline examining the subject of choosing a college and career.

TOPIC OUTLINE

Choices—In College and After

Thesis: The decisions I have to make in choosing college courses depend on larger questions I am beginning to ask about myself and my life work.

I. Two decisions described
   A. Art history or chemistry?
      1. Professional considerations
      2. Personal considerations
   B. A second year of French?
      1. Practical advantages of knowing a foreign language
      2. Intellectual advantages
      3. The issue of necessity
II. Definition of the problem
   A. Decisions about occupation
   B. Decisions about a kind of life to lead
III. Temporary resolution of the problem
   A. To hold open a professional possibility: chemistry
   B. To take advantage of cultural gains already made: French

168

A sentence outline is similar in organization to a topic outline. It differs from a topic outline in that every topic and subtopic is translated into a complete sentence, stating the central idea of the particular topic. The sentence outline has two advantages over the topic outline: (1) It forces the writer to study his material carefully so that he has something specific to say for each head and subhead; and (2), much more effectively than the topic outline, it conveys information in logical sequence to the reader. The topic outline merely states a series of subjects, rather like titles, which the writer intends to say something about. The sentence outline actually summarizes what he has to say.

Here is an example of a sentence outline, based on the topic outline we have just examined:

SENTENCE OUTLINE

Choices—In College and After

Thesis: The decisions I have to make in choosing college courses depend on larger questions I am beginning to ask about myself and my life work.

I. I have two decisions to make with respect to choosing college courses in the immediate future.
    A. One is whether to elect a course in art history or in chemistry.
        1. Since at one time I planned to be a chemical engineer and still have this career much in mind, professional considerations would indicate the choice of chemistry.
        2. On the other hand I enjoy art and plan to travel to see more of it; I need training in art history if I am going to be more than just another ignorant museum-goer.
    B. The second decision is whether to continue for a second year of French, beyond the basic college requirement.
        1. French might be practically useful to me, both in business (including engineering) and in the travel I hope to undertake.
        2. Furthermore I am eager to put to actual use, in the

169

         reading of good books, the elementary French I have already mastered.

    3. But how necessary are these considerations in the light of other courses I might take instead?

II. My problem can be put in the form of a dilemma involving larger questions about my whole future.

    A. On the one hand I want to hold a highly trained position in a lucrative profession.

    B. On the other hand I want to lead a certain kind of life, with capacities for values not connected with the making of money.

III. I will have to make a decision balancing the conflicting needs I have described.

    A. I will hold open the professional possibilities by electing chemistry.

    B. I will improve and solidify what cultural proficiency in another language I have already gained, by electing French.

A solid outline will help you see exactly where your essay is headed. Equipped with this road map, you may now wish to consider the range of destinations or subjects available to you.

SOME TYPES OF SUBJECT

To write about certain subjects—the Battle of the Bulge, the making of solar panels—we need to consult encyclopedias and other reference books in the library. For the moment, however, the essay based on personal experience, or, at most, on sources of information more readily available than those in the library, is an excellent field for experiment. The various kinds of writing discussed in the following passages should reveal a bit of the raw material most writers have immediately at hand.

Autobiographical Narratives

"The Story of my Life" or "How I Spent My Summer Vacation" are of course favorite topics of instructors in beginning composition courses. The resulting essays prove to be useful in getting to know the students. But there are dangers for the writer. Beware of writing a narrative account of your life, listing in chronological order such items as when and where you were born, who your parents are, where you went to school, and so on. Instead, try telling about the development of your interest in music, your social life, or your attitude toward a career. Alternatively, isolate one aspect of your character: intelligence, sense of humor, pride, aggression. Remember that it is not you but your reader who must be interested in your portrait and do not announce, "Self-respect is the dominant trait of my character" and expect the world to hang on your lips waiting for the next pearl. Recount instead an incident, as does the author of the following example, to show your self-respect at work.

There were many times when I had to exercise a great deal of ingenuity to keep out of trouble. It is a southern custom that all men must take off their hats when they enter an elevator. And especially did this apply to us blacks with rigid force. One day I stepped into an elevator with my arms full of packages. I was forced to ride with my hat on. Two white men stared at me coldly. Then one of them very kindly lifted my hat and placed it upon my armful of packages. Now the most accepted response for a Negro to make under such circumstances is to look at the white man out of the corner of his eye and grin. To have said: "Thank you!" would have made the white man *think* that you *thought* you were receiving from him a personal service. For such an act I have seen Negroes take a blow in the mouth. Finding the first alternative distasteful, and the second dangerous, I hit upon an acceptable course of action which fell safely between these two poles. I immediately—no sooner than my hat was lifted—pretended that my packages were about to spill, and appeared deeply distressed with keeping them in my arms. In this fashion I evaded having to acknowledge his service, and, in spite of adverse circumstances, salvaged a slender shred of personal pride.

—RICHARD WRIGHT, *The Ethics of Living Jim Crow*

A single memorable incident is often a better choice than a number of sketchily treated events in your life. And

171

be wary of the obvious incidents everyone has talked about: the camping trip, the auto accident, the big fire downtown (unless, of course, you are asked to write about these). Much more effective is some apparently minor incident, so developed with concrete detail that it acquires importance in the telling.

The best of learning came on the morning radio, which I learned to love. Every town of a few thousand people has its station, and it takes the place of the old local newspaper. Bargains and trades are announced, social doings, prices of commodities, messages. The records played are the same all over the country. If "Teen-Age Angel" is top of the list in Maine, it is top of the list in Montana. In the course of a day you may hear "Teen-Age Angel" thirty or forty times. But in addition to local news and chronicles, some foreign advertising creeps in. As I went farther and farther north and it got colder I was aware of more and more advertising for Florida real estate and, with the approach of the long and bitter winter, I could see why Florida is a golden word. As I went along I found that more and more people lusted toward Florida and that thousands had moved there and more thousands wanted to and would. The advertising, with a side look at Federal Communications, made few claims except for the fact that the land they were selling was in Florida. Some of them went out on a limb and promised that it was above tide level. But that didn't matter; the very name Florida carried the message of warmth and ease and comfort. It was irresistible.

—JOHN STEINBECK, *Travels with Charley*

Have you ever found yourself in a situation where you are the victim of some random act of violence? Consider the difficulties involved in trying to recall and to narrate such an incident. Note how this writer vivifies his account through the use of concrete detail, realistic dialogue, and the present tense.

The athletic meet takes place in a city-owned stadium far from the school. It is an important event to which a whole day is given over. The winners are to get those precious little medallions stamped with the New York City emblem that can be screwed into a belt and that prove the wearer to be a distinguished personage. I am a fast runner, and so I am assigned the position of anchor man on my class's team in the relay race. There are three other seventh-grade teams in the race, two of them all Negro, as ours is all white. One of the all-Negro teams is very tall—their anchor man waiting silently next to me on the line looks years older than I am, and I do not recognize him. He is the first to get the baton and crosses the finishing line in a walk. Our team comes in second, but a few minutes later we are declared the winners, for it has been discovered that the anchor man on the first-place team is not a member of the class. We are awarded the medallions, and the following day our home-room teacher makes a speech about how proud she is of us for being superior athletes as well as superior students. We want to believe that we deserve the praise, but we know that we could not have won even if the other class had not cheated.

That afternoon, walking home, I am waylaid and surrounded by five Negroes, among whom is the anchor man of the disqualified team. "Gimme my medal, mo'f—r," he grunts. I do not have it with me and I tell him so. "Anyway, it ain't yours," I say foolishly. He calls me a liar on both counts and pushes me up against the wall on which we sometimes play handball. "Gimme my mo'f—n' medal," he says again. I repeat that I have left it home. "Le's search the li'l mo'f—r," one of them suggests, "he prolly got it *hid* in his mo'f—n' *pants.*" My panic is now unmanageable. (How many times had I been surrounded like this and asked in soft tones, "Len' me a nickle, boy." How many times had I been called a liar for pleading poverty and pushed around, or searched, or beaten up, unless there happened to be someone in the marauding gang like Carl who liked me across that enormous divide of hatred and who would therefore say, "Aaah, c'mon, le's git someone else, *this* boy ain't got no money on 'im.") I scream at them through tears of rage and self-contempt, "Keep your f—n' filthy lousy black hands offa me! I swear I'll get the cops." This is all they need to hear, and the five of them set upon me. They bang me around, mostly in the stomach and on the arms and shoulders, and when several adults loitering near the candy store down the block notice what is going on and begin to shout, they run off and away.

    —NORMAN PODHORETZ, *My Negro Problem—and Ours*

173

Narrating any event calls for the use of *chronological organization*. Each stage of action will be marked by the passage of time (note the beginning of the second paragraph in Podhoretz's account), which means that the writer has a handy way to break his or her story into paragraphs. In recounting a Sunday softball game, for instance, you need simply divide the action into paragraphs about the early, middle, and late innings. There is little chance that you will misplace events or that you will give in to the temptation to wander off base. Remember that although the score of the game is of interest to your readers, they are more likely to be caught up in the detailing of a spectacular hit, catch, or error. Careful *selection* of details—the way players are dressed, the taunts thrown at umpires or coaches—gives readers the same feeling they experience in reading good fiction. The point of the story should come through the narration rather than be imposed on it. If a narrated incident is part of a larger expository or argumentative essay, let it serve as an example whose application to the essay's main idea is clear without being overstated.

As we have said, the one danger in narration is that you are likely to digress from the main elements of the story. Exploring the marital problems of the softball players is likely to change the focus of the account unless the game is being played by recently divorced couples. To avoid digression, keep the *purpose* or *objective* of the story firmly in mind; let that purpose guide you in the selection of details.

Descriptions

Description, telling what is to be seen, heard, tasted, touched, smelled, and possibly surmised, seems so clear-cut a task that its chief pitfall sometimes escapes notice until it is too late. The problem is *unity*, the importance of each element relating coherently to the others. A verbal picture may be unified by a summarizing statement that ties the components together or by a dominant and consistent attitude toward the images described. A visual scene

174

assembled on the page as through a fish-eye lens with every detail simultaneously and indiscriminately distinct is usually confusing. What is more, it is impersonal; there is nothing in it to connect writer and reader, and only a very confident, or very rash, writer throws away the bond of understanding with the reader. That bond may be preserved in a point of view. In description the phrase has more specific meaning: where the writer is sitting, standing, lying, or crouching while describing and evaluating. What does this point of view that surprisingly means exactly what it says have to do with unity? Remember that the reader is seeing through Someone Else's eyes, and, if Someone Else is admiring the blaze in the third-floor kitchen and, at the same time, noting how the fire truck takes the corner at Broad and Fremont, the reader is going to have a headache. Do not give readers headaches! A shift in point of view is permissible if the reader is given warning that a shift is coming or occurring, but the shift should be for a purpose, to contribute to a conclusion, not just because a lot of facts or impressions present themselves with the price of admission.

. . . The things I liked best about the Polo Grounds were sights and emotions so inconsequential that they will surely slide out of my recollection. A flight of pigeons flashing out of the barn-shadow of the upper stands, wheeling past the right-field foul pole, and disappearing above the inert, heat-heavy flags on the roof. The steepness of the ramp descending from the Speedway toward the upper-stand gates, which pushed your toes into your shoe tips as you approached the park, tasting sweet anticipation and getting out your change to buy a program. The unmistakable, final *"Plock!"* of a line drive hitting the green wooden barrier above the stands in deep left field. The gentle, rockerlike swing of the loop of rusty chain you rested your arm upon in a box seat, and the heat of the sun-warmed iron coming through your shirtsleeve under your elbow. At a night game, the moon rising out of the scoreboard like a spongy, day-old orange balloon and then whitening over the waves of noise and the slow, shifting clouds of floodlit cigarette smoke. All these I mourn, for their loss constitutes the death of still another

175

neighborhood—a small landscape of distinctive and reassuring familiarity.

—ROGER ANGELL, *The Summer Game*

The art of description is comparable to painting or photography. A successful artist has an "eye" for a compelling scene, recognizing how to represent an arrangement of flowers or people in a dramatic, eye-catching way. After a close look at paintings like *The Last Supper* or Van Gogh's *Sunflowers* you suddenly realize that the impact of such works can be traced to the selection and arrangement of details.

Like narrated incidents, descriptions too provide their own ready-made form of organization. Living rooms can be described from top to bottom, or bottom to top, street scenes from foreground to background. Profiles of personalities may follow a pattern that guides the eye from least significant details (physical features) to most significant facts (typical expressions or actions). These organizational guides keep the writer from transforming a descriptive sketch into a jumble of impressions guaranteed to strain the reader's eyes and attention.

Two approaches may be used in the art of describing: the objective and the impressionistic. An *objective* piece of description details a scene or subject as a camera might, with all the features in place. Such an approach characterizes much scientific writing, since the findings of investigators must be presented to others for verification. We also want a precise, realistic accounting of events from journalists, who in a sense are taking our place at major events like political speeches or catastrophes. As we shall see later, the objective method is of special value in outlining any process involving steps or stages; when changing a washer on a leaky faucet, the amateur plumber is likely to want simple, clear description of the unfamiliar objects required for the job.

The following passage is a good example of the scientific approach to description. Note in particular the attempt to take you as reader on a kind of voyage of discovery.

The Greenland whale is one of the most wonderful animals in the world, and the baleen, or whale-bone, one of its greatest peculiarities. The baleen consists of a row, on each side, of the upper jaw, of about 300 plates or laminae, which stand close together transversely to the longer axis of the mouth. Within the main row there are some subsidiary rows. The extremities and inner margins of all the plates are frayed off into stiff bristles which clothe the whole gigantic palate, and serve to strain or sift the water, and thus to secure the minute prey on which these great animals subsist.

—CHARLES DARWIN, From *On the Origin of Species*

Impressionistic or *subjective* description is interpretive in nature. The writer makes us aware of a certain impression the object or scene has made on him or her. An emotional response is sought from the reader of such descriptive passages. In creating this mood the writer of subjective description will also tend to use more figurative language than the objective writer. For example, metaphors and similes help to set a scene by comparing what is observed to something else the reader may be better aware of. A *simile* is a comparison in which the writer uses *like* or *as*, emphasizing a particular trait in the thing or person described: *He had a temper like a wildcat; Her forehand was as fast as a whiplash. Metaphors* draw parallels by suggesting analogies or likenesses between one object and another: *He had a volcanic temper; Her serve boomed out of a cannon.* Metaphors and similes are indispensable in both kinds of description, and both kinds may also be found together in essays containing some form of description.

In the following selection the writer describes a high school basketball game in some nameless small town. Is the description primarily objective or impressionistic? How can you tell?

Friday night. Girls in dark skirts and white blouses sit in ranks and scream in concert. They carry funnels loosely stuffed with orange and black paper which they shake wildly, and small megaphones through which, as drilled, they direct and magnify their

177

shouting. Their leaders, barely pubescent girls, prance and shake and whirl their skirts above their bloomers. The young men, leaping, extend their arms and race through puddles of amber light, their bodies glistening. In a lull, though it rarely occurs, you can hear the squeak of tennis shoes against the floor. Then the yelling begins again, and then continues; fathers, mothers, neighbors joining in to form a single pulsing ululation—a cry of the whole community—for in this gymnasium each body becomes the bodies beside it, pressed as they are together, thigh to thigh, and the same shudder runs through all of them, and runs toward the same release. Only the ball moves serenely through this dazzling din. Obedient to law it scarcely speaks but caroms quietly and lives at peace.

—WILLIAM GASS, "The Church"

Profiles

A favorite assignment for teachers of writing is to ask students to create a profile or portrait of an "unforgetable" character. Depending heavily on the techniques of description, a profile is a short biographical sketch that relies for its effect on a few well-chosen, vivid facts and details. When you draw on autobiographical material for a subject, the aim is to isolate a single circumstance worth discussing. In a profile very nearly the opposite process is followed; you portray the whole person in terms of several selected traits or acts. The subject of a successful portrait need not be famous—or notorious; as a matter of fact, the writer of a profile often takes some totally obscure person and tries to convince the reader that he or she is worth knowing.

The following selection reveals how a professional writer solves the problem of introducing a personality into her narrative and to the reader who will be asked to trace his path through the rest of the study. In one paragraph we have an unmistakable impression of the figure's physical appearance, personality, and behavior. (The Jean referred to is King Jean of France.)

In France's misfortunes a young man of twenty, Charles, King of Navarre, grandson of Louis X, saw his opportunity. Whether he really aimed at the French crown, or at revenge for wrongs done him, or at stirring trouble for its own sake like Iago, is a riddle concealed in one of the most complex characters of the 14th century. A small slight youth with glistening eyes and a voluble flow of words, he was volatile, intelligent, charming, violent, cunning as a fox, ambitious as Lucifer, and truly more than Byron "mad, bad and dangerous to know." Seductive and eloquent, he could persuade his peers or sway a mob. He allowed himself the same unbridled acts of passion as Jean and other rulers, but, unlike Jean, he was a plotter, subtle, bold, absolutely without scruple, but so swerving and unfixed of purpose as to undo his own plots. His only constancy was hate. He is known to history as Charles the Bad.

—BARBARA W. TUCHMAN, *A Distant Mirror*

While you may not want to attempt a portrait of some distant historical figure like Charles the Bad, another possible project is to write a profile of a distinguished citizen or personality in your community, one whom you have known fairly well. Select one you have liked and admired. Go to the library and consult some local "who's who" for background facts. Then organize your profile on the basis of a number of the following divisions.

    I. An interview, in which you introduce your subject and give a quick picture of his or her appearance
   II. A glimpse of the subject at work
  III. A transition to the facts about this person's career, education, and so on
  IV. The subject's dominant traits
   V. A typical professional performance (a major article or speech)
  VI. What others say about the subject

You need not use all of these divisions, but if you want to compress, remember that I, III, and V are essential.

If you want to do a more ambitious biographical piece, one that will take you to some of the reference books in the library, try writing a biographical sketch of (1) the author of a book you are reading; (2) a community leader; (3) the man or woman who represents you in Congress; (4) a well-known scientist who is connected with your college or university. You will find more detailed assistance for writing such papers in Chapter 6 of this section. Be careful to give all your borrowed information in your own words! To lift commentary verbatim without acknowledging the author is to commit *plagiarism,* the name for passing stolen ideas, and the penalties are usually severe.

When Senator John F. Kennedy, shortly before he became president, wrote his book about several distinguished past and present members of the Senate, he called it *Profiles in Courage,* and he was using the word *Profiles* in this more ambitious sense. Here is a passage from his profile of Senator Robert A. Taft, in which you will note the combination of incidents, quotations from others, and personal testimony from the writer's own experience that can make a persuasive piece of writing in this genre.

So Bob Taft, as his biographer has described it, was "born to integrity." He was known in the Senate as a man who never broke an agreement, who never compromised his deeply felt Republican principles, who never practiced political deception. His bitter public enemy, Harry Truman, would say when the Senator died: "He and I did not agree on public policy, but he knew where I stood and I knew where he stood. We need intellectually honest men like Senator Taft." Examples of his candor are endless and startling. The Ohioan once told a group in the heart of Republican farm territory that farm prices were too high; and he told still another farm group that "he was tired of seeing all these people riding in Cadillacs." His support of an extensive Federal housing program caused a colleague to remark: "I hear the Socialists have gotten to Bob Taft." He informed an important political associate who cherished a commendatory message signed by Taft that his assistant "sent those things out by the dozen" without the Senator ever seeing, much less signing them. And a colleague recalls that he did not reject the ideas of his friends by gentle indirection, but by coldly and unhesitatingly terming them "nonsense." "He had," as William S. White has written, "a luminous candor of purpose that was extraordinarily refreshing in a chamber not altogether devoted to candor."

It would be a mistake, however, to conclude from this that Senator Taft was cold and abrupt in his personal relationships.

180

I recall, from my own very brief service with him in the Senate and on the Senate Labor Committee in the last months of his life, my strong impression of a surprising and unusual personal charm, and a disarming simplicity of manner. It was these qualities, combined with an unflinching courage which he exhibited throughout his entire life and most especially in his last days, that bound his adherents to him with unbreakable ties.

—JOHN F. KENNEDY, *Profiles in Courage*

Book or Film Review

More and more in recent years, the tempo of book publication has increased to the point where no one can expect to read all the new books, even those restricted to a particular field of interest. Readers, therefore, must depend on the reports of others to select the particular books they may want to buy and read. The same is true of movies. To meet this demand for quick and ready information, there has developed in newspapers and magazines a special kind of review: a very short, informal description of a book (film), with some brief information about the author (director), and at least an implied evaluation of his or her work. You will find such brief reports in *Time,* in *The New Yorker,* and in several other magazines and newspapers that are likely to reach serious readers of books and moviegoers.

Sometimes such an informal review can be accomplished—or at least attempted—in a single paragraph. In the examples below you will note the almost breezy tone adopted by the anonymous reviewers. But beneath the informality there is much serious purpose, and much important information is presented in short and palatable form. Note how similar in style are these two reviews, one of a film, the other of a book.

EYES OF LAURA MARS (1978)—This New York-set thriller operates on mood and atmosphere, and it moves so fast, with such delicate changes of rhythm, that its excitement has a subterranean sexiness. Faye Dunaway, with long, thick, dark-red hair, is Laura Mars, a celebrity fashion photographer who specializes in the chic and pungency of sadism; the pictures she shoots

181

have a furtive charge—we can see why they sell. Directed by Irvin Kershner, the film has a few shocking fast cuts, but it also has a scabrous elegance and a surprising amount of humor. Laura's scruffy, wild-eyed driver (Brad Dourif) epitomizes New York's crazed, hostile flunkies; he's so wound up he seems to have the tensions of the whole city in his gut. Her manager (René Auberjonois) is tense and ambivalent about Laura—about everything. Her models (Lisa Taylor and Darlanne Fluegel), who in their poses look wickedly decadent, are really just fun-loving ding-a-lings. As for Dunaway, constantly kneeling or sprawling to take photographs, her legs, especially her thighs, are far more important to her performance than her eyes; her flesh gives off heat. Tommy Lee Jones is the police lieutenant who represents old-fashioned morality, and when the neurotically vulnerable Laura, who has become telepathic about violence, falls in love with him, they're a very creepy pair. With the help of the editor, Michael Kahn, Kershner glides over the gaps in the very uneven script (by John Carpenter and David Z. Goodman, with an assist from Julian Barry). The cast includes Raul Julia, Rose Gregorio, Meg Mundy, and Bill Boggs (as himself).

—From *The New Yorker*, May 5, 1980, p. 24.

SOLDIERS OF THE NIGHT by David Schoenbrun. Dutton, $15.95. The French Resistance during World War II was divided and disorderly, with a lack of formal discipline that steadily worried Allied military commanders. In spite of their supposed disabilities, the various Resistance groups fought bravely, sabotaged brilliantly, and delivered invaluable information about German units and positions. Their casualties were very high indeed. They have never had full credit for their work because the authorities—De Gaulle, England, and America—all feared that when peace came, these wily fighters might foment civil war. The object was to brush them under the rug as quickly as possible. Mr. Schoenbrun has filled a real gap with his fine reconstruction of the whole Resistance movement, for he covers both the activities of those gallant and stubborn patriots and the framework of international strategies and suspicions within which they were obliged to operate. An exciting and moving story, intelligently told. Illustrations, index.

—From *The Atlantic Monthly*, Aug. 1980, p. 84.

In attempting such a brief review yourself, you should keep in mind at least three purposes. First, you should indicate something of the author's or director's reputation or qualifications. Second, you should summarize the contents of the book or film in a brief survey of the chief points of its argument or plot. Third, let your reader know whether you think the work good or bad. The modest reviewer also provides some reason for his or her judgment.

Directions and Processes

The "how to do it" and "how it was done" literature of America is impressive in extent, and some of it, at least, is of impressive literary quality. The ability to give accurate directions is extremely important and should be cultivated just as strictly as the more creative kinds of writing. Here are a few exercises that you may find useful:

1. Take two points that lie far apart in your locality, such as your home and a distant shopping center. Draw up a short set of directions by which a total stranger might arrive at your home starting from the center. *Do not* use any of the points of the compass— North, South, East, or West—in your instructions. Depend entirely on an accurate description of landmarks and distances.
2. Explain to an unmechanical friend how to start and operate a power mower. Do not use a single technical term without explaining it in clear, untechnical language.
3. Tell one of your younger friends what he is to do to register in college. Take him from one building to another, and explain every step of the procedure in words that he cannot fail to understand.

Setting out directions is a useful exercise not only in clarity but in establishing order. All instructions have a clear beginning and a virtually unalterable sequence in which they must be given if they are to work. It is no good explaining how to change an ordinary household fuse without first telling where the fusebox is.

An explanation of a process is not necessarily a set of

183

directions to be followed by someone. Thousands of such explanations are written merely because there are people who like to know how things work. If you try one of the following subjects, you might try making it an interesting explanation as well as a set of directions to be followed:

1. Measuring wind velocity
2. Photographing children
3. Coming about in a sailboat
4. How to change a tire
5. Making Christmas cards
6. Format in the school paper
7. How to model clothes
8. Operating a motorcycle
9. Transplating wild flowers
10. Making a banana split

As you move from step to step in the process, be sure that each term is explained fully. Let us say you have chosen to explain how to change a tire. *Lug nut* may well be an unfamiliar term to novice tire changers; a short description of this vital part is in order. Any unfamiliar act, such as reversing the direction of the jack handle, must also be explained in detail. If a switch or lever must be thrown to change the direction of the jack, it is necessary to indicate precisely where it is located. For any step in the process, an explanation of the reason behind it can build the reader's confidence. Placing the jack under the front or rear bumper instead of next to the wheel opening is necessary for safety's sake, so the car will not slip off the jack in mid-change. Such explanations, delivered at times with deft touches of humor ("After jacking up the car, stand back and give it a moment to decide whether or not it wants to drop on your foot"), help the harried victim relax and glimpse the overall project more clearly. Finally, make sure your readers are aware not only of what to do but of what *not* to do. To return to our tire-changing project, it would be wise to warn against loosening the nuts holding the tire until the whole wheel is off the ground. Doing so beforehand could lead to the tire falling suddenly and unexpectedly on the head of the poor tire changer.

One world of activity in which "how to do it" writing plays an important role is sports. The following example describes in precise, simple language the flutter kick in swimming. The author's problem is to distinguish the art of the flutter kick from the natural, instinctive motion of kicking without repelling the reader with a barrage of intricate and unfamiliar detail.

In the flutter, the water is squeezed, thrust, and kicked away, imparting a forward drive. It is most effective when the power comes from the hips and thighs, the rest of the legs controlled but relaxed, the knees slightly bent, the ankles loose. The ankles may be turned slightly inward in pigeon-toed fashion and should be completely relaxed so that they flop loosely, the toes pointed to eliminate resistance.

The kick is, of course, a series of beats, the legs moving alternately up and down. As it is lifted toward the surface, the leg is relaxed at the knee and bends slightly, the bend increasing until the leg is near the surface. The downward thrust is a whiplash motion in which the whole leg is straightened, imparting a snap to the lower leg and the ankle. The effect is to drive the water down along the thighs and snap it away; or, to look at it in another way, the legs both in the upward and in the downward beat catch hold of the water and drive the body forward.

The first rule for practicing the flutter kick is to make the thighs do the lifting and thrusting. If those big muscles in the thighs and lower back do the work, the kick will not be as tiring as it would be if it were primarily a knee kick, incorrectly used by many swimmers. By applying force from his thighs, the swimmer will give an undulating movement to his legs somewhat like that of a piece of rope when one end of it is snapped. At first there should be little, if any, bending of the knees. The swimmer can let his legs twist inward slightly, rolling the knees closer together and pointing the toes inward and downward.

—HAROLD S. ULEN AND GUY LARCOM, JR.,
The Complete Swimmer

A good test of a "how to do it" article is this: can you, from reading it, put the process into operation yourself? Experiment with the example just given only if you have an exceptionally big bathtub, but the test of "Can you do it?" is generally appropriate in the case of an unfamiliar

185

process. It is particularly appropriate when you are reading an account of a process that is utterly unfamiliar to you.

Here is Vilhjalmur Stefansson's explanation of the method used by Eskimos in catching fish under ice:

In getting ready to fish through ice you fasten your floats to one edge of the net and your sinkers to the other, so that one edge of the net shall be held at the surface of the water and the other down vertically. Then you cut two holes in the ice about forty feet apart (for that is a common length for Eskimo nets) and each a foot or eighteen inches in diameter. Between these two holes you cut a series of smaller holes just big enough to stick your arm into the water, and perhaps six to eight feet apart. Next you take a stick of dry, buoyant wood that is eight or ten feet long. You shove it down through one of the end holes until it is all in the water, when it floats up and rises against the ice. You have a string tied to the stick and this stick you fasten to one end of the net. Then you lay the string so that, while one end is still visible at your hole, the other end is visible below the next hole six or eight feet away. You now go to the second hole, put your hand into the water and slide the stick along under the ice until you can see it through the third hole. The stick, of course, pulls the string in after it and by the time you have worked the stick along to the furthest hole your net is set. You now take a rope that is about ten feet longer than the net and tie each end of the rope to one end of the net so as to make an "endless chain," the net being under the water and the rope on top of the ice.

During the night the holes all freeze over. You allow the small holes to remain frozen permanently but each time you go out to tend the net you open the two end holes and pull the net out of one of them. As you pull the net out the rope part of your endless chain is pulled into the water. When you have picked all the fish out of the net, you pull on your rope and thus drag the net back into the water.

—Vilhjalmur Stefansson, *Hunters of the Great North*

As we have said, a complex operation can be described with the purpose of putting the reader into a position to perform it himself. That is the implication in Stefansson's account, as his repeated *you* suggests. (It is also, we may remind *you,* the implication in *The Macmillan Handbook of English.*)

Definition

One of the best ways to convince readers of your authority and knowledge is to define a word or term for them. This act saves them a trip to the dictionary and gives you a premise from which to argue or pursue some larger question, as Ms. Foote does in the essay we have reprinted in Chapter 1.

There is a great temptation among beginning writers to quote straight dictionary definitions of words or terms at the opening of their essays. But such a step is not always the best one to take. Consider a word like *justice.* Most readers have a vague idea of its meaning, so to quote from the dictionary will only invite boredom, especially if you do not plan to disagree with or challenge Webster. Instead of taking the easy way, an inventive writer will begin by recounting an incident in which justice—or injustice—was done. Rather than focusing on questions of etymology, this approach gives the reader a *working* or *contextual* definition from which may be extracted a variety of applications. Granted, a particular denotation can sometimes surprise: *assassin,* for example, derives from the word *hashhashin,* used to identify drug-crazed killers in Turkey. If a writer were trying to prove that assassins are often fanatics, such a detail would help. Here, as in all other forms of composition, a clear sense of purpose will guide the selection of approach. On the whole, the writer who finds many applications of a word or term is most likely to hold the interest of readers while building a successful essay.

As we have suggested, it is sometimes effective to structure an essay by *contrasting* words or by discussing certain words by means of their opposites. *Loyalty* would be better illustrated by pointing out the many instances of *disloyalty* in human history, or in your own experience. *Love* and *hate, poverty* and *wealth, good* and *evil* are familiar pairs of opposites that have been treated by many writers.

187

The task faced by the writer of the following paragraph involves tracing similarities between two states—love and death—that are apparently far apart. Such an ability reveals a mind that has thought long and hard on a topic and still sees complexities that a simple dictionary definition cannot resolve. This writer has also seen that the act of *contrast* requires some degree of *comparison* and vice versa. The essay that sets out to find similarities in apparently dissimilar things is hard to bring off but compelling when done with skill.

The relation between death and love has an impressive history in literature. In Italian writing, there was the frequent play upon the words *amore,* love, with *morte,* death. The connection also has its biological analogies in nature. The male bee dies after inseminating the Queen. More vivid is the case of the praying mantis: the female bites off the head of the male as he copulates, and his death throes unite with his copulatory spasms to make the thrusts stronger. Inseminated, the female proceeds to eat him to store up food for the new offspring.

—ROLLO MAY, *Love and Death*

The story of the unfortunate male praying mantis shows the stark efficiency of a process that subsumes both love and death. In a few detailed and informed sentences, May has convinced us of the intimate connection between two apparently opposed states.

Besides comparison and contrast, the best way to define a word or term is to narrate an incident in which the meaning of the word or term is exemplified. *Friendship,* for instance, may be generally understood by your readers. However, if you tell them how your friend Jack or Joan lent you bus fare to go home for your sister's wedding, drove you to the bus station, and on the way helped you pick out a fitting gift, your tale reveals the many dimensions of friendship in action. An essay that mixes personal anecdotes with more famous accounts—Mercutio's willingness to fight and die for his friend Romeo—would not only define the word but entertain and instruct readers.

Here is an anecdote that succeeds in defining the term

power in dramatic terms. The tale is both unusual and revealing.

A most vivid illustration of the meaning of the term *naked power* occurred in the late 1960's, when China was engaged in its famous cultural revolution. Students and Red Guard members at Peking University were striking against the school's outdated curriculum and its reactionary faculty and administrators. Posters covered campus walls and lists of demands were presented to the university's officials on a daily basis. In a major coup, the students managed to bring Chairman Mao to the campus to speak at a weekend rally. Amid chants of the Chinese equivalent of Student Power, Mao asked the students to estimate their numbers: "30,000" came the shouted reply. "And," asked Mao, "how many are the administrators and faculty?" When the students realized that the question invited them to exercise the power of numbers, they moved quickly to satisfy their goals.

We will present examples of effective opening and closing paragraphs later in this chapter. For the moment we suggest that a useful way to begin an essay of definition is to cite the need to define a term before the essay can proceed. Note the authoritative "I know what I am talking about" tone in the following sentence: "Although most of us have a general understanding of socialism, the term needs to be defined specifically before tracing its application to Polish society." In concluding the essay you might remind the reader that a concept like socialism, when understood in practice, differs considerably from the dictionary definition of the word. If you have traced the evolution in meaning of a certain word, as Ms. Foote does in "Notes on the Distaff Side," your conclusion might show how the word has evolved into a meaning that is not only different from the original meaning but quite opposite to it. Whatever approach you choose, avoid simply restating your introduction.

A final hint: Humorous definitions—one-liners—can often arrest attention and help guide your reader to a fuller understanding of the essay's main idea. H. L. Mencken, the exceptional American satirist, had a kind of obsession for such one-line definitions, and we quote a few of them to close this section on definition.

A cynic is a man who, when he smells flowers, looks around for a coffin.

Democracy is the art of running the circus from the monkey cage.

Wealth—any income that is $100 more a year than one's wife's sister's husband's.

Comparison and Contrast

Most of us follow the habit of making comparisons on a daily basis. Think of how you have compared last night's dinner at the Chinese Gardens with last month's feast there. How did this John Travolta movie hold up against *Saturday Night Fever?* Was last summer's vacation at Hogback Lake as much fun as this year's trip to Disney World? In making such comparisons we are looking for similarities—good service, crisp egg rolls—and differences—a smaller crowd last month, a more promising fortune from the cookie this time. To put it another way, comparison is a form of analysis or evaluation that requires the writer to identify similarities and differences in the person, thing, or event being observed.

There are at least three good reasons for writing comparison essays:

1. To demonstrate that one thing or event is *better* than another. There must be significant points of similarity—two movies starring John Travolta—in order to draw a comparison of this kind. However, brought off well, such a comparison will find you defending the reasons behind your choice of films or Chinese dinners with specific examples.
2. To point out how two similar persons, things, or events are *in fact different.* You might be comparing two totalitarian regimes, such as those in Vietnam and Russia. In this situation the aim is not to show that one is better than the other, but to discuss how

the differences influence the behavior of the two countries.

3. To uncover *surprising similarities* in two apparently different persons, things, or events. The advantage of this act of comparison is that your readers are led to reconsider something from a new perspective, which results in greater respect for your powers of observation. You might try comparing human and animal behavior, reading and television viewing, driving a car and managing a household. Reflection on specific details will start the engine of your mind and get the essay rolling.

As we have said, reviews of movies or books often involve comparison between the reviewed work and another by the same author or director. Keep the preceding purposes in mind as you consider writing reviews or critiques.

Organizing Comparison Essays. The effectiveness of a comparison paper is directly related to careful organization. There are some accepted guides to organizing such essays, and these guides might well be copied out and kept handy.

1. Separate Comparison. If you plan to compare the leader of a democratic country with the leader of a communist nation, your essay may function best by discussing each leader separately, letting your readers make the comparison or selecting important points to discuss in your conclusion. You should compare each leader in the same areas: First, assess Ronald Reagan's stance on the world situation, on defense, on peace, then examine Leonid Brezhnev on the same points. The same order of areas should be followed for each analysis, keeping in mind that your readers will be better able to follow your drift if you do so.

2. Similarities/Differences Comparison. If you choose to write about two events—an early Beatles concert and a recent Heart concert—the best method may be to consider all the similarities between the two, then all the differences. This method works best with persons, things, and events that are not on the surface strikingly different. Rock concerts belong to the same *class* of events, whereas democratic and communist governments belong to different classes. You might begin this type of essay by noting that the age of the audiences, the levels of sound, and the general attitudes toward rock music were the same at the two concerts but that the nature of the instruments, lyrics, and performance styles has changed considerably over the years. Just remember that your categories are *Similarities* and *Differences,* not *The Beatle Concert* and *The Heart Concert.*

3. *Alternating Comparison.* Certain comparisons work best when the writer breaks down the essay into topics and compares the persons, things, and events on this basis. For the essay on political leaders, you may keep the same topics—attitudes toward the world situation, defense, and peace—but you discuss the similarities and differences between the two leaders under the general topics. Sentences in this type of comparison essay tend to be constructed in the following way: "Whereas Reagan sees the countries in NATO as a buffer against Soviet aggression, Brezhnev tends to regard them as menacing enemies armed with American-made weapons." In order to pursue the alternating method, you will have to decide on general topics with some care: Is there, for instance, enough information about Reagan's stance on defense? But once the decision is made (three or four topics should suffice), the essay almost writes itself.

No matter what method you choose you should begin by writing down the names of the two persons, things, or events to be compared, then proceed to list details about each under the headings. This technique will build up the substance of the paper and start you thinking about the subject in a comparative way. Comparison methods can be adopted in both essays of exposition and argumentation; they work especially well in persuading readers that one particular book, movie, or political system is better than another.

6 *Problems of*

Composing

The methods or approaches outlined in Chapter 5 give you some notion of how to go about organizing your thoughts into an effective pattern. In this chapter we provide some more practical advice on how to begin filling the blank space of the page with words that will win your reader's attention. We also illustrate the steps involved in conducting an argument, reproduce a sample essay, and offer some suggestions for revising and proofreading the final draft.

BEGINNINGS AND ENDINGS

Every writer faced with the task of setting his or her ideas down on paper is conscious of the overwhelming importance of an effective beginning. It seems as important as first impressions in the first interview with your employer, or the introduction to your future parents-in-law. There is something terrifying about it because it must be got over first and because its success, or lack thereof, is bound to color everything that follows. In writing, students spend entirely too much time getting started.

"The best way to begin is to begin. Do not write introductions. Just plunge in." All this is sound advice, but not very helpful to the beginner. You might as well be told to learn to dance by plunging in—some persons do dance that way, after all. You need to know what to do after plunging in. Another piece of advice, possibly more helpful, goes this way: "Just write down anything about your subject. Keep going until you get well into your first main topic. Then, in revision, cross out the first two paragraphs." This advice rings true, but it may result in lopping off a good idea or two. A cleansing and healing of the afflicted part may prove as effective as amputation and will certainly hurt less. Learn to diagnose ailments before prescribing surgery.

There are, however, a number of specific devices that writers may use to introduce their subject appropriately and interestingly, just as there are similar devices for the easier task of appropriately ending their paper. Anyone glancing over a recent file of a serious magazine in which various kinds of articles appear—*Harper's,* for instance—is sure to find repeated examples of particular techniques for beginning as well as for ending. As the following selections will show, there is usually a close logical and rhetorical relation between the two. To connect your beginning and ending is one obvious way to give your paper *organization.*

Eight possible ways to begin (among many) are illustrated below. In each case the author's ending is also quoted. Their relation is worth study. As always, your choice of any particular technique depends not only on personal taste but on the kind of article you are writing and the kind of reader you are addressing. In studying these illustrations, note how the various beginnings and endings are in part responses to the particular subject and tone that the author has chosen.

The Dramatized Example or Incident. A familiar opening is a dramatized example or incident from which a larger generalization is to emerge. Here is such an introduction in the first few sentences of an essay on jogging.

Just as I'm putting on my sneakers and adjusting my headband, my stomach begins revolting. You'd think after nearly two years of running I'd be used to it now. I never quite get my breath until I'm a full mile into the run. Then, I guess, my body consents because there's no turning back.

Most people like to jog. Not me.

The author proceeds to argue that she does not jog but instead runs, some six miles a day. In the course of the essay we discover that she is not simply describing her experiences in the course of a typical jogging session; she is extolling a particular approach to life. This point is dramatically restated in her concluding paragraph.

As I zip by the mirror-image houses, I see duplicity everywhere, in the lines on the people's faces, in the Eliotesque coffee cups. When I reach home, there's always some lunatic standing on my front lawn ready to chat, saying something or other about a neighbor's dog. And above it all, I feel my mind shaking hands with my body.

—PATRICIA BREEN-BOND, "Running in the Rain"

The Anecdote. A related technique is to begin with an anecdote, true or fictitious, but told in the manner of the storyteller. Note how the author of the following passage transforms a true anecdote into something of a fable by means of the storyteller style. Here is effective narration at work.

When the Inquisitors summoned Galileo before them, they told him he must not find that the earth revolves around the sun. Galileo had been observing the heavens through a telescope: he had become convinced that the evidence warranted his conclusion. But the Inquisitors did not look through the telescope. They knew all about astronomy from reading the Bible. So against Galileo's telescope the Inquisitors employed another instrument: the rack. And by the rack, which could inflict pain on the astronomer's body, they undertook to cure the astronomer of his scientific error. Thus they prohibited the exploration of the heavens by the exercise of their physical power.

The essay then develops the thesis that the forces which move mankind forward, represented by Galileo's desire to explore the heavens, are like birds trying to free them-

195

selves from cages devised by forces symbolized by the Inquisitors' rack. The author concludes by recalling the image of oppression and the impulse for freedom.

It is a hope engendered in the human heart during the long ages in which the slowly emerging impulses of civilization, beset by barbarism, have struggled to be free.
— WALTER LIPPMAN, "The Will to Be Free"

The Autobiographical Incident. A similar opening technique is the illustrative incident taken from a moment in the writer's own life. Here the writer mixes autobiographical fact and humor to launch an essay on the effects of war.

I was born on the first day of the second month of the last year of the First World War, a Friday. Testimony abounds that during the first day of my life I never smiled. I was known as the baby whom nothing and no one could make smile. Everyone who knew me then has told me so. They tried very hard, singing and bouncing me up and down, jumping around, pulling faces. Many times I was told this later by my family and their friends, but, anyway, I knew it at the time.

The essay closes with a reference to the remarks of a famous British statesman on the end of World War I. Thus the writer provides a framework for her assertions about her early sophistication—she smiled only when she was bemused.

Since that time I have grown to smile quite naturally, like any other healthy and house-trained person, but when I really mean a smile, deeply felt from the core, then to all intents and purposes it comes in response to the words uttered in the House of Commons after the First World War by the distinguished, the immaculately dressed, and the late Mr. Asquith.
— MURIEL SPARK, "The First Year of My Life," *The New Yorker*

The Stereotype Refuted. A common device for opening an essay is to summarize stereotyped beliefs about a given subject, then proceed to refute them. Effectively done this opening can impress your audience with your learning and audacity. Here is a typical example.

The past few years in America have seen the gradual disintegration of the illusion that we are not a violent people. Americans have always admitted being lawless relative to Europeans, but this was explained as a consequence of our youth as a nation—our closeness to frontier days. High crime rates prior to World War II were regarded in much the same manner as the escapades of an active ten-year-old ("America is all boy!"), and a secret contempt suffused our respect for the law-abiding English. Today the chuckle is gone, the respect more genuine, for the casual violence of American life has become less casual, and its victims threaten to include those other than the disadvantaged.

The author then sets about to explain American violence as a reaction to sudden social change. He concludes by restating the opening reference to our general unwillingness to admit that we are threatened by "radical" plans to do something about our social dilemma.

The predominant feeling is that there is more change than anybody can tolerate already, so how can anyone even *consider* a radical reevaluation of the whole system. Or, to paraphrase a cartoon by Mell Lazarus: "I know I need to see a psychiatrist, but the idea scares me too much now—I'll go when I'm less anxious." Apparently, the idea not only scares us—it makes us mad enough to kill somebody.
—PHILIP SLATER, *The Pursuit of Loneliness*

The Surprise Opening (Serious). A variation on the use of the stereotype is to begin an essay with a surprising or even shocking statement, one that is distinctly *not* a stereotype. Sometimes such a beginning may take the form of open hostility toward authority, as in this case.

Humanists for thousands of years have attempted to construct a naturalistic, psychological value system that could be derived from man's own nature, without the necessity of recourse to authority outside the human being himself. Many such theories have been offered throughout history. They have all failed for mass practical purposes exactly as all other theories have failed. We have about as many scoundrels in the world today as we have ever had, and *many more* neurotics, probably, than we have ever had.

Then, having lured us into his argument with this shocker, the author must document his charges, and he concludes by reminding us of the important distinction between theory and practice, culture and the individual.

A teacher or a culture doesn't create a human being. It doesn't implant within him the ability to love, or to be curious, or to philosophize, or to symbolize, or to be creative. Rather it permits, or fosters, or encourages or helps what exists in embryo to become real and actual. The same mother or the same culture, treating a kitten or a puppy in exactly the same way, cannot make it into a human being. The culture is sun and food and water: it is not the seed.

—ABRAHAM MASLOW, "Psychological Data and Human Values"

The Surprise Opening (Humorous). Another kind of shock opening, far less aggressive in tone, can be achieved by putting forward an argument that is absurd on the face of it. Can the writer *mean* it? we ask. The writer in the following example gives us a ludicrous but somehow apt definition of bachelorhood.

The confirmed bachelor can be defined as the man who has the courage of his lack of convictions. Once he hasn't made his mind up, he really sticks to it. Swinging more and more wildly from his loosening trapeze, he is another reeling acrobat in the disorganized circus of American love and marriage.

By turning to a more somber tone at the close of his essay, Herbert Gold makes us realize that although the bachelor in pursuit of the ideal woman is a romantic idealist, there is another side of his personality that is lonely and poignant.

198

Usually he does not find the girl of his dreams. That ladder to the stars lies folded in a closet somewhere. Another evening has been spilled away with a swell kid whose name he will soon forget.

We do not see him during those moments when he is alone in his apartment, wondering why. *Alone.* Back home alone to his cold bed, his vacant hopes, and his Dacron shirt drying in his bathroom.

—HERBERT GOLD, "The Bachelor's Dilemma"

Questions to Be Answered. We spoke previously of the rhetorical question, the question with only one possible answer, as an ending technique. It is also familiar as a beginning. But even more familiar, and clearly appropriate for many kinds of serious argumentation essays, is to begin by asking questions that do not have easy answers. The effort to provide answers, then, becomes the central concern of the essay. Here is an example in which a poet questions the very act of writing poetry in the modern age.

Why is it that nowadays, when poetry brings in little prestige and less money, people are still found who devote their lives to the apparently unrewarding occupation of making poems? Is the poet a quaint anachronism in the modern world—a pathetic shadow of the primitive bard who, unable for some reason to take active part in the life of his tribe, won himself an honorable place in the community by singing of the exploits of hunters and warriors?

While part of the appeal of this essay is that the author cannot find adequate answers to these questions, he concludes by pointing out that the poet, like the rest of us, requires some of the same qualities we need in our own less glamorous work.

Each new poem I begin is an attempt at making and exploring. Each finished one is, in effect, a way of praising life, a sacrifice in life's honor. I need devotion, discipline, sincerity, skill, and above all, patience, if the poem is to come to anything; but I also need something I cannot cultivate—call it luck.

—C. DAY LEWIS, "The Making of a Poem"

199

The Appeal of Importance. In all the beginnings we have discussed, the author has been responsible for convincing his or her reader that the article will be worth the reading, that it is important or significant or amusing. Sometimes, instead of asking questions or telling stories to arouse interest, an author may simply *tell* the reader of the subject's urgency.

There is only too much reason to fear that Western civilization, if not the whole world, is likely in the near future to go through a period of immense sorrow and suffering and pain—a period during which, if we are not careful to remember them, the things that we are attempting to preserve may be forgotten in bitterness and poverty and disorder. Courage, hope, and unshakable conviction will be necessary if we are to emerge from the dark time spiritually undamaged.

After describing the political and social pressures that menace the spirit of Western civilization, the author concludes by emphasizing the need to learn lessons from adversity, if only to preserve the value of wisdom for future generations.

It is to the possible achievements of man that our ultimate loyalty is due, and in that thought the brief troubles of our unquiet epoch become endurable. Much wisdom needs to be learned, and if it is only to be learned through adversity, we must endeavour to endure adversity with what fortitude we can command. But if we can acquire wisdom soon enough, adversity may not be necessary and the future of man may be happier than any part of his past.
—BERTRAND RUSSELL, "If We Are to Survive This Dark Time—"

PERSUASION: THE WHOLE ESSAY

The *persuasion* or *argumentation* essay is both the most difficult and most rewarding essay to compose. That is why we have chosen to outline its features in detail, taking you from start to finish. Such essays are difficult to do

200

because they demand that the writer take a position, state a thesis to be argued, then argue that thesis according to the dictates of reason and logic. They are rewarding because they allow the writer to express strongly held beliefs in a forum that is free of the distractions that attend spoken debates. Learning the techniques of argumentation will be of special value when you are asked to take a stand on questions like the continuation of the 55-mile-an-hour speed limit or on drinking for eighteen-year-olds. Research or library papers are also often assigned as questions calling for a thesis to be argued by the writer.

ORGANIZING A PERSUASION PAPER

The first step in organizing a persuasion paper is *to state the thesis as a question to be argued.* *Convince* or *persuade* are words that ought to appear in the sentence as you state it in the prewriting stage. This thesis should be specific enough to give your readers an idea of where the essay is headed, but broad enough to allow for flexibility in the actual conduct of the argument. The following statement of purpose might be used to get us started; it will appear in somewhat different form in the essay itself.

Purpose: To convince the reader that rather than being a simple romance set against the background of World War II, *Casablanca* is in fact a propaganda film meant to encourage greater support for the war effort.

Title: Love and Politics: *Casablanca* as a Propaganda Film

Central Idea: The love triangle in *Casablanca,* whose resolution even the actors did not know until the last day of shooting, is important mainly as an allegory for the events of World War II. Through touches of characterization and a series of gestures, we realize that Rick's decision to give up Ilsa is in fact symbolic of America's decision to give up its cynicism about the European war and join the fight against the anti-romantic, anti-democratic Nazis.

The next step is to decide how *to present your case* to readers on the lookout for hard evidence. How you will order your material depends on what you have to say and

201

on the sort of reader you are addressing. Two standard methods, outlined in the paragraphs that follow, are widely recognized by theorists of composition.

Inductive Order (Order of Easy Acceptance)

Often readers are best led toward an unconventional idea by starting with a presentation of numerous facts, instances, or observations that build up support for that main idea. For instance, if you are advocating the institution of student government in your school, you may get a more favorable response from your readers (administrators? trustees?) if you convince them first that a system of strict, paternalistic government has resulted in inattention to grading policies, student placement, and campus activities. If you are urging the establishment of teen-age night clubs, begin by picturing the present undesirable conditions in the neighborhood: students on the streets late at night, involved in vandalism and other misdeeds. Following the inductive order means stating your generalization *after* citing individual instances that illustrate the main idea.

Deductive Order ("from the general to the particular")

It is frequently possible to win over your reader with a well-worded generalization or premise, the truth of which is substantiated in the body of the essay by a series of specific examples. In logic the *syllogism* is a form of argument based on deduction. It consists of a *major premise*— "All men love peace"—a *minor premise*—"John Kennedy was a man"—and a *conclusion*—"John Kennedy loved peace." As you can see, this method of argument has certain advantages. If you accept the major premise, the other two propositions must also be accepted; the force of logic serves to drive the point home. Many readers also equate eloquent generalizations like "All men love peace" with truth, even though such assertions may not hold up under scrutiny. (How can the claim be verified, especially in light of the many wars in human history?) In order to use this method successfully the writer must be sure that the generalization or major premise is workable and defensible. This means that the process of deduction should be tested out before writing the essay; you cannot depend solely on the authority of your own voice to carry it through. A handy rule is to make sure your generalization ("All men love peace") has been carefully qualified ("*Most* men or *people* love peace") so that readers will not be able to point to obvious exceptions before you have had a chance to persuade them.

Logic

As the preceding paragraph hints, some knowledge of the conventions of logic is of considerable value in conducting the argument in a persuasion essay.

Most of us, however, are put off by the word *logic*. It connotes a cold, unfeeling, even devastating approach to life. Yet in writing for an audience that you are trying to sway, impress, cajole, or move in some way, logic can be a useful guide. It may even serve as the machete that you can wield to cut your way through a jungle of ideas or impressions in your own mind. One thing is sure: if you make too many errors in logic, your reader will soon begin to suspect the authority of your statements. Once lost, that reader is difficult to win back to your point of view with emotional appeals alone.

Below are a few of the more common errors in logic or reasoning. Try out your understanding of them by testing them against the arguments that appear in the editorial sections of newspapers or magazines.

False Analogy. *Analogy* is a means of arguing by comparing something to something else. Recently we have heard of a "war on poverty" conducted by the Federal government; and the argument in support of urgent funding for poverty programs has depended on the analogy. We are made to feel that we must *conquer* poverty and hunger before they conquer us.

203

False analogies result when the comparison does not rest on any basic similarities or when the analogy is substituted for a proof in an argument. To justify certain actions in governmental organizations by comparing the organization to a "team" that is out "to win" is an example of substituting an analogy for a proof. Government is not a game.

False Cause. *False cause* has several variations, but the most common one confuses cause with effect. Because American society is so impressed with statistics, we are often susceptible to false cause arguments that employ them. For instance, an irate speaker recently used the following statistics to "prove" that rock music is evil: "Of 1,000 girls who became pregnant out of wedlock, 994 committed fornication while rock music was being played." One wonders what the other six were doing!

The *post hoc, ergo propter hoc* fallacy is another example of false cause argument. Translated the phrase means "after this, therefore because of this," and it describes a statement asserting that two events are related because the first predicted the second. Those who claim there is a *direct* relationship between Herbert Hoover's election as president in 1928 and the stock market crash of 1929 are using the *post hoc* argument. By asserting that we came out of the Depression because we elected a *Democratic* president, an analyst of government is only compounding the error.

Begging the Question. Any argument that assumes the truth of the very point to be proved *begs the question*. One of the symptoms of this fallacy is circular reasoning, in which the conclusion of the argument simply restates the assumption. Those who claim that the country's moral fiber has been weakened by too much television watching and that we will grow strong again if we destroy television sets have assumed too much. They must first *prove* that the nation's morality has indeed become corrupted in the period since the invention of television.

Argumentum ad Hominem. An "argument against the person" might simply be called *avoiding the question*, since it draws attention to the character of the individual and not his or her assertion. We immediately think of *abuse* or *invective* as examples of *ad hominem* arguments: "He has never done an honest day's labor in his life, so how can he dare to introduce a bill improving the rights of the average worker?" But a speaker who uses emotional generalities to win our approval is also ignoring the question: "Many long years of loyal service to and love for this company qualify me to speak about what is best for its employees."

Non Sequitur ("it does not follow"). When the premises of an argument do not establish a firm basis for the conclusion, then the conclusion is called a *non sequitur*. Often the cause is a failure to provide a step in the argument: "I bought one of those cars and it turned out to be a lemon. The company later went out of business." More often the conclusion is based on irrelevant evidence: "Joe Namath uses those pantyhose, so they must be good." Notice how many companies attempt to "prove" the quality or popularity of their products by getting endorsements from famous people.

No doubt the most obvious error in argumentation is *overgeneralization*. It is not specifically an error in logic, though many people might claim that a failure to qualify any statements about events or people violates their sense of the real world. More important, hasty generalizations give the reader the impression that you have not taken the time to look closely at the evidence. They are the basis as well for *prejudice* and *bias:* "*All* Italians belong to the Mafia"; "The Irish are fighting with each other *all the time.*" We are especially susceptible to overgeneralization when our emotions are aroused. It was not until some time after World War II that many Americans chose to recognize that the Japanese had planned to inform us about the attack on Pearl Harbor *before* it took place, but their Washington ambassador was delayed because of problems in decoding the message from Tokyo.

When you find yourself using such words as *always, never, all, only,* and *every,* it is time to examine your statement in detail. Don't claim that *only* truck drivers sit in front

205

of their television sets, beer cans in hand and watching football, until you have checked around. If you claim that *most* women want a home and husband, make sure that at least two-thirds in fact do or you will not only be open to a charge of overgeneralization but also to a charge of sexism. To avoid such serious predicaments, and to improve your writing, take advantage of the numerous qualifying terms available to you. Select the ones that accurately describe the facts in your argument: "*Some* men feel pressured by the company's affirmative action policy in hiring"; "She *often* wants me to do the shopping so that she can have more free time." Remember that the reader will heed statements based on a realistic assessment of the facts more readily than loose generalizations of the kind he or she hears frequently in informal and uninformed conversation.

Fact, Belief, Opinion Distinctions

Facts may be verified by referring to our senses. We can see that a table is not a chair; we can taste the difference between sugar and salt. Factual statements may be substantiated by some arbiter—an encyclopedia, a dictionary, a yardstick. Not all facts are physical, that is, involve measuring or weighing or counting. Some facts are historical in nature; they may be verified by artifacts or signs of the event. If we claim that one third of London's population died during the plague years of 1601–1605, we can produce the plague bills or death lists as proof. In some cases we may not possess these pieces of evidence. There is no birth certificate to prove, for example, that Shakespeare was born on April 23, 1564. But the important point is that this date is widely accepted by scholars, since we do have the record of baptism, which traditionally took place three days after birth. Such verification is at least a prerequisite of good writing; proof convinces readers of the writer's authority on the subject.

Beliefs may be strongly held (e.g., "I believe in UFO's"), but they are not verifiable in any recognized way. Religious belief may be stated in certain contexts, but the sheer statement of it should not be mistaken for proof. Qualifying beliefs helps, yet if you find yourself in an area—creation of the world, for instance—where belief must be stated in place of argument, it is best to delete such avowals.

Opinions may well be verified but not under the guise of opinions. *Theory* might well be used as a synonym for *opinion:* Einstein's theory of relativity has been supported by mathematical calculations and other means. "Pigs are smarter than horses" stands as Johnny Carson's opinion about animal intelligence. He has had a running feud with announcer Ed McMahon over the issue, but the evidence— pigs playing chess, horses talking—can never be conclusive. Commonly held opinion may support one or the other opinion, but it would be impossible to survey even a sufficient sample of pigs and horses to settle the matter.

Casablanca: Steps in the Argument

To return to our proposed essay on *Casablanca,* the central idea (see page 201) requires that we use a deductive approach in trying to prove that the film's main purpose was propaganda and not the recounting of a sentimental love story. We will have to provide reasons or evidence for the claim that the film's intention is clear from the beginning.

The next step in the process is *to challenge the opinions or arguments that oppose yours.* You may have had to do some preliminary reading to discover just what those arguments are, but once done with that reading, select what you believe are the central points of contention and start refuting them. Here is where your knowledge of logic comes in handy. On the question of the 55 mile-an-hour speed limit, opponents might argue that there has been no significant reduction in fatal accidents since the limit was imposed. This sort of contention can be easily demolished by citing statistics kept by the National Safety Council; for the years during which the 55 speed limit has been in effect, there have been fewer accidents. Other claims, that cars get better mileage at 65 or that drivers break the law with abandon

207

because 55 is too low, can be brushed aside on the grounds of faulty logic. Gas mileage actually decreases beyond 50, and many people drove a dangerous 80 miles an hour when the limit was 70. A satiric or biting tone is not required to puncture these balloons of bad thinking, however. Readers are more likely to respond favorably to a reasoned, analytical tone that simply lets out the hot air without damaging the balloon.

The major claims against the thesis in our *Casablanca* essay are that it was intended as "escapist fare" and that the script writers were so casual about their task that even they never knew from day to day how the movie would end. While we begin by admitting that the mood and setting lend an air of escapism to the action, we then point out that the course of events inevitably leads to the conclusion that Rick (Humphrey Bogart), fashioned as a character meant to represent the "American character," will enter the struggle wholeheartedly on the side of the Allies.

In the process of refuting your opponent's arguments, be sure as well to recognize their validity when the facts support them. *Casablanca,* after all, was made by a Hollywood studio, not by the government; it had to entertain if it was to draw audiences into the theaters. But our response to that observation is that *escapist* is too strong a word, the implication of it being that the movie has no value other than to make its audiences forget their troubles. By conceding some of the opposing points, you not only provide a context from which to conduct your argument, but show your readers how fair-minded you are. Playing by the rules is after all one of the prerequisites for winners and losers alike.

Proving your thesis—the activity that constitutes the body of your paper—calls for care in arranging your arguments and opinions in an order that is likely to be persuasive. Do not begin with your most significant or telling point. By moving from the least to the most important argument, you prepare the reader's attention for the clincher. State your ideas in a straightforward, soundly qualified way; avoid being excessively clever or witty. As much as possi-

208

ble, educate your readers about the subject while informing them of the background for the controversy or question your essay attempts to settle. In our *Casablanca* paper we combine *external evidence* (Bogart made other movies the same year in which he played roles similar to the one he plays in *Casablanca*) and *internal evidence* (the number of scenes dominated by patriotic gestures) to support our thesis. We also focus considerable attention on the film's final scene, arguing that the teaming up of Rick and Louis as freedom fighters has been prepared for by similar scenes throughout the movie. Moving from scene to scene helps as well in organizing the notes that have been scattered all over the desk.

The final step in a persuasion essay is *to recapitulate your main points,* especially if the paper is long (7–10 typewritten pages). Listing those points can have the same impact on your audience as watching Evel Knievel jump over thirteen London buses on his motorcycle. It may be safer for you, however, to select two or three "buses" that your readers are likely to remember. This is the approach we use in the *Casablanca* paper, where the last paragraph reiterates our points about the movie's structure and intent and about Bogart's role as symbolic of American attitudes. Another way of ending a persuasion paper is to call on your readers to take some form of action: Write letters, picket, form action groups. If you do direct your readers to take some kind of action, be specific and outline the probable consequences of such action. Whatever way you choose to end the paper, do not simply restate the opening paragraph; that is a sure way to convince your readers that they have been standing still for the last half-hour.

OUTLINE AND "CASABLANCA" PAPER

Love and Politics:
Casablanca as a Propaganda Film

Thesis: Rather than being a simple love triangle set against the background of World War II, Casablanca is in fact a propaganda film meant, through its hero's conversion to freedom-fighter, to encourage greater support for the war effort.

209

I. There are two critical statements about <u>Casablanca</u>
that suggest it was intended mainly as a romantic
love story.
A. One is Charles Higham's assertion that the film
is "escapist fare."
1. Some support for Higham's position can be found
in the "free zone" atmosphere of Rick's club.
2. The musical theme "As Time Goes By" establishes
a mood of romantic escapism and timelessness.
B. The other observation is that the screenwriters
turned out scenes on a day to day basis, never
knowing how the film would end.
1. There is some evidence for the claim in the actors' and director's reminiscences.
2. This claim places considerable emphasis on the
outcome of the love triangle--it could have
gone either way.
II. These critical judgments overlook signs within and
without <u>Casablanca</u> that suggest its main purpose was
propagandist.
A. Rick's character is an allegory for the American
character.
1. Before the war Rick (America) had a love affair
with Ilsa (France) and escapism (isolationism).
2. When the war began Ilsa (France) betrayed him
(set up the Vichy regime), leaving behind a
cynical, hurt Rick.
3. The attack on Pearl Harbor, alluded to in the
film, marks a turning point in his and in America's attitude toward the war.
B. Humphrey Bogart had played similar roles in other
1942 films.
1. <u>All Through the Night</u> presents him as a New
York gangster who turns patriot.
2. <u>Sahara</u> finds him playing a tank commander who,
with a small band of Allied freedom fighters,
holds off a Nazi regiment.
III. The film's propagandist impact is achieved through a
series of patriotic gestures.
A. Rick helps and protects those trying to escape
the Nazis.
1. He lets a young man win at roulette so that he
and his new bride can leave Casablanca.
2. He will allow no Germans to gamble in his club.
B. Rick aids Victor Lazlo in doing his "work."
1. He lets the club band play the "Marseillaise"
to drown out a group of singing Nazis.
2. He gives Victor and Ilsa the exit visas in an
elaborate ruse.
3. He resigns his love for Ilsa to return with
Louis to perform instead as a "lover" of freedom.

210

Love and Politics:
Casablanca as a Propaganda Film

Robert F. Willson, Jr.

211

In The Art of the American Film, Charles Higham offhand-
edly assesses Casablanca (1942) as a film "contrived to
present war as a somewhat enjoyable if hazardous experience, exactly what audiences needed as escapist fare in
those harrowing times" (p. 142). Higham's use of the
phrase "escapist fare" can be justified, to be sure, by
pointing to the film's romantic fantasy about a jilted
night club owner who gives up his claim on a former mistress because she is now the wife of a world-renowned
freedom fighter he deeply admires. The broken love affair
has its one night of renewal, then gives way to the more
pressing demands of saving the world from fascism. Accompanying the love (or frustrated love) story is the atmosphere of expedience that prevails in Casablanca, where
lives are bought and sold to pay for exit visas. Rick's
club, the Café Américain, might be viewed as a kind of
free zone in which brandy and gambling and singing help
to ease the pain of struggling to keep beyond the Nazis'
grip. In this microcosmic world, however, the atmosphere
is relatively safe and the game of escape is played with
style and grace in expensive-looking evening clothes.
[Only Ugatti (Peter Lorre), who breaks the rules by
bringing the visas into Rick's club, suffers immediate
punishment.] Dooley Wilson's version of "As Time Goes By"
adds just the right touch of optimism, suggesting in its
lyrics that true lovers will always survive the momentary
distractions of global war. No doubt the chief appeal of
the movie to wartime audiences was its final note of
stiff-upper-lip courage represented by Bogart's romantic
gesture for the sake of Victor Lazlo's mission. Lazlo requires Ilsa's (Ingrid Bergman) devotion and unquestioning
love to bring help to a Europe victimized by fascist ar-
mies.

But to claim that Casablanca is simply "escapist fare"
is to ignore signs throughout the plot that indicate a
desire not to lead audiences away from the reality of war
but to engage them in its struggle. The impression that
the film took shape on a day-to-day basis, with none of
the actors ever knowing how Julius and Philip Epstein
would decide to end it, has been reinforced by many subsequent commentaries. (See Morris Beja, Film and Literature, p. 48.) Yet to say that the only interest in the
plot is whether or not Bogie will get the girl is to
denigrate the chief purpose of Casablanca, which is propagandist. Director Michael Curtiz and his writers wish
us to "read" Bogart's character not simply as that of an
unrequited and cynical lover but as representative of the
American "character" in its outlook toward war. What happens to Rick nicely parallels, in a politically allegori-
cal way, the course of prewar American behavior vis-
à-vis the European problem. Rick was an ex-patriot in
Paris, a time recalled in a drunken vision as the place
where he met and wooed Ilsa. Like America before the war,
his behavior during this interlude was carefree, romantic, with Europe (France) perceived as a place in which
young Americans drank too much, drove fast cars, and fell
in love. The advancing Germans changed all that, however;
fascism grew powerful and overwhelmed all that was frag-

212

ile and beautiful. In addition, Ilsa "betrayed" Rick, turning back to her lover Victor instead of running away to freedom with Rick. Although to press the parallel too schematically would be wrong, Ilsa's act could be identified with the perfidy of Europe, in particular the creation of the Vichy regime. Paris could no longer be regarded as a playground for Americans but was seen instead as a "betraying woman," hurdling masculine America into hardship and woe. Thus as the film reintroduces Rick to Ilsa in Casablanca, his attitude is negative and defensive. He sees her as the thankless mistress who returns to him now only because she needs his help. There can be little doubt that Rick's reaction is typically American: suspicious, cynical, but soft-hearted. Rick's sentiments in favor of the underdog--also typically American--prevail in the end. It is interesting to note that Bogart played similar roles in other films released in 1942; these parts seemed to suit the tough guy image he had by then established in earlier films. All Through the Night finds him cast as the leader of a lovable group of Brooklyn gangsters who turn patriots when they discover Nazi Fifth Columnists in a warehouse they have broken into. In Sahara Bogart is a tank commander carrying a mixed group of Allied soldiers back to friendly lines. He decides to hold off a whole regiment of Nazis when one of his charges wonders what would happen if they slowed the enemy down with a last-ditch stand. As Rick, Bogart's underdog instincts lead him to help Victor Lazlo, whose story of patriotism Ilsa narrates, and then to join the fight against the Nazis in the company of the corrupt but romantic police official Louis (Claude Rains). America forges a new alliance with her friend France, which is now turning away from the collaborationist position she took in the early stages of the war.

There are other indications of the film's propagandist purpose. Before he slides off into his alcoholic reverie about prewar Paris, Rick asks Sam: "This is December, 1941--what time is it in New York?" This time reference indicates that the film's action is supposed to be taking place at a turning point in America's involvement in the war. The Japanese attack on Pearl Harbor meant that we could no longer, as Rick does in this scene, drown ourselves in the drink of isolationism or hide from the terrible, personal reality of war. "As Time Goes By" qualifies as an ideal accompanying song for both Rick's emotional suffering and America's attitude toward the war. As the song says, "The world will always welcome lovers," suggesting as well "lovers of freedom." Rick is such a lover, and he will rejoin the struggle (he previously fought for the Loyalists in Spain and ran guns to Ethiopia) against an enemy who, like America's past enemies, threatens our love of freedom and fair play.

Indeed, the film requires us to understand the love of freedom theme through a series of gestures that can only be called patriotic. These gestures, recurring as they do throughout the film, help to confirm the theory that Casablanca could not have ended in any other way than it does, with Rick's reinvolvement as a fighter for freedom.

That he has been engaged in patriotic activities is clear
from the beginning, even if we were never told about his
actions in Spain and Ethiopia. As Rick sits in the gambling room of his cafe, his table is so situated that he
can approve or reject any person seeking admittance with
the slightest movement of his head. One notable incident
occurs as he informs a German merchant that his money
will be good at the bar, not in the casino. The gesture
makes no sense if Rick is indeed the amoral businessman
he describes himself as being. But he clearly has scru-
ples when it comes to supporters of the Third Reich.

Later, when he realizes that a young girl and her new-
lywed husband are being toyed with by Louis, who hopes to
bed the girl in return for the promise of an exit visa,
Rick fixes the roulette wheel so that the young groom can
win enough money to purchase the visa. This gesture, like
the earlier one, proves Rick's willingness to become involved in a limited way in the struggle. He stands up for
the underdog, even though he professes to have no interest in his cause. His act here neatly foreshadows his effort to aid Victor and Ilsa.

We realize fully that the cause does matter to Rick
when he meets Victor Lazlo. During their polite exchanges, Rick demonstrates his unqualified respect for
Lazlo's "work." But the gesture that confirms Rick's loyalty and love of freedom occurs in a climactic scene in
the club when the German Major Strasse (Conrad Veidt)
rises to lead his charges in an alcoholic chorus or two
of "Die Wacht am Rhein." Bursting with anger and frustration, Lazlo marches up to the orchestra leader and asks
him to play the "Marseillaise." It is not, however, until
the leader has received the characteristic nod from Rick
that he turns to strike up the patriotic hymn. The scene
is climactic because the voices of previously frustrated
patriots now break out loud and clear, drowning out those
of the Nazi oppressors. This is the only demonstration of
Lazlo's "work" in the film, but it is meant to convince
us--and Rick--that everything possible must be done to
aid Lazlo's flight to America. Only someone with his
charismatic powers can arouse the free world's leaders to
continue the struggle against Germany. Here the patriotic
thrust of Casablanca literally blares out at the audience: We must keep up the good fight especially now that
the tide of the war seems to be turning in our favor.

The final memorable gesture in the film is Louis's act
of dropping the bottle of Vichy water into the airport
wastebasket. It symbolizes the end of appeasement, something the Allied forces wished desperately would happen
in France. (In this regard, we could see Lazlo as a General De Gaulle, flying to England to encourage the underground with hortatory radio broadcasts.) Only after Rick
actually shoots Strasse, however, does he fully reveal
his intention to fight. Then Louis is willing to join his
friend in escaping to the Free French forces nearby. The
film's ending poses Rains and Bogart in an ironic portrait as "lovers" walking off to a new world in which
they will "make beautiful music together." Here then is

the image of two countries whose love of freedom finally overcomes their personal, temporal concerns. This ending could be characterized as inevitable, given the earlier indications of Rick's patriotism and of Louis' romantic bent. It certainly confirms the belief that <u>Casablanca's</u> personal love story was always meant to be secondary to the larger story of involvement in the fight for freedom. Bogie's character emerges as a romantic conception of the American character, cynical, self-possessed, but finally impulsive in its efforts to enter the battle on the side of the underdog.

Preparing the Final Draft: Revising, Proofreading

Our essay on *Casablanca* appears to be a polished piece. But every essay can stand one more look: for weaknesses in organization, transition, support; for errors in spelling, word choice, punctuation. Of all writing performances, revising is probably the most difficult to master. It is, however, one of the most crucial to a successful essay. Here are some suggestions for shaping your work of words into a finished product.

Try to complete a draft of a paper at least a day or two before it is due. This means giving up the bad habit of composing *and* typing the essay the night before handing it in. Then take from the remaining time an hour or two when you are at your most alert, when you are feeling efficient and sensitive. Pick up your manuscript and begin to read. As you do so, try to *pretend it was written by somebody else.* In your role as just another reader of this composition, make quick notes in the margin of everything that makes you hesitate, for any reason. Ask yourself, How can I tell that this essay was written by an amateur, not a professional? Here are some of the kinds of evidence you may notice: weak transitions between sentences and paragraphs, loose logical connections between ideas, inexact use of certain words, a vague pronoun or two (*it* and *this* are regular offenders), a nonstop sentence, a series of very short sentences, a failure to organize the whole essay around a single theme.

After you have made notes of this sort, take steps to

215

correct all these weaknesses, using your dictionary, thesaurus, and this *Handbook* as you need them. Then try reading your paper again, but this time read it *aloud,* and listen to yourself. A tape recorder can be very handy for this purpose, and for the general task of remembering certain details about your subject. If you do not have a recorder, ask your roommate, or your mother, to act as an audience for your pronouncements. Sometimes the person you choose will question points of your argument or style you have failed to notice. In the process you should be able to recognize more revisable items: harsh sound effects, awkward repetition of words, clauses and phrases that seem to have no connection with the main thoughts of sentences. When this analysis is completed, you are ready to begin shaping your final draft.

Attempts to make substantial changes while typing or writing this final copy are inadvisable, although you may notice one or two additional details for improvement. If you have carried out your rereading and revising process thoroughly, drastic changes during the copying will do more harm than good. But your final act of *proofreading* is absolutely essential. Now you are on the lookout, not for the logic and phrasing of your argument, but for those mechanical errors that so irritate and distract a reader. This is the time to make final corrections of punctuation and spelling. To many students such things seem trivial, and in a way they are, but, unfortunately, to ignore them is suicidal. The plain fact is that no matter how clever your words may be, if you spell them badly your reader (who is, after all, your instructor) will assume that you are ignorant and illiterate. You would assume the same thing about someone else's sloppy manuscript.

Finally, it is a fine thing to be proud of what you do. To hand in a clean, solid composition should be no less satisfying than to score a clean, solid winner on the tennis court or to execute successfully a difficult piano recital. A performance is a performance. Admit that it is and never be content with less than the best you can do.

216

The Whole Essay: A Checklist

The following are selected questions about the essay as a whole. They are worth raising *before* you hand in the finished work, as they are certain to occur to an experienced reader like your instructor. As with the questions raised about grammar and mechanics these possible problem areas must be attended to carefully if the impact of your writing is to be strong and persuasive.

1. If you follow the *deductive approach* (see, for example, page 202), have you included your thesis statement in the opening paragraph? Is the rest of the essay organized and documented most effectively to prove the thesis?

2. If you follow the *inductive approach* (see pages 202–203), have you at least hinted at your thesis in the introduction? How long must the reader wait until he knows where you stand? (A reader other than you should be asked about this matter.)

3. Does the concluding paragraph merely repeat the introductory one? (See "Beginnings and Endings," pages 193–200.) Have you given your reader a sense that the argument has moved toward a conclusion? Does the essay just stop, or does it have an ending?

4. Are your paragraphs arranged so that the reader has the impression of moving from *least* to *most* important points? At any stage does a paragraph seem to digress unnecessarily from the mainstream of your argument? (See page 134.)

5. Have you achieved smooth *transition* from paragraph to paragraph? Ask yourself, or your objective reader, whether or not the essay seems disjointed or choppy because the reader is forced to leap from topic to topic in successive paragraphs.

6. If you argue by means of *comparison* and *contrast* (see pages 191–192), are the similarities and differences discussed adequately explained? If the whole essay is a comparison and contrast of the American and

217

Russian forms of government, for example, have you presented a *balanced* picture and reached some definite conclusion? To conclude by stating that both forms of government feature advantages and disadvantages is to leave the reader hanging.

7. Is the *tone* of your essay consistent? If you intend a light-hearted examination of laws against drug use, don't suddenly turn preachy or crusading at the close of your paper. Be sure you understand how *you* feel about the subject before presenting an opinion to the reader.

8. Have you used *active verbs* throughout? Check the number of *passive constructions* and if they represent more than a third of the verbs and verb phrases in your paper, revise the affected sentences. (See page 495 in the "Handbook.")

9. Does your essay stand as a *reasoned process*, or does it consist of a series of unsupported assertions or opinions? Watch for clues in the openings of your sentences. "I believe . . . ," "I think . . ." are signs that the statements cannot stand alone and need your presence to convince the reader. (See pages 206–207.)

10. Have you sufficiently defined and narrowed the topic? If in looking over the paper you find it studded with overgeneralizations, you have probably taken on a topic that is too big. *Be sure to consult your instructor before beginning to be sure the subject can be covered adequately in the time and space allotted.* (See "Problems of Subject and Focus," pages 161–192.)

EXERCISES

EXERCISE 1, FOCUS. *Write out* summarizing sentences *and* titles *for the following statements of purpose. For the sake of the exercise, suppose that you have been asked to write 800-word essays.*

1. *Purpose:* To outline the steps involved in painting a bedroom.

2. *Purpose:* To tell the story of my first encounter with authority (police, boss, dean, and so on.).
3. *Purpose:* To define *affluence*.
4. *Purpose:* To compare this year's holiday (Christmas, Labor Day, July the 4th) with last year's.
5. *Purpose:* To prove that strict punishment of children is the best way to raise them.

EXERCISE 2, VIEWPOINT. *(1) Describe an incident in which you met a friend at an airport, bus station, disco, X-rated movie, or the like. Tell of the encounter first from your point of view, then from your friend's. (2) Select some other incident—an argument, a news event—and try narrating it from first a serious, then a humorous perspective.*

EXERCISE 3, DEFINITION. *Most one sentence definitions follow a three-part order according to which the thing to be defined is stated, then the class to which it belongs, and finally the specific differences that set it apart from other things in the same class. Here are some examples:*

A *car* is a *four-wheeled vehicle* designed *to transport up to eight people from one place to another.*

A *dog* is a *hairy four-legged animal* that *serves primarily as a domestic pet.*

A *house* is a *building with several rooms* in which *one family normally lives.*

A *six-shooter* is a *hand-held weapon* that *fires six shots.*

The third component in these definitions could be expanded or made up of different details, most of which would define the term adequately. The trick is to be as specific as possible in stating differences: note that our definition of a dog could also apply to a cat.

1. Write specific one-sentence definitions of the following words:

soccer	ambivalence	hammer
blender	groupie	fate
Marine	pants	phony

2. The student essay below attempts to define the term *bigot*. What techniques does he use? Does he make clear the distinctions between a bigot and, say, a hypocrite? What of the people he chooses as examples of bigots? Would some other term be appropriate for any of these? In the last paragraph does the writer go beyond simple definition? If so what is he saying?

BIGOT

[1] A bigot is a Klansman. A bigot is a property owner who has no rooms when he has many. A bigot is a wealthy person who has an idea that poor people exist, but really doesn't care as long as they remain separate. The word bigot means these things and many much uglier scenes. White bigots, black bigots, rich or poor--bigotry has no racial or economic boundaries. Poor people very often are bigoted against the wealthy. Snobbery and discrimination come to mind when I think of the word bigot. Hatred and contempt also describe it. Fear, though, may be the key word to understanding bigotry. A fear that someone might be bigger, darker, richer, or smarter than one's self. From that initial fear stems all the hatred and contempt most of us try to ignore.

[2] A bigot in today's society may not be too dangerous if he's not in a position of power. He goes through life with fear and hatred inside himself, but often his only outlet is his family. He screams at them about the black people because they won't work, the Catholics because they pray too much, the Jews because of their wealth, and the Polish people because they're dumb. Any person or group is vulnerable to attack from the bigot, ninety-nine percent of the time verbal and, most often, not to their face. This is not to say that a person with these feelings can't cause very real and serious trouble.

[3] In America's nineteenth century bigotry against Native Americans was, in fact, deadly. Many thousands of people, whites and Indians, were killed during the so-called "Indian Wars." The redman was a savage, a beast, lower than a dog in many people's minds. The white European bigots could not, and would not attempt to understand his religion, the way he dressed, the way he ate his food. Bigotry killed the American Indian.

[4] In this century too, we have been witness to many such instances of bigotry. Adolf Hitler turned Germany into a nation of bigots and killers the likes of which the world has never seen before. If a person wasn't blond-haired and blue-eyed, with certification to prove his pure Arianism, his hold on life was tenuous at best. The suffering the Jewish people underwent is unbelievable. Some of Hitler's subordi-

nates have said they didn't really know what was
happening, that mass murder was not an official policy of the Hitler regime. Official or not, it caused
many millions of people terrible suffering and
death. Although millions of black people have not
been murdered in the United States, they have suffered both physically and emotionally. Bigotry has
not been an official policy of our government any
more than that of Hitler's, yet it has caused the
black man to feel he does not belong and is not
wanted here.

[5] Bigotry is psychological. Something in our minds
tells us that we are right and they are wrong. We
cannot control the way someone thinks or feels. We
can control actions to a degree--hopefully to a high
enough degree to prevent another Indian massacre or
Jewish genocide. I doubt, though, that we can really
control bigotry.

[6] I do believe we can fight against it. Individuals
must first want to do away with bigotry and then
find the roots of their prejudices. When, as individuals, we begin to understand these prejudices,
then as groups, we can work to fight bigotry.

[7] Bigotry is like a cancer; it feeds on its victim
until both are destroyed. Bigotry and cancer are
both ruthless killers, each as deadly as the other.
But there is one major difference--the control of
cancer is foreseeable.

--TERRY SICKEL

EXERCISE 4, DESCRIPTION. *(1) Describe a scene that has
changed dramatically since you first knew it—a neighborhood, a
house or building, a room. Use metaphors and similes wherever
possible to make the description more vivid. (2) Write a description
of yourself as if you were the subject of a newspaper article. Try
to isolate some feature of your personality—a hobby, something in
your appearance—that might make you interesting to a newspaper
audience.*

EXERCISE 5, THE BOOK OR MOVIE REVIEW. *Write a
short, one-page review of a movie or book you have seen or read
recently. Then, compare that movie or book with another by the
same director or author. Make a decision about which is better
and why. Look over the suggestions for planning and writing in
the Comparison and Contrast section of this chapter.*

EXERCISE 6, DIRECTIONS. *Make a list of some operations
you believe you can perform better than anyone else: repairing a
stereo, baking bread, restringing and tuning a guitar, hanging wall-*

221

paper. Write the first draft of a process paper giving directions so clear that even your instructor might be able to perform the delicate task. Remember the goal of making the paper interesting and readable.

EXERCISE 7, BEGINNINGS. *Select a subject that you want to use for an essay of persuasion. Write four beginnings for it. With the help of your instructor pick out the most promising one and use it for your paper.*

1. Begin by using an imagined incident which illustrates the point of your paper or out of which a discussion may seem to arise.
2. Begin with evidence of the importance or the timeliness of your subject.
3. Begin with a shock or surprise opening.
4. Begin with a question or a series of questions.

EXERCISE 8, TOPIC OUTLINES. *Select three subjects from the list below and prepare a topic outline to show how a composition might be written on each of the subjects.*

Science fiction movies	Sexism	Urban crime
Presidential power	Freedom of speech	Depression
College education	Parental power	Rock music

EXERCISE 9, PROOFREADING. *Make a list of the errors you catch in your proofreading. Compare it with a similar list of corrections made by your instructor on your paper. Does this comparison suggest some hints for future proofreading? Are your missing errors of a particular kind?*

EXERCISE 10, ANALYSIS. *Here are two uncorrected student essays that may be analyzed in the same way your instructor reads and corrects your work. Consider some of the following questions in a written critique of the papers: Are the subjects adequately focused and limited? What order of presentation does each writer choose? Does the writer follow the principles of that order? Is the essay coherent? What types of beginnings and endings are used? Does the writer use more active verbs than passive ones? Is there anything in particular that the writer might do to improve the essay?*

UNCORRECTED STUDENT ESSAY 1[3]

Skewed Language

"Skewed language" is defined as biased or planted language. Many examples of skewed language can be found in English, especially with reference to women. The English language was formed to keep women in their inferior or secondary role.

Common examples of occupational names--postman, policeman, garbageman, fireman--give the impression that women can't hold these jobs. If a woman does hold a job, once thought to be only a man's job, she is labeled with lady or woman followed by the occupational name as in woman doctor, woman congressman, or lady engineer.

Our male-dominant standard of English is well illustrated in the words playboy and don juan. The feminine equivalents--loose woman or slut--have completely different connotations. While playboy is not degrading to the males, loose woman is certainly degrading to the females. Another example is the single male, the glamorous bachelor, as opposed to the single female, the old maid or spinster.

The English language also has many words that reduce women to animals. Chick, bunny, and mouse are common examples. Although some expressions for men also refer to animals, they are the big, strong animals like tiger, cat and fox, which show the dominance of male over female.

Throughout the entire English language, there are many derogatory and degrading words aimed at women but very few, if any, aimed at men.

UNCORRECTED STUDENT ESSAY 2[4]

Law and Disorder

To my thinking the movie <u>Law and Disorder</u> was written for today's times and people. Most people are becoming more and more concerned with the amount of violence and crimes that occur and the increase of crime each year. There are many ideas as to what can be done to combat crime and protect the citizen and one idea is to form a group and patrol your own neighborhood. This is the idea the movie used and tried to show what chould happen.

The crimes they used were possibly extreme or exaggerated, yet they do happen: a car is parked on a street and in five minutes is completely stripped; a man lowers himself by rope from the roof of an apartment building, climbs in an open window, takes the TV, ties it on the other end of the rope and he goes down to the next floor, while the TV goes to

---

[3] Reprinted by permission of the author, Cheryl Boes.
[4] Reprinted by permission of the author, Virginia Stoker.

the roof. All this happens while the occupant is in
the kitchen fixing a sandwich.

The people living in this neighborhood were getting more furious each time the police were unable
to protect them, so they decided to form a group to
help the police and patrol their own neighborhood.

I thought the movie was quite good in pointing out
some of the things that could happen. What began as
trying to help the police turned into the group trying to be or thinking they were the police. Instead
of wearing their own clothes they needed uniforms
that looked like police uniforms, then they needed
to act like policemen so they must drill. It was
like watching a group of children so excited about
their new game and one of the children has an idea
to go one step further and another step until it is
not at all what the game originally was. Not being
satisfied with walking the streets they purchased an
old police car with a siren that they put on top.
Now they could ride around like policemen and with
the radio go on police calls outside their neighborhood. They answered a police call and in trying to
be regular policemen one of their group was shot and
killed. Their police car had been shot at and they
were a group of very confused frightened men.

The ending was not at all what they had thought it
would be: I think they had hoped to be heroes and
instead one person was dead, and I don't think they
realized what they had done that caused his death.

To me the show was effective and I don't think it
could have ended any other way. It gave the problem,
the increase in crime and what we can do about it.
It took one of many answers and showed what could
happen.

EXERCISE 11, PAPER TOPICS. *These suggested paper topics
can be covered in essays of 500–1000 words. Before writing on
any of them be sure to review the appropriate section in this chapter.
Decide beforehand as well on your purpose, title, and central idea.*

1. Most television programs, especially soap operas, represent a picture of life that contrasts significantly with
   what we call reality. Analyze one of these programs,
   pointing out specifically how incidents in it differ from
   real life.
2. Write an essay in which you convince your reader that
   automobile companies should produce electric cars;
   or that businesses and industries should develop and
   use more underground space; or that the housing industry should build more solar-heated homes. Con-

struct the essay so that the opposing arguments are given due weight.

3. Point out the fallacies in the following statements. Then write an essay on one of them showing how the kind of thinking revealed in the statement is practiced in other areas of society.

The last two times we went to the game the Royals lost. We are not going to any more games so that they will be sure to win them.

Reagan's ideas are very conservative; he will not be able to get along with a Democrat-dominated Congress.

Experience proves that good guys finish last.

Carter's 1976 campaign speeches show that he believes in a strong defense for our country.

4. Decide on some event in your recent experience—an accident, a near accident, an argument, a victory in some sport or game—and write an essay detailing its causes and effects. Try to pinpoint the most important cause and effect.

5. Compose an interview with a friend, a famous person, or an imaginary personality. Write the interview as a question and answer exchange, aiming at a full representation of the person's likes and dislikes. Remember that your reader knows next to nothing about your subject.

6. Select a review of a film or book or musical or dramatic performance from some local newspaper or national magazine. Cut it out and tape it to a sheet of blank paper. Then write a critique of the review, showing what you learned from it, the writer's biases, and your own expectations. Decide whether the reviewer has satisfied your definition of the job.

7. Write closing paragraphs for the two essays that might follow these opening paragraphs. Make some reference to the beginning, but be sure not simply to restate the openings.

The scientific technique called behavior modification has lately fallen into disfavor—and deserves to. Not that it has ever been deemed particularly reprehensible to modify behavior. What else is the time-honored purpose of all persuasion and all education? We constantly seek to induce others to behave as they "ought" or as we would wish them to. And we accept that others freely and routinely do the same to us.

—ALBERT ROSENFELD, "The 'Behavior Mod' Squad"

What has happened to the art of conversation? By conversation I am not thinking merely of word exchanges between individuals. I am thinking of one of the highest manifestations of the use of human intelligence—the ability to transform abstractions into language; the ability to convey images from one mind to another; the ability to build a mutual edifice of ideas. In short, the ability to engage in a civilizing experience.

—GEORGE C. McGHEE, "The Lost Art of Conversation"

8. Think of certain words you hear used with different connotations or shadings of meaning. Write an essay on a particular word or set of words, describing the context in which the meanings occur. Some examples: *boss, nice, mean, funny, beautiful.*

9. Detail the steps in a process that everyone must go through at some time or another. Registering for classes is a good example; applying for a loan is another. In the rest of your essay outline a modification of this process, showing how specific changes would improve it.

10. Write an essay in which you take the position that television news reporting is inferior to newspaper or newsmagazine reporting. Try to think of at least four reasons for your stand and devote a paragraph to each. After completing a first draft, cut the paper into individual paragraphs and rearrange these on a blank sheet of paper. You may want to do this more than once. Was your original structure or ordering better than the later one(s)? Then write a final draft of the paper.

7 *Writing Themes*

About Literature

and Film

Themes about literature and film require the same careful planning, statement of purpose, supported arguments, and coherent organization as essays of persuasion. There are, however, some special features of such critical essays that call for a separate chapter on the subject. We have used the word *critical* in the last sentence to underscore the truth that writing themes about literature and film calls for the honing of evaluative, analytical tools. Like the science student looking through his or her first microscope, the beginning critic will have to learn to name what he or she sees and to describe its pattern or design. Both the critic and the scientist will also have to know how to determine whether or not the discovery is worthwhile.

You have no doubt seen at some time a television commercial in which a gray-haired, trustworthy-looking man tells an anxious patient in his most sincere voice that in his medical experience a certain painkiller outperforms all others. While he is delivering this testimonial there appears at the bottom of the screen the announcement: "This is a dramatization." From this statement we glean that the speaker is not a doctor and that the drug probably is not all that much better or different from others like

227

it. In a similar way, literature dramatizes incidents instead of directly stating them, as an essayist would. Poems, plays, novels, films—all of these literary forms subscribe to the same concept of implication; imaginative writers tell stories or describe emotions without forcing them to express certain morals, or testimonials. This does not mean that literature does not teach us something about life and human behavior. What we learn, however, comes not from direct pronouncement but by way of developing *themes,* the central or controlling ideas of literature. The first step of the critical writer is to locate these themes and to explain how they function in the work.

Because imaginative writers imply rather than state directly, the beginning critic must read the work or view the film, paying careful attention to its structure. Repeated contact will help make the work less imposing, an experience comparable to the reduction of tension you feel in the presence of your English instructor. Once a pattern is discerned—of words, actions, images—the critic must attempt to describe it in his or her own words. This process is called *paraphrase.*

PARAPHRASE

Paraphrasing a poem is of course less complex than summarizing *War and Peace* or *Shōgun.* In these instances, however, some statement of literal meaning provides the clay with which you will shape your essay. A review of the events in the plot of a novel like *David Copperfield* would prove of special value to your reader in a discussion of some particular scene or character. An essay on a selected poem may well include the paraphrase itself as a means of illustrating features of a difficult passage.

Here is a short passage spoken by one of Shakespeare's great villain heroes, and a paraphrase.

> Life's but a walking shadow, a poor player
> That struts and frets his hour upon the stage
> And then is heard no more.
>
> —*Macbeth*

Paraphrase: Life is like an actor who plays out his short part and then exits.

As you see, the paraphrase guts Shakespeare's lines of their poetic strength and beauty. But a paraphrase is essentially a translation; it is important for the translator to grasp the basic meaning of the passage. Often, unfortunately, the nuances of the original are lost. In the case of a novel, short story, or film, the act of paraphrase involves describing what happens to the main character or characters in the work.

Explication

Explication is the next step following paraphrase. The word means more than just *explaining,* although a good explication gives the reader a better understanding of the work. *Explication* also means "analysis" or "interpretation." It is the writer's chance to look for that implied theme or meaning we spoke of earlier. In the case of the *Macbeth* passage, a possible explication might be

For Macbeth at this point in the play, life has become an illusion that has deceived him, much as an actor deceives an audience about the role he is playing. In Macbeth's case the choice of metaphor is significant, since he now realizes that the Witches have led him to believe incorrectly that he is invincible. This speech marks the fatalism that will direct his behavior in the final scenes. Macbeth is a victim of equivocation, a major theme in the tragedy.

This explication relates the passage to the speaker's character and indicates how the imagery supports the central idea of the play. The writer has begun a process of interpretation that could lead into other areas as well: the role of the Witches, Macbeth's past behavior, and his relationship with his wife. Limited by the writer's purpose, explication is really the essence of critical writing. But it cannot proceed until the writer has attempted some sort of paraphrase.

229

Some Critical Approaches: Form First

Whether writing about poems, plays, novels, or films, the beginning critic should be aware that there are some standard topics or subjects that might be profitably investigated. Before the actual writing, however, it is important to determine the form or genre of the work you intend to discuss. Once you discover that the poem in question is, say, a sonnet, you will recognize its fourteen lines and particular rhyme scheme as *conventions* of the form. This discovery will help to avoid the trap of comparing a sonnet to an epic poem or an elegy. A detective novel like Raymond Chandler's *The Big Sleep* should likewise not be compared to the romantic epic *War and Peace* just because both are novels. Tolstoy's monumental work intends to chronicle the spectacular adventures of a Russian family in the Napoleonic age. Chandler, on the other hand, writes about a hard-boiled detective trying to solve an elaborate murder mystery in 1940's Los Angeles. Determining form will help you to understand the boundaries of a particular literary world, leading to comparisons with other worlds of a similar kind. You can get some help for this investigation into form from introductions, book jackets, and histories or anthologies of literature. We list some useful books at the end of the chapter.

Theme Approach

Unlike the well-controlled persuasion essay you might write for your English course, a work of literature may not be so easily boiled down into a central thesis that can be stated in one sentence. The quote from *Macbeth* that we paraphrased in a sentence implies the theme of illusion and reality, but it also introduces the idea of fatalism or determinism, a theme that especially dominates the close of the action. An effort to locate and state one theme is also likely to distort the work to some degree, leading us to relate everything else in it to that theme. In addition some poems, like this *haiku* (a poem of seventeen syllables

230

originated by the Japanese), cannot be said to present a theme but instead aim at recounting emotions or reactions:

> The piercing chill I feel:
>   my dead wife's comb, in our bedroom,
>   under my heel. . . .
> —TANAGUCHI BUSON (trans. by Harold G. Henderson)

Discussing this poem's imagery, an approach we will examine later, would yield considerably more than analysis of its theme.

To write a successful essay on theme in a literary work or movie, you need to recognize first that the theme you select is likely to be one of several that might be identified. Your task is to convince the reader that *your* theme is significant and essential to an understanding of the work. Shakespeare's *Macbeth,* for example, is a study of a man who becomes so driven by ambition that he ignores all moral restraints and kills the rightful king of Scotland to win the crown. In order to persuade your reader that this is the correct way to read the play, you should begin with the three-step prewriting formula we have outlined elsewhere.

Purpose: To convince the reader that the theme of ambition in in *Macbeth* best illustrates the fate of the hero and the state.

Title: The Magnetic Crown: Ambition in *Macbeth*

Thesis: Macbeth is so completely blinded by ambition that he violates the significant moral and ceremonial laws that hold society together, destroying himself and nearly destroying the state.

Armed with these guides, you can begin to gather supporting details as you would for any persuasion essay. The Witches tempt Macbeth by promising him the kingship, but Macbeth himself decides to kill the king. Lady Macbeth reinforces Macbeth's ambition and helps him to commit the murder, but after the killing of Banquo, Macbeth's

231

idea, she too becomes a victim of ambition. Macbeth murders Duncan while the king is both asleep and resting in Macbeth's own castle, thereby violating moral, familial, and social laws and customs. Macbeth's ambition blinds him to the reality that he has no heirs to inherit his tainted crown. He soon experiences the paranoiac fear that tells him other lords—Banquo, Macduff—seek to depose him; as a result, he launches a reign of terror and murder that nearly destroys Scotland. We have obviously struck a rich vein in the play; its yield gives to the essay the concreteness and evidence that make for good critical writing.

In the process of exploring the theme of ambition you should recognize the existence of other themes in *Macbeth.* For instance, there are references throughout to free will and fate. In fact, some commentators on the play believe the Witches direct Macbeth to kill King Duncan, thereby sealing his fate. Given this reading, the theme of fate or determinism becomes central to the action. While acknowledging this interpretation, however, you might point out that the Witches' prophecy only complements Macbeth's own ambition; the murders of Duncan, Banquo, and others are not controlled by any supernatural force. A sound, thoughtful argument will convince the reader that the theme of ambition is more central to *Macbeth* than any of the other pretenders.

A caution: Be sure that the theme you choose is in fact an established pattern in the work. Try as well to be as specific as possible in stating the theme: "Love in *Romeo and Juliet*" is obviously too broad. Such a title will leave the reader asking about the difference between love as a *subject* and some depiction of love (Shakespeare calls it "star-crossed" in *Romeo and Juliet*) as a *theme.*

Structure Approach

Any essay about the structure of a literary work or film must pay attention to the elements or parts that make up the work or film. If you choose to write such an essay, your task will require analysis of such parts as chapters (novels), scenes (plays or films), stanzas (poems), and a discussion of how they function in the whole design. For example, an examination of the structure of *Macbeth* might reveal the growing isolation of the hero as the scenes in which he appears after the banquet (III.iv) find him alone. Or you might argue that the structure of the plot moves slowly toward greater tension and conflict (called *rising action*) until the *climax* of the banquet scene, after which events transpire rapidly and the action "falls" to a resolution or *dénouement* with the killing of Macbeth. Another possibility is to show that the main incident of the final scene—the beheading of Macbeth—is meant to recall the opening of the play, in which the traitor Cawdor, whose title Macbeth inherits, is beheaded. Essays following these patterns of organization demonstrate how the themes of the work are presented through the structure or design. An essay on alternating comic and serious scenes in Shakespeare would be concerned with the way a particular mood is created.

There are at least three recognized ways of talking about structure. Concentrating on any or all of these will help you to grasp more firmly just what literary structure is.

1. Setting. Determining where the action takes place will get you started thinking about how setting is related to structure. If events begin in one place and the action then shifts to another, the writer may logically discuss how the two settings are similar and different. More particularly, you might compare the way the main character behaves in each setting. In *Huckleberry Finn,* for example, the main structural thread is the Mississippi River, on which Huck and Jim travel to freedom. Their river life is also meant to contrast with their experiences on shore, where they are often victims of prejudice or blind rage. In *Macbeth,* the hero's castle, where much of the action takes place, is a scene of tension and terror that is contrasted with the atmosphere in England, a healthy, well-governed realm. Alternating settings can establish a pattern in which we as readers observe significant differences or similarities between characters and events. Of special interest is the way in which setting is associated with the main character, how it compares with or even determines his or her own nature.

2. Time Sequences. Events in plays, films, novels, and short stories are narrated chronologically as a rule. A sequence of events covers a period of time with some sense of beginning, middle, and end. Novels like *David Copperfield* take the reader from the hero's birth to his maturity; others, like *In Cold Blood,* concern only a short, intense period in the lives of killers and victims. The passing of time in *Macbeth* is somewhat indefinite, although we can say with some certainty that Shakespeare attempts to compress time in order to create a fast pace that nicely parallels Macbeth's breakneck rise to power. Through flashbacks authors suspend time to allow for the sketching in of details about character and motivation. A study of time sequence might examine variations in the pace of time's passing, interruptions for flashbacks and their relation to the main time sequence, or gaps in time between events. This latter technique is a favorite one in films, where narration is often not as careful as it is in fiction.

3. Emotion and Suspense. Imaginative writers and filmmakers often build their works on the principle of suspense, keeping their readers and viewers emotionally involved in the action. One way to achieve this effect is to arrange scenes or chapters so that gradual discovery and suspension of our emotions are achieved. A classical example of suspense is the plot of *Oedipus Rex* by the Greek playwright Sophocles. The hero seeks out the cause of drought and sickness in his kingdom at the opening of the tragedy. As the play progresses we realize that he is the cause of the curse on his land: He has unwittingly murdered his father and married his mother. The perfect example of a philosophical murder story, *Oedipus Rex* reveals parts of its terrible truth through witnesses who are brought in for questioning. The last witness, a shepherd who knows the true story of Oedipus's birth, clinches the case against the king, who then blinds himself in remorse for his deed. Sophocles scores a brilliant coup by making the audience aware of Oedipus's guilt long before he is. This effect is known as *dramatic irony,* a significant part of good dramatic structure.

Novelists may manipulate our feelings toward particular characters by skillful arrangement of parts or scenes. In Dickens's *Great Expectations* the hero Pip first encounters the convict Magwitch in a graveyard. This opening scene of terror is firmly impressed on our minds as Pip describes his fears and feelings of guilt for having helped Magwitch escape. When Magwitch later appears in the novel, emerging almost from the grave, Pip expects him to expose his guilt to the world. In fact, Magwitch turns out to be Pip's unknown benefactor, providing money for his education and career in return for Pip's assistance. Like the hero, we too are surprised and elated because Dickens has prepared us to think of the old convict as selfish and an enemy to happiness. The structure of *Great Expectations* could in fact be described as following a pattern of *reversal,* with each chapter establishing a mood that is "reversed" or modified in the next. The result is greater pleasure for the reader.

As we have said, your evaluation of the structure of a film or literary work will concern how each part (chapter, scene, stanza) contributes to the whole. What is the cumulative effect of the ordering of incidents on the overall work?

A caution: Do not simply recount events in the plot and suppose you have written an essay on structure. You must evaluate these events, compare them to others, and point out how the pattern reinforces the themes of the work.

When recounting events in a literary work or film remember to use the *present tense:* "Macbeth *responds* to Banquo's ghost by *throwing* his goblet at him." Assume that the story is unfolding for the first time as you read it, and this perception will prevent you from lapsing into the past tense.

Character Approach

An essay on a character or characters can be both easy to handle and indicative of the author's ability to portray rounded personalities. In essence, such an essay follows the process of *description*, focusing on the details of appearance, manner, and behavior that are depicted in the work. But the essay goes beyond description and into evaluation when you attempt to prove some thesis about the character. Analyzing Macbeth, you might argue that he is a tragic figure because he possesses so many traits of greatness that are eventually destroyed by his ambition. In gathering information about him, you need to consider first his own speeches and actions. The early part of the play, for example, is marked by his serious reflections on the Witches' prophecies. When Lady Macbeth urges him to murder King Duncan, Macbeth delivers speeches in which he depicts the moral horror of such a deed. After the murder, however, his speeches and actions become those of a frightened, hallucinating villain, vowing to destroy all real and imagined enemies.

In addition to Macbeth's speeches and actions, we have his relations with other characters as a means of studying him. His friendship with Banquo seems firm at the play's opening, but soon after Macbeth becomes king the two are separated by mutual suspicion. Macbeth eventually has Banquo killed because he fears the Witches' prophecy that Banquo's heirs will become kings. Macbeth's relationship with Lady Macbeth is probably the most complex and fascinating one of its kind in literature. She at first dominates him, literally shaming him into the murder of Duncan with taunts about his manhood. But with the murder of Banquo we see her influence declining until, overwhelmed by suppressed guilt, she suffers the fate—madness and death—that should have visited Macbeth. He instead grows more isolated and tyrannical.

In any analysis of character, some attempt should be made to comment on the work's main theme or themes.

236

Macbeth's transformation from hero to tyrant can be neatly tied to the theme of ambition, the force that destroys his humane qualities of imagination and compassion. You may also want to say something about how successful the writer is in depicting a believable character. In *Macbeth* the hero could have easily slipped into a stereotyped villain, but Shakespeare takes pains to differentiate him from the stereotype by exploring the inner recesses of his mind. The soliloquy, a speech of self-assessment delivered while the speaker is alone on stage, proves to be a useful device for individualizing character in drama.

Point of View

In fiction the author has a choice of ways to narrate the story. The adoption of a particular *point of view* is especially crucial to our understanding and perception of character. The following are standard points of view that you should be aware of before assessing character in a work of fiction.

Omniscient Narrator. As an omniscient narrator the author acts as a god who is able to see into the minds and reveal the thoughts of all the characters. He is free not only to manipulate the characters and action but also to comment, often ironically, on the behavior of his creations. A masterpiece of omniscient narration is Henry Fielding's *Tom Jones,* a comic novel about the raucous adventures of a foundling child. Here is a description of Miss Bridget, a none too attractive woman supposed to be Tom's mother, and her affection for a none too attractive man named Captain Blifil:

> Tho' Miss Bridget was a Woman of the greatest Delicacy of Taste; yet such were the charms of the Captain's Conversation, that she totally overlooked the Defects of his Person. She imagined, and perhaps very wisely, that she should enjoy more agreeable Minutes with the Captain than with a much prettier Fellow; and forewent the Consideration of pleasing her Eyes, in order to procure herself much more solid Satisfaction.

237

Fielding uses highly inflated and general diction to tell us, while winking his eye, that Miss Bridget is out to snare this man at all costs because it might be her last chance. An omniscient author might achieve a similar effect by contrasting the inner thoughts of two characters.

Objective Narrator. This technique of narration allows the reader to see and hear the characters in action, without any comments by the narrator. One character may describe and interpret the action of others, but these opinions must then be judged against his or her prejudices: this speaker is not the author. Whatever conclusions are drawn from the action must be based on details presented in the dramatic setting the author establishes. Ernest Hemingway uses the dramatic point of view with particular effect in his novels about expatriates and members of the lost generation.

I mistrust all frank and simple people, especially when their stories hold together, and I always had a suspicion that perhaps Robert Cohn had never been middleweight boxing champion, and that perhaps a horse had stepped on his face, or that maybe his mother had been frightened or seen something, or that he had, maybe, bumped into something as a young child, but I finally had somebody verify the story from Spider Kelly. Spider Kelly not only remembered Cohn. He had often wondered what had become of him.

An omniscient narrator would not waste time identifying Robert Cohn as a middleweight boxing champion, but because Jake is a character in the story he is telling he feels free to voice his suspicions about this intruder. The passage actually tells us as much about Jake as it does about Robert Cohn.

First-Person Narrator. The point of view of this narrator is that of a main character who tells the story using the first-person pronoun *I*. This *I* should not automatically be taken for the author, although in William Styron's novel *Sophie's Choice* the main character Stingo's experiences as a fledgling writer living in Brooklyn seem to parallel those of the author. In both fiction and poetry it is probably

238

wise to consider the first-person narrator as a character with a life and viewpoint that are separate from those of the author. The main character's way of speaking and behaving will greatly affect the language and style of the work. Holden Caulfield, the young hero of J. D. Salinger's *The Catcher in the Rye,* uses a colloquial style that seduces us into seeing the adult world as made up of "phonies" in spite of our better judgment. Huck Finn also has a disarmingly frank style that makes him as intriguing as the events and characters he describes. Although most first-person narrators are major characters, there are some works in which minor figures assume that role. In F. Scott Fitzgerald's *The Great Gatsby,* Nick Carroway holds a position of relative unimportance compared to the role of *his* hero Gatsby. An essay on the first-person narrator in a particular novel might usefully discuss how the novel would change should the narration shift to an omniscient or dramatic point of view.

Caution: Be sure you identify the point of view before beginning to write about a character. The way in which that character has been created will determine his or her role in the work.

Imagery Approach

As we pointed out in the discussion of description, imagery refers to the picture-making quality of language. Pictures are made with *metaphors* and *similes,* both of which are, in effect, comparisons of one thing to another. Here is a striking simile from *Macbeth:*

> And pity, like a naked, new-born babe
>   striding the blast . . .
> Shall blow the horrid deed in every eye.

The use of *like* or *as* signals a simile. Shakespeare compares pity to trumpet-blowing cherubim spreading word of Macbeth's murder of King Duncan throughout the realm. In order to qualify as a simile the statement has to compare two things that are dissimilar in kind. "Your car is like mine" is not a simile; "Your car is like a metal ladybug" is a simile. Similes usually limit or refer to only one trait the two things have in common: pity in the *Macbeth* quote has the effect on us of children crying out. Metaphors drop the linking word *as* or *like*—"Pity *is* a naked, new-born babe"—and also allow for a greater number of similarities or connotations. Macbeth's "Life's but a walking shadow" could mean that life is an illusion or that it is ghostlike, with the connotation of *sinful* or *damned* attached. Both connotations can apply at the same time, since they are not mutually exclusive but in fact complementary.

Here are some examples of similes and metaphors from different kinds of poems:

> He watches from his mountain walls,
> And like a thunderbolt he falls.
> > —ALFRED, LORD TENNYSON, "The Eagle"

> Her feet beneath her petticoat
> Like little mice stole in and out,
> As if they feared the light. . . .
> > —SIR JOHN SUCKLING, "A Ballad Upon a Wedding"

> The wind stood up and gave a shout. . . .
> > —JOHN STEPHENS, "The Wind"

> Old age is
> a flight of small
> cheeping birds
> skimming
> bare trees
> above a snow glaze.
> > —WILLIAM CARLOS WILLIAMS, "To Waken an Old Lady"

Tennyson's eagle is compared to a thunderbolt falling on an unwary victim. Suckling tries to catch the bride's timidity on her wedding day by observing that her nervous feet look like frightened mice. These similes point to specific qualities in the comparison: speed and nervous movement.

240

Stephens's metaphor catches the wind's power, its loudness: Is it also calling out defiantly to us? Williams allows even more room for connotation in his metaphor. We hear the shrill sounds sometimes associated with aged voices, and we observe a winter scene of bareness and stark whiteness that is associated with death. Could the flight of the birds represent the eternal desire to escape the winter season of death?

If you are analyzing the imagery in a long poem or play or short novel, your best approach is to describe a pattern of such imagery. In *Macbeth,* for instance, blood imagery literally drenches the play. With what events and characters is blood associated as the play develops? Are there different types of blood images: innocent blood, the blood of traitors, blood lines? Is Shakespeare trying to paint the picture of a hero actually drowning in the blood of his victims? Images depicting the sea, colors, storms, birds, and so forth are common in many works of literature and are usually arranged in a comprehensible design. In some works an image may be repeated without any change in the formula. Papers dealing with repeated images might comment on how repetition transforms the image into a *symbol,* an action or object that implies a meaning beyond itself. The crown in *Macbeth* comes to symbolize the hero's ambition as we see it used by the Witches to mock his murder of Duncan and Banquo and his usurpation of the throne. Common symbols are flags, roses, swords, crosses, doves, and spider webs.

An essay on imagery or symbolism should attempt to show how the pattern is related to the work's main theme or themes. Blood imagery clearly pictures the results of Macbeth's ambition, especially in the murders of innocents like Banquo and Macduff's wife and children. There is also an element of irony in the pattern, since Macbeth's own blood has not produced a male heir to whom he can pass on his tainted crown. This connection with the main theme should be hinted at throughout the paper, not sprung on the reader in the last paragraph.

241

Perhaps the most difficult and yet satisfying critical essay is the study of a particular work or author's style. This kind of essay is difficult because it requires close reading and listing of qualities. You must pay attention, for example, to a writer's characteristic way of presenting characters, describing scenes, or making sounds. Like the attempt at assessing imagery, the stylistic essay is looking for patterns, an exercise that may well prove tedious when scouring the pages of *War and Peace.* But such an essay can prove especially rewarding when you feel you have unlocked the mystery of a writer's style. Your next encounter with his or her work should be more pleasurable precisely because you know what to look and listen for.

In beginning the essay on style, it is best to choose a representative sample of the work for analysis. A speech or soliloquy in a play, a character description in a novel, a whole short poem—these are manageable selections to study. Your conclusion will suggest how the passage or section is representative of the whole work.

Once you have decided on a sample, the next step is to examine its *diction.* The words chosen by writers tell us a good deal about their purposes. Formal words and constructions create a slow-paced, distanced tone that colors the way we perceive characters and events. Specific or concrete words create a mood of realism in a work; abstract or general words tend to cast events in a philosophical mold. (The way in which an author arranges words and images in fact creates a world for the literary work or film; this world must be understood on its own terms by anyone pretending to criticize it.) When denotative words predominate, the style is more likely to be descriptive of a material, realistic world; an abundance of connotative words, on the other hand, signals a more poetic, sometimes fantastic setting for events. Even the length of words can establish a particular rhythm that comes to distinguish the work. Consider the effect of the following passages on your ear:

242

The small, sleek car sped past and almost blew us off the road. We lost it in the dust cloud raised up ahead. Our rage was spent on two beers at the bar.

With supercilious pomposity the guardian of morals from our local tabloid unleashed a tirade of devastating adjectives on the inventive but unfortunately inept performance of Molière's satiric comedy by the community repertory company.

The differing sounds and rhythms clearly point to different voices, the latter assuming the stance of an educated, somewhat jaundiced commentator on the arts scene.

After words, *sentences* should be the next object of study in a paper on style. Questions about length are valid here too: Are the sentences varied in length? Are they predominantly short or long? Do they employ many points of punctuation? You will also want to consider types of sentences. If the author repeats questions, exclamations, or commands, the emerging pattern will affect the work's style in particular ways. Hamlet asks many questions besides "To be or not to be"; most of them are similarly philosophical and hard to answer. As a result the play seems to be full of unsolvable puzzles. In poetry and poetic drama, like *Hamlet,* word order will also affect style. Inverted sentences arrest the eye, focusing attention on a particular word: "Fate is the hunter" places greater emphasis on the word *fate* than does "The hunter is fate." Types of sentences give similar clues about style. A string of simple declarative sentences in a novel establishes a mood of reportial detachment. Sentence fragments—"Not me!" "Never again!"—create a mood of heightened emotion. As in the analysis of words, the central question is, "What pattern emerges in the passage?" Remember too that even though some poetic lines do not contain punctuation, the rules of sentence structure still apply.

Finally, you will want to determine the *sound effects* in a literary work or film. Poetry and poetic drama depend heavily on language that makes certain sounds, since the words in the work are meant to be spoken aloud. (Yes, poetry should be read aloud to determine sound and rhythm patterns.) To a lesser extent, fiction too depends on sound effects, although the narrative or story-telling purpose keeps the reader moving with language rather than stopping too frequently to listen to it. Sound effects and music obviously play a big part in movies; these features should be considered in any film review that pretends to give a full impression of the work.

Two favorite devices of imaginative writers concerned with sound effects are *alliteration* and *assonance*. Alliteration is the repetition of words that begin with the same letter or sound. It is an especially effective device for expressing a strongly felt emotion. Read aloud the following passage from John Donne's *Holy Sonnet XIV:*

> Batter my heart, three-personed God, for You
> As yet but knock, breathe, shine, and seek to mend.
> That I may rise and stand, o'erthrow me, and bend
> Your force to break, blow, burn, and make me new.

We can actually hear the sound of a battering ram in the *b* alliteration here. The speaker thinks such violent force is necessary to break through to his sinful heart. Alliteration should be saved for such special purposes in your own writing; excessive use of it is often the sign of amateur writing. Assonance is the repetition of internal vowel sounds in more than one word. Note the slow pace that marks the opening passage of Thomas Gray's *Elegy Written in a Country Churchyard:*

> The curfew tolls the knell of parting day,
> The lowing herd wind slowly o'er the lea. . . .

Rhyme can also contribute to the overall effect of poems, especially if the rhymed words repeat a particular sound. *Day* and *lea* in Gray's poem repeat the *a* sound that is later picked up in such words as *shade* and *grave*, both of which contribute to the funereal atmosphere.

As we said earlier, stylistic analysis of any passage should demonstrate how that section is representative of the whole work. You will note too that after the study of diction, sentence form, and sound effects is finished, the critic is obliged to relate these elements to the work's tone. Both tone and style will to a great extent be decided by the genre or form as well. Shakespeare's *Macbeth* is a tragedy, and its diction can be seen to conform to a pattern of formality and seriousness that befits the tragic form. In conducting your analysis, try to identify the stylistic traits that are unique to the author in question.

Caution: Do not simply list types of sentences or sound effects. Make the evidence part of a larger generalization or thesis that can be supported.

There are other approaches to critical writing besides those we have discussed here. The book or film review is treated in Chapter 5, "The Problems of Subject and Focus." The persuasion essay on *Casablanca* in the next chapter has sections that analyze particular scenes with an eye toward classifying them, another kind of critical activity. We suggest that you turn to these sections for further information and that you consult some of the books we have listed at the end of this chapter.

The short essay reproduced here illustrates how the analysis of character, imagery, and structure can be employed in the close reading of an individual passage.

HAMLET'S SELF-REVELATION:
A READING OF HAMLET, I, v, 95–109

Remember thee?	95
Ay thou poor ghost, whiles memory holds a seat	96
In this distracted globe. Remember thee?	97
Yea, from the table of my memory	98
I'll wipe away all trivial fond records,	99
All saws of books, all forms, all pressures past,	100
That youth and observation copied there,	101
And thy commandment all alone shall live	102
Within the book and volume of my brain,	103
Unmixed with baser matter, yes, yes, by heaven:	104
O most pernicious woman!	105
O villain, villain, smiling, damned villain!	106

My tables, meet it is I set it down   107
That one may smile, and smile, and be a villain,   108
At least I am sure it may be so in Denmark.   109

[1]   In this passage from Act I of *Hamlet*, Hamlet is alone on stage immediately after the ghost has left, and so the character addressed is the ghost, at least at first. Actually, the speech is a soliloquy, because Hamlet almost immediately seems to be talking to himself or to the open air. Although he speaks about the ghost, about his mother (who is the "most pernicious woman"), and about his uncle (the "villain"), *the real subject of the speech is himself.** His thoughts show his disturbed condition, his selection of words indicates his background as a student, and the rhythm in the concluding part of the speech shows his forthcoming preoccupation with the "ills that flesh is heir to."†*

[2]   *First of all the speech shows that Hamlet has been greatly disturbed by the Ghost's message that Claudius is a murderer.* Whereas previously the young prince has been melancholy, feeling the need to do something but with no reason for action, he is now promising the Ghost to remember him and his desire for revenge. If one assumes that Hamlet is a person of normal sensibility, thoughts of murderous vengeance would necessarily create confusion. Such disturbance, which Hamlet himself feels in his "distracted globe" (97), is shown by his resolution to wipe away "all trivial fond records" from the "table" of his memory (99, 98), and then by his action of writing in his "tables" that "one may smile, and smile, and be a villain" (108). Surely this contradiction between intention and action demonstrates his disordered state.

[3]   *Just as the contradiction reveals Hamlet's troubled mind, the diction reveals his background as a student and therefore it shows that Shakespeare has completely visualized and perfected Hamlet's character.* The words are those to be expected from a student whose mind is full of matters associated with school. *Table, records, saws of books, copied, book and volume of my brain, baser matters, tables, set it down*—all these smack of the classroom,

---

From *Rebels and Lovers: Shakespeare's Young Heroes and Heroines*, ed. Alice Griffin (New York University Press, 1976), p. 321.

   * Central idea.
   † Thesis sentence.

where Hamlet has so recently been occupied. And in lines 96 through 104 there is a complicated but brief description of Renaissance psychology, a subject that Hamlet has just been learning, presumably, at Wittenberg. Briefly, he states that his mind, or his memory, is like a writing tablet, from which he can erase previous experience and literature (the "pressures past" of line 100), and which he can then fill with the message that the ghost of his father has just transmitted to him. Even in the distracted condition of this speech, Hamlet is capable of analyzing and classifying what is happening to him. This is the reflexive action of a scholar.

[4]   *An additional indication of Hamlet's mental condition, perhaps a subtle one but certainly in keeping with Shakespeare's poetic genius, is the rhythm of the speech.* The full impact of what Hamlet is saying is that by wiping away all previous experience from his memory, and by thinking only about death and vengeance, his mind is taking a morbid turn. The last part of the speech is rhythmically consistent with this condition. There are many trochaic rhythms, which would have been described in Shakespeare's day as having a *dying fall.* There are thus falling rhythms on

$$\acute{\;}\quad\circ\quad\acute{\;}\quad\circ$$
$$\text{yes, by heaven}$$

and

$$\acute{\;}\quad\circ\quad\acute{\;}\quad\circ\qquad\acute{\;}\quad\circ\quad\acute{\;}\quad\circ\quad\acute{\;}\quad\circ$$
$$\text{O villain, villain, smiling, damned villain!}$$

The last two lines end with trochees *(villain, Denmark).* This rhythm is unlike most of what went before, but will be like most of what follows, particularly the interjections in the "To be or not to be" soliloquy and the conclusions in that soliloquy (on the word *action*).

[5]   *Since this passage reveals Hamlet's character so clearly, it is relevant to the rest of the play.* From this point onward Hamlet will constantly be spurred by this promise to the ghost, that the ghost's "commandment all alone shall live / Within the book and volume of . . . [his] brain" (102, 103) and Hamlet will feel guilty and will be overwhelmed with self-doubt and the urge for self-destruction because he does not act on this promise. His attitude toward Claudius, which previously was scornful, will now be vengeful. His budding

love for Ophelia will be blighted by his obsession with vengeance, and as a result Ophelia, a tender plant, will die. Truly, this passage can be regarded as the climax of the first act, and it points the way to the grim but inevitable outcome of the play.

EXERCISES

EXERCISE 1, PARAPHRASE AND EXPLICATION. *Paraphrase the following poem. Then write a short paragraph of explication. Remember that paraphrasing calls for restating the central idea or theme in other words. Explication requires evaluating any deeper or larger meaning in the passage. Be sure to look up any words you do not understand.*

> What is our life? A play of passion,
> Our mirth the music of division.
> Our mothers' wombs the tiring-houses be
> Where we are dressed for this short comedy.
> Heaven the judicious sharp spectator is,
> That sits and marks still who doth act amiss.
> Our graves that hide us from the searching sun
> Are like drawn curtains when the play is done.
> Thus march we, playing, to our latest rest,
> Only we die in earnest, that's no jest.
> —SIR WALTER RALEGH

EXERCISE 2, THEME. *Select a short story or poem and write a 500-word essay about its central theme. Show how any lesser themes are related to what you believe is the main theme.*

EXERCISE 3, STRUCTURE. *Select a novel or play and outline its setting, time sequence, and emotional or suspenseful features. Show how these elements are coordinated to create the structure of the work.*

EXERCISE 4, CHARACTER. *Select a major character from a novel, play, or film. Identify the point of view employed by the author (director) in presenting the character. Then describe the important ways in which the character is developed: author's descrip-*

tion, dialogue, inner monologue, comments by other characters, and so forth.

EXERCISE 5, IMAGERY. *Write an essay of 500–1000 words on one image pattern in a poem, short story, novel, or film. Make sure you show how this pattern is related to the main theme or themes.*

EXERCISE 6, STYLE. *Analyze the style of the following paragraph. After you have finished commenting on the diction, sentence form, sound effects and rhythm, identify the tone and mood of the passage. If possible read the whole work and indicate how this passage fits the overall style.*

I do therefore humbly offer it to public consideration, that of the hundred and twenty thousand children already computed, twenty thousand may be reserved for breed, whereof only one-fourth part to be males; which is more than we allow to sheep, black cattle, or swine; and my reason is, that these children are seldom the fruits of marriage, a circumstance not much regarded by our savages, therefore one male will be sufficient to serve four females. That the remaining hundred thousand may, at a year old, be offered in sale to the persons of quality and fortune through the kingdom; always advising the mother to let them suck plentifully in the last month, so as to render them plump and fat for a good table. A child will make two dishes at an entertainment for friends; and when the family dines alone, the fore and hind quarter will make a reasonable dish, and, seasoned with a little pepper or salt, will be very good boiled on the fourth day, especially in winter.

—JONATHAN SWIFT, From "A Modest Proposal"

SUGGESTED FURTHER READING

CIRCLOT, J. E. *A Dictionary of Symbols.* Trans. Jack Sage. New York: Philosophical Library, 1976.
GUERIN, WILFRED L., EARLE G. LABOR, LEE MORGAN, JOHN R. WILLINGHAM. *A Handbook of Critical Approaches to Literature.* 2nd ed. New York: Harper & Row, 1979.

HOLMAN, C. HUGH. ed. *A Handbook to Literature.* 3rd ed. New York: Odyssey Press, 1972.

JAMES, HENRY. *Theory of Fiction.* Ed. James E. Miller, Jr. Lincoln: University of Nebraska Press, 1972.

KENNEDY, X. J. *An Introduction to Poetry.* 3rd ed. Boston: Little, Brown, 1974.

MONACO, JAMES. *How to Read a Film.* New York: Oxford University Press, 1977.

PERRINE, LAURENCE. *Story and Structure.* 5th ed. New York: Harcourt Brace Jovanovich, 1978.

ROBERTS, EDGAR V. *Writing Themes About Literature.* 4th ed. Englewood Cliffs, N.J.: Prentice-Hall, 1977.

WIMSATT, W. K., JR. and CLEANTH BROOKS. *Literary Criticism: A Short History.* New York: Knopf, 1957.

8 | *The Research*

Paper

IMPORTANCE OF
THE RESEARCH PAPER

The research paper is an important and extended exercise in writing. It is best understood as an essay or report derived from the collection of data by research. *Research* is grand search. It means looking for a particular kind of information on a particular kind of subject in a particular kind of medium, and sorting the relevant findings according to some plan. Although the preparation of a research paper may depend on concentrated study of books, articles, and reports in the library—the study, in short, of someone else's research—it may be written after almost any kind of information-gathering exercise. Careful observation of your family's patterns of behavior on rainy days is, in this sense, a form of research.

There are many values and skills to be acquired from writing a research paper:

1. Practice in preparing the term papers that will be required in many of your college courses.
2. Acquisition of interesting and perhaps useful information about a special subject.
3. An increase in the ability to distinguish between facts and opinions.
4. An improved ability to *judge* material as well as to find it, to evaluate its worth, to organize it, and to present it in attractive form.

These skills are useful whether you compose a report for your speech class, a speech for the AMA or Young Democrats, or an article for the school newspaper.

THE USE OF THE LIBRARY

Although we must always take into account differences in size and organization of different libraries, a study of the resources of a library can still be taken up under three main headings: (1) the card catalog, (2) the general reference library, and (3) the guides and indexes to periodicals and bulletins.

The Card Catalog: Basic Guide to the Library

The starting point for exploration of the library is, logically, the *card catalog,* a collection of cards listing every book (including reference books), bulletin, pamphlet, and periodical the library owns.

The cards are arranged alphabetically according to authors, titles, and subjects. In other words, a large and complete library will have every book listed on at least three separate cards. You can therefore locate a book if you know the author's name, or the title, or the subject with which it deals. A listing in the card catalog, however, is no more than a record that the library believes it owns the work in question. A book on the shelves is worth two in the catalog, so remember that books should be checked out of the library by due process, not carried out surreptitiously under a coat.

Magazines and bulletins are usually listed by title—that is, the card catalog will tell you whether or not the library owns a certain magazine or series of bulletins. The card for a given magazine or bulletin will tell you which volumes are bound and shelved (and usually the call number to be used in asking for them), and which are stacked unbound in a storeroom. In most libraries there will be a duplicate list of periodicals for use in the reference library room. For detailed information about the contents of periodicals, bulletins, and newspapers you will have to consult the periodical indexes. These are listed and explained on pages 261–264.

Here is a typical library card.

```
ML3551  Rosen, David M
.R68
        Protest  songs  in  America,  by  David  Rosen.
    Foreword  by  David  Manning  White.  [Westlake
    Village,  Calif.]  Aware  Press  [1972]

        154  p.  20  cm.  $3.75
        Bibliography:  p.  151-154

        1.  Protest  songs--History  and  criticism.
        2.  Songs,  American--History  and  criticism.
        3.  American  ballads  and  songs.  I.  Title.
```

1. ML3551.R68 is the call number, according to the Library of Congress system. (See pages 255–256.)

2. "Rosen, David M" is the author's name, last name given first. The date of the author's birth (and death) may or may not appear on a card.

3. "Protest songs in America . . . [1972]" gives the title of the book, the author, the writer of the foreword, the place of publication, the publisher, and the copyright date.

4. The next line explains that the book contains 154 pages, that the shelf size (height on the shelf) of the book is 20 centimeters, and that its price is $3.75. Pages 151–154 contain a bibliography of related works.

5. The titles at the bottom of the card tell under what subjects the book may be found in the catalog. You can find this work by looking under Protest songs—History and criticism; Songs, American—History and criticism; American ballads and songs; and under the book title.

The card just examined is an *author card.* A *title card* is just like an author card, except that the title is typewritten at the top.

A *subject card* is an author card with the subject typed, usually in red, above the author's name at the top.

```
American ballads and songs

PS3515  Huston, John, 1906--
.U83        Frankie and Johnny.  Illustrated by Covar-
        rubias.  New York, B. Blom, 1968.

        160 p.  illus.  18 cm.
        Reprint of the 1930 ed.

        1. American ballads and songs.  I. Covarru-
        bias, Miguel, 1904-1957, illus.  II. Title.

    PS3515.U83FS 1968 812.54                    68-57190
Library of Congress                                 MARC
```

On the card just illustrated are two or three items not found in the specimen author card.

1. Both the Library of Congress and the Dewey Decimal call numbers are listed: PS3515.U83FS and 812.54. (Both numbering systems are described in the section that follows.)
2. "Library of Congress" indicates that the Library of Congress has a copy of the book.
3. The numbers and letters at the lower right are for the use of librarians in ordering copies of this card. They are of no interest to the general user of the card catalog.

To find information about a certain periodical consult your library's Serial Record. This collection of cards will tell you where to find the periodical in the library and how many and which volumes are available.

Call Numbers. A call number is a symbol or group of

symbols used by a library to designate a particular book. It consists frequently of two parts: the first, or upper, is the classification number, the second, or lower, the author and book number. The call number is typed on the upper left-hand corner of the card-catalog card, on the spine or binding of the book, and often inside the book's front or back cover. In most libraries, before you may take out a book, you must fill out a *call slip*. On this slip should appear the call number, the name of the author, and the title of the work. Your signature and whatever supplementary information the library requires complete the call slip.

For the undergraduate, a knowledge of the systems used in devising call numbers is relatively unimportant. To satisfy a natural curiosity on the part of many students, however, the following brief explanation is given.

Two classification systems are used by libraries in this country: the Library of Congress system and the Dewey Decimal system.

The Library of Congress System. The Library of Congress system, found more frequently in college than in public libraries, uses the letters of the alphabet, followed by additional letters and Arabic numerals, as the basis of its classification.

A	General works	M	Music
B	Philosophy—Religion	N	Fine arts
C	History—Auxiliary sciences	P	Language and literature
		Q	Science
D	History and topography	R	Medicine
E and F	American history	S	Agriculture
G	Geography—Anthropology	T	Technology
		U	Military science
H	Social sciences	V	Naval science
J	Political science	Z	Bibliography and library science
K	Law		
L	Education		

The following table shows the larger subdivisions under one of these main classes:

G Geography—Anthropology

G	Geography (General)
GA	Mathematical and astronomical geography
GB	Physical geography
GC	Oceanology and oceanography
GF	Anthropogeography
GN	Anthropology—Somatology—Ethnology
	Ethnogeography (General)

	51–161	Anthropometry—Skeleton—Craniometry
	400–499	Customs and institutions (Primitive)
	537–686	Special races
	700–875	Prehistoric archeology

GR	Folklore
GT	Manners and customs (General)
GV	Sports and amusements—Games

	201–547	Physical training
	1580–1799	Dancing

The Dewey Decimal System. The Dewey Decimal system, devised by Melvil Dewey, uses a decimal classification for all books. The entire field of knowledge is divided into nine groups, with an additional group for general reference books. Each main class and subclass is shown by a number composed of three digits.

000	General works	500	Natural science
100	Philosophy	600	Useful arts
200	Religion	700	Fine arts
300	Sociology	800	Literature
400	Philology	900	History

The following table shows the first subdivision under the literature class and the beginning of the intricate system of further subdividing under the 820 group.

800	Literature		
	810	American	
	820	English	
		821	English poetry
		822	English drama
			822.3 Elizabethan drama
			822.33 Shakespeare

830   German
840   French
850   Italian
860   Spanish
870   Latin
880   Greek
890   Minor literatures

The Reference Library

The reference library consists of all the general reference works, such as encyclopedias and dictionaries, and collections of pamphlets, bibliographies, guides, maps, and pictures that are to be consulted for some specific information rather than to be read in their entirety. Reference books ordinarily may not be taken from the library. The following list of reference books should be a starting point for your exploration of possible subjects. It is wise to know what they are, where these books are shelved, and how they can be used to the best advantage. The date given is usually the date of the latest revision. In this rapidly changing world, the date of publication may be very important in a reference book.

General Encyclopedias. A student using the *Britannica* and the *Americana* should consult the annual supplements, the *Britannica Book of the Year* and the *Americana Annual,* for additional information.

Encyclopaedia Britannica. 30 vols., 1975. Chicago: Encyclopaedia Britannica, Inc. Since 1940 the *Britannica* has been kept up to date by continuous revisions. The 15th ed. is divided into a macropedia (19 vols.), consisting of long, fully detailed articles, and a micropedia (10 vols.) of dictionarylike format. Both are arranged alphabetically. A single-volume propedia, or index, is arranged according to topic. The micropedia and propedia may be used as indexes to macropedia articles.

Encyclopedia Americana. 30 vols. New York: Americana Corporation. Like the *Britannica,* the *Americana* is now kept up to date by continuous revision. Hence the date is necessary with any reference to it.

257

Collier's Encyclopedia. 24 vols., 1973. New York: Crowell Collier, and Macmillan Publishing Co., Inc. Continuously revised. Although written in a popular style designed for the general rather than scholarly reader, it is objective and authoritative.

Special Encyclopedias. A special or limited encyclopedia is available for almost any subject of importance that one can think of. You may find a long list by looking under "encyclopedias" in the most recent annual volume of the *Cumulative Book Index.* Many of these special encyclopedias, once useful and authoritative, have not been revised recently. The information they contain is now dated. Others are valuable as historical records. Here are a few examples of this type of reference book:

The Catholic Encyclopedia. 15 vols. New York: McGraw-Hill Book Company, 1967. Although this work deals primarily with the accomplishments of Roman Catholics, its scope is very general. It is useful for subjects dealing with medieval literature, history, art, and philosophy.

The Jewish Encyclopedia. 12 vols. New York: Funk & Wagnalls, 1925.

McGraw-Hill Encyclopedia of Science and Technology. 15 vols. incl. yearbooks. New York: McGraw-Hill Book Company, 1960, 1966, 1971.

Encyclopedia of World Literature in the Twentieth Century. 3 vols. New York: Frederick Ungar Publishing Co., 1971.

Yearbooks. In addition to the general yearbooks listed here, there are yearbooks for many specialized fields. See the *Cumulative Book Index* or *Books in Print* for titles.

Britannica Book of the Year. Chicago: Encyclopaedia Britannica, Inc., 1938 to date.

Americana Annual. New York: Americana Corporation, 1923 to date.

Chambers' Encyclopedia Yearbook. London: International Learning Systems Corporation Limited, 1970 to date.

World Almanac and Book of Facts. New York: The New York World-Telegram and Sun, 1868–1967; Newspaper Enterprise Association Incorporated, 1967 to date.

Information Please Almanac. New York: Macmillan Publishing Co., Inc., 1947–1959; McGraw-Hill Book Company, 1960; Simon & Schuster, Inc., 1961 to date.

Economic Almanac. New York: National Industrial Conference Board, 1940 to date.

Statesman's Year-Book. London: Macmillan & Co., Ltd.; New York: St. Martin's Press, Inc., 1864 to date.

The Official Associated Press Almanac. New York: Almanac Publishing Company Incorporated, 1970 to date. (First published as *The New York Times Encyclopedia Almanac.*)

Guides to Reference Books. The following are the principal bibliographies of reference texts.

BARTON, MARY NEILL, and MARION V. BELL. *Reference Books: A Brief Guide.* 7th ed. 1970.

The Bibliographic Index. 1937 to date.

GATES, JEAN KAY. *Guide to the Use of Books and Libraries.* 2nd ed. 1969.

SHORES, LOUIS. *Basic Reference Sources: An Introduction to Materials and Methods.* 1954.

WINCHELL, CONSTANCE M. *Guide to Reference Books.* 8th ed. 1967.

A World Bibliography of Bibliographies. 4th ed., 5 vols. 1965–1966.

The Harper Encyclopedia of Science. Rev. ed. 1967.

Constance Winchell's *Guide* offers the best source of reference books in your field of interest. More specialized bibliographies and indexes can also be found in this volume.

Biographical Information. Biographical information can also be secured with the help of various periodical indexes (such as the *Readers' Guide to Periodical Literature*) and in very compressed form in your own desk dictionary.

Dictionary of American Biography. 20 vols., plus 3 supp. vols. New York: Charles Scribner's Sons, 1928–1973.

Dictionary of National Biography. 22 vols., plus 7 supp. vols. London: Oxford University Press, 1885–1971. The word *national* is sometimes confusing to students; it refers to the "nationals" of the British Empire, more recently known as the British Commonwealth of Nations.

259

Current Biography: Who's News and Why. New York: H. W. Wilson Company, 1940 to date. Published monthly, with six-month and annual cumulations.

Webster's Biographical Dictionary. Springfield, Mass.: G. & C. Merriam Company, 1971, 1976. A one-volume pronouncing biographical dictionary of over 40,000 names. It includes living persons.

Who's Who in America. Chicago: A. N. Marquis Company, 1899 and biennially to date.

Who's Who. London: A. & C. Black, Ltd.; New York: Macmillan Publishing Co., Inc., 1849 to date.

Biography Index. New York: H. W. Wilson Company, 1947 to date. This is a guide to biographical information in books and magazines.

Dictionaries and Books of Synonyms. The following books are useful for study of the changing meanings of words and for the discovery of synonyms.

New Standard Dictionary. New York: Funk & Wagnalls, 1935 to date.

New Century Dictionary. 3 vols. New York: The Century Company, 1927–1933. Based on the original *Century Dictionary,* 12 vols., 1911.

Oxford English Dictionary. New York: Oxford University Press, 1933. A corrected reissue of *A New English Dictionary on Historical Principles,* 1888–1933. The purpose of this work is to give the history of every word in the English language for the past 800 years. It contains many quotations illustrating meanings of words in various periods and full discussions of derivations and changes in meanings and spellings.

Dictionary of American English on Historical Principles. 4 vols. Chicago: University of Chicago Press, 1936–1944. This is especially useful to the student who wishes to learn the historical changes in the use and meaning of words in American English.

Webster's New Dictionary of Synonyms. Springfield, Mass.: G. & C. Merriam Company, 1968. A dictionary of discriminated synonyms with antonyms, analogues, and contrasted words.

HAYAKAWA, S. I. *Modern Guide to Synonyms and Related Words.* New York: Funk & Wagnalls, 1968.

KLEIN, ERNST. *A Comprehensive Etymological Dictionary of the En-*

glish Language. 2 vols. Amsterdam, New York: Elsevier Publishing Co., Inc., 1966–1967.

PARTRIDGE, ERIC. *A Dictionary of Slang and Unconventional English.* 2 vols. New York: Macmillan Publishing Co., Inc., 1967.

Roget's Thesaurus of the English Language in Dictionary Form. Rev., greatly enl. ed. New York: G. P. Putnam's Sons, 1965.

Gazetteers and Atlases. In a world of rapidly changing national boundaries and of former colonies emerging as independent nations, gazetteers and atlases are out of date almost as soon as they are printed. Most of the following works, however, are kept up to date by reasonably frequent revisions. Check the date on the book you are using.

The Columbia Lippincott Gazetteer of the World. A revision of *Lippincott's Gazetteer* of 1905. New York: Columbia University Press, 1962.

Rand McNally Commercial Atlas and Marketing Guide. Chicago: Rand McNally Company.

Encyclopaedia Britannica World Atlas. Chicago: Encyclopaedia Britannica Company, 1959. Rev. annually.

National Geographic Atlas of the World. 3rd ed. 1970.

The Times Atlas of the World. Rev. ed. 1968.

Books of Quotations. When you are in doubt about the source or wording of a passage that you can only vaguely recall, search out the complete passage in a book of quotations. These volumes are thoroughly indexed by key words.

BARTLETT, JOHN, and E. M. BECK. *Familiar Quotations.* 14th ed. Boston: Little, Brown and Company, 1968.

STEVENSON, BURTON. *The Macmillan Book of Proverbs, Maxims, and Famous Phrases.* New York: Macmillan Publishing Co., Inc., 1941.

———. *The Home Book of Quotations.* 10th ed. New York: Dodd, Mead and Company, 1967.

Guides and Indexes to Periodicals and Bulletins

Magazines and Bulletins. Indexes to magazines, bulletins, and newspapers are usually shelved in the reference room of the library.

When searching for something published in a magazine, you need to know two things: (1) Does the library subscribe to that periodical? (2) In what issue was the article published? The answer to the first question is on a card, found in either the general catalog or an additional special card file in the reference room. For an answer to the second question, look into a periodical index. (Your reference librarian can help you to locate these resources.)

Bulletins are listed in most indexes. In compiling your bibliography remember that a bulletin is treated as a periodical if it is published at regular intervals (that is, as a series), and as a book if it is a separate, single publication.

There is a special index for material published in newspapers. See pages 263–264.

Poole's Index to Periodical Literature, 1802–1881, and supplements from 1882 to 1906. A subject index only. Materials such as poems and stories are entered under the first word of the title. Only volume and page numbers are given; dates are excluded.

Readers' Guide to Periodical Literature, 1900 to date. Entries are under author, title, and subject. Besides volume, paging, and date, it indicates illustrations, portraits, maps, and other materials. Since for the student seeking a general topic this is the most important of the indexes, a sample of its entries follows:[1]

ALEXANDER, Donald Crichton
　　Top tax official on rebates, refunds, audits; interview. il por U.S. News 78:19–20 Ap 14 '75
　　　　　　　　　　about
　　IRS's $287 billion man. il por Time 105:60–1 Ap 7 '75 *
ALEXANDER, John
　　George Washington shopped here. il Sat Eve Post 247:22–3 Mr '75
ALEXANDER, Tom
　　Battered pillars of the American system: science. il Fortune 91:146–7+ Ap '75
　　Plate tectonics has a lot to tell us about the present and future earth. il Smithsonian 5:38–47 F '75
ALEXANDER and Baldwin, Inc
　　Hawaiian company invests its sugar profits. por Bus W p80–2 Ap 14 '75

---

[1] Reproduced by Courtesy of H. W. Wilson Company.

ALEXANDER Botts, detective; story. See Upson, W. H.
ALEXANDER Sprunt Jr sanctuary. See Bird sanctuaries—South Carolina
ALEXEYEV, Vasili. See Alekseev, V.
ALEXIAN brothers. See Brothers (in religious orders, congregations, etc)
ALFORD, Albert L.
   Education amendments of 1974. il Am Educ 11:6–11 Ja '75
ALFRED the Great, king of England
   Golden dragon, by A. J. Mapp, Jr. Review
      Harper 250:104–5 Ap '75. J. Gardner
      Smithsonian 5:108+ Mr. '75. B. Farwell *
ALGAE
   Polarizing fucoid eggs drive a calcium current through themselves. K. R. Robinson and L. F. Jaffe. bibl il Science 187:70–2 Ja 10 '75
   Toxicology and pharmacological action of anabaena flos-aquae toxin. W. W. Carmichael and others. bibl il Science 187:542–4 F 14 '75
      See also
   Plankton
   Seaweed

Specialized Periodical Indexes. These include the following:

Social Science and Humanities Index (formerly the *International Index to Periodicals*), 1907 to date. This is the best index to periodical journals. It also indexes some foreign-language journals, especially those in German and French.
Agricultural Index, 1916 to date.
Art Index, 1929 to date.
Biography Index, 1947 to date.
Book Review Digest, 1905 to date.
Education Index, 1929 to date.
Index to Legal Periodicals, 1908 to date.
Music Index, 1949 to date.
Public Affairs Information Service, 1915 to date. Indexes, periodicals, books, documents, and pamphlets relating to political science, sociology, and economics.
Quarterly Cumulative Index Medicus, 1927 to date. *Index Medicus,* 1879–1926. An author and subject index to periodicals, books, and pamphlets in the field of medicine.

Index to Newspapers. *The New York Times Index* can be used as an index to any daily newspaper in the United

States, since the same stories will probably be found in all daily papers on the same day they appear in the *Times.* The London *Times Index* is a good source for articles of all kinds.

New York Times Index, 1913 to date.
Index to The Times [London], 1906 to date.

THE RESEARCH PAPER

The research paper, variously known as the *investigative theme,* the *term paper, library paper,* or the *research article,* is an exposition, based on research in a library, presenting the results of careful and thorough investigation of some chosen or assigned subject. You will no doubt also have occasions to write term papers based not on library research but on laboratory experiments, questionnaires, or your own critical reactions to something you have read; papers of that sort are organized and written like any other expository paper. Some English departments require a long analytical discussion based on material collected and printed in what is often known as a *source book* or *casebook.* This type of paper, which is sometimes called the *controlled-research* or *controlled-sources* paper, solves certain problems inherent in the research assignment, such as the need to plumb the library or assemble original data. Where the controlled-sources method is used, the instructor's directions should be followed exactly. The information that follows applies primarily to papers based on library investigation.

Summarized here are the values or purposes of the research paper:

1. It will teach you how to use the library efficiently.
2. It will acquaint you with the methods of scholarly documentation—that is, the use of bibliography and footnotes.
3. It will increase your ability to take usable notes.
4. It will teach you how to organize and combine material from a number of different sources.

5. It will give you practice in presenting material in a way that will appeal to your readers.

The research paper can be a project full of frustrations, however, unless you follow orderly procedures. Below is a commentary on the various steps that constitute an orderly, efficient approach to the job.

Decide on a General Subject or Field of Investigation

As soon as the research paper is assigned, many students will ask themselves: "Now what subject do I know something about?" A major in English may want to investigate some author or literary movement. A student in forestry may be especially eager to investigate the new uses of forest products. A student of home economics may wish to write on nutrition or consumer redress. In some ways this attitude is commendable; it approaches in method the theory of the "honors course" now so popular in colleges—the independent investigation in depth of some special field related to a student's major interest. But in other ways this attitude is a mistake. A student should indeed be interested in the subject of his investigation, but his interest may as well involve the thrill of exploring an unfamiliar field.

Of course, if the subjects are assigned the problem of choice does not exist, but if the student has a choice, either unrestricted or limited, the choice should be based on a knowledge of both what is desirable and what must be avoided. The following kinds of subjects are *not* workable; they lead only to frustration:

1. Subjects that are too broad. Broad or general subjects are starting points. They must be limited or narrowed to usable dimensions.
2. Subjects on which little has been published anywhere.
3. Subjects on which the local library has little material.
4. Subjects that are so technical that the writer cannot understand his material, much less present it intelligibly to others.
5. Subjects that are too narrow or too trivial for a paper of the suggested length.

265

6. Subjects indistinguishable from those selected by your classmates.

It is impossible to list all the general interests that will appeal in every instance. The lists given here are merely suggestive:

1. Something related to the course you are taking or expect to take in college, such as literature, history, medicine, or political science.
2. Something coming out of your experience, such as your work during summer vacations, your military service, your travel or stay in a foreign country, the occupations of your parents. But remember that these are only the starting point for your library work.
3. Something related to your hobbies, your special talents, or your reading interests, such as photography, archeology, exploration, sports, aviation.

The advice of your instructor may be the last word on your choice of subject. If you have freedom of choice, however, or if you are urged to present several choices for your instructor's approval, the following list of general fields may help:

1. Archeology	12. Music
2. Art	13. Mythology
3. Aviation	14. Nature
4. Biography	15. Photography
5. Crime	16. Psychology
6. Drama	17. Sciences
7. Education	18. Sports
8. History	19. The theater
9. Language and literature	20. Utopias
10. Medicine	21. Warfare
11. Movies	22. Welfare

Make a Preliminary Check of the Library and Do Some General Reading

Before making a final decision on the general subject, it is best to spend an hour or two browsing in the library to see whether the subject will be satisfactory and to get an idea of how it can be limited. First look in the card catalog. Then check through some of the periodical indexes to ascertain the extent of the available published material in the selected field. Notice in what types of periodicals the information is to be found, and make a preliminary check, either through the general card catalog or through a special list of periodicals, to see which of the sources are available in the library. Look in the *Britannica* to see what it has on the topic. If there is only a limited amount of information on hand and several persons want access to it simultaneously, efforts at research will run into frustrating delays.

Limit the Subject

After selecting a general field of interest, you will, with the help of your instructor, select some part or aspect of it that can be effectively presented in the given space and time. If you are interested in American literature, you may decide to write about Robert Frost or Sylvia Plath. You may find it convenient to limit your subject still further and to investigate the early poems of Frost or the suicidal tendencies expressed in the works of Plath. These are merely suggested topics. The variety of possible topics is vast. How you limit a broad subject depends partly on the time or the space allowed, partly on the thesis of the paper, partly on the extent of available material. A scholarly probing of a very minor area is one thing; a more general presentation of facts, such as might be read before a club or a seminar, is another. In choosing a subject, always remember that it is impossible to narrow or limit a subject by excluding details. A research article should be interesting. Interest comes from the concrete details, the examples, and the imaginative touches in the writing. Note how this balance is achieved in articles on science or medicine in *Time* magazine.

Now let us take two or three of these general fields and suggest in each of them several topics narrowed down to what can be presented adequately in the time and space prescribed.

267

GENERAL SUBJECT: MOVIES

1. Hollywood stars
2. Famous directors
3. Horror movies—their history
4. The Western hero
5. Novels into films
6. The art movie
7. The history of film technology
8. The gangster film
9. Movies and '30s society
10. Silent comedies

GENERAL SUBJECT: WARFARE

1. Caesar's battles
2. Famous ancient sea fights
3. The strategy of siege
4. Air battles of World War I
5. World War II generals
6. War in literature
7. American antiwar movements
8. Modern weapons of war
9. The American draft system
10. Nuclear arms limitation

Prepare a Working Bibliography

A bibliography is a list of books, articles, bulletins, or documents relating to a given subject or author.

When you begin working on a research paper, arm yourself with a supply of 3 × 5 cards or slips of paper. On these cards make a list of references—one and *only one* to each card—that you hope will be useful. Collect the references from the card catalog, the encyclopedias, and the periodical indexes. Since there is always a great deal of wastage and frustration in defining a specific area of research, take out insurance by getting more references than you expect to use. As you proceed with your reading, refine the bibliography by adding new references and by discarding those you find useless.

Bibliographic Forms. It is unfortunate that bibliographic forms have not been standardized as completely as have the parts of an automobile. Recently, however, the Modern Language Association has moved toward standardization in the general field of literature, language, and the social sciences. The Association's most recent publication or bibliographic forms is called the *MLA Handbook for Writers of Research Papers, Theses, and Dissertations.* As its long title indicates, this handbook may be used by undergraduates, graduates, and professionals in the preparation of research papers and theses. The forms of bibliographies and footnotes used here are based on the *MLA Handbook,* insofar as the recommendations of the MLA are applicable to undergraduate work.[2]

(There are other forms used for bibliographies and footnotes, however, and your instructor may well recommend modifications of the MLA style. Use the form requested.)

Every bibliographic reference consists of the three parts necessary for a complete identification of the printed work used, and these parts are generally arranged in this order:

1. *The author's name.* (Write the last name first only where lists are to be alphabetized. If an article or pamphlet is unsigned, begin with the title.)
2. *The title.* (If it is a book, underline the title. If it is an article, essay, poem, short story, or any subdivision of a larger work, enclose it in quotation marks.)
3. *The facts of publication.*
   a. For a book, give the place of publication (with the abbreviated state, if needed for clarity, as *Garden City, N.Y.*), the name of the publisher in full, and the date.
   b. For a magazine article, give the name of the magazine, the volume number, the date, and the pages.
   c. For a newspaper article, give the name of the newspaper, the date, the section if the sections are paged separately, and the page.

Sample Bibliography Cards

The sample bibliography cards that follow illustrate the arrangement of items and the punctuation in various types of references.

---

[2] *The MLA Handbook for Writers of Research Papers, Theses, and Dissertations* (New York: Modern Language Assn., 1977).

ARTICLE IN AN ENCYCLOPEDIA

Initials of the author identified in vol. I. Date of copyright from back of volume. Title of article in quotes. Underline title of reference book.

> Atkinson, Richard J. C.
>
> "Stonehenge." Encyclopaedia Britannica, 1958, XXI, 440–441.

BOOK BY A SINGLE AUTHOR

Copy call number. Underline title of book.

> PN1993.5 Bergman, Andrew
> .U6
> B38   We're in the Money:
>
>   Depression America and Its Films.
>
>   New York: New York University Press, 1971.

BOOK BY TWO OR MORE AUTHORS

All names after the first are in normal order.

> PN45 Wellek, René, and Austin Warren.
>
> .W36
> 1962 Theory of Literature.
>
>   New York: Harcourt, Brace, 1949.

BOOK EDITED BY MORE THAN THREE PERSONS

et alii ("and others") abbreviated *et al.* (Do not underline.)

270

```
Ref.      Spiller, R. E., et al., eds.,
PS88      2 vols.
 .L522
1974      Literary History of the United States. 4th
          ed. rev.

          New York: Macmillan Publishing Co., Inc.,
          1974
```

BOOK EDITED

```
 811      Millay, Edna St. Vincent.
.M611x
          Collected Poems. Ed. by Norma Millay

          New York: Harper & Brothers, 1956.
```

SIGNED MAGAZINE ARTICLE

VIOLENCE

Assassinations and the bicentennial. P. P. Moulton. il
   [illustrated] Chr. Cent. 90: 1120–2 N 14 '73

```
Moulton, P. P.

"Assassinations and the Bicentennial."

Christian Century, Nov. 14, 1973, pp. 1120–22.
```

UNSIGNED ARTICLE

WATERGATE case

After surrendering tapes, new pressures on Nixon. il por
   [portrait] US News 75: 19–21 N 5 '73

```
"After surrendering tapes, new pressures on Nixon."

U.S. News and World Report, Nov. 5, 1973, pp. 19–21.
```

271

NEWSPAPER ARTICLE

James, John: The New Directors; illus. J 27, 1973, F Ed.,
p 7

James, John

"The New Directors."

Detroit <u>News</u>, Jan. 27, 1973, Final Ed., p. 7.

Bulletins are treated like books if they are published occasionally, and like magazine articles if they are issued periodically (at regular intervals).

OCCASIONAL BULLETIN

Parker, William Riley. <u>The</u> <u>MLA</u> <u>Style</u> <u>Sheet</u>. 2nd ed. New
York: MLA, 1970.

PERIODICAL BULLETIN

"New Trends in Testing," <u>Educational</u> <u>Research</u>, HEW, Nov.
1974, 27-28.

Reading and Taking Notes

It is a good idea, before you begin to read and take notes, to collect a few fairly promising bibliography cards. Take your cards with you to the library. Look up several of your references. You might start with the encyclopedia articles, or with books that give an overview of your subject. The aim in this reading is to develop a preliminary understanding of the subject you are interested in exploring. Read for general information. While exploring, note those topics that seem to be most closely related to your particular subject. If your subject is the impact of a certain type of movie from the Thirties on social attitudes, be sure to record information about the backgrounds of screenwriters, directors, and the actors themselves. These topics, properly arranged, will become your first rough outline. They will be the headings to use on your note cards when you begin taking notes.

Reading and Skimming. The tortures of research, the dead ends, the crucial articles that turn out to be irrelevant, the books that cannot be located, plague everyone. But there will be fewer frustrations and less wasted time if you remember that what you have learned about writing must apply also to your reading. Good writing produces work organized so that its contents are evident quickly, easily, without confusion, without wasted effort. Those who write books, chapters, essays, or articles in magazines follow the same principles of writing that you have learned— so that *you* may get the information you want, easily, quickly, without confusion, without wasted effort. Here are some aids to quick reading and comprehension:

1. In a book examine first the table of contents, Preface, Foreword, or Introduction, the index (if it has one), the chapter headings, and the topics of the lesser divisions.

2. In an essay or article look for a formal statement of plan or purpose at the beginning. If it is a rather long essay or article—one of those five-part essays used by magazines for serious discussions, for example—look at the beginning of each part for a hint of the contents.

3. Glance through the essay, reading a topic sentence here, another one there, until you come to what you want. The process is called *skimming*.

Evaluating Your Sources. To expect a college freshman writing his or her first research paper to have the experience necessary to evaluate all sources is not exactly fair or reasonable. But any college student can learn a few hints or signs that will help distinguish the totally unreliable from the probably reliable. *The student should first realize that not all that gets into print is true.* Some—perhaps most— of it is as true and as reliable as honest and informed men and women can make it. Some of it is mistaken or biased opinion. The following suggestions will help in the evaluation of sources:

1. The first aid is the date of publication of the book or article. In some fields, such as chemistry, physics,

and medicine, information even a few months old may be outdated. *Try to get the most recent facts possible.*

2. To a certain extent, judge the information by the authority of the publication in which it appears. The *Britannica,* for instance, selects its authors with more care than does a newspaper.

3. A long, thorough treatment of a subject is probably more accurate than a short treatment of it, or a condensation.

4. Finally, if it is possible, find out something about the reputation of the author. Obviously a careful checking of authorities is a necessity in a scholarly thesis written for publication, and a desirable but often unattainable ideal in a freshman term paper. In practice, however, a college library can usually be trusted to winnow out most of the chaff before it buys. When in doubt ask your librarian for help.

The Topic Outline. Once the dimensions of a subject area have been established by preliminary exploration, it is time to organize the subject according to a *topic outline.* A topic outline, however, should consist of more than a simple record of information; it should also begin to sift the information in terms of what an intelligent, mature person approaching the matter with an open mind will most appreciate being told. A writer must always keep his reader in mind. What information is actually available is, of course, the primary restriction on any topic outline. From that point the topic outline is the result of selecting material appropriate to the writer's objective and the reader's interest. "Selecting" is the key word. A tabulation of everything ever thought about a subject is no more a topic outline than is a list embracing every conceivable perspective some imaginary reader might like to see explored. The writer must pick and choose, add to and discard from the working outline, until the paper is set in its final form. But if the first topic outline is bound to undergo change, it is nonetheless important as a necessary guide for note-taking. It is therefore better that its preliminary form include too much than too little.

Use of Note Cards. When you go to the library you should have with you a generous supply of note cards. These may be either the 3 × 5 cards that you use for your bibliography or some slightly larger, such as the 4 × 6 size. If you cannot obtain cards, cut notebook paper into quarters to make slips approximately 4 × 5 inches in size. Just as carry-on baggage should not be stowed in an aircraft's baggage rack, notes should not be written in a notebook. One loose piece of paper to each note is the only format permitting easy and frequent rearrangement.

Methods of Identifying Notes. Notes must be identified if you are to avoid confusion later on. Two simple methods of identifying notes are presented here:

1. As you take notes, write at the top of a card the topic under which the information falls. At the bottom of the card write an abbreviated reference to the source of your information. This reference may consist of the author's last name, an abbreviated title, and the exact page reference.

2. The second method is to number all the bibliography cards. Any number system will do as long as the numbers are not duplicated. Then instead of the reference at the bottom of the note card, write the number of your bibliography card and the page number. Of course, whichever method is used each note card must relate to a topic in the working topic outline.

Be sure to use the method that is recommended by your instructor.

The Form of Notes. A sample note card is given below, but before you study it, consider the following suggestions for note-taking:

1. Most notes will be in the form of a summary. Get what is essential and get it accurately, but do not waste words. In order to avoid any chance of inadvertent plagiarism, try to paraphrase what you read—that is, try to *use your own words, not the words of your source.* But dates, figures, and such matters must obviously be quoted accurately.

275

2. If you wish to quote the exact words of an author, copy your material in the form of direct quotations. Ordinarily you should not use direct quotations from your sources if a summary will serve. But if you wish to preserve the words of your source because of unusually apt or precise language, or for some other adequate reason, quote your source exactly. If you leave out a part of a quoted sentence, indicate the omission by means of spaced periods (. . .) called *ellipsis periods* or *suspension points*. Use three spaced periods, leaving a space between the word and the first period, if you omit words in the sentence, and four spaced periods (which include the period ending the sentence) if your omission follows a complete sentence. If you omit a paragraph or more, use three spaced periods centered on the card and in a line of their own, with space above and below the ellipsis.

3. Let your first unbreakable rule be: "One topic to a card." Do not include in your notes on the same card material relating to two or more topics. You may have as many cards as you wish covering the same topic, but take care to label each card and cite the exact source of your notes on each card.

4. Make your notes accurate and complete enough to make sense to you when they become cold.

5. Use headings or topics that represent actual divisions of your outline. Too many topics will merely result in confusion. Let the working outline be your guide.

6. Finally, remember that every note card must have three pieces of information: (1) the heading or topic, which shows you where the information belongs; (2) the information itself (in quotation marks if you use the words of your source); (3) the exact source of the material (including page reference).

Plagiarism. In writing a paper based on research, it is very easy for a student to fall into unintentional plagiarism. Therefore, he or she should understand exactly what *plagiarism* is, and how it can be avoided. The procedure outlined in this chapter should help you to steer away

276

from *borrowing without giving proper credit* through careful note-taking. In taking notes be sure to rephrase the author's material in your own words; do not merely alter a word here and there. The danger is that if you do alter only a few words, the language of your source will carry over into the final paper. To prevent this transference, rephrase and summarize in your notes. You will naturally do more rephrasing when you write your first draft and the final draft, thus reducing the possibility of copying. Since plagiarism can be a serious offense (in some cases students have been expelled for committing it), ask your instructor to explain his or her definition of the word, and to give you assistance in any doubtful instances.

Sample Note Cards. If you follow the instructions on pages 275–276, you will have little trouble in taking usable notes. These samples are summaries. No sample cards are necessary for anything as obvious as a direct quotation.

Prepare the Final Outline

For most of you, the final outline is not the one you will write the paper from. In other words, the outline is usually in a state of flux until the paper itself is finished. It is subject to change until the last moment. If something that looked good at first later seems to be out of place, throw it out and improve the outline. The outline is a working blueprint, a simplified diagram of your paper, but it is no help to anyone if it forces you to construct something that at the last moment you feel is wrong. Change it if it needs changing.

For the conventions of the formal outline, turn back to Chapter 5 in this section. Then examine the outline preceding the sample research paper in this chapter.

Write a First Draft of the Paper

In the process of writing a paper based on research in the library, most writers—whether students or professionals—work up the outline slowly and gradually as they col-

II, B. Phrases, Clichés

Phrases of Shakespeare's creation:
"tower of strength"
"yeomen service"
"to the manner born"

Gordon, The English Language, p. 31

II, A. Words, Figurative Use

Shakespeare was the first writer to use "cap" in the sense of taking off or touching one's cap as a token of respect.

Brewer, Dictionary of Phrase and Fable, p. 185

---

lect notes. The whole process is one of synthesis, of gradual putting together, of sifting and rearranging, which of course includes throwing away unusable material as well as filling in unexpected gaps. It is time to begin writing when the working outline adequately defines the limits of the paper's content and when an approach to the subject, and possibly to the reader, is clear. It may be that you even have thought of an interesting beginning. So, take your note cards and outline at this point, and, on the table in front of you, spread out your note cards for your first section. Read them over to freshen in your mind the sequence or flow of thought—and then you are on your own.

As you write, whenever you come to borrowed material, either quoted or paraphrased, include the reference in parentheses in the right place in the text or between horizontal bars running from margin to margin, the first immediately below the material. Later, copy your footnotes, in the approved form, at the bottom of each page as you prepare the final draft of your paper.

When you quote verse, you may run two lines together in your quotation if you indicate the end of a line by a slash (/), but if you quote more than two lines you should center the quotation on the page. If you quote prose of some length, you should separate the quotation from your text by indention. *No quotation marks are used when quotations are marked by indentions.* Ask your instructor if single or double spacing is required for indented quotations. Study the sample research paper at the end of this chapter for examples of these conventions.

Write a Final Draft with Footnotes

The Final Draft. Go over your first draft carefully before adding the footnotes and copy it for final submission. Keep the following principles in mind: (1) unity and direction of the paper as a whole; (2) interest, supplied by fact and example; (3) organization of the paper as a whole and of the separate paragraphs; (4) correctness of sentence structure; and (5) correctness of punctuation and spelling.

Footnotes: Where Needed. Whether in a college term paper or in a scholarly research article, footnotes are required:

1. *To acknowledge and identify every direct quotation.* Quoted material, as we have indicated earlier, should always be quoted exactly, word for word, except where dele-

279

tions are indicated and either enclosed in quotation marks or indented. Footnotes are not used with familiar sayings or proverbs; everyone knows that these are quoted. (Expressions such as "all the world's a stage" or "all that glitters is not gold" are examples. But be careful to avoid these clichés; the library paper, like any other essay, requires aptness and freshness of language.)

2. *To acknowledge and identify all information that has been used in the paper or thesis in paraphrased, reworded, or summarized form.* Of course, facts of general knowledge need not be credited to any one source.

3. *To define terms used in the text, to give additional information that does not fit into the text, and to explain in detail what has been merely referred to in the text.*

4. *To translate unusual foreign phrases.*

Numbering and Spacing Footnotes. To indicate to the reader that a footnote is being used, place an Arabic numeral immediately *after* the material referred to and a little above the line. Do not put a space before the number or a period after it, either in the text or in the footnote. Place the same number *before* and a little above the line of the note at the bottom of the page. Each note should be single-spaced, and there should be one line of space between notes.

Footnotes should be numbered consecutively, starting from *1,* in a paper intended for publication; in a typed or handwritten paper, however, it is often required that they be numbered beginning with *1* on each page. Some instructors and editors prefer that footnotes appear on a separate sheet(s) at the end of the essay. Use the style your instructor recommends.

The Form of Footnotes. The first time you use a footnote to refer to any source, give the same information that is given in the bibliographic entry, and the exact page from which your information is taken: the author's name (but in the natural order, *not* with the last name first), the title of the work, the facts of publication, and the exact page reference. The punctuation in the footnote is changed in one important respect—instead of periods, as in the bibliography, commas and parentheses are used to separate the three parts of the reference. Later references to the same source are abbreviated. If only one work by an author is used in your paper, the author's name with the page reference is enough. If more than one work by the same author is used, the author's name and a shortened form of the title (with exact page reference, of course) will suffice. Book publishers' names are given in the shortest intelligible form—*Macmillan,* not *Macmillan Publishing Co., Inc.*—when they are included.

The forms illustrated here are those recommended by the *MLA Handbook* (1977), with the addition of the publishers' names. For scientific papers the forms are slightly different, and the student who writes papers for publication in scientific journals should follow the rules set up by those journals.

Models for Footnotes—Book

BOOKS BY ONE AUTHOR

¹ Andrew Bergman, *We're in the Money: Depression America and Its Films* (New York: New York University Press, 1971), p. 18.

² Philip Roth, *The Great American Novel* (New York: Holt, Rinehart and Winston, 1973), p. 200.

LATER REFERENCES

³ Bergman, p. 21. (The MLA recommends use of *p.* or *pp.* [*pp.* is the plural abbreviation] only with works of a single volume.)

⁴ Roth, *Novel,* p. 218. (Latin reference tags, such as *ibid., loc. cit.,* and *op. cit.,* are now considered redundant. See pp. 284–285.)

TWO OR MORE AUTHORS

⁵ René Wellek and Austin Warren, *Theory of Literature* (New York: Harcourt, Brace, 1949), p. 45.

EDITED BOOK

⁶ Christopher R. Reaske, ed., *Seven Essayists: Varieties of Excellence in English Prose* (Glenview, Ill.: Scott, Foresman, 1969), p. 75.

BOOK EDITED BY MORE THAN THREE EDITORS

⁷ M. H. Abrams et al., eds., *The Norton Anthology of English Literature* (New York: Norton, 1968), I, 33.

REPRINTED BOOK

⁸ L. C. Knights, *Drama and Society in the Age of Jonson* (1937; rpt. New York: Norton, 1968), pp. 146–149.

BOOK REVIEW

⁹ Cyrus Colter, rev. of *The Unfinished Quest of Richard Wright,* by Michel Fabre, *New Letters,* 40 (Spring, 1974), 108–114.

DISSERTATION

¹⁰ Hugh J. Ingrasci, "The American Picaresque Novel Between the World Wars," Diss. Michigan 1972, p. 10.

TRANSLATED WORK OF TWO OR MORE VOLUMES

¹¹ H. A. Taine, *History of English Literature,* trans. H. Van Laun (New York: 1889), IV, 296.

Models for Footnotes—Articles

ARTICLE IN A JOURNAL

¹² Jay Halio, "Three Filmed *Hamlets,*" *LFQ,* 1 (1973), 316–320. (Note that the journal's name, *Literature/Film Quarterly,* is abbreviated, and *p.* or *pp.* is not used for page numbers.)

ARTICLE IN AN ENCYCLOPEDIA

¹³ Richard J. C. Atkinson, "Stonehenge," *Encyclopaedia Britannica* (1958), XXI, 440.

ARTICLE FROM A MONTHLY MAGAZINE

¹⁴ H. Keppler, "New Look at Eclipses," *Modern Photography,* Nov. 1963, 93.

ARTICLE IN A WEEKLY MAGAZINE

[15] Muriel Spark, "The First Year of My Life," *The New Yorker,* 2 June 1975, pp. 37–39. (When the volume number is not given, the page number is identified by *p.* or *pp.*)

UNSIGNED MAGAZINE ARTICLE

[16] "An End to Kindness," *Time,* 2 June 1975, p. 43.

SIGNED NEWSPAPER ARTICLE

[17] John James, "The New Directors," Detroit *News,* 27 Jan. 1973, Final Ed., p. 7, cols. 1–4. (The edition and column numbers are not essential, but they are helpful pieces of information. The city where the paper is published is not generally underlined.)

ARTICLE IN AN EDITED COLLECTION

[18] Mary Lascelles, "Shakespeare's Pastoral Comedy," in *Pastoral and Romance: Modern Essays in Criticism,* ed. Eleanor Lincoln Terry (Englewood Cliffs, N.J.: Prentice-Hall, 1969), p. 119.

Miscellaneous

INTERVIEW

[19] Tom Jones, personal interview on popular music, Kansas City, Mo., 6 Jan., 1972.

QUOTATION CITED IN A SECONDARY SOURCE

[20] Gourmet Fields, "The Most Delectable Food I Ever Tasted," as quoted in *W. C. Fields by Himself,* ed. Ronald J. Fields (Englewood Cliffs, N.J.: Prentice-Hall, 1973), pp. 4–5.

ARTICLE REPRINTED IN A COLLECTION

[21] Robert B. Heilman, "Wit and Witchcraft: An Approach to *Othello,*" *The Sewanee Review,* 64 (Winter 1956), rpt. in *Shakespeare: Modern Essays in Criticism,* ed. Leonard F. Dean (New York: Oxford University Press, 1961), pp. 294–310.

FILM

[22] *The Taming of the Shrew* (1966), dir. Franco Zeffirelli; s. Elizabeth Taylor, Richard Burton. USA/Italy: Royal Films Interna-

tional F.A.I. Prod. (There is as yet no standardized form for footnoting films. The above citation includes as much information as is available, though the main elements are the title, date of release, director, country, and production company.)

RECORDING

[23] Bob Dylan, "Desolation Row," *Highway 61 Revisited* (Columbia Records, 1965).

Roman Numerals. Because Roman numerals have a restricted use, students are sometimes unfamiliar with them. The following brief explanation may be helpful:

The key symbols are few in number: 1 = I, 5 = V, 10 = X, 50 = L, 100 = C, 500 = D, 1,000 = M.

Other numbers are formed by adding or subtracting. The three main principles involved are as follows: (1) A letter following one of equal or greater value is added value. (2) A letter preceding one of greater value is subtracted value. (3) When a letter stands between two of greater value, it is subtracted from the last of the three and the remainder is added to the first. Try this explanation with the following examples:

RULE 1

2 = II	20 = XX	200 = CC
3 = III	30 = XXX	300 = CCC
6 = VI	60 = LX	600 = DC
7 = VII	70 = LXX	700 = DCC

RULE 2

4 = IV	40 = XL	400 = CD
9 = IX	90 = XC	900 = CM

RULE 3

19 = XIX	59 = LIX	1,900 = MCM

Abbreviations in Footnotes. Although the number of abbreviations used in research papers at the graduate-school level is large—and often confusing to the lay reader—only a few are of immediate concern here.

284

anon. Anonymous.

c., ca. *Circa,* "about." (Used with approximate dates.)

cf. *Confer,* "compare." (should not be used when *see* is meant.)

ch., chap. Chapter.

chs., chaps. Chapters.

col., cols. Column, columns.

ed. Edited, edition, editor.

e.g. *Exempli gratia* [ĕg · zĕm′plī grā′shĭ · à], "for example."

et al. *Et alii* [ĕt ā′lĭ · ī], "and others."

f., ff. And the following page (f.) or pages (ff.).

ibid. *Ibidem* [ĭ · bī′dĕm], "in the same place." (*Ibid.* refers to the note immediately preceding. *The MLA Handbook* recommends substituting either the author's name or an abbreviated title; either is unambiguous and almost as brief as *ibid.*)

i.e. *Id est,* "that is." Do not use for "e.g."

l., ll. Line, lines.

loc. cit. *Loco citato* [lō′kō sī · tă′tō], "in the place cited." (*Loc. cit.* refers to the same passage cited in a recent note. It is used with the author's name but is not followed by a page number.)

op. cit. *Opere citato* [ŏp′ĕ · rē sī · tā′tō], "in the work cited." (*The MLA Handbook* calls this "the most abused of scholarly abbreviations," and recommends instead the use of the author's name alone or with an abbreviated title.)

The Fair Copy. After you have finished your final draft, you should prepare a clean copy for submission. Chapter 6, in Section I of this book, gives some general rules that you should follow unless your instructor has some other preference. The sample research paper at the end of this chapter will also assist you.

Prepare a Final Bibliography

Your final bibliography should include all the articles and books cited by your paper in the footnotes, plus whatever additional source information your instructor specifies. A bibliography can be prepared quickly and simply by gathering the bibliography cards for the footnotes in the final draft and arranging the citations taken from them in alphabetical (index, not dictionary) order by author, or by title when no author is given.

To alphabetize titles in index order, remember that (1) initial articles *(a, an, the)* are disregarded and (2) alphabetization is by word, with short forms of the same word coming first no matter what letter the second word starts with. For instance, *New York* always precedes *New Yorkers:*

New York: Days of Adventure
New York: The Fast Pace
New York Audiences
New York Critics

To alphabetize names in index order, you will also need to bear in mind a few variations from dictionary order. *Mc-* and *M'-* are alphabetized as if spelled *Mac-*. When two authors have identical last names, alphabetize by first names first, second names next: *Norman, Marie B.* precedes *Norman, Mary A.* An initial takes precedence over a spelled name that begins with the same letter, and a last name followed by a single initial takes precedence over a last name followed by two initials: *Norman, M.* precedes *Norman, M. B.,* and both precede *Norman, Mary A.* Use the titles (or dates, if titles are identical) to alphabetize a number of works by the same author writing alone. When there are collaborators, use the following order: (1) single author; (2) author and collaborator; (3) author "et al."; (4) title; (5) date, with the earliest first:

JONES, A. B. *My Life and Times.* New York: Jones Publishing Company, 1975.
—— and TOM SMITH. *Friendly Enemies.* New York: Jones Publishing Company, 1973.
—— et al. *Relatives.* New York: Jones Publishing Company, 1973.
—— et al. *Topical Essays.* New York: Jones Publishing Company, 1971.
—— et al. *Topical Essays.* New York: Jones Publishing Company, 1974.

286

The form of the individual entries has already been treated on pages 269–272. See also the bibliography accompanying the sample paper that follows.

Sample Outline and Library Paper

The following sample outline and library paper are reproduced here, not as perfect models to imitate, but as examples of conscientious and competent work.[3] (The student has used a *sentence* outline here; for a sample of the *topic* outline, turn back to p. 168.)

```
Words, Words, Words: Shakespeare's Contribution to Our
                          Language
Thesis Sentence: Although Shakespeare is widely recog-
nized as a literary genius, his work as well constitutes
a major contribution to our language, giving us the words
to create satisfying images and to express insights into
human nature.
  I. Shakespeare's vocabulary and the language richness
     of his age created the right atmosphere for his
     contribution.
     A. Shakespeare's vocabulary was large and diverse.
        1. General estimates put it at 20,000 words.
        2. About 90% of his vocabulary was made up of
           native words.
     B. The Elizabethan age was one in which the language
        changed rapidly.
        1. The Elizabethans were language conscious—they
           loved sermons and speeches—and Shakespeare took
           advantage of this condition.
        2. Shakespeare was also part of the transformation
           from Middle to Early Modern English.
 II. Shakespeare was the inventor of many words and
     phrases.
     A. He used words to which he gave original connota-
        tions.
        1. Greek and Latin derivatives like "obscene" and
           "pedant" were given special meanings.
        2. Ordinary words like "bump" and "dwindle" are
           attributed to him.
        3. Figures of speech were given meanings—"coxcomb"
           meaning "fool"—that they retain today.
        4. Shakespeare invented many compound words—"hot-
           blooded," "hell-black"—that have continued in
           use.
     B. Many new phrases were introduced in his works.
        1. Phrases like "heart of gold" have been repeated
           so much that they are now regarded as clichés.
        2. Certain phrases—"beat it," "fall for it"—have
           been twisted into slang.
```

[3] Reprinted by permission of the author, Jennifer Borron.

  3. Some clichés have achieved the status of proverbs: "the devil can quote scripture."
  4. We now use certain quotations—"Beware the Ides
   of March" and "What's in a name?"—as signs of
   literary sophistication.
III. Shakespeare's works are the sources of expressions
 that have become identified with character or social
 types, books, and derivative plays.
  A. Shakespeare's individualized characters have been
   transformed into stereotypes.
   1. "Romeo and Juliet" is the tag for stereotyped
    young lovers.
   2. "Shylock" is used as a derogatory label for
    moneylenders.
  B. Book titles often have their origins in lines
   from Shakespeare.
   1. The Sound and Fury was taken by Faulkner from
    Macbeth.
   2. Brave New World is a line from The Tempest.
  C. Adaptations of the plays have provided new, well-
   recognized expressions.
   1. Kiss Me, Kate is based on The Taming of the
    Shrew.
   2. West Side Story is a musical version of Romeo
    and Juliet.
IV. Shakespeare should be recognized as the writer who
 has most strongly influenced today's language.
  A. His works continue to have widespread popularity,
   especially as sources of quotations.
  B. In a sense, the wheel has come full circle, since
   Shakespeare was equally influential in forming
   the language of his own age.

288

Words, Words, Words:
Shakespeare's Contribution to Our Language

By
Jennifer Borron

English 120-B
August 1, 1980

Words, Words, Words: Shakespeare's Contribution to Our
Language

As we know it today, English is one of the richest languages in the world. Studies of its evolution have shed
light on the number of literary figures who have given so
much of their vocabulary to us; they are responsible for
much of this enrichment. Included in these ranks are men
like Chaucer and Milton. However, the one name that
stands out with unequalled greatness in linguistic contribution is William Shakespeare.

No other person has had such influence on the way a
language is spoken or written. Henry Bradley confirms
this claim in The Making of English: "Shakespeare has no
equal with regard to the extent and profundity of his influence on the English language."[1] Bradley's opinions do
not stand alone in the field of literary criticism and
the study of the history of the English language. James
C. Gordon, who has written extensively on the etiology of
English, regards Shakespeare as the greatest single benefactor of our language. Furthermore, he considers Shakespeare's works "so familiar to so many that our cultivated tradition, both literary and colloquial, is studded
with . . . phrases of his creation."[2] The extent of the
research done on Shakespeare's use of words and phrases
illustrates his great reach into almost every profession
dealing with language.

Why has Shakespeare had such an impact on how we use
our language? Largely the answer lies in the size of his
vocabulary, which is generally accepted as consisting of
about twenty thousand words. Not only was he an ingenious
inventor, twisting meanings to create entirely new meanings or turning nouns into verbs, he also had a command
of word use in the writings of certain authors before and
during this time. Shakespeare's knowledge of classical
and foreign literary sources furthered the success of his
creativity in writing. Yet despite this acquaintance with
foreign and classical works, the semanticist Mario Pei
proposes that "his vocabulary is about ninety percent native, . . . [giving] the world a full realization of the
potentialities of . . . English. . . ."[3] Because of Shakespeare's extensive resources, he is one of the heaviest
contributors to the language's vocabulary, but Pei admits
"it is often difficult to distinguish between the words
he accepted and gave currency to, and those he personally
coined."[4] An article dealing with Shakespeare's vocabulary
in the literary journal, Notes and Queries, assumes that
once a word was part of his vocabulary, it was never
lost.[5]

Shakespeare's enrichment of our tongue also stems from
the period of time in which he lived. Shakespeare wrote
most of his plays during the reign of Queen Elizabeth,
the Elizabethan Age. The primary characteristic of the
age was a sort of "language-consciousness,"[6] which allowed
men like Shakespeare to lay the foundations of Modern English. The Elizabethans were frequently exposed to ser-

-2-

mons and public speeches, which stimulated their interest in the sound and sense of the language. James D. Gordon speculates that Shakespeare knew of this consciousness and took advantage of it when writing.[7] His awareness of the effect of language went along with what is called in The Riverside Shakespeare "the fundamental state of the language, which was just ripe for Shakespeare's formative use of it."[8] The Elizabethan Age was in fact in the transitional period between Middle and Modern English. Gordon, in The English Language: An Historical Introduction, calls Shakespeare's language "Early Modern English."[9] Using Shakespeare as an example of a writer who contributed to the change of the language from one period to another illustrates his importance in the history of English.

According to Stuart Robinson, a good part of Shakespeare's "legacy to the language" comes from his supremacy in word-making.[10] A brief survey of the Oxford English Dictionary leaves one astonished at the number of quotations indicating William Shakespeare as the first user of a given word. Some words can be easily recognized as his inventions--the compound from "star-crossed," for example--but others give no indication of their originator.

Many Greek and Latin derivatives were introduced for the first time in Shakespeare's plays. L. K. Barnett's book, The Treasure of Our Tongue, cites a long list of words that entered English in this manner: "accommodation," "apostrophe," "frugal," "pedant," and "premeditated," to name a few. Other classical words that Shakespeare popularized are: "assassination," "dexterously," "dislocate," "indistinguishable," "misanthrope," "obscene," "reliance," and "submerged."[11] In Origins of the English Language, Joseph M. Williams asserts that "Shakespeare's use of new words illustrates an important point in connection with them. This is the fact that they were often used, upon their first introduction, in a sense different from ours, closer to their etymological meaning in Latin."[12] Whether or not Shakespeare had an intimate knowledge of Latin is not known, but we do know he had a poet's sense of the appropriate word for the feeling or idea he was trying to convey.

Shakespeare not only borrowed and made familiar words of classical origin, he is also credited with a lengthy list of ordinary words. According to G. Blakemore Evans, editor of The Riverside Shapespeare, "It was he who introduced such ordinary words as 'lonely' and 'laughable,' invented such onomatopoeic vocables as 'bump,' borrowed from their classical cognates 'monumental' and 'aerial,' not to mention 'critic' and 'pendant,' without which his students would be at a loss."[13] George H. McKnight attributes to Shakespeare: "'dwindle,' 'credent,' 'baseless,' 'multitudinous,' and 'courtship.'"[14] James Gordon adds "'control,' 'countless,' and 'exposure.'"[15] Since the words were drawn from his plays, it is easy to see how "ducat" was extracted from Shylock's exclamation in The Merchant of Venice[16] and "confectionary" was drawn from

-3-

the name "Count Confect" in Much Ado About Nothing.[17] This
list seems to substantiate an impressive contribution,
but it must be remembered that these words are known as
Shakespeare's, as is the case with any other author, only
because they have not been found in any previous works,
not because he first used them in his writings.

Although the group is smaller, figurative words used by
Shakespeare have carried into modern English the meaning
he originally intended them to have. For example, Brewer's Dictionary of Phrase and Fable lists the verb "to
cap. To take off, or touch one's cap to, in token of respect; also to excel."[18] This meaning, Brewer adds, comes
from Hamlet (II, ii): "as in 'on fortune's cap we are not
the very button.' "[19] Thus it is used by Shakespeare to
refer to a mark of excellence. Similarly, "to beetle" and
"to bone," meaning "to overhang" and "to filch," are attributed to Shakespeare's Hamlet.[20] Asimov's Guide to
Shakespeare states that Shakespeare gave the word "cox-
comb" the figurative connotation of "fool" that it still
retains.[21]

It was fashionable in Shakespeare's day to create certain new words by hyphenating others. One can imagine the
large number of compounds that appeared in Modern English
at that time. Mario Pei submits a list of compound words,
such as " 'foam-girt,' 'heartsick,' 'needlelike,'
'everburning,' 'lack luster,' 'hot-blooded,' and 'hell-
black,' "[22] that can be traced directly to Shakespeare.

Although word contributions are important pieces of evidence of Shakespeare's gift to the language, Bradley believes "the greatness of his influence [lies] in the multitude of phrases derived from his writing."[23] For the
most part these phrases were introduced through his
plays, very few coming from his sonnets and long poems.
Over the centuries they have been quoted and alluded to
so much that Shakespeare's phrases have turned into
clichés.

The OED defines a cliché as "the French name for a
stereotype block."[24] In English the term has come to refer
to phrases that are well worn from repetition. With this
definition a seemingly endless list of clichés are noted
as Shakespeare's phrases. Among the more familiar expressions, Pei lists " 'heart of gold,' the naked truth,'
foregone conclusion,' 'to break the ice,' 'to breathe
one's last,' 'to tell the world,' 'to wear one's heart on
one's sleeve,' and 'the milk of human kindness.' "[25] James
Gordon lists other phrases of Shakespeare's creation,
such as " 'tower of strength,' 'yeoman service,' and 'to
the manner born.' "[26]

It seems reasonable that the better-known plays would
produce a greater number of phrases which have become
clichés. Such is in fact the case. From Julius Caesar
comes "dish for the gods," "lean and hungry look," "live-
long day, and "it's Greek to me."[27] Mark Antony's speech
to the crowd at Caesar's funeral has become so familiar

-4-

that we use "lend me an ear" to signify "pay attention to what I am about to say."[28] Hamlet is so well known that " 'flaming youth,' 'not a mouse stirring,' 'to smell to heaven,' " not to mention "something rotten in the state of Denmark," have all become common phrases.[29] From Othello we extract the phrase "crocodile tears." Isaac Asimov declares, "Any mention of crocodiles would irre-sistibly bring tears to mind, for the most famous . . . legend concerning [the animal] is that it sheds tears over its prey while swallowing it."[30] Hence the expression connotes a form of hypocritical sorrow. The theme of Othello is one of hypocrisy and jealousy alike. When Iago declares, "O beware, my lord, of jealousy!/It is the green-eyed monster, which doth mock/The meat it feeds on" (III.iii.165-67), we have Othello becoming a victim of jealousy, popularly identified with the phrase itself.[31]

Some slang phrases have resulted from corruptions of Shakespeare's clichés. From A Golden Book of Phrases, Stuart Robinson compiles examples like: " 'beat it,' 'done me wrong,' 'fall for it,' 'not in it,' and 'not so hot.' "[32] One would certainly not imagine Shakespeare as the originator of these expressions, and we are also likely to think of someone else as the source of "swear a mild oath by the dickens."[33]

The proverbial phrase is another form of cliché, exam-ples of which we can find in Shakespeare. The proverb and cliché are similar, although the proverb tends to convey a more heavily moral message. In the case of Shakespeare, his "aphorisms have turned into proverbs: 'the devil can quote scripture,' and 'misery makes strange bedfellows' come, with slight modification, from The Merchant of Venice (I.iii.98) and The Tempest (II. ii. 40) respectively."[34] Another, more famous proverb from The Merchant of Venice warns us, "All that glitters is not gold."[35] Shakespeare not only coined phrases that became clichés and slang expressions, his language also imparted to us his wisdom concerning human nature.

Many other Shakespearean phrases have become familiar to us as direct quotations. The Oxford Dictionary of Quotations devotes a large section to Shakespeare's writ-ings. Our speech would be incomplete without the flavor-ing of his phrases, which have become favorites of rheto-ricians and orators who call upon them to express ideas more eloquently. Quoting Shakespeare is considered a sign of literary sophistication. Our public speech would cer-tainly lack some of its character could we not recall the Soothsayer's words in Julius Caesar (I.i.18) exclaiming, "Beware the ides of March,"[36] or Banquo's prophecy in Mac-beth (I.iii.123), "the instruments of darkness tell us truths. . . ."[37] Without Shakespeare young lovers would not be able to express the intense emotion echoed in Juliet's "What's in a name? That which we call a rose/By any other name would smell as sweet" (II.ii.42-43).[38] Neither could actors refer to the Seven Ages of Man nor boldly exclaim:

-5-

"All the world's a stage,/And all the men and women merely players" (As You Like It, II.vii.129-30).[39]

From Shakespeare's cast of "players" have emerged stereotypes, a phenomenon comparable to the transformation of his original phrases into clichés. Romeo and Juliet stand among the ranks of the world's great lovers, and we picture Caesar through Shakespeare's portrayal of the character, rather than through historical accounts that more accurately portray him. " 'Benedick,' the name of Shakespeare's bachelor par excellence . . . has undergone only very slight modification in coming to represent a '(newly) married man.' "[40] Isaac Asimov affirms that "Shylock" is not a Jewish name, nor was there ever a Jew named "Shylock," but the characterization of the man is so powerful that Shakespeare's invention has entered into English as the name for any grasping, hard-hearted creditor.[41]

Furthermore, Shakespeare has entered our lives in ways more subtle than direct contributions. Knowledge of his works has led authors like William Faulkner and Aldous Huxley to borrow his words for titles of their books. Faulkner extracted a line from Macbeth for the title The Sound and Fury[42] and Huxley mined Miranda's speech in The Tempest (V.i.183-84) for his book, Brave New World.[43] The rhyme "Jack and Jill" bears a striking resemblance to a passage in A Midsummer Night's Dream, and King Lear is said to have inspired Robert Browning's Gothic poem "Child Harold to the Dark Tower Came."[44] Cole Porter named his musical version of The Taming of the Shrew, Kiss Me, Kate, after Petruchio's words in that same play; Romeo and Juliet's saga was transported in its entirety to New York City of the 1950's in West Side Story.

Viewing Shakespeare's works as a whole, it is not possible to comprehend just how great a part he plays in our speech and writing. It is not until we divide into categories the mass of information that has been collected dealing with his influence on language that we begin to realize the extent to which our imaginations are possessed by him. Looking at the contributions from a literary perspective barely touches on Shakespeare's effect on the English language. Words and phrases of his creation can be added to a list that includes examples of his influence on syntax, grammar, and the evolution of spelling changes in English. While his works have taken on the reputation of literary classics, they should also be studied as sources of words and phrases that are still in use and applicable to our time.

Over the course of history, English has undergone a series of changes. Each has enriched and expanded our language to the point that it is one of the most widely spoken tongues in the world. As the British Empire grew, so did the language, along with an awareness of its writers. Today this awareness has grown to the point that Shakespeare is synonymous with the brilliance of the English language. His profound influence on that language is evi-

denced daily in ordinary conversation. As he himself
said, "The wheel has come full circle."

Footnotes

[1] Henry Bradley, The Making of English (London: Macmillan and Co., Ltd., 1904), p. 153.
[2] James D. Gordon, The English Language: A Historical Introduction (New York: Thomas Y. Crowell Company, 1972), p. 31.
[3] Mario Pei, The Story of the English Language (London: George Allen and Unwin, Ltd., 1967), p. 61.
[4] Pei, p. 61.
[5] Edward Slater, "Word Links with The Merry Wives of Windsor," Notes and Queries, 22 (Apr. 1975), 169.
[6] Pei, p. 58.
[7] Gordon, p. 31.
[8] G. Blakemore Evans, ed., The Riverside Shakespeare (Boston: Houghton Mifflin, 1974), p. 8.
[9] Gordon, p. 103, n. 2.
[10] Stuart Robertson, The Development of Modern English (New York: Prentice-Hall, Inc., 1936), p. 400.
[11] Lincoln Kinnear Barnett, The Treasure of Our Tongue (New York: Knopf, 1964), p. 151.
[12] Joseph M. Williams, Origins of the English Language: A Social and Linguistic History (New York: The Free Press, 1975), p. 288.
[13] Evans, p. 11.
[14] Gordon, p. 31, n.1, citing George Harley McKnight, Modern English in the Making (New York: Appleton-Century-Crofts, 1925), p. 188.
[15] Gordon, p. 31, n.2.
[16] Isaac Asimov, Words from History (Boston: Houghton Mifflin Co., 1968), p. 69.
[17] Isaac Asimov, Asimov's Guide to Shakespeare, 2 vols., (New York: Avenel Books, 1978), I, 557.
[18] E. C. Brewer, ed., Dictionary of Phrase and Fable (New York: Harper & Row, 1970), p. 185.
[19] Brewer, p. 184.
[20] Brewer, pp. 95, 133.
[21] Asimov, Guide, I, 593.
[22] Pei, p. 61.
[23] Bradley, p. 153.
[24] The Compact Edition of the Oxford English Dictionary, 2 vols., (New York: Oxford University Press, 1971), I, 496.
[25] Pei, p. 143.
[26] Gordon, p. 31.
[27] Pei, p. 143.
[28] Brewer, p. 359.
[29] Gordon, p. 31.
[30] Asimov, Guide, I, 353.
[31] Evans, p. 24.
[32] Robertson, p. 470.

[33] Evans, p. 11.
[34] Evans, p. 11.
[35] Brewer, p. 472.
[36] The Oxford Dictionary of Quotations, 2nd. ed. (London: Oxford University Press, 1955), p. 448.
[37] The Oxford Dictionary of Quotations, p. 456.
[38] The Oxford Dictionary of Quotations, p. 477.
[39] The Oxford Dictionary of Quotations, p. 427.
[40] Thomas Pyles, The Origins and Development of the English Language (New York: Harcourt Brace Jovanovich, 1971), p. 307.
[41] Asimov, Guide, I, 510.
[42] Evans, p. 25.
[43] Evans, p. 24.
[44] Asimov, Guide, II, 36.

Bibliography

Asimov, Isaac. Asimov's Guide to Shakespeare. 2 vols. New York: Avenel Books, 1978.
——. Words from History. Boston: Houghton Mifflin Co., 1968.
Barnett, Lincoln Kinnear. The Treasure of Our Tongue. New York: Knopf, 1964.
Bradley, Henry. The Making of English. London: Macmillan and Co., Ltd., 1904.
Brewer, E. C., ed. Dictionary of Phrase and Fable. New York: Harper & Row, 1970.
The Compact Edition of the Oxford English Dictionary. 2 vols. New York: Oxford University Press, 1971.
Evans, G. Blakemore, ed. The Riverside Shakespeare. Boston: Houghton Mifflin, 1974.
Gordon, James D. The English Language: A Historical Introduction. New York: Thomas Y. Crowell Company, 1972.
McKnight, George Harley. Modern English in the Making. New York: Appleton-Century-Crofts, 1928.
The Oxford Dictionary of Quotations, 2nd ed. London: Oxford University Press, 1955.
Pei, Mario. The Story of the English Language. London: George Allen and Unwin, Ltd., 1967.
Pyles, Thomas. The Origins and Development of the English Language. New York: Harcourt Brace Jovanovich, 1971.
Robertson, Stuart. The Development of Modern English. New York: Prentice-Hall, Inc., 1936.
Slater, Edward. "Word Links with The Merry Wives of Windsor." Notes and Queries, 22 (Apr. 1975), 169–71.
Williams, Joseph M. Origins of the English Language: A Social and Linguistic History. New York: The Free Press, 1975.

A HANDBOOK OF

WRITING AND

REVISION

9 | *Grammar*

and Usage

§1. SENTENCE FRAGMENTS

Fragmentary sentences should be avoided in expository writing.

A grammatically complete sentence is a pattern of communication in words that is based on a verb with its subject. The essential core of a complete sentence is at least one verb with its subject or subjects. Structurally the sentence must be an independent unit, capable of standing alone. Dependent units, such as phrases, clauses, appositives, and similar groups of words, are not sentences, and should not be written as sentences. When any one of these dependent units is written and punctuated as a sentence, it is called a *sentence fragment.*

Ineffective Sentence Fragments

An *ineffective sentence fragment* may be revised by (1) attaching the fragment to the sentence with which it logically belongs, (2) completing its form by adding the necessary words, (3) rewriting the passage.

The four main types of ineffective sentence fragments are listed below and their corrections indicated by examples:

299

1a. A dependent clause should not be written as a complete sentence.

1

If you remember that a dependent clause usually begins with a connective that relates it to the main clause, you can guard against some types of fragments. For adjective clauses look for the relative pronouns *who, which,* and *that,* and the relative adverbs *when, where,* and *why.* For adverb clauses look for the subordinating conjunctions *after, although, as if, because, before, if, since, though, unless, when, where,* and *while.* Noun clauses are almost never miswritten as fragments. Another helpful fact to remember is that the fragment usually *follows* the main clause, to which it may be joined in correction.

FRAGMENT

He spent his life preaching social justice. *Which was a startling concept in his day.*

REVISION

He spent his life preaching social justice, which was a startling concept in his day. [Add fragment to main clause.]

FRAGMENT

The animosity that his ideas excited is incredible. *Although a few brave men praised him.*

REVISION

The animosity that his ideas excited is incredible, although a few brave men praised him. [Add clause to sentence.]

FRAGMENT

The officer came to the alley where the man was last seen. *And where the stolen jewelry was probably hidden.*

REVISION

The officer came to the alley where the man was last seen, and where the stolen jewelry was probably hidden. [The second *where*-clause also modifies *alley*.]

300

1. SENTENCE FRAGMENTS

1b. A verbal or a prepositional phrase should not be written as a complete sentence.

FRAGMENT

The two boys took the first trail to their left. *Hoping it would take them to a river.*

REVISIONS

The two boys took the first trail to their left, hoping it would lead them to a river. [Join phrase to main sentence.]

The two boys took the first trail to their left. They hoped it would lead them to a river. [Supply subject and verb to make the fragment a sentence.]

FRAGMENTS

They trudged along the trail all day. *Without a rest. Without stopping to eat what food was left.*

REVISION

Without a stop to rest or to eat what food they had, they trudged along the trail all day. [You may also revise by putting the prepositional phrases after the main clause.]

FRAGMENT

The railroad made Virginia City a lumber center. *Its population leaping from three hundred to five thousand in three years.* [This is a participial phrase, of the special type called the absolute phrase. See page 86.]

REVISION

The railroad made Virginia City a lumber center. Its population leaped from three hundred to five thousand in three years. [Change the participle to a verb to make a complete sentence. You may also join the phrase to the main clause.]

1c. An appositive phrase should not be written as a complete sentence.

Guard against this fault especially when the phrase is introduced by such words as *namely, for example, such as,* and the like.

301

1

FRAGMENT

Some games are called contact sports. *Namely, football, basketball, and ice hockey.*

REVISION

Some games, namely football, basketball, and ice hockey, are called contact sports.

FRAGMENT

New problems face the woman entering college. *Such as budgeting her money and her time for study.* [*Budgeting* is in apposition with *problems.*]

REVISION

New problems, such as budgeting her money and her time for study, face the woman entering college. [Place the appositive near *problems,* not at the end of the sentence.]

FRAGMENT

We found the case transferred to Juvenile Court. *A development that completely puzzled us.* [*Development* is in apposition with the whole idea expressed in the main clause.]

REVISION

We found the case transferred to Juvenile Court, a development that completely puzzled us. [Add the appositive to the main clause.]

1d. Any verbless chip or fragment of a sentence, whether you can classify it or not, should not be allowed to stand as a sentence.

Some fragments are written because the writer was in too much of a hurry to think; others are written because the writer has carried over into writing the exclamatory nature of very informal speech. The following examples will make the points clear:

FRAGMENTS

Just a lazy weekend vacation. No work. No worries. That's what he promised me.

302

1. SENTENCE FRAGMENTS

REVISIONS

Just a lazy weekend vacation with no work or worries—that's what he promised me. [The dash indicates a sharp break in the construction.]

What he promised me was a pleasant weekend vacation, with no work and no worries.

FRAGMENT

Unexpectedly I dropped in on her daughter. *Just a friendly call, no party.* [The writer of this was making notes, not sentences.]

REVISION

Unexpectedly I dropped in on her daughter. I intended this to be just a friendly, informal call. [Make a sentence out of the fragment.]

Note: Fragments are allowable when reproducing conversation or when asking or answering questions. Since these situations occur mainly in novels or short stories, expository writers should be wary about their appearance in essays. For example, the asking and answering of rhetorical questions in an argumentative essay creates a sort of bogus dialogue that can wear the reader's patience thin:

How often should the President answer letters? Always. When? As soon as all the evidence is in.

It may be strategic to quote a patch of dialogue for illustration's sake, especially if you are trying to convey a particular mood for a scene you are describing.

One can easily imagine the sort of conversation that took place in the White House during those harrowing days:

President: "I suppose you've listened to the tapes."
Jones: "Yes, often."
President: "Hear anything damaging?"
Jones: "Everything."

1

EXERCISES

EXERCISE 1, RECOGNIZING SENTENCE FRAGMENTS.
Copy the following sentences. Some of them are complete. Some are fragments. If a sentence is complete, underline its subject once and its verb twice. If the group of words is a clause, encircle the subordinating connective. If it is a verbal phrase, encircle the verbal.

1. *Main Street* being Sinclair Lewis's first really important novel.
2. Although he had already published two or three full-length stories.
3. A native of Sauk Center, Minnesota, he wrote about the people he knew best.
4. At first, the natives of Sauk Center were very indignant.
5. Resenting his slurs against them and their way of life.
6. They insisted that his novel was not a true picture of their town.
7. That his characters were caricatures and his town a monstrosity.
8. Finding that his fame brought them notice and recognition.
9. Gradually capitalizing on their notoriety in profitable ways.
10. Merchants adopted "Gopher Prairie" as a sort of brand name for several of their commercial enterprises.

EXERCISE 2, ELIMINATING SENTENCE FRAGMENTS.
In some of the following word groups you will find sentence fragments. Eliminate each fragment either by joining it to the main clause or by rewriting it as a complete sentence. Be able to tell whether rule 1a, 1b, or 1c applies.

1. Last summer, while on our way from New York to Denver, we stopped at University Park, Pennsylvania, to visit a friend of ours. Whom we had not seen since our college days.
2. The college is now a state university, and the town, once called State College, is now known as University Park. Names of towns being subject to quick changes.

3. The town is not exactly inaccessible, as some say. Neither is it close to a modern expressway.
4. The drive to the city took us across several ranges of hills. The road at times narrow and curving but never difficult to take at reasonable speeds.
5. I was amazed at the extent and attractiveness of the campus. Situated as it was in the beautiful Nittany Mountains.
6. We found our friend in the college infirmary, where he had his office. And where he has worked with the students for many years.
7. His face showed at once that he had aged and gained weight. And his hair, or what was left of it, having turned gray.
8. He said he could leave his office early, drive us around the campus, and then take us out to dinner. Which was an offer that we accepted with many thanks.
9. Talking with an old friend usually revives old memories. Such as campus riots, football games, and wartime experiences.
10. Leaving him the next morning, we felt that he had led a happy, useful, and rewarding life. A fact that we spoke about during most of that day.

2

§2. RUN-TOGETHER SENTENCES

When two or more complete sentences are combined in a single sentence, they must be properly separated from one another.

A sentence made up of two or more independent, coordinate clauses, properly joined and punctuated, is called a *compound sentence.* (See pages 90–91.) The usual means of joining these independent clauses are (1) a semicolon, (2) a conjunction, (3) a comma and a conjunction, (4) a semicolon and a conjunction. (See also §§13 and 14.)

2a. The comma splice or comma fault may be corrected in several ways.

The use of a comma to join independent, coordinate clauses is called a *comma splice* or a *comma fault*. It should be avoided in college writing. A comma splice may be corrected in one of the following ways. The student should choose the method of revision that produces the most effective sentence.

1. The comma splice may be corrected by *subordinating one of the two independent sentences.* (If you put both statements in the same sentence, you must believe that one is closely related to the other. A subordinate clause can express this relation specifically.)

SPLICE

We all went home after the picnic, it had started to rain.

BETTER

We all went home after the picnic because it had started to rain.

SPLICE

The food was fine except for the salad, I didn't like it.

BETTER

The food was fine except for the salad, which I didn't like.

2. The comma splice may be corrected by *inserting a coordinating conjunction after the comma.* (These conjunctions are *and, but, for, or, nor, yet.*)

SPLICE

We were looking for a shady spot, we couldn't find one.

BETTER

We were looking for a shady spot, but we couldn't find one.

3. The comma splice may be corrected by *using a semicolon*

2. RUN-TOGETHER SENTENCES

instead of a comma if the sentences are close enough in meaning to be combined into a compound sentence.

SPLICE

We finally found a satisfactory place, it was breezy but quiet.

BETTER

We finally found a satisfactory place; it was breezy but quiet.

If you wished instead to subordinate, then the sentence would look like this:

We finally found a satisfactory place, which was breezy but quiet.

4. The comma splice may be corrected by *using a period to separate the two coordinate clauses.* In simple examples, such as the ones we are discussing here, the danger of this alternative is a series of very short sentences that look choppy.

CORRECT BUT CHOPPY

We finally found a satisfactory place. It was breezy but quiet.

Note that the choice of a solution for the run-together sentence, like all choices in writing, can affect the tone of the statement. In the last revision above, the choice of two very short sentences makes the speaker sound matter-of-fact and distanced, almost like a police officer reporting details of an investigation. The decisions you make about grammar relate directly to the way your words affect the reader.

LEGITIMATE COMMA JUNCTIONS

The use of a comma to join coordinate clauses is more common in novels, stories, and some types of journalistic writing than in expository prose. The clauses so joined

307

are likely to be short and simple, and are most likely to occur in the following situations:

1. *When the clauses are arranged in the "a, b, and c" order.*

EXAMPLES

The shrubs were leafy and well-shaped, the walks had been carefully raked, and the fountain shone in the sunlight.
The dog growled, the cat spat, the mouse fled.
The batter swung, the catcher dove, and the ball rolled to the backstop.

2. *When the series of statements takes the form of a climax.*

EXAMPLES

I came, I saw, I conquered.
The sun is growing warm, frogs are waking in the marshes, planting time will soon be here.

3. *When the statements form an antithesis, or are arranged in the "it was not merely this, it was also that" formula.*

EXAMPLES

It was more than just murder, it was a massacre.
To give in to them now not only would mean defeat, it would mean accepting their savage way of life.

Two familiar situations in writing invite the comma splice. One such danger point is immediately following tags such as *he said* in dialogue.

DIALOGUE

"That's right," said Paul. "I'd almost forgotten her name." [A period is the usual punctuation, although a semicolon is occasionally used.] "No one remembers the good things I have done," she complained; "no one ever does." [Semicolon used here.]

"Yes, I know, sir," said Tony. "I warned him to be careful." [Period used here.]

2. RUN-TOGETHER SENTENCES

The other danger concerns conjunctive adverbs such as *however, moreover,* and so on.

ADVERBS

The prisoner told a long story of atrocities; however, his companion did not agree with his version of what had happened to them. [Use a semicolon before the conjunctive adverb. By using a semicolon and relocating the adverb within the second clause, you can achieve a smoother transition: ". . . atrocities; his companion did not agree, however, with his version . . ."]

When I registered for engineering, I had two high school subjects to make up; moreover, I had forgotten most of the algebra I ever knew. [Use a semicolon before the conjunctive adverb.]

2b. The fused sentence may be corrected by the same methods as the comma splice.

The fused sentence is one in which two sentences are run together with no punctuation at all between them. It is an extreme example of the same carelessness that produces the sentence fragment and the comma splice.

In the following pairs of sentences, the first is a fused sentence followed by a unified one. Notice how familiarity with sentence combining techniques like subordination can help you out of such corners.

At first I wondered if I should speak to her she seemed to be so wrapped up in her thoughts.

She seemed so wrapped up in her thoughts that at first I wondered if I should speak to her. [Subordination]

I almost decided to walk by and pretend I did not see her she might think I was intruding.

Fearing that she might think I was intruding, I almost decided to walk by and pretend not to see her. [Subordination]

I was lonesome I decided to speak and I said hello in a weak voice.

As I was lonesome, I decided to speak to her, and I said hello in a weak voice. [Subordination]

309

EXERCISES

EXERCISE 1, SUBORDINATING CLAUSES. *Correct each of the following sentences by subordinating one or more of the run-together coordinate clauses.*

1. Some people like an ocean voyage in winter, they want to escape the frost and snow at home.
2. A few are likely to be bored on a ship it is such a closed-in community.
3. The weather may be fine for days, however, it may change abruptly, everyone gets seasick.
4. The food is usually rich and plentiful, it would be a crime not to enjoy it.
5. Deckchairs are the rule in sunny weather, in bad weather one stays below.
6. Who would not appreciate seeing the islands of the West Indies, we have heard so much about them?
7. The stewards on shipboard are uniformly pleasant and efficient, they have been so well trained, they know exactly what to do.
8. Vacations at sea are within the reach of many people today they were a luxury for a privileged class not so very long ago.
9. Air travel is much faster, of course, nevertheless a week on a ship can be far more restful.
10. Most people are glad to get home, however, you can tell by looking at their happy faces as they step ashore.

EXERCISE 2, SUBORDINATING WITH PHRASES AND APPOSITIVES. *Revise each of the following sentences by using subordination of a rank below that of a subordinate clause (a phrase or an appositive).*

1. Success in life, they say, requires two principal qualities, they are perseverance and innate talent.
2. This is like most such generalizations it is hard to put to practical use.
3. A person has perseverance, or innate talent, how can you distinguish?

4. Many people apparently have perseverance and talent, they still do not conspicuously succeed.
5. Such statements are misleading they are so simple, they sound falsely profound.
6. Luck must have something to do with success, ask any millionaire about it.
7. Money seems to be the only measure it is the one most people accept.
8. There are only three recognized classes of successful people in America they are corporation executives, Presidents, and sports stars.

EXERCISE 3, REVISING AN INFORMAL PARAGRAPH.
Here is a paragraph composed in a style approximating informal speech. Rewrite it by revising its fragments and run-together sentences in any way you think appropriate.

I'm disgusted with him. The liar. Telling me all the time how honest he was, too. He wanted to borrow my car, I knew he didn't even have a license, his roommate told me that. I should have said no to him, I know I should. Right to his face. I'm soft-hearted, you know how I am. In spite of all past disappointments. I wonder where my car is, it's been quite a long time now. That thief.

Notice again, as you do this exercise, how the tone changes with the changes in grammar. Is the speaker in your revision more angry than the original speaker, or less? Is he closer to his imaginary listener, or further away?

§3. SUBJECT–VERB AGREEMENT

A verb must agree in number with its subject.

Once it is understood that a singular verb matches a singular noun and a plural verb a plural noun, there is nothing very difficult in recognizing that "The *boys are* playing in the yard" is standard English, whereas "The *boys is* playing in the yard" is not. As long as subject and verb lie close together, and it is obvious whether the subject

3

is singular or plural, there should be no problem in applying the principle of agreement in number. Confusion arises when the complexity of a sentence or the peculiarity of a subject obscures the immediate relation between subject and verb. Problems in agreement fall into three main categories:

1. When several other words intervene between the subject and verb, or when the word order is unusual, the writer or speaker may forget for the moment just what the subject is and so make an error.

2. When the subject seems to be simultaneously singular and plural—"everybody," "gymnastics," "the whole family," "either of us," "a group of people"—or when its number seems to be a matter of choice, the writer can easily become confused over the number to be reflected in the verb.

3. Because usage differs according to situation or occasion, the writer may not know which rule best suits a given occasion. The forms recommended in this book, however, are appropriate and correct in all varieties of English— formal or informal, written or spoken. In very informal situations, other forms may *also* be current.

It is often helpful to make a quick diagram of the grammatical subject and verb of a sentence.

3a. Plural words that intervene between a singular subject and its verb do not change the number of the subject.

EXAMPLES

The *racket* of all those engines *was* deafening. [*Racket was,* not *engines were.* "Of all those engines" is a phrase modifying *racket,* and this of course does not make *racket* plural.]

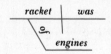

312

One of the many techniques he explained to us *was* that of repelling. [*One* technique *was repelling.*]

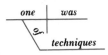

3b. When words are added to a singular subject by *with*, *together with*, *as well as*, *in addition to*, *except*, and *no less than*, the number of the subject remains singular.

EXAMPLES

The *teacher*, as well as his principal, *was* exonerated. [*Teacher was*]

The *boy*, together with three companions, *was* discovered the next day. [*Boy was*]

These expressions may be logically considered as introducing modifiers of the subject. They do not have the force of *and*, which is the word that compounds a subject and makes it plural.

3c. In sentence patterns that depart from the typical subject-verb-complement order, watch for the following situations in particular.

1. The Subject Following the Verb. Mental transposition into normal order will clarify agreement of subject and verb.

EXAMPLES

Scattered over the floor *were* the *remains* of the evening's feast. [*Remains were scattered*]

Browsing peacefully in her vegetable garden *were* a large *elk* and three mule *deer*. [*Elk and deer were*]

2. Introductory *It*. Introductory *it*, as in "It is the people who matter," is always followed by a singular verb,

313

3

no matter whether the noun that follows is singular or plural. *It* in such cases is an expletive, often called the *preparatory subject*, preparing the way for the real subject to come. Nevertheless it controls the verb. No one would say, "It are the people." (The preparatory subject is often used as a carry-over from spoken English. In the first example below note how much more direct the statement becomes after eliminating "It is . . . that" and rearranging word order: "We must consider her happiness." When you find yourself using the "It is" or "There are" constructions to excess, try rephrasing your sentences without them.)

EXAMPLES

It is her *happiness* that we must consider. [*It is happiness.* But try rephrasing: We must consider her happiness.]

It is the *colleges* that must take up the burden. [*It is colleges.* Rephrased: Colleges must take up the burden.]

3. Introductory *There*. In present-day English, usage seems to be divided in regard to the number of the verb when the preparatory *there* introduces a sentence.

In sentences in which the noun that follows the verb is *plural,* most writers and speakers will use a plural verb.

EXAMPLES

There *are,* if I counted right, exactly *thirteen* persons at this table. [*Persons are*]

There are, you must admit, several *degrees* of guilt. [*Degrees are*]

4. Introductory *What*. *What* as a preparatory subject may be either singular or plural according to what the writer means. If it serves in the sense of *the one thing that,* it is singular, and the only caution to observe is that all related verbs should respect its singular status—even when its subjective complement consists of more than one thing.

3. SUBJECT-VERB AGREEMENT

3

EXAMPLE

What is interesting about this model *is* the seven speed settings available. [*The one thing about this model is. . . .*]

It is usually clear when *what* must be plural.

EXAMPLE

For *what are* doubtless good reasons, responsibility for maintaining the reservoir has been transferred from the Sewage Authority.

Even with logic on your side, it is advisable to avoid constructions like the following:

Pterodactyls were not birds; *what* they were *was* reptiles. [Balance is preserved by saying simply, ". . . they were reptiles."]

When the subject following the verb consists of a number of nouns, the first of which is singular, there is a tendency to make the verb singular.

EXAMPLES

In a club like ours, there *is* one president, one meeting place, and one set of rules for everyone.

At the party, where there *was* a great guitarist and a good selection of wine, we saw several old friends.

There *is* enough gold and silver in those hills to make digging worth your time.

3d. The verb agrees with its subject, not with its subjective complement.

If the difference in number between subject and complement produces an awkward sentence, it is better to rewrite.

RIGHT

The one last *object* of her love *was* three Siamese cats. [Not *object were*]

315

REWRITTEN

She had nothing left to love except her three Siamese cats.

RIGHT

Our *worry was* the frequent storms that swept the lake. [Not *worry were*]

REWRITTEN

We worried because storms frequently swept the lake.

3e. A compound subject joined by *and* takes a plural verb.

Again, do not be distracted by unusual word order or by intervening phrases.

EXAMPLES

The *rest* of the manuscript and the *letter* from Whitney *seem* to have been destroyed in the fire. [Not *seems*]

A heavy *coat* or *windbreaker* and a fur *cap are* recommended as additional equipment. *Are* both an *overcoat* and a *parka* necessary? [Not *overcoat and parka is*]

When several singular subjects represent the same person or thing, however, a singular verb is used.

EXAMPLES

Our *ally* and *neighbor* to the south, the Republic of Mexico, *maintains* a quiet border.

My *friend* and *colleague* Paul *races* cars as a pastime.

But notice the difference that an article *(a, an, the)* can make.

EXAMPLES

The blue and gold sweater is very attractive.
The blue and the gold sweaters are very attractive.
A red and white rose is in bloom.
A red and a white rose are in bloom.

316

3f. When subjects are joined by *neither—nor, either—or, not only—but also,* **the verb agrees with the nearer subject.**

When both subjects are singular, the verb is singular; when both subjects are plural, the verb is also plural. But when one subject is plural and the other singular, *formal usage* prescribes that the *nearer subject* dictates the number of the verb. In informal usage there is a tendency to make the verb *always plural.* One way to avoid an awkward sentence—as well as an awkward decision—is to recast the sentence entirely.

FORMAL

Neither the *students* nor their *teacher is* adequately prepared.

Neither *you* nor *I am* going there now.

INFORMAL

Neither the *students* nor their *teacher are* adequately prepared.

You aren't going there now and neither *am I.*

RECAST

Both the *students* and the *teacher are* inadequately prepared.

You and *I aren't* going there now.

3g. After *each, every, each one, everyone, everybody, anybody, nobody, none, either,* **and** *neither* **the singular verb is used in formal English.**

EXAMPLES

Each of us *is* willing to pay *his* or *her* share of the expenses. [Note that *his* or *her,* referring to *each,* is also singular.]

Every American *knows his* or *her* duty.

Has anyone seen her?

I wonder if *anybody knows* who wrote the song.

The rule as stated here represents the practice of most writers. Exceptions can easily be found, in both formal

317

3

and informal writing. In an attempt to interpret usage, it is said that the *intention* of the writer determines whether the singular or the plural is to be used. But that is a razor-edge distinction for a student to make. When you say, "*Each* of the boys *tells* a different story," the choice is clear, but it is a less obvious matter of right between "*None* of the boys *is* telling the truth," and "*None* of the boys *are* telling the truth." You may justify the first as formal usage and the second as informal usage. The simplest solution is to say, "All the boys are lying."

3h. With a collective noun a singular verb is used when the group named by the noun is regarded as a unit; a plural verb is used when the noun is regarded as indicating the individuals of a group.

Common collective nouns that are tricky are *class, band, number, family, group, public, committee.*

EXAMPLES

The *number* of failures *was* surprising. [*The number* is usually construed as a single unit.]

A *number* of students *are* failing this term. [*A number* refers to individual items or members of a group and is therefore plural.]

The whole *family is* here. [The modifier indicates that *family* is considered as a single unit.]

The *family are* all attending different churches. [Here the reference is to the individuals of the family.]

Since there is considerable range for individual choice in the use of collective nouns, *consistency* must be the student's guide. Once you have spoken of a group as a single unit, you should not, without some explanation, refer to it as a plural.

EXAMPLES

The *platoon are* removing their knapsacks. *They are* getting ready for a mock charge.

The *class was* assembled promptly and proceeded with *its* assignment.

318

3i. When the subject is a title, the name of a book, a clause, a quotation, or some other group of words expressing a single idea, the verb is singular.

EXAMPLES

The Tramp's Cup is a collection of David Ray's poems.

All men are created equal is a statement of dubious truth.

This rule also applies to expressions signifying number, quantity, distance, time, amount, or extent. When the subject is expressed as a unit, the verb is singular.

EXAMPLES

Twenty years is a long time to wait for an editor to make up his mind.

Five hundred words is long enough for most daily themes.

Thirty miles is a tiring day's run.

But when the amount is meant to be made up of separate units, the plural verb is used.

EXAMPLES

The first *ten years* of every marriage *are* the hardest.

There *are five hundred words* in his essay.

3j. Several words ending in *-s* are governed by special rules of usage.

A number of nouns ending in *-ics* are considered singular when they refer to a branch of study or a body of knowledge (*linguistics, physics, mathematics, civics, economics*), but are usually plural when they refer to physical activities, qualities, or phenomena (*acoustics, acrobatics, tactics, phonetics, athletics*). Other words likely to cause trouble are listed below.

Usually singular: *news, measles, mumps, gallows.*
Usually plural: *scissors, riches, slacks, means, falls* [water].
Either singular or plural: *headquarters, politics, sports*

319

3

3k. A singular verb is used with a relative pronoun referring to a singular antecedent, and a plural verb is used with a pronoun referring to a plural antecedent.

EXAMPLES

It is important to associate with *students who are* honest. [*Who* refers to *students,* a plural noun.]

He is the only *one* of the family *who intends* to go to college. [*Who* is singular because it refers to *one.*]

Now notice the difference between the last example above and the following construction: "He is one of those boys who are always getting into trouble." If you shift this about to read, "Of those boys who are always getting into trouble, he is one," you can see that *who* refers to *boys* and is therefore plural. But in practice the singular verb is very common, especially in speech: "He is one of those boys who is always getting into trouble."

EXERCISES

EXERCISE 1, RECOGNIZING SUBJECTS AND VERBS. *Some of the difficulty with agreement, as we have seen, is simply a matter of making sure just what the subjects and verbs in sentences are. In the following sentences write S above each subject and V above each verb.*

1. As he said, there were a police officer and a crowd of people in front of our house.
2. The police officer, as well as most of the crowd, was looking up at the sky.
3. One of several things that I worried about was a fire.
4. Neither burglars nor a fire is ever far from a homeowner's thoughts.
5. Every one of my neighbors is worried about fires.
6. My friend and neighbor George swears that we have poor fire protection.
7. Smoke, as well as fire and water, causes much damage to a burning house.

320

8. Looking up toward the treetops in front of our house were three small boys.
9. The number of people inspecting our residence was growing steadily.
10. The news that finally reached us was reassuring; the excitement was about a kitten frantically trying to descend from its perch on a tall tree.

EXERCISE 2, CORRECTING ERRORS IN SUBJECT-VERB AGREEMENT. *Correct the errors in each of the following sentences. Tell what rule applies.*

1. The outcome of all those meetings and conferences were the appointment of a committee.
2. In colleges and in governments there is usually a type of person that love to serve on committees.
3. This committee, with the Dean of Administration, serve as a check on other committees.
4. There seems to be several explanations why this was called a standing committee.
5. If my mathematics is correct, this committee sat from two to six the first day.
6. Four hours are a long time for a standing committee to sit.
7. Each of the members have a different cause to champion.
8. Neither the dean nor the chairman admit saying, "A camel is a greyhound designed by a committee."
9. One man complained that the acoustics in the auditorium was poor.
10. The outcome of all their deliberations were that the questions under discussion should be referred to a new committee.

EXERCISE 3, RECOGNIZING AND CORRECTING ERRORS IN AGREEMENT. *Some of the following sentences contain errors; some are correct. Point out each mistake that you find, correct the sentence, and tell what rule applies.*

1. The teacher remarked that his use of obscenities were unfortunate.

321

4

2. Either you or I am going to tell him to watch his language.
3. Linguistics are not exactly his strong point; he is much better at athletics.
4. Athletics, whether you believe it or not, do require some skilled teaching.
5. The salary of a football coach, fifty thousand a year, is much more than the average professor earns.
6. There seems to be several reasons·why this is so.
7. The public know that a good fullback is hard to find, and it is willing to pay the price required.
8. But many a good fullback were lost to the world because he could not pass his entrance examinations.
9. My uncle is one of those who do not believe that a knowledge of poetics is useful in a business office.
10. After his long career as a little-known author, one of his novels were made into a motion picture.

§ 4. PRONOUNS

Be careful to use the right form of the pronoun.

Nouns in modern English change their form for the plural and for the possessive. Plurals are discussed in § 19. The possessive forms are discussed in § 15. There are very few problems connected with the form changes of nouns.

Some pronouns, however, change their forms for person, number, and case, and thereby cause the student of the English language numerous difficulties. In English there are three cases: the *nominative* or *subjective,* the *possessive,* the *objective.* There are also three persons: the *first* person indicates the speaker; the *second* person indicates the one spoken to; the *third* indicates the one spoken about.

The forms of the personal pronoun are shown in the table below:

322

4. PRONOUNS

	FIRST PERSON	SECOND PERSON	THIRD PERSON Masc.	Fem.	Neuter
Nominative:	I	you	he	she	it
Possessive:	my, mine	your, yours	his	her, hers	its
Objective:	me	you	him	her	it

4

PLURAL NUMBER

	FIRST PERSON	SECOND PERSON	THIRD PERSON
Nominative:	we	you	they
Possessive:	our, ours	your, yours	their, theirs
Objective:	us	you	them

The relative and interrogative pronoun *who* has only three forms:

Nominative:	who, whoever
Possessive:	whose
Objective:	whom, whomever

There are also a number of *indefinite* pronouns, such as *another, anybody, anyone, anything, both, each, either, everybody, everyone, everything, few, many, neither, nobody, none, one, somebody, someone.*

The intensive pronouns (used for emphasis) and the reflexive pronouns (used to point the action back toward the subject) are *myself, himself, herself, itself, yourself, yourselves, ourselves, themselves.* Be careful not to overuse these intensive pronouns.

INTENSIVE

The general *himself* gave the order. I *myself* will carry it out.

REFLEXIVE

"You can easily hurt *yourselves*," I said, but they picked *themselves* up.

323

MISUSED

Everyone, including *myself,* was surprised by the announcement. [The objective case, *me,* is appropriate.]

My wife and *myself* were invited to Harry's party. [My wife and *I*]

Nominative Case

4a. The nominative case is used when the pronoun is the subject of a verb.

You should watch out for three trouble spots in connection with the use of the nominative case:

1. A parenthetical expression, such as *they think, they say, we believe,* etc., between *who (whoever)* and the verb may confuse the writer.

EXAMPLES

Jones is one senior who we think could teach this class. [Not *whom we think,* but *who could teach*]

A young man who we believe was the driver of the car is being held.

Who did you say brought us these cherries? [Not *whom did you say*]

We agreed to accept whoever they thought was the best foreman. [Not *whomever*]

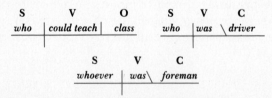

2. The fact that a *who* or *whoever* clause follows a preposition may lead the writer into using the wrong case.

EXAMPLES

Send a card to *whoever* asks for one. [Not *to whomever. Whoever* may seem to be attracted into the objective case by its position

324

after the preposition. But it is the subject of the verb *asks*. The whole clause is the object of the preposition.]

Settle the question with *whoever* wrote the report. [Not *with whomever,* but *whoever wrote*]

3. In clauses of comparison, with *than* and *as,* the nominative is used with the implied verb.

EXAMPLES

She can usually see more in a painting than *I* [can see]

No one knows that better than *she* [knows it]

Few can play as well as *they* [do] on that field.

Comparison between two clauses, the verb of one of which is implied, constitutes what is called an *elliptical* sentence.

4b. In standard literary English, the nominative-case form is used when the pronoun is a subjective complement after the verb *be*.

In conversation, "it's me" is generally accepted, and in most conversational situations "it's *I*" or "it is *I*" would sound affected and silly. As for "it's *us*" or "it's *them*," probably the best advice—*in conversation*—is to follow your ear and your sense of propriety. You should do the same when writing dialogue. Outside quotation marks, however, standard written English requires the nominative in all such uses.

EXAMPLES

It is *we* who must bear the burden of the tax program, even though it was *they* who initiated it.

It was *he* (or *she*) who made the plans for the rained-out picnic.

Possessive Case

4c. The apostrophe is not used with personal pronouns to form the possessive case; the apostrophe is used,

325

however, with those indefinite pronouns that can be used in the possessive.

The possessive forms of the personal pronouns are *my, mine, your, yours, his, her, hers, its, our, ours, their, theirs.*
The possessive forms of the indefinite pronouns are *anybody's, anyone's, everybody's, nobody's, no one's, one's, somebody's.*

WRONG

The furniture is *their's,* but the house is *our's.*
The bush is dying; *it's* leaves are covered with volcanic ash.

RIGHT

The furniture is *theirs,* but the house is *ours.*
The bush is dying; *its* leaves are covered with volcanic ash.

Note carefully the distinction between *it's,* which means *it is,* and *its,* which is the possessive form of *it.* Note also that when *else* follows the indefinite pronoun, such as *anybody, somebody, someone,* the apostrophe and *s* are added to *else,* not to the pronoun.

RIGHT

It's [contraction of *it is*] *anybody's* guess *whose* [possessive form of *who*] car will win this race.
Would you like to ride in somebody *else's* car?
It is best to trust someone *else's* judgment on Hitler's leadership.

4d. In standard English the general practice is to use the possessive form of the pronoun when it precedes a gerund.

Please note that here we do not use *general* in the sense of *universal.* We mean, "Most do; some don't." It is easy enough to find exceptions in the writing of reputable authors.

326

4. PRONOUNS

I cannot understand *his refusing* to do that for me.

Her driving off so abruptly was hard to understand.

I told them about *your resigning* from office.

In these sentences the verbals *refusing, driving, resigning* are gerunds. They are used as object, as subject, and as object of a preposition, in that order. When the verbal is a participle, however, the objective case is correct.

We saw *them waving* a white flag. [Them in the act of waving]

I found *him using* my typewriter. [Him in the act of using]

With nouns introducing or modifying gerunds, usage varies. There are situations in which the possessive is desirable; there are others in which it is difficult or clumsy, and therefore it gives way to the objective.

The family resisted the idea of Liberace's *leaving* home.

The prospect of *nations fighting* one another again is again conceivable.

It was hard to imagine so many *buildings being constructed.*

4e. Instead of the apostrophe-*s* form, the *of*-phrase may be used to show possession when the situation calls for it.

1. Ordinarily, the *of*-phrase is used for inanimate objects: "the back of the building," "the top of the heap," "the hem of the dress" (*not* "the dress of my sister"). However, notice such forms as "in an hour's time" and "a week's pay." In some cases either form may be used; in other cases only one form is possible.

4

2. The *of*-phrase may also be used when the simple possessive form would separate a noun from its modifier.

EXAMPLE

The trustworthiness of a man who never thinks twice is highly questionable. [Not "The man's trustworthiness who never thinks . . ."]

The reassurances of a driving instructor who doesn't own a car are difficult to accept. [Not "The driving instructor's reassurances who doesn't . . ."]

The double possessive is a construction long established in standard English.

EXAMPLES

friends of Kara's   that old passion of mine   a colleague of his

Objective Case

4f. The objective case of the pronoun is used when the pronoun is the direct or indirect object of a verb or verbal.

DIRECT OBJECT

We liked *him*. Paul called *her*. The plumber tried to pay *him*. Punishing *him* did little good. The FBI indicted *them*.

INDIRECT OBJECT

The sheriff's wife served *them* their dinners. I offered to find *him* a good lawyer.

The need for objective case in a pronoun object that immediately follows a verb or verbal is easy to recognize. A fault is obvious in sentences such as "I saw *she* at the game" and "My father bought *we* a new surfboard." Three kinds of construction, however, may pose some difficulty.

1. *Who* and *whom* may be confused when they appear out of their normal subject-verb-object pattern. In ques-

328

tions, *who* beginning the sentence is used in informal speech for both the subject and the object forms, but formal writing requires *whom* as object.

CONVERSATIONAL

Who did you want to see?

I'd like to know *who* they're going to elect.

FORMAL

Whom can we trust at such a moment in history? [We can trust *whom*.]

Franco was the one *whom* they finally selected. [They selected *whom*.]

2. When the pronoun is the second of two objects connected by *and*.

EXAMPLES

The pilot told John and *me* to make the decision to jump. [Not *John and I*]

Everyone was astounded when the bowlers' association chose for membership both *her* and *me*. [Not *her and I*]

3. When the pronoun is the object of an implied verb, after *than* and *as* in clauses of comparison.

EXAMPLES

He always gave Jack more attention than [he gave] *me*.

Mary told me more about her secret life than [she told] *him*.

By reviewing paragraph 3, § 4a, you can observe the difference when the nominative pronoun is used as the subject of the implied verb in similar constructions:

EXAMPLE

Mary told me more about her secret life than *he* [told me about his].

329

4g. The objective case form is normally used when the pronoun is the object of a preposition.

Here again trouble arises not when the pronoun immediately follows a preposition, as in "I said to *her*" [not, of course, to *she*], but when the pronoun comes before its preposition or when it is the second of two objects.

EXAMPLES

It is difficult to predict *whom* the people will vote for. [For *whom*]

Whom could we turn to at a time like this? [To *whom*]

There was some controversy between *him* and *me*. [Not *him and I*]

Informal, conversational usage accepts *who* as the objective form, especially in questions, in which the pronoun may begin a sentence or a clause, such as "*Who* did you call for?" of "*Who* are you talking to?" But it is *not* acceptable, in either speech or writing, to use a nominative pronoun linked with a noun in the objective case, as in "of we citizens" or "between we men and women." Be wary, in fact, of using these constructions in formal writing, even with the proper objective pronoun. "A body of us citizens went to see the mayor" is not a very effective, serious sentence. "We concerned citizens went to see the mayor" is a better sentence.

4h. The objective case is proper when the pronoun is the assumed subject or the complement of the infinitive *to be*.

EXAMPLES

Everyone wanted *him* to be the leader of the shark-hunting trip.

The woman whom I thought to be *her* turned out to be someone else.

4i. A pronoun should agree with its antecedent in number, gender, and person.

330

4. PRONOUNS

The antecedent of a pronoun is the word or words to which the pronoun refers. If the antecedent is singular, the pronoun should be singular; if it is plural, the pronoun should be plural.

EXAMPLES

First one woman cast *her* vote.

Then three men cast *their* votes.

An old man cast *his* vote.

Mary and her lamb had left *their* house early.

The responsibility will probably fall to *me, who am* the oldest one present. [The awkwardness that agreement seems to cause here can be avoided by a simple revision: "I am the oldest one present."]

We prefer to speak to *you, who are* the president.

Here as elsewhere, when questions of usage arise, we must distinguish between what is customary in formal usage and what is accepted in conversational, informal situations. We shall discuss the problems of agreement in terms of certain typical trouble spots that often require more than one kind of answer.

1. In situations that call for more or less formal English, it is customary to use a singular pronoun to refer to any of the following: *anybody, anyone, everyone, everybody, nobody, no one, somebody, someone, person.*

In informal English, especially in conversation, these words, although they take singular verbs, are quite generally felt to be collectives (plural in sense), and the pronouns referring to them are often plural. In addition, all sorts of special situations arise. For instance, *each, every, everybody, everyone* have a general meaning of "all, or a group, but taken individually." Apparently it is the "group" sense that is dominant in influencing the number of the pronoun referring to one of these words. In some cases, when the group consists of both males and females, the speaker uses the plural form because he feels that neither *his* nor *her* is quite accurate. Finally, in some situations, such as in this sentence, "Everybody started to laugh, but in a moment *they* realized that the speaker was not joking," the singular form just would not make sense.

FORMAL AGREEMENT

England expects every man to do *his* duty. [No question of gender here]

Everyone must do *his* part in this war.

Nobody has a right to think that *his* happiness is more important than the happiness of others.

OFTEN ACCEPTED IN CONVERSATION

Somebody must have left *their* coat here after the party.

Everyone ought to feel that *their* vote really counts.

By "often accepted," however, we do not mean universally accepted, even in conversation, and in any case a stricter agreement is required in formal written English.

2. Either a singular or plural pronoun may be used to refer to a collective noun, depending on whether the noun designates the group as a whole or the members of the group. *Consistency is the governing principle.* The construction should be either singular or plural, but not both.

INCONSISTENT

The cast *is* giving *their* best performance tonight. [The verb is singular but the pronoun is plural.]

The team *is* now on the floor, taking *their* practice shots at the basket. [Again, verb and pronoun indicate a shift in number.]

CONSISTENT

The cast *is* giving *its* best performance tonight.

The team *are* on the floor now, taking *their* practice shots. [The team is thought of as being more than one person.]

332

4. PRONOUNS

Other collective nouns to watch for are *faculty, legislature, student body, union.*

3. Ordinarily one of the masculine pronouns, *he, his, him,* is used to refer to one of these "group taken individually" words. *He or she, his or her, him or her* are now generally accepted as substitutes.

EXAMPLES

Every *person* in the audience was requested to put *his* [or *his or her*] loose change in the basket.

It has also been common and correct to use one of the masculine pronouns when the antecedent of the pronoun gives no indication of gender but might refer to either a man or a woman.

EXAMPLES

Every *author* is responsible for proofreading *his* book.

The good *cook* invents *his* own dishes.

To follow this practice is still correct; however, it is also correct (and sometimes desirable) to acknowledge both genders in the pronoun.

EXAMPLES

The *writer* must make up *his or her* mind on the question.

What secretary would let the boss dictate to *him or her* during the lunch break?

The average homeowner hasn't a moment to call *his or her* own; *he or she* spends *his or her* free moments struggling to keep *his or her* private castle from decaying until it is offensive to *his or her* neighbors.

The last example shows the awkwardness of sustaining the doubled pronoun construction throughout frequent references. When the *he and she*'s begin to pile up and overwhelm everything else in a sentence or paragraph,

333

the awkwardness can be overcome by using a plural construction. "Average homeowners haven't a moment to call *their* own; *they* spend their free moments . . . to keep *their* . . . to *their*. . . ." It may sometimes be best to recast the whole to avoid the need for pronouns altogether.

Note: The shorthand device *he/she* should never be used in any sort of formal exposition; it has no oral equivalent and labels its writer as someone who has no thought for the sound of words. Never use the device in essays written for class.

4. In modern usage, the relative pronoun *who* is used to refer to persons and occasionally to animals, but *whose* may refer to persons, animals, or things, especially when *of which* produces an awkward construction. The relative pronouns *that* and *which* may refer to persons, animals, places, things, and ideas.

EXAMPLES

My brother, *who* is an art critic, particularly admires modern painting. It is a taste *that* I cannot understand. He once gave me a painting, *which* I hung upside down in my room. It is a masterpiece *whose* meaning is obscure, at least to me. But my best friend, *whose* critical taste I admire, thinks it is magnificent. Taste in art is something *that* I find hard to fathom.

For at least a century many respected writers have used *that* and *which* interchangeably as relative pronouns, often making their choice on the assumption that *which* is somehow more refined than *that.* Between the two words, however, there is a distinction that very precise writers may wish to observe. *That* is a *restrictive* relative pronoun. It introduces a clause that particularizes or identifies the antecedent so that the antecedent may not be mistaken for anything else.

EXAMPLE

Bring me the umbrella *that* is drying in the hall. (There may be half a dozen umbrellas lying around, but I want only the one *that* is drying in the hall.)

334

4. *PRONOUNS*

In a *nonrestrictive* clause, one that adds information about an antecedent but does not single the antecedent out, *which* is the proper, formal relative pronoun.

EXAMPLE

Bring me my umbrella, *which* is drying in the hall. [*Drying in the hall* is only one of many details—color, size, style—the speaker might have offered. Note too that a nonrestrictive clause, unlike a restrictive one, is usually enclosed by commas.]

See "A Guide to Usage," page 546.

5. When *one* is the antecedent, American usage prefers *he* and *his* (or *he or she, his or her*) to the repetition of *one,* which is regarded as too formal.

TOO FORMAL

One must not lose one's temper when one is being criticized for one's choice of shoes. [Most people would regard this as affected. The formality, however, does avoid the problem of identifying *one* in any particular gender.]

ACCEPTED FORMAL ENGLISH

A person must not lose his temper when he is being criticized for his choice of shoes.

If one were to read between the lines, he would quickly detect the irony in Swift's proposal to use babies as food.

The informal equivalent of these expressions is the second person pronoun.

INFORMAL

You mustn't lose your temper when being criticized for your taste in clothes.

6. Pronouns used in apposition are the same case as their antecedents.

EXAMPLES

The reward was divided among us three, George, Tom, and *me.* [Not *I*]

335

They had told *us*—*him* and *me*—to report to headquarters immediately.

EXERCISES

EXERCISE 1, CASE OF PRONOUNS. *In the following sentences, tell whether each of the italicized pronouns is used as the subject of a verb, the complement of a verb or verbal, or the object of a preposition.*

1. *I* wonder whether *you* will walk downtown with Harris and *me*.
2. *We* must visit a lawyer *whom we* talked to last week.
3. *I* usually try to bring along *whoever* wants to come, if *he* asks *me*.
4. *Neither* of *us* is quite sure what the lawyer wants *us* to do.
5. *Who* else do *you* suppose would care to come with *us*?
6. A woman can often be of assistance to *us* men in such cases if *she* wishes.
7. *It* was *she* who helped *us* last time.
8. *Everyone* knows a lawyer can be difficult for those of *us* victims who are unsure of *themselves*.
9. If *he* says, "Try to remember *whom* you met that day," I am likely to forget *whoever* it may have been.
10. *You* are more quick-witted than *I*, so come along.

EXERCISE 2, CORRECTING PRONOUN ERRORS. *Correct every error in the use of pronouns in the following sentences. Assume that your corrected sentences are to appear in a college theme, not in informal conversation.*

1. Lorraine, who is more energetic than me, is the person they should have for the job of president.
2. We voters, of course, are the only ones who's preference matters.
3. Of all we people whom I think should be available for office, Lorraine is the first who comes to mind.
4. But the whole question, as I say, is up to we voters, who will cast our ballots on Friday.

5. When a person casts their ballots, they have to consider very carefully who they should vote for.
6. At any rate Lorraine is the person whom I feel sure will be most adequate to serve us all, and everybody will be pleased with their new leader.
7. If I were her I would be overjoyed at their showing so much confidence in me.
8. Yesterday a member said to Lorraine and I that they would probably give her or me their vote.
9. You probably know to who I am referring.
10. No one could be more pleased by such information than me, who is always eager to serve.

EXERCISE 3, FORMAL AND INFORMAL ENGLISH. *For each of the following sentences, provide two versions, one of which can be, but need not necessarily be, the form given here. One version should be appropriate to conversational speech, and one appropriate to graceful, formal, written English. In some cases (as in the first sentence), you should revise wording that may be formally correct but that is awkward or stuffy. In some cases you may feel that your two versions should be identical; after all, good written prose and good conversation may employ in very many instances exactly the same language. Do not be afraid to remove pronouns altogether in the interests of realistic speech or graceful prose.*

1. It is I who am best prepared of all those whom you have available for the task which we have been discussing.
2. I wonder who he's talking to—me?
3. One should not exaggerate one's virtues in order to impress one's listener with one's superiority.
4. Who is it? It is I.
5. Some people whom I know intimately are likely to assert that which they know with altogether too much passion.
6. Everybody has their own opinion about that.
7. I wonder who he's going to call on next.
8. Somebody left their raincoat on this rack; he will have to come and get it.
9. Those to whom I have spoken on the subject which is before us have made the point that all is lost which

5

is not pursued vigorously, and I am bound to agree
with their opinion.
10. Whoever I need, I get.

§ 5. ADJECTIVES AND ADVERBS

**Distinguish between adjectives and adverbs and use the
correct forms of each.**

*Adjectives modify nouns. Adverbs modify verbs, adjectives, other
adverbs, or groups of words, such as phrases and clauses,* even
when they are whole sentences. One superficial sign of
distinction between the two is that most adverbs end in
-ly. A few adjectives, such as *friendly* and *lovely,* also have
the *-ly* ending, and a number of common adverbs, such
as *fast, far, here, there, near, soon,* do not. Usually these are
not hard to recognize.

ADJECTIVE

That's a *friendly* gesture.

He is a *violent* man.

She is a *lazy* person.

ADVERB

Butter it *only* on one side.

She learns *fast.*

I shook him *violently.*

He sat *lazily* in the sun.

The wine should arrive *soon.*

Actually the difference between adjectives and adverbs
depends not on a distinctive form or ending but on the
way the words function in sentences. Thus a number of

338

familiar words are used as either adjectives or adverbs, depending on function. In the list below, note that *when the word modifies a noun, it is used as an adjective; when it modifies a verb, an adjective, or another adverb, it is used as an adverb.*

EXAMPLES

	ADJECTIVES	**ADVERBS**
deep	We dug a *deep* well.	He dug down *deep*.
early	I am an *early* bird.	They sent us home *early*.
fast	He is a *fast* walker.	He walks much too *fast*.
little	It is a *little* game.	The game is *little* understood.
right	I wish I had the *right* answer.	I wish I could do it *right*.

```
  S   |   V   |   O             S    |    V      |    O
  I   |  had  | answer          I    |  could do |    it
            \ right                        \ right
```

5a. The clumsy or awkward use of a noun form as an adjective should be avoided.

In our flexible language, as we have seen, words commonly used as nouns can also function as adjective modifiers, as in a *bird* dog, a *house* cat, an *ivory* tower, an *iron* rod, a *silk* dress, a *flower* pot, the *New York* streets, the *boat* people. These are natural and legitimate uses. The objection is to awkward or ambiguous uses, as in the following examples:

AWKWARD

We heard a communism lecture.

It was really a heart attack sign.

Then we heard the mayor of Disneyland's speech.

She's really a fun person to be with.

BETTER

We listened to a lecture explaining communism.

It was a symptom of a heart attack.

Then we heard the speech made by the mayor of Disneyland.

You'll have a lot of fun in her company.

5b. Use the adjective after certain linking verbs, such as *be, become, appear, seem, prove, remain, look, smell, taste, feel.*

A linking verb is completed by a subjective complement, either a noun or an adjective. The adjective complement describes the subject.

The woman was *quiet.* [The *quiet* woman]

woman	was \	quiet

The little boy appears *happy.* [The *happy* little boy]

Hyacinths smell *sweet.* [*Sweet* hyacinths]

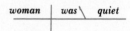

hyacinths	smell \	sweet

This water tastes *bad.* [*Bad* water]

water	tastes \	bad

The report proved *true.* [*True* report]

With some of the verbs, when the word in the predicate refers to the manner of the action and not to the subject, it is, of course, an adverb, and the adverb form must be used.

340

5. ADJECTIVES AND ADVERBS

The Martian appeared *unexpectedly.*

The man felt *carefully* for the door.

She looked *quickly* at me.

We tasted the water *suspiciously.*

5c. Use the adverb form for a word that modifies a verb, an adjective, or another adverb.

ADVERB MODIFYING A VERB

He dresses *well* [not *good*], but his manners are poor.

During the summer I improved my tennis game *considerably.* [Not *considerable*]

Although he talks *cleverly* [not *clever*], his arguments are shallow.

ADVERB MODIFYING AN ADJECTIVE

My uncle was *really* [not *real*] happy to see us again.

It was *awfully* [not *awful*] generous of you to help us out.

ADVERB MODIFYING ANOTHER ADVERB

He slid down the hill *considerably* [not *considerable*] faster than he had crawled up.

He *almost* [not *most* or *mostly*] always jogs before breakfast.

Most of the difficulties center in a few words, of which the following are typical: *bad—badly, good—well, sure—surely, real—really, most—almost, awful—awfully, considerable—considerably.*

The words *most* and *almost* present a special problem. In formal usage, *almost* is the accepted modifier in such expressions as: almost all were saved; summer is almost here; we almost never see him; almost everyone respects him. But in informal conversation, *most* is widely used in

341

5

those situations. In your writing it is best to follow formal usage.

5d. Certain colloquial uses of adjective and adverb should be avoided: *type, like, -wise.*

UNDESIRABLE

This *type* screw won't go into that *type* wood.

Hers is not a power-*type* serve.

BETTER

This kind of screw will not go into that kind of wood.

Hers is not a powerful serve.

UNDESIRABLE

I slid down the hill *like,* and then I saw this, *like,* glow in the sky.

It was *like* hours, you know, before the bus came.

BETTER

I slid down the hill, and then I saw a glow in the sky.

It was hours before the bus came.

UNDESIRABLE

Moneywise I was in favor of it, but *fraternitywise* I was against it.

Timewise we were in real trouble.

BETTER

The proposal was good financially, but I disapproved of it in the interest of the fraternity.

We had almost no time left.

5e. When an adverb has two forms (the short and the -ly forms), any difference in their use or meaning is determined by idiom.

5. ADJECTIVES AND ADVERBS

The following adverbs—and a few others—have two forms:

bright—brightly	high—highly	near—nearly
cheap—cheaply	late—lately	right—rightly
close—closely	loose—loosely	tight—tightly
deep—deeply	loud—loudly	wrong—wrongly

The adverbs in these pairs are not always interchangeable. Nor is there any quick and easy way of learning how to distinguish them in meaning and function. Using them in sentences, as in the following, will help.

IDIOMATIC	INEFFECTIVE IDIOM
Lately the son has been staying out late.	Late the son has been staying out lately.
The dog crept close to me.	The dog crept closely to me.
Nobody was near.	Nobody was nearly.
He was highly respected.	He was high respected.
The woman slowly opened the door.	The woman slow opened the door.
Go slow. Drive slow. Go slowly. Drive slowly.	

5f. Observe the distinction between the comparative and the superlative.

The positive form of an adjective or adverb assigns a quality to the word it modifies, as in "a *big* bed," "he walked *rapidly*." The comparative degree is formed by adding *-er* to the positive or by using *more* or *less* with the positive, as in "a *bigger* bed," "he walked *more rapidly*" (not *rapider*).

The superlative degree is formed by adding *-est* to the positive form, or by using *most* or *least* with the positive. The superlative degree ranks the modified word highest or lowest in a class. It implies that there are at least three things in a class: "a *big* bed," "a *bigger* bed," "the *biggest* bed." [See also § 33.]

343

5

The comparative degree, then, is used when referring to two persons or things; the superlative degree is used when three or more persons or things are involved.

COMPARATIVE

He was *taller* than his brother.

Of the two boys, John was the *more intelligent* and the *more cooperative*.

She learned *faster* than I [not *me*].

SUPERLATIVE

He was the *tallest* boy on the basketball team. [More than two]

John was the *most intelligent* and the *most cooperative* boy in school. [Highest in a group consisting of more than two]

She learned *fastest* of us all.

Some words are compared irregularly:

many	more	most		much	more	most
bad	worse	worst		good	better	best
little	less *or* lesser	least		well	better	best
little	littler	littlest				

Adjectives of more than two syllables rarely take *-er* and *-est* to form comparatives and superlatives. Forms such as *famouser* or *magnificentest* are not modern English. In formal writing, it is best not to use comparative or superlative forms of adjectives that name qualities thought of as absolute, such as *more perfect, most perfect, most unique.*

Those who object to modification or qualification of *unique, perfect, complete, black,* and other words that express absolute states or qualities may use *most nearly unique, more nearly* or *most nearly perfect, most nearly complete, most nearly black,* and so on. When the makers of our Constitution wrote, "We the people of the United States, in order to

344

form a *more perfect* union . . . ," they may have had *more nearly perfect* in mind. Or they may have accepted usage without giving it much thought.

In modern English one does not combine two superlatives to form a kind of super-superlative. The same principle applies to comparatives.

WRONG

That is the *most unkindest* thing you could have said.

RIGHT

That is the *most unkind* thing you could have said.

WRONG

He finally reached the *more remoter* regions of the country.

RIGHT

He finally reached the *remoter* regions of the country.

EXERCISES

EXERCISE 1, RECOGNIZING ADJECTIVES AND ADVERBS. *Copy the following sentences. Underline each adjective once and each adverb twice.*

1. Her spirits were high because the sun shone bright on her graduation day.
2. You may be right, but the little boy climbing the mountain does not appear lazy.
3. The aged teacher was considerably provoked because the bright students protested loudly against the assignment.
4. When he awoke after a deep sleep, he noticed that the cold morning air smelled fresh and sweet.
5. All decisions regarding high policy must be highly respected, whether they are right or wrong.
6. Then, too, a lively conversation with the kindly old man was an awfully pleasant price for a delicious dinner.

5

5

7. The room smells stuffy, the milk tastes sour, the oil-cloth feels gritty, the toast appears sooty, and the prospect for a happy day looks poor.
8. The housekeeper is coming early, I am sure, because everything looks wrong in my room.
9. Really, I feel well, although I did not sleep well last night.
10. Things look bad everywhere today.

EXERCISE 2, CORRECTING ADJECTIVE AND ADVERB ERRORS. *Correct the error in the form or use of the adjective or adverb in each of the following sentences.*

1. In the window she saw a gown that was richer and luxuriouser than anything she could imagine.
2. His manners were gentlemanly and he spoke friendly to me, but I could not trust him with the gun in his hand.
3. All the players felt unhappily after losing the game, and the alumni sure felt bad about it too.
4. You have been so good to me that I feel cheaply because I cannot repay you.
5. Lately he has taken to driving his sports car real fast.
6. I am most ready; my paper is near finished.
7. There is considerable merit in your paper ideawise, but structurewise it is badly arranged.
8. When I compare it with the one written by Anne on paperweights, it is real hard to say which is worst.
9. He held the bat closely to his chest and then hit the ball highly in the air.
10. Sit tight; the doctor is near ready to see you.

EXERCISE 3, CHOOSING CORRECT ADJECTIVE AND ADVERB FORMS. *In each of the following sentences select the correct form of the adjective or adverb.*

1. I was (really carefully, real careful, really careful) about mounting the horse with red in his eye.
2. In spite of his education, he still does not read (well, good).

3. We drove (slow and careful, slowly and carefully) over the icy roads.
4. When we lost our way, Tracy (sure, surely) felt (bad, badly).
5. Like most careful persons, he takes his driving (real serious, really seriously).
6. Eugene is the (tallest, taller) of the two forwards on the team.
7. Tony did (good, well) on his English test.
8. Tony is (carefuller, more careful) than Eugene.
9. Eugene's history essay was (more perfect, more nearly perfect) than Tony's.
10. Harriet looked (curious, curiously), but actually she was only amused.

6

§ 6. VERB FORMS

The appropriate form of the verb should be used.

A student who is uncertain about the right form of a verb turns to the dictionary for help. We omit guides for pronunciation:

lay, *v.t.* [LAID, LAYING]
lead, *v.t.* [LED, LEADING]
lie, *v.i.* [LAY, LAIN, LYING]
look, *v.i.*

A dictionary gives what are known as the *principal parts* of a verb, or as many of them as are necessary. Verbs are *regular* or *irregular,* and this distinction controls the amount of information that the dictionary gives. The regular verbs form their past tense and their past participle by adding *-d, -t,* or *-ed* to the present: "I *looked,*" "I *have looked.*" Therefore only one part *(look)* is sufficient. But the irregular verbs change the present stem form to make the past tense and the past participle: "I *lie* on the floor," "I *lay* on the floor," "I *have lain* on the floor." The dictionary gives as many principal parts as are necessary to indicate all the forms of the verb—or its *conjugation.* In the case of *lie,* the dictionary lists all the principal parts— namely, the past tense, the past participle, and the present participle. When the dictionary does not list the past participle of an irregular verb, it is assumed that it is the same as the past tense, as in "I *lead,*" "I *led,*" "I *have led.*"

An abridged conjugation of the verb *take* follows. For other forms and their uses, see §6a. The principal parts of *take* are *take, took, taken, taking.*

INDICATIVE MOOD

ACTIVE VOICE		**PASSIVE VOICE**	
Singular	*Plural*	*Singular*	*Plural*
PRESENT TENSE			
I take	we take	I am taken	we are taken
you take	you take	you are taken	you are taken
he takes	they take	he is taken	they are taken
PAST TENSE			
I took	we took	I was taken	we were taken
you took	you took	you were taken	you were taken
he took	they took	he was taken	they were taken
FUTURE TENSE			
I shall (will) take	we shall (will) take	I shall (will) be taken	we shall (will) be taken
you will take	you will take	you will be taken	you will be taken
he will take	they will take	he will be taken	they will be taken
PRESENT PERFECT TENSE			
I have taken	we have taken	I have been taken	we have been taken
you have taken	you have taken	you have been taken	you have been taken
he has taken	they have taken	he has been taken	they have been taken

348

6. VERB FORMS

PAST PERFECT TENSE

I had taken	we had taken	I had been taken	we had been taken
you had taken	you had taken	you had been taken	you had been taken
he had taken	they had taken	he had been taken	they had been taken

FUTURE PERFECT TENSE

I shall (will) have taken	we shall (will) have taken	I shall (will) have been taken	we shall (will) have been taken
you will have taken	you will have taken	you will have been taken	you will have been taken
he will have taken	they will have taken	he will have been taken	they will have been taken

IMPERATIVE FORMS: take, be taken
INFINITIVE FORMS: to take, to have taken, to be taken, to have been taken
GERUNDS: taking, having taken, being taken, having been taken
PARTICIPLES: taking, taken, having taken, being taken, having been taken

Tenses

6a. The correct tense forms of the verb should be used.

1. The Present Time. Present time may be expressed by three main verb forms. The *simple present* tense form usually expresses general or habitual action: "I *work*," "he *teaches*," "she *lives* in Albany," "they *drive* a Mazda." To express action as going on at the present time we use the *progressive* form of the present: "I *am working*," "he *is teaching*," "she *is living* in Albany," "they *are driving* a Mazda." There is also a present auxiliary form, "do," which is used for emphasis (I *do work*), for negations (she *does* not *teach*), and for questions (*does* she *live* in Albany?).
2. The Past Time. Past time is usually expressed by the *past tense*, as in "I *studied*," "she *played* the piano," "he

6

taught," "I *worked.*" Past time may also be indicated by the present tense form (called the *historical present*), as "The captain *looks* at me, and I *stare* back at him, and he *says* to me . . ." It is a device that should be avoided in writing, except as part of dialogue, or in narrative writing that expresses vivid feelings and sense impressions.

3. The Perfect Tenses. The *present perfect* tense shows that an act has been completed prior to the present.

EXAMPLES

The attendants *have taken* all the tickets.

All the tickets *have been taken.*

The *past perfect* tense shows that an act was already completed before some specified or understood time in the past.

EXAMPLES

I *had heard* about the crash before you told me.

He *had* already *paid* his respects to the deceased.

The *future perfect* tense, which is less common than the others, indicates a future act as having already taken place, in relation to some specified or understood time in the future.

EXAMPLES

He *will have counted* the money by the time the police arrive to collect him.

By late this afternoon the money *will have been counted.*

4. The Future Time. Future time may be indicated in several ways. It may be indicated by the *present tense with an adverb or an adverbial phrase of time.*

EXAMPLES

We *arrive* in Chicago in *thirty minutes.*

Our wedding *takes* place *next June.*

350

6. VERB FORMS

The future may also be indicated by using *going to* or *about to* with the verb.

EXAMPLES

We *are going to stay* overnight in Chicago.

He *is about to declare* himself a candidate.

Shall—Will, Should—Would. Finally, and most obviously, the future may be indicated by using *shall* or *will* with the verb. Attitudes toward the use of *shall* and *will* have provoked controversy because the words are another illustration of the language in rapid change, and when usage changes quickly, controversy often arises. But the distinction between *shall* and *will,* once considered vital to educated English, now no longer seems so important. In modern informal speech, most people use *will* and *would* (or the contractions *I'll, he'll, he'd, you'd*) for all expressions of the future, and many do the same in writing. Others, at least in writing, use *shall* and *should* for the first person singular and plural, and *will* and *would* for the second and third persons. Once again, these seemingly trivial choices have their effect on tone: to maintain the *shall—will* distinction is to add a slight touch of traditional formality to the style.

Those who do maintain the distinction observe, in general, the following rules: for simple future, *shall* with the first person, *will* with the second and third persons; for the emphatic future, *will* for the first person, *shall* for the second and third persons.

EXAMPLES

I shall discuss the uses of verbs, and you will write the appropriate forms.

You will have to study diligently if you are to put them to good use.

In asking questions, *shall* is ordinarily used with the first and third persons and *will* with the second person when

351

a request for permission is implied: *"Shall* I wrap it up for you?" *"Shall* he take you home?" *"Will* you do it?" A note of formality may be imparted to a question if the speaker uses the form that he anticipates in the answer: *"Shall* you be at the meeting?" "I *shall."*

To express habitual or customary action, *would* is generally used in all three persons; *should,* however, may be found in the first person.

EXAMPLES

She *would* read in the library instead of playing tennis with her friends.

He *would* sit in his rocker and knit all day long.

I *would* [*should*] be grateful for your advice.

Should is often used in the sense of *ought,* although in some sentences *ought* may imply a slightly stronger sense of obligation.

EXAMPLES

He really *should keep* his mouth shut. [He *ought to* . . .]

The policy *should have been defined* long before this. [The policy *ought to have been defined* . . .]

You *ought* to stop throwing cream pies at celebrities.

Sequence of Tenses. Use the tenses that show the correct relation of time between the main verb and the subordinate verb. When, for example, a verb indicates action that took place before the action of the main verb, and the main verb is in the past tense, then the subordinate verb must of course be past perfect.

EXAMPLES

After I *had talked* with him for a while, he *was* more agreeable.

When they *had run* ten miles, they *decided* to stop.

352

6. VERB FORMS

Be careful to use the correct tense of infinitives and participles. Notice in the following examples that the time indicated by the verbal is always in relation to the time expressed by the main verb. That is, a present infinitive indicates the same time as the main verb, even when the main verb is past.

EXAMPLES

I was very pleased *to hear* from you. [Not *to have heard*]

She intended *to go* home, but she did not make it. [Not *to have gone*]

With participles, a past tense of the participle must be used to indicate a time previous to the main verb.

EXAMPLES

Having played tennis all day, we were tired. [Not *playing*]

Talking as we walked along, we soon arrived at the cliff's edge. [Not *having talked*]

Careless Shifts in Tense. In telling a story or recounting an event, it is undesirable to shift from past to present or from present to past unless there is a real change in time of the action being described. For this reason the historical present should be used with care. (See also § § 31 and 33.)

CARELESS SHIFT

I *went* out the door and *walked* slowly down the street, where the traffic *seemed* even more noisy than usual. Suddenly a man *approaches* me from an alley. "Look!" he *says,* and *forces* a piece of paper into my hand; but when I *looked* at it I *saw* nothing. I *continued* my walk.

THE SUBJUNCTIVE

6b. The subjunctive mood is used in a number of situations in formal writing.

The only uses of the subjunctive the student need be concerned about in speech and writing are the following:

353

6

1. In *if*-clauses expressing doubt or impossibility of the condition (usually referred to as "condition contrary to fact").

EXAMPLES

If she *were* here, you would not dare insult her.

Were he with us today, he would be gratified at this scene. [This word order now has a somewhat old-fashioned ring.]

Were we to pursue the investigation, you would soon become uneasy.

Note that when the condition is *not* contrary to fact, the subjunctive is not used.

EXAMPLES

Either he was here or he was not. If he was here, then he must know that his stereo was stolen.

If she did go swimming, she must have noticed the piranhas.

2. In *that*-clauses expressing a wish, request, or command.

EXAMPLES

The president has ordered that all prisoners *be* treated equally.

I demand that he *come* here at once. [Again, note the relative formality of these sentences using the subjunctive. *Compare:* I want him to come here at once.]

3. In main clauses to express hope, wish, or prayer, usually in traditional and stereotyped patterns.

EXAMPLES

The Force *be* with you.

Long *live* rock and roll!

"The rules *be* damned!" shouted the losing coach.

6. VERB FORMS

With regard to the form of the verb, we can say that for most verbs the subjunctive form differs from the indicative in only the third person singular of the present tense.

INDICATIVE		SUBJUNCTIVE	
I take	we take	if I take	if we take
you take	you take	if you take	if you take
he takes	they take	if he take	if they take

[*Note: If* here is only an indicator of the subjunctive mood. *Should* is also sometimes used for the same purpose.]

EXAMPLES

We recommend that he *take* the entrance examination.

The remark about his hairpiece could hurt, should he *take* it the wrong way.

The verb *to be* is a special problem. The problem may be simplified by saying that the subjunctive of *to be* uses:
1. *Be* in all forms of the present tense.
2. *Were* in all forms of the past tense.
3. *Have been* in all forms of the present perfect tense.

EXAMPLES

Be it ever so noisy, there is no place like the dorm.

Were you as busy as I was at that moment, you would not have asked me to help you.

Voice

6c. The passive voice of the verb should not be overused.

In most writing, and especially narrative and descriptive writing, the active voice is preferred as more direct, vivid, and emphatic than the passive voice. It is obviously simpler and clearer to say "I hit the intruder on the nose" than

6

"the intruder was hit on the nose by me." But the passive voice has its legitimate uses, as the first sentence in this paragraph should testify. It is indispensable when *the action of the verb is more important than the doer, when the doer of action may not be known,* or *when the writer may wish to place emphasis on the recipient of the action rather than on the doer.*

EXAMPLES

Twenty thousand dollars was collected from a number of sources.

Another man was fired last night.

All the bridges were destroyed during the war.

It is not the passive voice in itself that is objectionable—it is the overuse or misuse of it. Constant repetition of passive verbs can create an effect of deadness in the action of the prose, as if nothing *did* anything but instead sat around waiting for something *to be done to it.*

The passive voice becomes the scapegoat if not the actual criminal when there is a shift in point of view in a group of sentences. Notice what happens in the following sentences:

CONFUSED

One person may be writing a letter; a book absorbs the attention of another. As usual someone sat in her chair sound asleep. Constant whispers could have been heard by the lecturer. [The effect here is similar to that found in a carelessly edited film, where an actor exits screen left and reappears screen right without any visible reason for the flip. Continuity is lost.]

CONSISTENT

During the lecture, one person is writing a letter; another is reading a book. As usual someone sits sound asleep. Several people are whispering constantly.

The passive voice, on the other hand, may be useful in enabling a writer to maintain his point of view through several sentences.

356

SHIFT IN POINT OF VIEW

She sat absorbed in her book. A frown could be seen on her face. Then a long whistle from outside interrupted her thoughts. She glanced in annoyance toward the window. Then she smiled as if what she saw there amused her. It was Spot, the whistling beagle.

CONSISTENT POINT OF VIEW

As she sat there frowning, absorbed in her book, her thoughts were interrupted by a long whistle from outside. Annoyed, she glanced through the open window. Then she smiled at what she saw there. It was Spot, the whistling beagle.

6

EXERCISES

EXERCISE 1, PRINCIPAL PARTS. *With the help of your dictionary, if necessary, find the principal parts of the following verbs. List the form given, the past tense, the past participle, and the present participle or gerund; for example,* begin, began, begun, beginning.

bear	dive	know	raise	spring
blow	drink	lay	ride	sting
break	drive	lead	ring	swim
bring	eat	lend	rise	take
burst	get	lie	set	throw
buy	go	lose	shake	wake
choose	grow	prove	sink	write

EXERCISE 2, TENSES. *Make necessary corrections of tenses in the following sentences.*

1. I was eager to have learned German since I planned to go to Berlin.
2. I told everyone I bought my ticket two days before.
3. Learning the language in a few weeks, I was ready to go at last.
4. I should have purchased a round trip ticket, but I failed to do so.
5. Will you be in Berlin at any time this summer?

6

6. The year before, I had traveled in England so that I could have spent some time with a friend of mine in London.
7. Shall I try it once more?
8. By midnight we shall have reached our first destination.
9. I was pleased yesterday to have heard from you at last.
10. Knowing what a good correspondent you are, I look forward to hearing from you soon.

EXERCISE 3, THE SUBJUNCTIVE. *In the following sentences select the correct forms from those given in parentheses.*

1. I requested that an invitation (be, is, was) sent to them immediately.
2. We all wish we (are, were) with you at this time.
3. He demanded that their rock throwing (cease, ceased, ceases) at once.
4. We suggested that he (withdraw, withdraws) these demands.
5. He looks as if he (is, were) angry, but one cannot be sure.
6. I know he (is, were) angry because I heard him swear.
7. My suggestion is that he (bring, brings) you along with him.
8. Finally someone made the motion that the whole discussion (is, be, was) dropped.
9. If Jack (is, were) here at last, you (should, would) not treat me this way.
10. Since Jack (is, were) here at last, you will not treat me this way.

EXERCISE 4, PASSIVE AND ACTIVE VOICE. *In the following sentences change the passive constructions to active ones where appropriate. Remember that there are some legitimate uses of the passive.*

1. I am seen at the corner disco every night.
2. Another operator was fired last night for playing Glenn Miller records.

3. Bernie Lablatt attracts everyone's attention when he dances with Natalie Strobe.
4. Frantic whispers can be heard by the manager when the chandelier stops spinning.
5. I was bumped into at least twice by Alice Cooper.
6. All the wooden tables were imported from France.
7. A smile could be seen on Lorna's face when they showed the clip from *Disco Drive-in*.
8. At least ten thousand dollars is made there every night.
9. Claude claimed that illegal sales were taking place downstairs.
10. In her usual witty way Mindy observed that a swinging time was had by all.

6

10 *Mechanics*

§ 7. MANUSCRIPT: FORM AND REVISION

7a. In the preparation of manuscript, follow standard procedures and any special instructions given you by your English instructor.

1. *Use standard typewriter paper or, for handwritten papers, the 8½ × 11 ruled theme paper.* Most English departments require composition students to use regulation typewriter paper, unruled if the themes are typewritten, ruled if the themes are handwritten. If you use narrow-ruled notebook paper for a theme, write on every other line.

2. *Write legibly.* If you write by hand, make your writing easy to read. Write with a good pen and use black or dark blue ink. Do not use red, violet, or green ink. Form all letters distinctly, especially those that might be confused with other letters. Dot your *i*'s and cross your *t*'s. Do not decorate your letters with unnecessary loops and flourishes. Indicate paragraphing clearly by indenting about an inch.

3. *Type legibly.* If you use a typewriter, see that the ribbon is fresh and the type clean. Adjust your margin properly. *Always double-space your typing.* Space five spaces for paragraph indentions, one space between words, and two spaces after the end punctuation of a sentence. If you must delete material in typing, use one of the convenient correction tapes or liquids. *If you must cross out any considerable portion of your material, type your page over again.* Never begin a line with a punctuation mark, such as a comma, a period, a question mark, or an exclamation point, that belongs at the end of the preceding line.

360

7

4. *Label your themes correctly.* Use the method of labeling papers recommended by your instructor. Follow his or her instructions exactly. If the themes are to be handed in on flat, unfolded sheets of paper (the method preferred by all publishers), the correct place for the name, the page number, and the theme number is the upper right-hand corner of each page. Of course, you should never write on the back of the paper.

5. *Be careful about the correct placement and capitalization of the title.* Write the title on the first line of the first page only, or about two inches from the top of the sheet. Center the title on the page. Capitalize the first word and all important words in the title. The usual practice is to capitalize all nouns, pronouns, verbs, adverbs, and adjectives, and all prepositions that stand last or contain more than five letters. Do not underline the title or enclose it in quotation marks, unless the title is a quotation, and you wish to emphasize that it is quoted. Do not use a period after it, but you may use a question mark or an exclamation point if the sense of the title calls for either of these marks. Leave a space of about an inch between the title and the first line of your theme. Do not repeat the title on succeeding pages.

6. *Use proper margins.* Leave margins of an inch at the top and at the left of each page. Do not crowd your words at the right or at the bottom of the page. Some instructors like a wide margin at the right as well as at the left of the page so as to have room for comments and corrections. After the first page, begin writing on the first line.

If you are quoting verse, center your quotation on the page and follow the line arrangement of the poem from which you are quoting. *No quotation marks are needed.* If the quotation does not end a paragraph, begin the next line of your composition flush with the left margin.

7. *Make deletions and corrections clearly.* Parentheses and brackets are never used to delete or cross out a word. These marks have other uses.

To delete material, draw a horizontal line through it. In typing, material may be deleted by typing a capital *M*

7

over it—if the section to be crossed out is not too extensive. Otherwise use some kind of liquid white-out or correcting tape.

If you wish to insert a correction in your text, mark the point of insertion with a caret (∧) and write the inserted material above the caret.

7b. Revise your manuscript carefully, both before you hand it in and after it has been returned to you for correction.

1. *Go over the first draft of your paper and copy it for final submission.* In revising your first draft, you should consider the following checklist:
   a. Has the paper an objective, a central idea, a direction?
   b. Is the content made interesting by facts and examples?
   c. Is the organization, in the whole paper and in the separate paragraphs, as logical as possible?
   d. Are there obvious errors in sentence structure to correct, such as the period fault, the comma splice, failure of verbs and subjects to agree?
   e. Are the punctuation and spelling correct?

2. *Revise your paper carefully after the instructor has returned it to you.* Make every correction indicated or suggested by your instructor. If he or she refers you to a handbook section, first study the section carefully to see how it applies to your error. Then, in pencil or a distinctive color of ink, draw a horizontal line through the word or words you wish to cancel, and in the space above, between the lines, write the revised version. If for any reason you do not have the time to revise the returned paper, at least make sure that you know what the faults indicated are and how you would revise them had you the time.

On pages 365–366, you will find the process of correction and revision illustrated.

On page 365 are two paragraphs of prose filled with elementary errors. The instructor has used section numbers from this "Handbook" to show the student where each kind of error is discussed and the correction explained. If the instructor had wished to be more explicit, he or she would have underlined the points of error.

On page 366, the same selection appears. This time the instructor has used correction symbols, according to the system indicated on the inside of the back cover of this book. The student has revised his sentences, in response to the instructor's corrections, by writing between the typewritten lines.

If your instructor indicates by a note or a comment in the margin that some part of your page is confused, undeveloped, or illogical, rewrite the section criticized. Whenever the revision is short, you may write between the lines. When you rewrite a number of sentences or paragraphs, however, you should first make your corrections on the face of your manuscript, and then recopy the entire page.

3. Once you have revised a page or an entire theme, it is a good idea to ask your instructor's opinion of the revision. Of course, the instructor may require you to hand in the revision, in which case it is an even better idea.

§ 8. CAPITALS

A *capital letter* is a kind of punctuation mark, designed to draw the reader's attention to itself for a particular reason. These reasons have been formalized in standard practice. There is justification, then, for the appearance of every capital, and they should not be abused in overcapitalization.

8a. Capitalize the first word of every sentence, including fragments punctuated as sentences, and the first word of any group within a sentence that is understood as a sentence in its own right.

363

8

What now? Who knows? Nobody.

He replied, "There is little hope left."

The main question is, When do we eat?

Do *not* capitalize the first word of (a) an indirect quotation, (b) a direct quotation that is not a complete sentence or that is made a structural part of the new sentence in which it is quoted, (c) the part of a direct quotation that follows dialogue tags such as *he said,* unless the part begins a new sentence.

EXAMPLES

Everyone said that the statement was untrue. [Indirect quotation. *Compare:* Everyone said, "The statement is untrue."]

Some people feel, like the singer in Rush's ballad, that "love is a game people play." [Direct quotation made a structural part of the new sentence]

"I wish I could tell you," he added, "what I really mean about that."

In quoting poetry or any other document, follow the original exactly in respect to capitalization. In writing out a title, capitalize the first word and all other words except conjunctions and prepositions of less than five letters. An exception is a short preposition ending the title, which should be capitalized: *When the Lights Were Turned On.* For further information on the special problems of titles, see § 10a.

8b. Proper nouns and adjectives are capitalized.

A *proper noun* names some particular person, place, or object; a *common noun* indicates one of a class of persons, places, or objects. In practice the distinction is usually not difficult.

Capitalize:

1. Names of persons, places, buildings, ships, and so on: John H. Farley, Wisconsin, the Washington Mon-

Why College?

12	Why did I come to college. That is a hard question,
2	it cannot be answered in a few words. From one point of
19	view, it seems abserd that I should be here without
15/19	knowing why I am here. Its true my parents allways
	wanted me to go to college. They probably never quite
	analyzed their reasons for wanting me to go. They wanted
1	me to better myself. To learn a profession or a trade.
11	They felt that a well educated person would be able to
6/29	lead an easier life than they lived. Knowing the hard
6/13	life they lived their attitude seems reasonable to me.
13	From another point of view however, it seems logical to
	me that I should come to college to find out why I came
	to college. I am not sure that I can find all the an-
	swers. My college work may give me one answer to my
1	question. Or maybe several of the many possible answers.
37	While I do not expect to find all the answers, after
19	four years here I may know more definately what the
	question means.
28	I have talked with other freshmen about their rea-
19/21	sons for comeing to college. They have many solutions.
1	Most of them talk about economic security. Which of
	course is a legitimate objective. Others talk about a
25a	life of service to others. If you talk long enough about
	the subject, you will hear about cultivation of the mind
	and the emotions. These are ideas I will try to discuss
	here.

SAMPLE THEME MARKED BY THE INSTRUCTOR

365

Why College?

Ques. Why did I come to collegeₚ? That is a hard question,
RS ~~it~~ *which* cannot be answered in a few words. From one point of
Sp view, it seems *absurd* ~~absurd~~ that I should be here without
Pn/Sp knowing why I am here. It's true my parents ~~allways~~ *always*
wanted me to go to college. They probably never quite
analyzed their reasons for wanting me to go. They wanted
PF me to better myself, *by learning* ~~To learn~~ a profession or a trade.
Pn They felt that a well-educated person would be able to
Tnse *Dng* lead an easier life than they *have* lived. ~~Because I know~~ ~~Knowing~~ the hard
Tnse
C life they *have* lived, their attitude seems reasonable to me.

C From another point of view, however, it seems logical to
me that I should come to college to find out why I came
to college. I am not sure that I can find all the answers. My college work may give me one answer to my
PF question, *or* maybe several of the many possible answers.
Gl *although* ~~While~~ I do not expect to find all the answers, after
Sp four years here I may know more ~~definately~~ *definitely* what the
question means.

Sub *As I talk* ~~I have talked~~ with other freshmen about their rea-
Sp/Ex sons for ~~comeing~~ *coming* to college, *I encounter many ideas.* ~~They have many solutions.~~
PF Most of them talk about economic security, ~~Which~~ *which* of
course is a legitimate objective. Others talk about a
Wd *Rep* life of service to ~~others~~ *humanity* If you talk long enough about
the subject, you will hear about cultivation of the mind
and the emotions. These are ideas I will try to discuss
here.

SAMPLE THEME AS CORRECTED BY THE STUDENT

ument, the *Constitution,* Middletown Township, China-town, Israel.

2. Names of political and geographic divisions if they are part of a proper name: Union of South Africa, Northwest Territory, Dominion of Canada. [But *not:* a union of states, the territory toward the northwest]
3. Names of historic events or epochs: the Middle Ages, the Black Death, World War I, the Depression, the Sixties.
4. Names of nationalities, religious groups, and lan-guages: English, Mormon, Slavic, Japanese. [Note that these can be used either as nouns or as adjec-tives.]
5. Adjectives derived from proper names: Byronic, Freudian, Scottish. [A few adjectives, used in special senses, such as *roman* or *italic* type, are often consid-ered common rather than proper.]
6. Names of organizations: United States Steel, the Red Cross, Congress of Industrial Organizations, United Nations, Phi Beta Kappa.
7. Days of the week, names of the months and of particu-lar holidays: Easter, Good Friday, Veterans Day, the second Monday in March.

As a rule, difficulties arise only when the same word is used both as a proper noun and as a common noun; some of these difficulties are discussed in § § 8c and 8d below.

8c. Any title used preceding a name or as a substitute for the name is capitalized.

A *title* is always capitalized preceding a name; following a name, it is capitalized only to show particular respect or distinction.

EXAMPLES

Captain Townsend; Prince Philip; Pope John Paul; Alexander Haig, the Secretary of State; *but:* D. H. Jones, the chairman of the committee.

367

Notice that these words are *not* capitalized when they are not used as a title for a particular, named person. The article *a* is usually a signal that a common noun follows.

8

EXAMPLES

A queen's consort is usually a prince.

He was promoted to captain.

When will they elect a new pope?

He is a good prospect for a vice-president's position.

Abbreviations after a name, such as Esq., Ph.D., M.D., F.R.S., are usually capitalized and not spaced. The following, however, are correct either with or without capitals: Jr., jr., Sr., sr. (*and note also* No., no.; A.M., a.m.; P.M., p.m.). Be consistent.

8d. Common nouns are capitalized only when they are used in the sense of proper names.

1. Capitalize *North, South, East, West, Northwest, Far East* only when these words refer to specific geographical divisions. Do not capitalize them when they refer to directions.

EXAMPLES

The South is gaining industrially at the expense of the Northeast.

I turned south at the crossroads.

She lives north of the city.

2. Capitalize the words for educational and other institutions only when they are a part of some name, not when they are used as common nouns.

EXAMPLES

The school was near Memorial Hospital, not far from the University of Maryland.

I attended high school there. It was called Beaverbrook High.

Many universities are looking for a good president.

368

I would like to work for the Smithsonian Institution or the Metropolitan Museum, but not all museum work interests me.

8

3. Capitalize the names of particular courses of study, such as *Mathematics 120, Physical Education 485b*. But do not capitalize such terms when they are used to refer to general areas of learning: *mathematics, physical education, history, law.* Remember, however, that names of nationalities and languages are always capitalized: *French history, English literature, Mexican art.*

4. Capitalize words denoting family relationships (*mother, father, uncle, grandfather*) only when these words stand for an individual who is called by that name. Again, be alert for the signal of a common noun, such as an article or possessive preceding the word.

EXAMPLES

A mother is often a twenty-four-hour laborer. My mother was such a person. One day I said to her, "Do you work as hard as Grandmother did, Mother?" She only replied that mothers have always worked hard. She is not a candidate for the women's movement.

The dictionary can often be useful in determining standard practice of capitalization. But in most doubtful cases, as these examples illustrate, it is necessary to recognize just how a word serves in a particular context.

EXERCISES

EXERCISE 1, SUPPLYING CAPITALS. *Copy the following sentences, supplying capitals when necessary.*

1. north central airlines serves many communities in the great lakes region.
2. there are many colleges and universities in the region, including minnesota and the university of wisconsin.
3. wisconsin is famous for its courses in journalism, but

8

it also offers programs in all the liberal arts including english, anthropology, history, physics, and so on.

4. the badgers, as the football team is called, find players from the fond du lac area and from many schools along lake michigan.

5. everyone knows that in the middle sixties wisconsin's football team contributed much to building the "big ten image."

6. the university's president has been an important figure in midwest history, especially because of his efforts to bring federal and state support to the school in madison.

7. I have tried to convince my brother to take north central when he flies west to visit us in wisconsin.

8. during world war II barracks were built on the campus to house united states soldiers, many of whom were of norwegian ancestry.

9. the state capitol is located in the center of town, and the legislators have adopted a romantic attitude about madison's beauty.

10. the governor and other public officials are still trying to overcome the bad publicity engendered during the days of student rioting.

EXERCISE 2, SUPPLYING CAPITALS. *Here is a piece of administrative English, of the sort that might appear on a college bulletin board. Again, supply capitals where necessary, and only where necessary.*

registration for the fall term will take place in walker hall from monday at 9 a.m. till wednesday at 4 p.m. all students will bring high school records and identification cards with them. the following courses will not be offered this year: economics 130, english 110, french 111, chemistry 120. students expecting to major in physical science should see professor adkins. those expecting to enter law school must elect political science 430. please talk without delay to the professor who has been designated as your adviser.

§ 9. ABBREVIATIONS AND NUMBERS

9

9a. In ordinary writing, abbreviations are usually avoided (with a few standard exceptions).

The following are usually written out, although in footnotes, bibliographies, tabulations, and addresses they may be abbreviated to conserve space:

1. Names of countries and states: Canada [not *Can.*], West Virginia [not *W.Va.*], North Dakota [not *N.Dak.*].
2. Names of the months and days of the week: September [not *Sept.*], Monday [not *Mon.*], Friday [not *Fri.*].
3. Christian names: Charles [not *Chas.*], Robert [not *Robt.*], Edward [not *Edw.*].
4. Names of college courses, titles of professors, and other words frequently abbreviated in campus conversation: professor [not *prof.*], educational psychology [not *ed. psych.*], political science [not *poli. sci.*].
5. The titles *The Reverend* [not *Rev.*] and *The Honorable* [not *Hon.*], at least in formal situations. These titles are used with the person's full name, not with just the last name.
6. The following words: number, volume, chapter, page, and [not &], street, avenue, manufacturing, company, mountain, Christmas.

POOR

He was looking forward to Xmas vacation next Dec.

BETTER

He was looking forward to Christmas vacation next December.

POOR

This class meets on Tue., Thurs., and Sat.

BETTER

This class meets on Tuesdays, Thursdays, and Saturdays.

371

9

POOR

He worked in N.Y. for the Macmillan Pblg. Co.

BETTER

He worked in New York for Macmillan Publishing Co., Inc. [It should be remembered that sometimes a company name is properly composed of abbreviations and ought to be written accordingly, e.g., Macmillan Publishing Co., Inc. As there may be a legal reason for the use of abbreviations in company names, try to find out what the company's letterhead says and use that.]

POOR

Some day she hopes to be a prof. of poli. sci.

BETTER

Some day she hopes to be a professor of political science.

POOR

Wm. and Chas. live on Jerome Ave., near Dilmore St.

BETTER

William and Charles live on Jerome Avenue, near Dilmore Street.

The following abbreviations are customary and appropriate:

1. Titles before proper names: Dr., Mr., Mrs., Ms., M., Messrs., Mme., Mlle.

2. Certain designations after names: Jr., jr., Sr., sr., D.D., M.D., Ph.D.

3. With dates only when necessary for clearness: A.D. and B.C.: Octavian lived from 63 B.C. to A.D. 14. (Note that B.C. follows the year, A.D. precedes it. It has been argued by some non-Christians that the abbreviations B.C. and A.D. misrepresent a true, universal reckoning of history. The alternatives proposed are B.C.E. (Before the Christian [or Common] Era) and C.E. (the Christian [or Common] Era).

4. Certain expressions usually abbreviated in informal and in technical writing, though written out when a more

372

formal effect is desired: i.e., e.g., viz., etc. These actually stand for *id est, exempli gratia, videlicet, et cetera,* but they are written out as *that is, for example, namely, and so forth.*

5. Names of government agencies and certain other well-known organizations: TVA, CARE, NATO, PUSH. Note that the last three of these are pronounced as single words, rather than as series of letters. Abbreviations pronounced as words are known as *acronyms.* Note also the omission of periods. When in doubt about the punctuation, consult your dictionary.

Observe that it is not customary to space after periods within most abbreviations, except that initials representing names *are* spaced: A. L. Jones.

9b. In general writing (i.e., writing that is not statistical), most numbers are written out whenever they can be expressed in one or two words, or in a simple phrase.

She is about twenty-five years old.
She earned nearly eight thousand dollars last year.
She was able to buy three and a half acres of land.

For the use of the hyphen with compound numbers see § 11.

A *number* beginning a sentence is usually spelled out. If it cannot be easily written out, recast the sentence so that the number does not stand at the beginning. Be consistent and avoid referring to eight thousand dollars as $8,000 later in the same essay.

EXAMPLES

Thirty-five persons attended the hanging. [Not *35 persons . . .*]
She paid a price of $4,550 for the pony. [Not *$4,550 was paid . . .*]

9

9

9c. Figures (or numerals) are used for the following:

1. Dates: March 20, 1981; *not* March twentieth, nineteen hundred eighty-one. [Note that the day of the month is separated from the year by a comma.]
2. Street and room numbers: 415 State Street; *not* four hundred fifteen State Street; Union Hall 216, *not* Union Hall two hundred sixteen.
3. Page numbers: page 334; *not* page three hundred thirty-four.
4. Decimals, percentages, mathematical and technical statistics: 0.7, *not* zero point seven; 27%, *not* twenty-seven percent; $\frac{1}{25}$, *not* one twenty-fifth.
5. Several numbers occurring in the same paragraph or section, if the numbers refer to different quantities of the same thing and if one of the numbers would ordinarily be given in figures.

EXAMPLE

These systems are at distances ranging from 100,000 to 1,500,000 light years, their diameters range from 4,000 to 45,000 light years, and the total luminosities from 20 to 500 million times the luminosity of the sun.

Notice in the last example that commas are used to separate the figures into units—thousands, hundred thousands, millions—for clearness and convenience in reading. Commas are *not* used, however, in dates, serial numbers, telephone numbers, or social security numbers. In some of these it is customary to use hyphens to divide complex numbers into groups. *Example:* "My Social Security number is 381-36-2160."

EXERCISES

EXERCISE 1, CORRECTING ABBREVIATION ERRORS. *Correct the errors in the use of abbreviations in the following sentences.*

9

1. Our route took us through Mich., Wis., and Minn.
2. The Stoic philosopher Seneca lived from 4 B.C. to 65 A.D.
3. This author was not born until after 1917 A.D.
4. English lit and math are my best courses.
5. We were in Vt. and Mass. for the rock festival.
6. Thos. Jones took me to the game with Hancock Hi.
7. I think that our chem labs are poorly designed.
8. One of the profs there said they were firetraps.
9. Professor L.B. White and Doctor A.G. Black are my chem lecturers.
10. Rev. Holmes was our convo speaker.

EXERCISE 2, IDENTIFYING ABBREVIATIONS. *Identify each of the following abbreviations. Consult your dictionary.*

1. ad lib	6. ESP	11. UNESCO
2. ASCAP	7. f.o.b.	12. S.R.O.
3. BMR	8. q.v.	13. USAFI
4. CIO	9. TNT	14. NCAA
5. colloq.	10. S.J.	15. op. cit.

EXERCISE 3, SPELLING OUT NUMBERS. *In the following sentences circle the numbers that should have been written out in words.*

1. He will inherit the estate when he reaches the age of 21.
2. The estate consists of a ranch, some stocks, and $35,600 in bonds.
3. Brenda was given an expensive car on her 18th birthday.
4. Her sister Diana, who is 16, is in love with a boy 3 inches shorter than she.
5. Margaret's birthday parties are poorly attended, for she was born on December 26, 1950.
6. Although a member of the 4-H Club for 6 years, she does not know what the four *H*'s stand for.
7. Timmy, an 8th grader, told her his scholastic average for 2 years is 86.55.
8. He has just bought a 90mm lens for his Exakta, which is a 35mm single lens reflex camera.

9. In 1940 McMillan and Abelson produced element 93, named *neptunium* after the planet Neptune.
10. 36 men can be housed in the dormitory at 218 South 36th Street.

§ 10. ITALICS

Italics are used to set words apart in a variety of situations.

The word *italics* refers to print. In handwriting or in typing, a word to be understood as in *italics* is underlined.

TYPEWRITTEN

In the May 1979, issue of <u>Horizon</u> there is a review of Franco Zeffirelli's <u>The Champ</u>.

PRINT

In the May 1979, issue of *Horizon* there is a review of Franco Zeffirelli's *The Champ.*

In business letters, instead of being underlined, the words are usually typed in capitals, as: HORIZON, *THE CHAMP.*

Usage varies greatly in regard to the use of italics. The principles or statements of usage in this section refer to more or less formal usage. Newspapers, as a rule, do not use italic type. The *New York Times Book Review* follows British practice and uses quotation marks for titles of books. The *Atlantic* italicizes the titles of books, magazines, and newspapers, but uses quotation marks for titles of essays and short stories. If you are writing for publication, the only sure guide is the style sheet of the magazine you are aiming at.

The following rules are usually observed in college papers of a formal nature.

10a. When referred to in formal writing, titles of books, plays, newspapers, magazines, musical composi-

tions, and works of art as well as names of ships are usually underlined in manuscript and printed in italics.

EXAMPLES

Huckleberry Finn	*Scientific American*
Queen's *News of the World*	the Portland *Oregonian*
Michelangelo's *Pietà*	the *Queen Elizabeth II*

Quotation marks are generally used for titles of chapters or subdivisions of books and for titles of short stories, magazine articles, newspaper articles, and short poems.

EXAMPLES

The stories in Maugham's *East and West,* such as "Rain" and "The Letter," could have appeared in a magazine, such as the *Atlantic,* before being published in book form. Later, as a play, *Rain* enjoyed a long run.

The Kansas City *Star* ran a story titled "Gone With the Wind" about tornado damage.

The definite article *the* and the name of the city before the title of a newspaper are usually not italicized: the St. Louis *Post-Dispatch.* Some periodicals, however, prefer the italicized article: *The New Yorker.* [Note that *The* in such use requires a capital.]

10b. Foreign words and phrases that are still not Anglicized are italicized (underlined) when used in writing.

A number of terms pronounced like foreign words are nevertheless considered so much a part of our language that italics are *not* used. Examples include: cliché, staccato, blitzkrieg. Some dictionaries will tell you if a word is still considered foreign and therefore must be italicized. Different dictionaries use different symbols for this purpose.

377

10c. In formal writing, words, letters, and figures, referred to as such, are usually italicized.

You have seen this procedure exemplified many times in this book, where italics have been used to mark off a word being discussed *as a word*. But in informal writing, quotation marks may be used for the same purpose. As always, be consistent in the form selected. In definitions, the word to be defined is commonly set in italics (underlined) and the definition is enclosed in quotation marks.

FORMAL STYLE

Poll is a term that has a meaning quite different from the one it began with. In Middle English the word was spelled *polle* and meant "head," or more particularly, the "top of the head," for that was the part of a person that could be seen above the crowd when a count of "heads" was being taken.

—WILFRED FUNK, *Word Origins*

INFORMAL STYLE

Many people confuse "imply" and "infer."

The European "7" is written differently from ours.

10d. Italics may be used to give special emphasis to a word or phrase.

The use of italics or underlining for emphasis can be badly abused in formal writing, where it is likely to appear as a weak effort to give importance to words that ought to be important without such mechanical help. Furthermore, excessive underlining has associations with trivial dialogue, often of a juvenile flavor. ("Hey, *man,* you should have seen her *wheels.* I mean you should have *seen* them. *Outasight!*") In a similar way, italics have been liberally used by some novelists, notably J. D. Salinger, to suggest the up-and-down stresses of emotional speech. "I was *born* here. I went to *school* here. I've been *run over* here—*twice,* and on the same damn *street.*"

But in formal exposition, it is conventional to use italics

378

for emphasis far more sparingly, usually only when the sentence would not be immediately clear without them.

EXAMPLES

Emotions represented in literature are, neither for writer nor for reader, the same as emotions in "real life"; they are "recollected in tranquillity"; they are "expressed"—that is, released— by analysis; they are the *feelings* of emotions, the perceptions of emotions.
—RENÉ WELLEK AND AUSTIN WARREN, *Theory of Literature*

In the comic vision the *unformed* world is a river, traditionally fourfold, which influenced the Renaissance image of the temperate body with its four humors.
—NORTHROP FRYE, *Fables of Identity*

EXERCISES

EXERCISE 1, ITALICS AND QUOTATION MARKS. *Copy the following paragraph, underlining for italics and adding quotation marks where necessary. Use the formal conventions.*

Webster's New World Dictionary, like other such works, includes helpful lists of synonyms for many familiar words. Listed under crowd, for example, you will find throng, multitude, swarm, mob, host, and horde, with precise differences indicated. An introductory article called Guide to the Use of the Dictionary is of further assistance to the reader searching for a mot juste. A subsection of this article, titled The Synonymies, treats antonyms as well, and concludes: "the antonym sad heads a synonymy that includes melancholy, dejected, depressed, and doleful, all antonymous to happy."

EXERCISE 2, ITALICS AND QUOTATION MARKS. *Copy the following paragraph in the same way, underlining for italics where necessary and adding quotation marks in the proper places.*

Joseph Heller's Catch-22 has become the novel that speaks for many disenchanted, distrustful people. It reflects the alienation of American intellectuals in a much more encompassing

379

11

way than did Eliot's The Wasteland. Heller had achieved only minor success in his first work, a play called We Bombed in New Haven, but his anti-war novel struck a chord in the hearts of many frustrated Yossarians. If Eliot appealed to a Lost Generation, Heller is the spokesman for what might be called the Skeptical Generation. This group, for whom Catch-22 has become a slogan, could never hear America, the Beautiful or read Leaves of Grass with the same enthusiasm as their pre-World War II counterparts. It will take more than regular teaching of the Gettysburg Address to return American youth to the state of relative innocence it possessed before writers like Heller arrived on the scene.

§ 11. SYLLABICATION AND HYPHENS

11a. The awkward division of a word at the end of a line of handwritten or typewritten manuscript should be avoided.

In printed matter, where a perfectly even right-hand margin is mandatory, we have become accustomed to a number of word divisions at the ends of lines. In handwritten or typewritten papers, however, it is usually unnecessary to divide many words. For clearness and ease in reading, it is wise to observe the following cautions about dividing words at the end of a line:

1. Never divide words of one syllable, such as *eighth, rhythm, signed, burned.* Note that the *-ed* ending in the past-tense form must not be split off as a syllable when it is not pronounced as a syllable.

2. Never divide a word so that a single letter is allowed to stand by itself, either at the end of a line or the beginning of the next line, as in *a- / mount, a- / round, e- / lope, greed- / y, read- / y.*

3. Try to avoid dividing proper names, as in *Ed- / ward,* or *John- / son.*

4. Try not to separate a name and the initials that go with it, as in *E. B.-/ White.*

5. Try to avoid dividing the last word of a paragraph or a page. In print such a division is often necessary, but in manuscript is can be easily avoided.

11b. If a division of a word is necessary, the division should be made between syllables and a hyphen placed at the end of the line.

Assume that your reader is pronouncing your sentence aloud and divide words so that both parts are pronounce-able. You must divide correctly between syllables and your best resource in doing so is your dictionary, where syllables are clearly indicated. The following cautions should be of additional help:

1. Divide compound words on the hyphen, and try to avoid a second hyphen: self- / evident, *not* self-evi- / dent; college- / trained, *not* col- / lege-trained.

2. In words with prefixes, divide on the prefix: non- / sensical, pre- / caution, ante- / diluvian. Note that these words are ordinarily written solid; they are not hyphenated compounds.

3. In words with suffixes, divide on the suffix: child- / ish, dog- / like, youth- / ful, fall- / ing, yell- / ing.

4. As a rule, when a word contains double consonants, divide between the two consonants: ac- / com- / mo- /date, in- / ter- / ro- / gate. In such examples as *fall-/ ing* and *yell-/ ing,* however, the rule about double consonants conflicts with the rule about suffixes; the rule about suffixes takes precedence.

11c. Two or more words forming a compound adjective preceding a noun are hyphenated.

EXAMPLES

A broad-shouldered, long-legged man; a rough-looking center; ready-made opinions; a twin-screw engine; in up-to-date condi-

381

11

tion; a well-traveled highway; a two-thirds majority; an old-fashioned soda; a three-dog night; the Russo-Finnish border.

When a compound modifier consists of two or more words with a common beginning, the following style is used: *A three- or four-room addition, Anglo- and Franco-American, paid in five- and ten-dollar bills.*

The following are usually not hyphenated: compound modifiers that follow the noun; compounds in which an adverb ending in *-ly* is used.

EXAMPLES

The man was well known for fiddling. [We met a well-known poet.]

His information was up to date. [He planned an up-to-date revision of the book.]

It was a loosely worded statement. [Her explanations were loosely worded.]

In order to express certain ideas more emphatically, professional writers may sometimes invent their own hyphenated phrases. While this practice has the stylistic advantage of grabbing the reader's attention, it is best for beginning writers to follow it sparingly.

EXAMPLE

This habit of the I-want-it-and-I-want-it-now buying public leads many record producers to turn out popular-but-slick albums. [Would *spoiled* or *catered to* work better than the compound modifying *public?* Isn't the second compound more descriptive than the first?]

11d. Compound numbers from twenty-one to ninety-nine are hyphenated.

EXAMPLES

Twenty-seven dollars, thirty-four inches

Fractions, when used as modifiers, are hyphenated. When one of the terms of the fraction is already a compound, however, no additional hyphen is used, as in *four twenty-fifths, twenty-one fortieths.* Such simple fractions as *one half, two thirds,* and so on, are often written without a hyphen, but *one-and-a-half* always follows the hyphenated form.

11

EXAMPLES

The bill was finally passed by a two-thirds majority.

One half of the pie was already eaten.

Paul normally employs about one one-hundredth of his brain.

11e. Hyphens are used with the following classes of compound words.

1. With prefixes *ex-* (in the sense of "former") and *self-:* ex-president, ex-minister, self-regard, self-help, self-pity.
2. When two functions that are usually distinct are united in one person or thing: cleaner-polisher, secretary-treasurer, publisher-editor, city-state.
3. With prefix *semi-* when second element begins with *i:* semi-independent, semi-invalid, semi-retired.
4. With suffix *-like* when first element ends with *ll:* bell-like; when first element is a proper noun: American-like, Garbo-like.
5. With groups making or containing prepositional phrases: son-in-law, man-of-war, jack-in-the-pulpit.
6. To prevent confusion with similar words: re-form [to form again], reform [to change or amend]; re-count [to count anew], recount [to tell]; re-creation [a second creation], recreation [play, sport, diversion].
7. When the second element of a compound word is a proper noun: anti-American, pre-Renaissance, pro-Russian.

When in doubt about the correct form of a compound, consult *Webster's New Collegiate Dictionary, The American College Dictionary, Webster's New World Dictionary,* the *American Heritage Dictionary,* or *The Random House Dictionary.*

11

EXERCISES

EXERCISE 1, SYLLABICATION. *Indicate which of the following words you should not divide at the end of a line. Show how you would divide the others. Give your reason in each case.*

1. agreed	6. sorely	11. brushed
2. precedence	7. speedy	12. elect
3. preeminent	8. unit	13. bankbook
4. through	9. across	14. squeezed
5. thorough	10. action	15. stringy

EXERCISE 2, COMPOUND WORDS. *With the aid of a dictionary determine which of the following should be written solid, which with a hyphen, and which are separate words.*

1. air raid	16. good bye
2. air raid shelter	17. half brother
3. all inclusive	18. half crazed lion
4. all right	19. half written theme
5. ante date	20. partly written paper
6. ante bellum	21. in as much as
7. anti climax	22. infra red
8. any body	23. north west
9. basket ball	24. post office
10. book store	25. score board
11. by law	26. text book
12. by pass	27. inter collegiate
13. post Renaissance	28. under graduate
14. dining room	29. week end trip
15. every thing	30. well made car

11 | *Punctuation*

The purpose of punctuation is to help make clear the meaning of printed or written language.

To some degree punctuation symbolizes the pauses in oral speech, but it does so crudely and artificially. It is still useful to read a sentence aloud with attention to its meaning, and punctuate the pauses you hear in your own voice. But correct punctuation has also come to reflect the grammatical structures of sentences, as well as the particular conventions of the age. Therefore, a comma does not always represent a drop or pause in the speaking voice, and the various marks of punctuation do not consistently distinguish among the various subtle drops that our voices so naturally perform. Like most other conventional patterns of behavior, the conventions of punctuation have to be learned.

The practice of writers has been codified into a number of rules or principles of punctuation. These rules or principles govern a very large number of typical situations in writing. At times, however, certain marks are optional, depending on the writer's particular attitude toward what he or she is saying and on decisions of publishers. On the whole, nevertheless, college students can have success if they follow codified usage. When in genuine doubt, resort to common sense.

Punctuation, then, is more than a series of rules: *it offers one more way of clarifying expression.* Even in the many situations where one has a choice—for example, to include a comma or leave it out—one's choice need not be arbitrary. The rhythm of one's prose style will be very largely con-

385

trolled by the use or omission of punctuation marks where no rule clearly applies.

12

§ 12. END PUNCTUATION

The Period

12a. A period is used after a declarative or imperative sentence, or after an indirect question, but not after a direct question.

EXAMPLES

I had no idea where I had been or how I got there. [Declarative]

Always know where you are. [Imperative]

The legislature asked how the firm spent the money. [Indirect question]

The legislature asked, "How have funds been dispersed?" [Direct question, ending with a question mark]

Note the difference, in the last two examples, in the way the human voice is used. At the end of the indirect question there is a drop in voice level characteristic of all declarative sentences. But a rise in pitch at the end of a sentence—How have the funds been dispersed?—is usually a sign of a question, to be symbolized by a question mark.

12b. Most of the common abbreviations require a period.

EXAMPLES

Mr., Mrs., Ms., Dr., St., Jr., a.m., B.C., Mass.

Increasingly, the period is not used with certain groups of letters or acronyms standing for organizations or government agencies. Note that the letters are written without spacing.

EXAMPLES

UN, USSR, CIA, TVA, FCC, NAACP, SALT, DOE, NOW

386

12. *END PUNCTUATION*

Usage is divided in regard to some of the older abbreviations consisting of the initial letters of words, though the tendency is toward omitting the period. Consult your dictionary when in doubt.

EXAMPLES

Y.M.C.A. *or* YMCA; r.p.m. *or* rpm; A.M.A. *or* AMA

12c. Spaced periods (ellipsis marks or suspension points, usually three within a sentence, four at the end of a declarative sentence to include the necessary closing period) are used to indicate the omission of words from a quoted passage, or pauses or hesitation in dialogue.

EXAMPLES

We the People of the United States, in order to . . . secure the Blessings of Liberty to ourselves and our Posterity, do . . . establish this Constitution for the United States of America.
—PREAMBLE TO THE U.S. CONSTITUTION

The fates of secret agents throughout the world fit a similar mold. . . . Their mother agencies—the CIA's and KGB's—regard every one of them as dispensable.

"Now let me think. . . . Yes. . . . I suppose so."

The Question Mark

12d. A question mark is used after a direct question but not after an indirect question.

Note the distinction in voice level discussed under § 12a. Most of our problems in using the *question mark* are mechanical ones, involving other punctuation surrounding the mark in special cases.

EXAMPLES

What will I do if Miss Byrne is there? What will I say to her? she asked herself, but did not wait for an answer. [Quotation marks are sometimes omitted when unspoken thoughts are quoted.]
—MICHAEL MCLAVERTY, *School for Hope*

387

Wasn't it Paul Clapton who said, after the long, hot drive to Santa Fe, that he would "never climb into that van again"? [Note relation of question mark to quotation marks when part of a phrase is quoted in a question.]

After we landed we learned, with a tremendous surge of pride, that as the waters rose around them, those green troops, soldiers from far northwestern states mostly, stood in ranks on the canted decks singing a popular song of the war, "Where Do We Go from Here, Boys?" [A question mark ends the sentence if the last part is a quoted question.]

—IRVIN S. COBB

Instead of asking "What would a good education consist of?" many professors of education are asking "What do most college students want?"; instead of asking "What books are wisest and best and most beautiful?" they conduct polls to determine which the largest number of students have read with least pain. [Some writers would have put commas after each *asking*. Note that a question mark is used with a title if it is a question.]

—JOSEPH WOOD KRUTCH, "Is Our Common Man Too Common?"

A single question mark is used after a double question—that is, a quoted question following a question. (See also § 16.)

EXAMPLES

Who wrote "Where have all the aardvarks gone?"

Why doesn't man simply ask, "Where will clean water and air originate in the future?"

A question mark within parentheses may be used to indicate doubt or uncertainty about the preceding figure or fact. This is a conventional practice in the case of a doubtful birth or death date.

EXAMPLE

Lucien Botha was born in 1779(?) and died in 1859.

But the use of a parenthetical question mark to indicate irony is the mark only of immature writing.

388

12. END PUNCTUATION

We had a great(?) time at that party.

A question mark is often used after commands or requests phrased as questions if a formal effect is desired, but a period is used for a less formal effect. A convenient test, once again, is to read the sentence aloud, checking for the rise in pitch characteristic of the last syllable of a question.

FORMAL

May I ask the entire pitching staff to reassemble here at four o'clock?

LESS FORMAL

Will all the hurlers meet here again at four o'clock, please.

The Exclamation Point

12e. An exclamation point is usually used after an expression that indicates strong feeling or emotion.

The student's temptation often is to overuse the *exclamation point,* creating a breathless or overexcited style not unlike that produced by an overuse of italics. (See § 10d.) Words such as *yes, no, oh, well, surely,* when beginning a sentence, are usually followed by a comma. Actually it is wise to avoid them in the opening position, except in dialogue. If *oh* introduces an expression of strong feeling, put the exclamation point at the end of the expression. Never use more than one exclamation point in a sentence.

EXAMPLES

"Good lord!" he gasped in amazement.

It is difficult to see how anyone in his right mind could have concluded *that!*

Oh, this is unforgiveable!

The hours dragged on at a turtle's pace. He had read every *National Geographic* in the waiting room. This was the last time

389

13

he would come to this doctor! What a way to treat a loyal dog lover!

EXERCISE

EXERCISE, END PUNCTUATION IN DIALOGUE. *In the following dialogue, supply commas, periods, question marks, and exclamation points where they are necessary. Be careful to place punctuation correctly in relation to quotation marks.*

1. "Did you know the ending would turn out that way" asked Dr Fisher
2. "No I didn't" she replied
3. The doctor asked her what other movies she had seen lately
4. "Oh not many" she said "Have you seen anything like this before"
5. "What makes you ask that" he replied
6. "Do you know who said 'Movies are getting better' " she asked
7. "Who was it that used to ask 'Why not try a good movie tonight' "
8. "Watch out" he shouted suddenly as they attempted to cross the street in front of the theatre
9. "Wasn't that Mr Wells in his MG Wow That was too close for comfort"
10. "I wonder" he observed "when the streets will ever be safe for pedestrians"

---

§ 13. THE COMMA

Of all the marks of punctuation, the *comma* has the widest variety of uses. Probably because the comma is used in so many situations, any attempt to codify the practice of writers and to state usage in terms of definite principles must give due weight to the exceptions. Yet, however important the differences of practice are, to the student the most important thing is that there is such a large area of

390

13

agreement. Most of the uses of the comma can be stated in terms of principles that reflect what most writers are doing.

The student should always remember, however, that these descriptions of usage must be interpreted with a little common sense. It is true, for instance, that writers place a comma after an introductory clause or phrase if they feel that this sentence element is not an integral part of the main clause—that is, if it is not closely restrictive—but no rule, only common sense, can tell a student when this clause is restrictive or nonrestrictive.

Generally, punctuation tends to be *close* (that is, with a liberal use of commas) in serious or formal writing, where precision is vital. It tends to be *open* (that is, using a minimum of punctuation) in informal description and narration and in journalistic writing.

Although the primary function of punctuation is to help make meaning clear, punctuation has another function, a rhetorical one. The comma—and to a certain extent the semicolon—may be used to indicate the degree of pause or emphasis or rhetorical balance or contrast of ideas. The important fact still remains, however, that before a writer can make punctuation a stylistic resource he or she must first become familiar with the general practice of writers.

Because of its wide variety of uses, the comma may appear to some a subject of puzzling complexity, although at times it is hard to see why young people of eighteen, who speak familiarly of isotopes and learn to pilot jets, should be bowled over by so simple a thing as a comma. At any rate, it is possible to simplify a simple subject further by dividing all comma uses into two groups. In one group we have the *to separate* uses; in the other group we have the *to enclose* uses. A picture of the whole thing makes it still simpler and clearer.

A TABLE OF COMMA USES

Usually to Separate		*Usually to Enclose*	
13a.	main clauses	13h.	nonrestrictive clauses
13b.	elements in series	13i.	parenthetical elements

13

13a. A comma is ordinarily used to separate coordinate clauses joined by *and, but, for, or, nor,* except when the clauses are short and closely related in meaning.

A writer is safe to apply this rule rather strictly in formal writing. At the same time it must be acknowledged that the use of a comma to separate main clauses has become almost optional. Journalistic writing discards the comma in this situation except to prevent misreading. At the formal level, the general practice is to omit the comma when the subject of the sentence does not change after the first clause. If there is any other clearly defined practice to help the beginning student, it is that the comma is obligatory before *for* (to prevent confusion with the preposition *for*) and recommended before *but.*

Evel Knievel, the motorcycle daredevil, attempted to jump across the Grand Canyon in 1976, and in 1980 the great abyss still yawns in open defiance.

For the boundary between sea and land is the most fleeting and transitory feature of the earth, and the sea is forever repeating its encroachments upon the continents. [Note, as in this sentence, that the conjunction *for* may be used to begin independent sentences. *But* is another conjunction frequently used in this way.]

—RACHEL CARSON, *The Sea Around Us*

The brilliance of a nova at its peak is usually not sufficient to make it visible to the naked eye, but supernovae surpass in brilliance the brightest of ordinary stars and some of them can be observed in full daylight. [Note that no comma is used before *and* because the subjects of the last two clauses are felt to be closely related.]

392

In a sense, the processes of fission and fusion are similar, for they both are used to convert mass into energy in an amount given by Einstein's equation. [Note comma before *for.*]

13

—DONALD J. HUGHES, "Atoms, Energy, and Peace"

They [the buildings of architecture] may be sophisticated, worked out with the greatest intellectual subtlety, designed like the Parthenon by known architects of genius; or they may, like some old stone barn in Pennsylvania, be the naïve, natural legacy of half-understood tradition, put up by an anonymous builder. [Note the semicolon before *or* in a compound sentence with a number of commas. See § 14 for further discussion.]

—JOHN E. BURCHARD, "Architecture and Building"

13b. Commas are used to separate words, phrases, or clauses in a series.

A *series* must have at least three members; usually the last is joined to the other by *and* or *or.* It is at this point, the point of the conjunction, that usage differs. Although the comma is generally used here in most formal writing, some writers do omit it. In informal writing there is a progressive tendency to discard the comma before the conjunction, except for clearness. In journalistic writing, the comma is regularly omitted.

Men, women, and children enjoyed the happy, carefree, and refreshing outing. [Nouns and adjectives in series] The Beatles stopped, looked, and then darted for cover. [Series of verbs]

In scarlet and blue and green and purple, three by three the sovereigns rode through the palace gates, with plumed helmets, gold braid, crimson sashes, and jeweled orders flashing in the sun. [Series of nouns]

—BARBARA W. TUCHMAN, *The Guns of August*

So our girl in this free country has, in truth, little choice. Security is the goal, and as soon as possible. Marry the boy right away, get the house right away, have the brood right away. No time for search of self, no time for experiments in love and life, no time for interior growth, no time for the great world outside. [Series of predicates]

—MARYA MANNES, *The Singular Woman*

393

13

What is the nature of man's consciousness, his feelings, his hopes and aspirations, his personality, his learning, logic, and memory?
—HAROLD G. WOLFE, "The Mind-Body Relationships"

Rock music can be heard on our radios, our television sets, and our children's stereos, and because there is no way to stop it, the sound has barged into practically every sports arena in the country. [Series with *and*]

Here is an example from serious writing in which the author omits the comma:

To be courageous, these stories make clear, requires no exceptional qualifications, no magic formula, no special combinations of time, place and circumstance.
—JOHN F. KENNEDY, *Profiles in Courage*

13c. Commas are used to separate consecutive adjectives preceding the noun they modify when the adjectives are coordinate in meaning.

The comma is correct only when the adjectives are *coordinate*—that is, when each of the adjectives refers directly and independently to the same noun. When an adjective modifies the whole idea that follows it, it is not separated from it by a comma. If you can substitute *and* for the comma, the comma is correct. Note in the following examples that *and* would be a natural substitute for each comma used:

with slow, powerful strokes . . . these cold, treeless heights . . . the still, dimly lighted street . . . this bold, gleaming structure . . . his exuberant, energetic brother . . . their dull, inglorious lives . . . the muddy, tired, discouraged soldiers

A safe practice is to omit the comma with numerals and with the common adjectives of size and age:

the little old lady from Pasadena . . . a dirty old senior citizen . . . the spreading chestnut tree . . . a large red-haired woman . . . four tiny black dots

394

More generally, a comma should not be used when one of two adjectives associated with a noun modifies the other adjective or the other adjective and the noun together.

EXAMPLES

Ground roast coffee . . . dark brown earth . . . pure spring water . . .

13d. The comma is used to separate words and phrases that might be incorrectly joined in reading.

This rule applies to the following situations:

1. When the conjunctions *for* and *but* might be mistaken for prepositions.

The SWAT team waited in anxious silence, for the messenger seemed to be in a desperate hurry. [Waited in anxious silence for the messenger?]

All hands slid down the ropes, but one sailor seemed to be caught in the rigging. [All slid down the ropes but one sailor?]

2. When a noun might be mistaken for the object of a verb, verbal, or preposition before it.

After washing, the doctors filed into the dining tent. [*Not* After washing the doctors]

Before starting to eat, the chaplain bowed his head in prayer. [*Not* Before starting to eat the chaplain]

Above, the sun burned a dull red; below, the sand radiated heat like a furnace. [*Not* Above the sun . . . below the sand]

When we left, the Bickersons were still playing their endless game of pinochle. [*Not* When we left the Bickersons]

13e. Ordinarily, a comma is used to set off a modifier that precedes a main clause, especially when the introductory element is long and not closely connected with the main clause in meaning, when it is not *restrictive*.

395

13

In punctuating modifiers that precede the main clause you should depend on your good sense as well as on rules. You should decide whether or not the sentence will be clearer with the introductory modifier set off by a comma. Length of clause alone will not prescribe when to use a comma and when not to use it. Frequently very short clauses are set off for emphasis. In general, if the introductory element is not clearly restrictive, put a comma after it. The following distinctions will help you:

1. Use a comma when you begin with a fairly long (usually over five words) nonrestrictive adverbial clause:

When it came time to pack up the weapons, we discovered that one of the grenades was missing.

Because the car's wheels should touch the pavement when it is moving, your Jaguar should not be pushed over 120 miles per hour.

If we are not six feet tall, we can at least console ourselves with the knowledge that we are not three feet tall.

2. Use a comma to set off an introductory participial phrase modifying the subject or an introductory *absolute phrase* (see "Parts of Speech," page 86):

Stopping often to gaze back or to browse in ripe raspberries hanging beside the trail, we ascended to the top. (Phrase modifies *we*.]
— EDWIN WAY TEALE, *Journey into Summer*
The fire being over, the students returned to the classroom. [Absolute phrase]

3. Set off short introductory prepositional phrases only when they are definitely nonrestrictive, such as *transitional phrases* (see "Parts of Speech," page 83).

NO COMMA
Up to this point we are on safe ground.
During the ceremony a dog strayed into the room.
In the spring the ground is covered with poppies and beer cans.

COMMA USED

In addition, such experiences are educational.

Of the small islands, the nearest is heavily populated.

In the first place, his idea for dog galoshes is not new.

Long introductory prepositional phrases may be set off if the writer believes that a comma is an aid to clearness:

In addition to the picture information it sends out, a television station also transmits sound.

> —LOUIS N. RIDENOUR, "Electronics and
> the Conquest of Space"

In the biological and physical as well as the sociological sciences, statistics have become, as they never were before, the most important tool of investigation.

> —JOSEPH WOOD KRUTCH

4. A short introductory clause is usually not followed by a comma. It may, however, be set off for greater emphasis or for clearness.

When he gives us a test he usually leaves the room. [Informal]

If the deputy comes I will tell him to look for you in the shop. [Informal]

13f. A comma, or commas, may be used to indicate transposed or contrasting sentence elements.

EXAMPLES

A boy, thin, ragged, and very frightened, had wedged himself behind the crate. [*Note:* A, thin, ragged, and very frightened boy had. . .]

Inequality, by arousing jealousy and envy, provokes discontent. [*Not transposed:* Inequality provokes discontent by arousing jealousy and envy.]

He [Shakespeare] knew that Hamlet's dilemma, between the flesh and the spirit, was at the heart of every human being's private tragedy, and he made Hamlet so terrifyingly real, with his courtesy and his violence, his intelligence and his self-hatred,

13

his inconsistencies and his terrors, that every generation since has been able to recognize in him its own image. [Note here how commas set off balanced elements.]

—MARCHETTE CHUTE, *Shakespeare of London*

She insisted on blue, rather than white, gowns and tuxedoes. [Contrasting sentence elements]

13g. Commas are used to set off mild exclamations, sentence adverbs (i.e., which modify the entire sentence), and the responsives *yes* and *no* when they begin a sentence.

EXAMPLES

Yes, he assigned another essay for Friday.

Evidently, you will not have the paper ready for him.

Unfortunately, I will have to stay up all night to write it.

Mary said, "Well, what excuse can I give him?"

Oh, you will think of something to say before Friday.

13h. Commas are used to set off nonrestrictive clauses. They are not used to set off restrictive clauses.

If the distintion between restrictive and nonrestrictive clauses is not already clear to you, think of restrictive clauses as "identifying" or "pointing-out" clauses. A restrictive clause helps to locate or identify its antecedent. It says to the reader, "I mean this particular person or object, and no other." It is close to its antecedent in meaning, so close that it cannot be separated from it by a comma. A nonrestrictive clause does not point out or identify; it merely gives additional information about its antecedent.

RESTRICTIVE CLAUSES

The board decided in favor of another candidate *who has had more experience.* [Not just another candidate, but one with more experience]

The teenager *who has a hobby* will never be lonely. [Not any teenager, but that particular kind of teenager]

398

Please bring me that book *that you see lying on the table.* [That particular book and no other]

NONRESTRICTIVE CLAUSES

The board decided in favor of Ms. Rossi, *who has had more experience.* [The name identifies the person; the clause does not need to identify or point out.]

Terry Fisher, *who has a hobby,* will never be lonely. [The name identifies him.]

Please bring me Styron's *Sophie's Choice, which you see lying on the table.* [The title identifies the book.]

Astronomy, *which is the study of heavenly bodies,* is a fascinating subject. [*Astronomy* identifies itself. It does not need a clause to tell which particular astronomy.]

My father, *who had not heard the question,* shook his head in silence. [A person has only one father. The clause cannot help identify him.]

Participial phrases may be either restrictive or nonrestrictive, depending on the meaning intended.

RESTRICTIVE

The young woman *standing near the door* is waiting to register. [That particular young woman]

A book *written by that author* is bound to be interesting. [Phrase points to a particular kind of book—one written by that author.]

NONRESTRICTIVE

Honor Miller, standing there by the door, is waiting to register. [Name identifies her.]

Raising his rifle quickly, he fired at the moving object. [Nothing in the phrase helps to identify the person.]

13i. Commas are used to set off parenthetical elements (interrupters), or words, phrases, and clauses used to explain, to qualify, or to emphasize.

In a sense, several of the sentence elements discussed under other rules are "interrupters" in that they tend to

399

13

break or interrupt the normal flow of a sentence, but strict classification is not here important. The parenthetical elements dealt with here may be classified as follows:

1. Conjunctive adverbs, such as *however, therefore, moreover, furthermore,* when they are used within the clause. In any style, an epidemic of *moreover*'s and *furthermore*'s is as bad as a plague of *and*'s and *but*'s.

EXAMPLES

An institution, *therefore,* may fail because its standards are too high.

In truth, *however,* it was probably not known until after the bodies were discovered.

And do not use a conjunctive adverb to force a connection. "She ate too many hot dogs; consequently, she was sick" is nauseous in more ways than one.

2. Directive and qualifying words and phrases. Some of the most common of these, such as *also, perhaps, indeed, too, at least,* may, in informal writing, be considered as close modifiers and therefore not set off by commas. Others are usually set off.

EXAMPLES

All of this, *of course,* is theory.

Her theory, *unluckily,* was disproved by the events that followed.

He would become, *in short,* a delinquent of the worst kind.

3. Parenthetical phrases and clauses. Most of these are parenthetical comments, but some are adverbial clauses that interrupt the sentence flow.

EXAMPLES

This, *I suppose,* is the essence of juggling.

Our interpretation of his motives is, *I think,* totally unfair.

If you must take risks on the lake, see to it that, *whenever storm warnings are up,* you at least have a life preserver on the boat.

400

It should be noted here that three types of punctuation are used with parenthetical elements. Parentheses are used for the most distant interrupters, dashes for something a little less distant, and commas for interrupters most closely related to the rest of the sentence. For a further discussion see § § 17 and 18.

EXAMPLES

The *Star Wars* cast *(a strange collection of men, women, and machines)* has managed to hold together through two films without appearing to age.

It isn't that the scene offends him, but he feels that he—*the shark's main course*—should have something to say about how the sequence is shot.

In painting, *especially modern painting,* it is sometimes difficult to distinguish between the Norse helmet and the woman's form.

13j. Commas are used to set off absolute phrases when they occur within the sentence.

EXAMPLES

A great dam came into view, *water boiling from its curved rank of spillways.*
　　　　—ANDREW H. BROWN, *National Geographic*
She stood there, *her damp face glowing with happiness,* and asked us all to be seated.

13k. Commas are used to set off appositives.

An *appositive,* or a word in apposition, is used to limit or qualify the meaning of another word, to stand for it, to add to its meaning, or to emphasize it. The name *appositive* refers to the fact that a word and its appositive stand side by side. Most appositives—with the exception of the types listed below—are to be set off by commas.

EXAMPLES

Stan Perkins, the *foreman* of the plant, was hurt yesterday. [Appositive with modifiers]

401

13

Other animals, such as the giraffe, camel, and brown bear, use a different type of locomotion. [Appositive introduced by *such as*]

—WILLIAM C. VERGARA, *Science in Everyday Things*

As he neared Fourth Street, another man, *a new one,* sprang up suddenly before him, *a short, heavy-set fellow,* stepping out of the shadows and striding directly toward him. [Notice how the use of appositives may add to sentence variety.]

—ROBERT M. COATES

Welles, *a director of considerable merit,* had to borrow large sums of money in order to transform *Othello, full of special scenery and lighting effects,* into a film with nightmarelike dimensions.

But do *not* use commas with many common expressions in which the appositive and its substantive are so close that they are felt as a unit:

Jack the Ripper, Jack the Giant-killer, Henry the Eighth, my son Harold, William the Conqueror, the word *appositive,* the novelist Roth.

Participles and occasionally adjectives may be placed for greater emphasis or for variety after the words they modify. When so placed they are said to be in the appositive position and are therefore set off by commas. See also § 13f.

EXAMPLES

During a pause in the game, one of the fans, *devotedly cynical,* shouted mock encouragement at the pitcher.

A sound, *loud and high-pitched like a jet engine's scream,* escaped from her throat.

The pitch, *slow and tantalizing,* is typical of Perry's hurling style, *the mark of a seasoned, devious veteran.* [Adjectives in the appositive position and then a substantive appositive]

Appositives may also be enclosed in parentheses or set off by dashes to indicate a greater degree of separation, if such distinction is desired. (See § § 17 and 18.) Sometimes dashes are used because of the presence of several commas.

402

EXAMPLES

It follows that every policy of the West that contradicts these fears—every Marshall Plan, every extension of economic aid to backward areas, every increase in social economic opportunity, every act of justice and reconciliation—breaks with the Communists' fundamental gospel—the fatality of history—and restores, triumphantly and creatively, the freedom of the West. [Note here not only the two appositives set off by dashes but also the use of two adverbs, *triumphantly* and *creatively,* in an unusual position.]

—BARBARA WARD, *Policy for the West*

The city is always full of young worshipful beginners—young actors, young aspiring poets, ballerinas, painters, reporters, singers—each depending on his own brand of tonic to stay alive, each with his own stable of giants.

—E. B. WHITE, *Here Is New York*

Appositives are sometimes introduced by such words as *that is, namely, such as, for instance, for example,* and the like. In long, formal sentences these words may be preceded by a colon or a semicolon. In ordinary writing, both formal and informal, *namely, that is, for example,* and *for instance* are usually preceded and followed by commas. *Such as* is not followed by a comma.

EXAMPLES

Short prepositions, such as *in, on, to, for,* are not capitalized in titles.

We know that white light—light from the sun, for example—is really a mixture of light of all colors.

There is only one proper thing for a driver to do when the car dies, namely, put up the hood and take a nap.

13l. Commas are used to set off substantives used in direct address.

EXAMPLES

Professor Holmes, your lectures are a constant delight to your class. [To begin a sentence]

403

Read the poem, *Mr. Taylor,* and tell me if it means anything to you. [Within the sentence]

"Please change places with me, Helen," I asked. [With quotation marks]

13

13m. An explanatory clause such as *he said* (a dialogue guide), when it interrupts a sentence of dialogue, is set off by commas.

EXAMPLES

"For your next project," said the instructor, "you will write an essay about the Blarney Stone."

Sean McCarthy raised his hand and said, "Did you know that Cormack McCarthy, one of my ancestors, built Blarney Castle in 1602?" [Dialogue guide begins sentence.]

"Most tourists," explained Eric Swensen, "do not know that the real Blarney Stone is impossible for them to reach."

"They are allowed to kiss a substitute stone," he added. "It works just as well." [Dialogue guide at end of one sentence and before the second sentence]

Also see § 16 for placing of quotation marks in relation to commas.

13n. Commas are used to separate elements in dates and addresses that might otherwise be confused.

EXAMPLES

Ms. Joan Staley, 27463 West Chicago Street, Livonia, Michigan 48150

Mr. Thomas Larkin, 316 Northeast 54th Street, Kansas City, Missouri 64148 [It is unnecessary to set off the Zip Code by commas because it is already distinct from the name of the state preceding it.]

March 17, 1981 [The comma is necessary only to separate 17 from 1981. If the date is written European style, 17 March 1981, there is no need for a comma; nor is there in the absence of the day of the month, March 1981. A comma should be used after the full citation of month, day, and year: "On March 17, 1981, the last prisoners. . . ."]

404

13. THE COMMA

William Shakespeare was born on April 23, 1564, in Stratford-upon-Avon, England.

CAUTION

No comma is needed following the year if only that date is cited: "He was married in 1582 to Anne Hathaway."

EXERCISES

EXERCISE 1, NONRESTRICTIVE CLAUSES. *Punctuate each nonrestrictive clause in the following sentences.*

1. I remembered that this was the day when every student was to be prepared for the worst.
2. Every year we have a homecoming day when everybody tries to impress parents and other visitors.
3. I awakened Toby Blair who was my roommate so that he would have time to dress more formally.
4. His everyday outfit which consists of jeans and a sweater seemed hardly appropriate.
5. His father and mother of whom he was very proud were coming to visit us.
6. We found them a room at the Green Mountain Inn where most of the alumni liked to stay.
7. I did not think that my parents who were vacationing in Mexico would come for the reunion.
8. I am happy to have a roommate whose parents adopt me on occasion.
9. I know a sophomore who gets letters and checks from two sets of parents.
10. This weekend which we spent with Toby's parents was a happy one.

EXERCISE 2, USING COMMAS AND SEMICOLONS. *Punctuate each of the following sentences. Decide whether to use a comma, a semicolon, or no mark at all. Be able to justify your decision.*

1. I have considered going into social work but my mother has tried to discourage me.
2. My mother is a practical person and she thinks that I am too young to know my mind.

405

13

3. I know something about the work for I have studied sociology and made trips to the state institutions.
4. During the summer I worked in the Red Cross office and I enjoyed the work.
5. A friend of mine is a social case worker and I have occasionally gone with her on her trips.
6. Her work is very interesting for it introduces her to all sorts of people.
7. She visits poor and hungry families but she does not actually take them baskets of food.
8. Sometimes she comes home very angry for she has no patience with drunken husbands.
9. She makes a careful study of each case and then she recommends the most suitable kind of assistance.
10. At times the Red Cross gives immediate help and then the happiness of the needy family is a welcome reward to the case worker.

EXERCISE 3, WORDS IN SERIES. *In the following sentences insert commas where they are necessary.*

1. Mark Twain was a journeyman printer a Mississippi River steamboat pilot and a famous writer and lecturer.
2. Few could compete with him in the ability to capture the lusty humor the spirit and the idiom of nineteenth-century America.
3. His humor his zest for life and his ability to see the ridiculous in everyday things endeared him to his readers.
4. Mark Twain was born in the Middle West lived in the Far West and died in New England.
5. He knew Bret Harte a poet short-story writer college professor and editor.
6. From his boyhood in Hannibal he found the materials for such characters as Tom Sawyer Huckleberry Finn and Becky Thatcher.
7. Mark Twain's best work reveals his genuine love of humanity his impatience with sham his irreverent bawdy humor and his hatred of all pretense and deceit.
8. During his stay in San Francisco he associated with

13

Bret Harte and Artemus Ward and other pioneers of the new literature of America.
9. He was attracted to Charles Farrar Browne, who was a humorist specializing in original spelling homely philosophy and shrewd comments on human nature.
10. As a tall imposing white-haired and white-suited celebrity he was well known in his later years through his popular appearances on the lecture platform.

EXERCISE 4, INTRODUCTORY ELEMENTS. *In each of the following sentences decide whether the introductory phrase or clause is to be followed by a comma or not.*

1. If a blind poet had not written a long poem about it few modern readers would have heard about the Trojan War.
2. Because the wife of a Spartan king ran off with a young Trojan many warriors perished before the walls of Troy.
3. Although the Homeric account may be the romantic version of the story the real cause of the war may have been political and economic rivalry.
4. After the sudden elopement of Helen and Paris the friends of King Menelaus of Sparta assembled to avenge the insult.
5. Having discovered a just cause to do what they liked to do even without cause the Greek heroes assembled at Aulis for the expedition.
6. Excited by hopes of an easy victory and thoughts of rich plunder the avengers gathered 100,000 men and 1,186 ships.
7. Unlike modern wars in which everybody loses ancient wars could often be profitable to the victors.
8. Ten long years having been wasted before the walls of Troy both sides were willing to try any stratagem to win or call the war off.
9. Deciding to put their faith in trickery instead of bravery the Greeks built a large hollow horse and pretended that it was an offering to their gods.
10. Convinced by a Greek spy that the horse would make them invincible the Trojans dragged it into the city

407

13

and with it enough armed Greeks to open the gates of the city to the invaders.

EXERCISE 5, DATES AND ADDRESSES. *Copy the following sentences. Insert commas where they are needed.*

1. Our friends used to live at 826 Elm Drive Harris Junction Illinois but they recently moved to 230 Warren Street Duluth Minnesota 55720.
2. Elinor Wylie was born in Rosemont Pennsylvania in 1887 and died in London England on December 16 1928.
3. Stephen Crane was born in Newark New Jersey on November 1, 1871 and died twenty-nine years later on June 5 1900 at Badenweiler in the Black Forest.
4. Mary's new address is 722 East McMillan Street Rosemont Indiana 43130.
5. All questions should be addressed to 38 Oak Street Southwest Fargo Texas 71350.

EXERCISE 6, COMMAS AND RULES. *Copy the following sentences. Supply every missing comma and tell what rule of usage applies.*

1. If you have never heard of Phineas Barnum you have missed knowing what naïve curious gullible America will believe.
2. In 1842 Barnum opened the American Museum which housed an exhibit of wild animals freaks and curiosities.
3. Although many of his freaks were ordinary persons decked out to fool the public some we must admit to his credit were real celebrities.
4. Phineas Barnum an American showman was born in Bethel Connecticut.
5. Stories are still told about people paying to gape at the tattooed lady the wild man of Borneo the sword swallower and the fire eater.
6. In 1871 having failed in a bid for Congress Barnum organized his famous circus publicized as "The Greatest Show on Earth."
7. Many years earlier he had publicized General Tom

408

13

Thumb a dwarf whose real name was Charles Sherwood Stratton.

8. Stratton strangely enough was a normal child of normal parents but at a very early age for reasons never known to medical science he seemed to stop growing.
9. Barnum who believed that you could fool all of the people all of the time depended on an extravagant flamboyant style of advertising new at that time but now general in show business.
10. Barnum internationally famous as a showman was also interested in serious affairs; in 1850 for example he brought to this country Jenny Lind the famous Swedish soprano.

EXERCISE 7, ALL USES OF THE COMMA. *Punctuate the following sentences. Tell what rule or principle of usage applies to each comma that you use.*

1. At the desk sat a slender red-haired woman who gave us more cards to fill out.
2. As we watched the woman reached for the telephone dialed a number and asked for somebody named Monty.
3. Her soft pleading voice dripping with honey she spoke words that would have melted a traffic policeman's heart.
4. My companion Paul Biggs a graduate of M.I.T. knew her for they had worked at the same summer resort in Vermont.
5. Vermont with hills lakes and rolling rocky New England scenery is a famous vacation region.
6. As he confided to me in whispers they had picnicked swum hiked and ridden horseback together over the famous Long Trail but their bridle paths as he said never became a bridal path to the altar.
7. Monty an elusive sort of character if we might judge from the overheard conversation finally agreed to some tentative arrangement.
8. The crisis having been postponed for the time the woman turned her attention to us and to her work.

409

9. She accepted our cards and with a fluttery momentary smile tossed them into a box.
10. "If you should ask me which I hope you don't" said Paul "I would tell you that our applications will never reach the manager."

14

§ 14. THE SEMICOLON

14a. A semicolon is used between the main clauses of a compound sentence when they are not joined by one of the coordinating conjunctions.

In weight, or length of pause, a *semicolon* is more than a comma and less than a period. The period separates sentences. The semicolon separates main clauses within a sentence. Its frequent use marks a dignified formal style, implying relatively long, balanced sentences, and for this reason an abundance of semicolons in an informal paper should be viewed with suspicion. On the other hand, the semicolon provides an excellent substitute for weak conjunctions between coordinate clauses, and it can often strengthen structures that are clearly parallel. It is in general an important device in developing a firm, economical style.

Ordinarily a semicolon should not be used to cut off a phrase or a dependent clause from the main clause.

EXAMPLES OF INCORRECT USE

In these days, as writing grows increasingly brisk if not openly journalistic; one sometimes wonders what has happened to the good old semicolon.

She was habitually critical of me; because my manners, she said, were like those of the inhabitants of Animal House.

Notice, however, that substituting the semicolon for the subordinating conjunction, when the relationship between the clauses is implicit, can afford stylistic advantage.

410

14. THE SEMICOLON

EXAMPLE

She was habitually critical of me; my manners, she said, were like those of the inhabitants of Animal House.

OTHER EXAMPLES OF CONVENTIONAL USE

And there you have the whole secret of Beethoven. He could design patterns with the best of them; he could write music whose beauty will last you all your life; he could take the driest sticks of themes and work them up so interestingly that you find something new in them at the hundredth hearing: in short, you can say of him all that you can say of the greatest pattern composers; but his diagnostic, the thing that marks him out from all the others, is his disturbing quality, his power of unsettling us and imposing his giant moods on us.

—G. B. SHAW

The frontier has been a predominant influence on the shaping of the American character and culture, in the molding of American political life and institutions; the frontier is the principal, the recurring theme in the American symphony.

—CLYDE KLUCKHOHN

This does not mean, of course, that the people are happy; the society to whose traditions they are adjusted may be a miserable one, ridden with anxiety, sadism, and disease.

—DAVID RIESMAN

When a pitcher sees a batter at the plate he thinks of a strike-out; when a batter sees a pitcher on the mound he thinks of a home run; when an umpire sees them both he thinks of trouble.

Often the verb in the second or third clause may be unstated, but understood to be the same as the verb in the first clause.

EXAMPLE

The humanist dismisses what he dislikes by calling it *romantic;* the liberal, by calling it *fascist;* the conservative, by calling it *communistic.*

—ROBERT GORHAM DAVIS

411

14b. A semicolon is used between the coordinate clauses of a compound sentence with one of the following conjunctive adverbs: *therefore, however, hence, accordingly, furthermore, nevertheless,* **and** *consequently.*

14

In modern prose, however, it is more common to find the conjunctive adverb placed within the second or third clause and enclosed in commas than to meet it as a conjunction at the beginning of its clause.

EXAMPLES

He had worked in the foreign service for two years without leave; hence he was tired and frightened almost beyond endurance.

He had worked in the foreign service for two years without leave; he was, consequently, tired and frightened almost beyond endurance.

From a running start Lance launched his body into a vigorous racing dive; however, he was about thirty feet from the pool at the time.

14c. A semicolon is used in place of a comma when a more distinct pause than the comma would give is desirable.

You may sometimes find published writers using the semicolon in ways that violate Rule 14a above. Although such exceptions do exist, they should not give you justification for adopting them in classroom work. Follow the rules outlined here as closely as possible.

EXERCISE

Commas Versus Semicolons. *In the following sentences, determine appropriate punctuation to be used in the places marked by brackets. Would you use commas, semicolons, or no punctuation at all?*

1. His hair was white and stood up wildly on his head [ ] nevertheless I was struck by a singular neatness in his appearance.
2. It was due, I suppose [ ] to his lofty stature and immaculate dress [ ] no doubt he has a careful attendant looking after him.
3. Like all distinguished men in political life [ ] he spoke with assurance, even with arrogance [ ] yet I could not help sensing some anxiety in his behavior.
4. I walked up to him then [ ] and held out my hand [ ] but he evidently failed to recognize me.
5. When a man has the weight of nations on his shoulders [ ] he may be forgiven for overlooking individuals [ ] but I admit I was angry.
6. It is one thing to be dignified and detached [ ] it is quite another to be downright rude.
7. I had arrived early [ ] as was my habit [ ] I therefore felt privileged to depart without delay.
8. The affair was not the worst I have ever endured [ ] but it was nearly so [ ] at such times one wishes one could escape at any cost.
9. Once I had arrived at the entrance [ ] however [ ] there was no turning back.
10. When I go to a place like that [ ] I go gladly [ ] when I return [ ] I come home even more gladly.

15

§ 15. THE APOSTROPHE

15a. An apostrophe and *-s* are used to form the possessive of a noun, singular or plural, that does not end in *-s*.

EXAMPLES

A man's will, women's rights, children's toys, a dog's life, the sun's rays, the earth's surface, Irene's husband, my mother-in-law's views.

413

15

When two or more names joined by *and* are represented as joint owners of something, in ordinary usage the last name alone takes the apostrophe.

EXAMPLES

Meier and Frank's store, Swenson and Carmody's Machine Shop, Nancy and Sally's mother, Larson, Jones, and Marshall's antique shop, Jon and Lorna's affairs.

But when separate ownership is meant, the apostrophe follows each noun. Of course, when both nouns and pronouns are used, the pronouns take the possessive-case form.

EXAMPLES

Nancy's and Sally's clothes are strewn all over the bedroom.

Mr. Marshall's and Captain Ford's egos were badly damaged in the collision.

Mr. Danby said that his, his wife's, and his daughter's possessions were saved before the ship sank.

Usage sanctions such group possessives as *the Queen of England's hats,* but sometimes it is better to dodge an awkward construction by rewriting it. The double possessive or genitive is established usage, as in "some relatives of Arlene's," "that old car of ours," "a friend of theirs," "that red coat of hers." [Note here that the *of*-phrase is used to indicate the possessive.] See §4e, "Pronouns."

15b. The apostrophe alone is used to form the possessive of a plural noun ending in -*s*.

EXAMPLES

Workers' rights, three months' wastes, students' diseases, the Smiths' house, foxes' tails.

15c. The apostrophe with -*s* is used to form the possessive of singular nouns ending in -*s*, if the resultant form is not unpleasant or difficult to pronounce.

414

EXAMPLES

James's cycle, Keats's poems, Jones's office; *but:* for goodness' sake, for conscience' sake, Demosthenes' orations.

15d. An apostrophe with -*s* is used to form the possessive of certain indefinite pronouns.

EXAMPLES

Anybody's game, somebody's hat, everybody's business, one's ideas, somebody's coat, another's turn.

The apostrophe should not be used with personal pronouns to form the possessive. See § 4c, "Pronouns."

EXAMPLES

If this coat isn't yours [not *your's*], it's probably hers [not *her's*].

The decision is ours [not *our's*].

The two dogs are theirs [not *their's*].

It's only a puppy; its [not *it's*] bark is worse than its [not *it's*] bite.

15e. An apostrophe is used to indicate the omission of letters or figures.

EXAMPLES

Hasn't, doesn't, weren't, o'clock, it's [it is], I'll, class of '84.

15f. An apostrophe and -*s* are used to form the plurals of figures, letters, and words referred to as words.

EXAMPLES

You have not dotted your *i*'s or crossed your *t*'s.

Your *m*'s, *n*'s, and *u*'s look alike.

He used too many *and*'s and *but*'s in his paper.

Be careful not to make your *3*'s look like *8*'s.

His jeans are more appropriate for the 60's than the 80's. [In formal writing, decade references should be written out: Sixties, Eighties].

Note that only the figures, letters, and words are set in italics. The 's are set in roman type. Some publications omit the apostrophe in these situations, but there may be confusion in a sentence like this: In his handwriting the *i*s and *u*s are but a wavy line.

15g. The apostrophe is often omitted in names of organizations, associations, buildings, etc.

EXAMPLES

The Authors League, Farmers Market, Pawnee State Teachers College, Mathematics Teachers Association, St. Elizabeths Hospital, Veterans Administration.

EXERCISES

EXERCISE 1, USE OF THE APOSTROPHE. *Copy the following sentences. Insert an apostrophe wherever it is correct.*

1. "Its almost ten oclock," said Toms cousin, "and hes not in sight yet."
2. "I wouldnt worry," replied Maries mother. "Theyre very busy now at Smith and Eberlys Department Store this season."
3. "Were hungry, Mom," said little Edie. "Arent you going to make us a sandwich?"
4. "Mind your *p*s and *q*s, young lady, and youll earn your *A*s and *B*s," remarked Marie apropos of nothing.
5. "If Dads not here pretty soon," said Tom, "hell be here in time for tomorrows breakfast."
6. "Its all in the days work. Once he took the Smiths ocelot to the doctors and decided to sit up all night with it," said Marie.
7. "Youre joking, of course," replied Tom. "You know that its leg was broken."
8. "Well, for heavens sake," exclaimed Maries mother, "it was somebodys responsibility, wasnt it?"
9. "Mother, did you say 'for Keats sakes' or 'for Keatss sakes'?" asked Marie. "Theres a fine difference, you know."

10. "I think everybodys so hungry hes getting silly," said
    Tom. "Whos going to make some hamburgers for us?"

EXERCISE 2, POSSESSIVE FORMS. *Write the possessive singular and the possessive plural of each of the following. Example:* child, child's, children's.

1. boy	11. attorney
2. baby	12. fox
3. Smith	13. wolf
4. mother-in-law	14. Powers
5. he	15. wife
6. goose	16. Berry
7. it	17. writer
8. woman	18. she
9. Williams	19. sailor
10. Allen	20. kangaroo

16

§ 16. QUOTATION MARKS

16a. Double quotation marks are used to enclose a direct quotation in dialogue and in reproducing short passages from other writers.

EXAMPLES OF DIALOGUE

Talking quietly as they left the theater, the two couples were trying to decide whether the film they had just seen was truly funny.

"The best scene in the whole movie was the car chase through the shopping mall," said Carl.

"No, it was just a big waste of money," answered Jeanne, Lorne's date.

"I wonder if Belushi and Aykroyd are planning a sequel," asked Lorne. "It seems logical to me to invent another Blues brother with his own orphanage to save."

"Yes," said Paula, "but who would be a good choice for the part?"

"Sammy Davis, Jr.," offered Carl.

417

Note that in dialogue a new paragraph is used with every change in speaker.

The writer must be careful not to leave out one set of quotation marks. Quotation marks come in pairs, one set at the beginning and one set at the end of every quoted part.

WRONG

"I have never really liked potted beef, said King Henry. It frequently gives me heartburn."

RIGHT

"I have never really liked potted beef," said King Henry. "It frequently gives me heartburn."

A familiar error in citing passages from others is to begin a quotation that never ends. By failing to close the quotation with the appropriate second set of marks, the passage from the quoted author and the comment by the quoting writer can become thoroughly confused.

WRONG

King Henry once observed, "I have never really liked potted beef. It frequently gives me heartburn. This remark has often been misquoted.

If a quotation consists of several sentences, the quotation marks are placed at the beginning and at the end of the entire quotation, not at the beginning and end of each separate sentence in that section.

"You'd have had your stomach full of fighting, young man," added Colonel Williams, "if Squire Sedgwick had not taken them just as he did. Squire," he added, "my wife shall thank you that she's not a widow when we get back to Stockbridge. I honor your courage, sir. The credit of this day is yours."
—EDWARD BELLAMY, *The Duke of Stockbridge*

If a quotation consists of several paragraphs, quotation marks are placed before each paragraph but at the end

418

of the last paragraph only. This convention applies to a continued speech by one speaker. If the speaker changes, his words are placed in a new paragraph or paragraphs. Short descriptive, narrative, or explanatory passages may be paragraphed with dialogue, especially if they are placed between sentences of dialogue spoken by the same person.

A quoted passage of several lines of prose or poetry—not a part of dialogue—may be indicated by indention. In typing it is often typed single-spaced; in print it may be set in smaller type than the rest of the text. No quotation marks are needed when indention is used.

No quotation marks are used with an indirect quotation.

DIRECT

"Yes," I said to him, "it's all right."

"I am relieved to hear it," he replied.

INDIRECT

I told him it was all right.

He said he was relieved to hear it.

16b. Single quotation marks are used to enclose a quotation within a quotation.

EXAMPLES

"Finally," she said, "I just turned to him and shouted, 'Leave me alone, won't you?' " [Note the position of the quotation marks in relation to other marks.]

"If the good Lord should tell me that I had only five minutes to live," said Justice Oliver Wendell Holmes, "I would say to him, 'All right, Lord, but I'm sorry you can't make it ten.' "
　　　—CATHERINE DRINKER BOWEN, *Yankee from Olympus*

16c. Quotation marks are used to enclose quoted titles of stories, poems, chapters, and other subdivisions of books, and, in newspaper style, the titles of books. (See § 10.)

419

16

16d. Quotation marks are used to enclose words spoken of as words.

Italics are used for this purpose, however, when the style is formal, although writers are not consistent in this practice. In informal writing, quotation marks are usually more common. See § 10c.

EXAMPLE

He was no doubt angry when sportswriters described him and his play in words such as "showboat," "hot dog," and "bush."

16e. Quotation marks are used to enclose words used in a special sense.

Often quotation marks are used to indicate to the reader that the writer, in repeating someone else's words, takes no stock in the manner in which they have been used and is about to offer his own opposing views.

EXAMPLES

National greed has disguised itself in arguments that "inflation" forces prices skyward. [The writer does not think that inflation is the cause.]

The press secretary claimed that the jungle village had to be "demolished" in order to be "saved." [The writer points out the obvious contradiction in the choice of words.]

Don't overuse quotation marks in an apologetic or self-conscious way, enclosing slang or other expressions that you feel may be inappropriate. If they are inappropriate, you should find better ones. If they are appropriate, they need no apology.

WRONG

He is often the victim of unhappy "attachments."

The "street cops" are watching for illegal sales of Dr. Pepper.

Hers is a "star-type" figure and personality.

420

RIGHT

He is often the victim of unhappy attachments. [The attempt at irony fails here].

The undercover police are watching for illegal sales of Dr. Pepper. [Do not try to bring in a slang term under cover of quotation marks].

She possesses the figure and personality of a star. [Avoid using *-type* constructions, especially as modifiers of nouns].

16f. Quotation marks are often used to enclose the definitions or meanings of words spoken of as words.

EXAMPLE

Miscellaneous further illustrations of elevation are *pretty* from an early meaning "sly," through "clever," to something approaching "beautiful"; *nice* from an etymological meaning "ignorant," through its earliest English sense "foolish," and later ones like "particular," to its present broad and vague colloquial meaning of "pleasant" or "acceptable"; and *fond* from "foolish" to "affectionate."
—STUART ROBERTSON, *The Development of Modern English*

See also § 10c.

16g. Commas and periods are always placed inside quotation marks.

This rule is a printers' convention. The period and the comma are the two marks that occupy the lower half of a line of print; all other marks—the colon, the semicolon, the question mark, and the exclamation point—stand the full height of the line. To have a comma or a period trail out beyond quotation marks looks bad. Remember the convention: periods and commas are *always* placed inside quotation marks. See § 16b for examples.

16h. The question mark, the semicolon, and the exclamation point go inside quotation marks if they belong to the quoted part. They go outside if they do not belong to the quoted part.

421

16

EXAMPLES

Did you hear him say, "I won't go"? [The question mark belongs to the main clause, or the entire sentence. Hence it stands at the end. But notice that no period is used in addition to the end punctuation.]

"Well, we'll see about that!" she exclaimed in anger.

"It is as much of a trade," says La Bruyère, "to make a book as it is to make a clock"; in short, literature is largely a matter of technique. [Note that the semicolon is not a part of the quotation. It belongs to the whole sentence.]

—IRVING BABBITT

16i. For dialogue guides (such as *he said*) with quoted dialogue, use the punctuation that the structure of the sentence calls for.

EXAMPLE

"The price is not a matter of profit," he said, stiffly; "it is a matter of principle." [Notice the semicolon to separate coordinate clauses in a compound sentence of dialogue. Most writers use a period and a following capital letter instead of a semicolon in this sort of construction. See § 16a for other examples of punctuating dialogue.]

The general practice is not to use a comma before a quoted part that is woven into the sentence or before a title. This is logical enough: note that the voice makes little or no pause before reading such quotations.

EXAMPLES

Her Volkswagen was the kind of car that "spends more time in the shop than on the road." She was sure that before the car was ready to drive again repairs would "cost a fortune."

Like Yeats's chestnut-tree in "Among School Children" (which when asked whether it is leaf, blossom, or bole, has no answer), a poem is to be seen not as a confederation of form, rime, image, metaphor, tone, and theme, but as a whole.

—X. J. KENNEDY, *An Introduction to Poetry*

EXERCISES

EXERCISE 1, COMPOSING A PARAGRAPH WITH QUO-
TATIONS. *Copy out a paragraph of formal prose that seems
to you interesting, for any reason. Then write your own paragraph
of comment, in which you quote three or four short phrases from
the original, punctuating properly as you do so.*

EXERCISE 2, QUOTATION MARKS AND PARAGRAPH-
ING. *Copy the following, punctuating and paragraphing correctly.*

Minnie pushed a few more letters into boxes, set down
her bundle, and walked to the counter. She gave Ellen a
roll of stamps and dropped the bills into a drawer. What's
Martin think he's going to do about that shark? she asked.
I don't know. I guess they'll try to catch it. Canst thou
draw out leviathan with a hook? I beg your pardon? Book
of Job, said Minnie. No mortal man's going to catch that
fish. Why do you say that? We're not meant to catch it,
that's why. We're being readied. For what? We'll know
when the time comes. I see. Ellen put the stamps in her
purse. Well, maybe you're right. Thanks, Minnie. She
turned and walked toward the door. There'll be no mistak-
ing it, Minnie said to Ellen's back.

—PETER BENCHLEY, *Jaws*

§ 17. COLON AND DASH

The Colon

**17a. The colon is used to separate an introductory state-
ment from a list of particulars.**

The *colon* is a mark of emphatic separation and should
not break grammatically related elements apart: should
not divide a verb from its object, an object or subject from
its appositives. Whatever precedes the colon, then, must
constitute a grammatically complete clause or statement.

423

17

RUPTURED SENTENCE

In the kitchen drawer she kept: a hammer, a screwdriver, a pair of pliers, some assorted nails, and a pneumatic drill. [A hammer . . . drill are all objects of *kept.* No punctuation is necessary to announce them.]

COMPLETE CLAUSE INTRODUCING A LIST

In the kitchen drawer she kept a few household tools: a hammer, a screwdriver, a pair of pliers, some assorted nails, and a pneumatic drill.

Exception: a list set out in tabular form introduced by an incomplete clause.

If you can answer my questions, I would like to know:
1. how often you teach the course,
2. what textbook you usually use,
3. how many students normally enroll in the course,
4. what price of textbook you consider acceptable,
5. whether you feel the enclosed book might prove a useful substitute for the text you now use.

These clauses begin with a lower case letter and are closed with commas. If even one of the clauses contained internal commas, it would be necessary to close each with a semicolon to avoid confusion. As the clauses in this case are considered part of the sentence beginning with "If you can answer," the last one terminates with a period. When every clause in a list is a complete one, as those in the example are not, the usual practice is to treat each as an individual sentence beginning with a capital and ending with a period. *The art is to compose the list so that its punctuation is consistent.*

17b. A colon introduces a long quotation.

EXAMPLE

Trillin adds humor to his essay by applying what might be called pseudoscientific tests:

> St. Louis meets the tests I devised several years ago to identify an Eastern city: a place where nobody on the city council ever

wears white patent-leather shoes, where there are at least two places to buy pastrami (every Western city has one place, usually called something like the New York Delicatessen), and where just about everbody eats supper after dark and calls it dinner.
—CALVIN TRILLIN, *The New Yorker*

(The preceding quotation, used for illustration, is somewhat shorter than those that ordinarily require a colon. Note as well that because the quotation is longer than a normal sentence, it is indented and single-spaced by the writer. When this is done, no quotation marks are required.)

17c. The colon may be used to separate main clauses when the second amplifies, restates, or interprets the first.

EXAMPLES

The Army's chief-of-staff met for two hours with the President; he told his commander what he wanted to hear: that the country's troops were ready at a moment's notice to destroy the alien saucers.

Modern science has not only purified this notion; it has also transformed it: a transformation that can be described by saying that modern science is *indifferent to nothing.*
—KARL JASPERS, *Is Science Evil?*

17d. In a formal business letter the colon rather than a comma is used after the salutation.

Dear Mr. Crushbum:
  The longline panty-girdle manufactured by your company, Binding Foundations, Incorporated, contains several serious defects. . . .

The Dash

17e. The dash is used to indicate a sudden, abrupt break in thought or structure.

425

17

The last shot—a rocket from our left-winger—was so powerful that the goalie—an experienced but cocky type—did not realize it was in the net until ten seconds after the red light blinked.

"I wish—I wish you'd let him know—please do—it was an accident." [In dialogue to give the effect of hesitation]

"I don't know whether she would like—" [Speech abruptly broken off]

17f. The dash is used for an explanatory or parenthetical phrase or clause that breaks into the normal flow of the sentence.

Three kinds of marks may indicate parenthesis—*the comma, the dash,* and *marks of parenthesis.* The degree of separation indicated by these marks varies from the lightest, for which commas are used, to the most definite and the most formal, for which parentheses are used.

EXAMPLES
There may be a better guitarist somewhere—in a small, obscure Spanish village—but when Segovia begins his performance you believe you are hearing notes and harmonies that can only be called divine.

Like the British paratroopers to the east, the Americans—in humor, in sorrow, in terror and in pain—began the work they had come to Normandy to do.
—CORNELIUS RYAN, *The Longest Day*

17g. The dash is used to introduce or to set off a long, formal appositive or summary.

EXAMPLES
There is no other dog in the world to match the Afghan hound—for elegant beauty, for friendliness, and for blinding speed. [Introducing an appositive]

These obstacles—jagged triangles of steel, saw-toothed gatelike structures of iron, metal-tipped wooden stakes and concrete

426

cones—were planted just below high- and low-tide water marks.
[To set off long appositive]

—CORNELIUS RYAN, *The Longest Day*

The dash may occasionally be found before such words as *namely* and *that is* introducing an appositive. See also § 13k.

EXAMPLE

Also you will find out about the queer fade-away, the slow curve, the fast in- and out-shoots that seem to be timed almost as delicately as shrapnel, to burst, or rather break, just when they will do the most harm—namely, at the moment when the batter is swinging.

—PAUL GALLICO

A dash may be used before such words as *all* and *these* introducing a summary, or summarizing appositive, after a series. The occasions for this use of the dash are infrequent.

EXAMPLES

Pop quizzes, dances, new friends, Frisbee contests—all these should be a part of your freshman year.

Good acting and a fast-paced plot—these are the key elements of a successful adventure film.

Caution: The dash must not be used indiscriminately for all other marks of punctuation. It should be saved for its special function, so that it will be effective when it is used.

§ 18. PARENTHESES AND BRACKETS

Parentheses

18a. Parentheses are used to enclose material that is supplementary, explanatory, or interpretive.

In theory, the general principle is that commas set off material that is fairly close to the main meaning of the sentence (see § 13i); dashes set off material more distant in meaning (§ 17g); and marks of parenthesis are used to indicate the most distant parenthetical relation. In practice, however, there is considerable variety among modern writers in the way parentheses are used. One traditional function is to enclose an explanation, a definition, or a set of examples to clarify a particular reference.

EXAMPLES

The book, *Ultra Goes to War,* by Richard Lewin, proves that breaking the German code (named "Enigma" after the machine itself) helped Montgomery defeat Rommel.

Many things may be legitimately inferred to exist (electrons, the expanding universe, the past, the other side of the moon) from what is observed.

—SIDNEY HOOK

Sometimes parentheses may be used to introduce a comment by the author about what he is doing, drawing the reader's attention to some particular device of style.

EXAMPLE

Almost every high-school graduate "knows" (I put quotation marks around the word) that air is primarily a mixture of oxygen gas and nitrogen gas. . . .

—JAMES B. CONANT

Finally, journalists are prone to enclose whole parenthetical sentences inside other sentences, sometimes at awkward points in the structure.

EXAMPLE

His message is a messianic mixture of tax talk and drop-off answers ("That's got to be changed" or "We have to change that," but few specifics). [Note that a colon would be more appropriate here]

—REPPS HUDSON

18b. Parentheses do not obviate the need for other punctuation in the sentence.

428

An expression enclosed in parentheses may be part of a clause, and the clause, including the parenthetical remark, must close with the appropriate punctuation, which is set *outside* and *after* the parentheses.

EXAMPLES

Routine maintenance of an automobile can be carried out by numerous agencies (a dealership, a service station, or the owner), but when the car's guarantee is at stake only work done by the dealer will be acceptable. [The comma necessary between independent clauses joined by a conjunction must follow . . . *owner*).]

What she referred to as "the statue's boots" were, in fact, greaves (armor for the shins). [The period follows . . . *shins*).]

Occasionally a parenthetical expression is a separate sentence adding information to the sentences preceding and following it. In such cases the parentheses *enclose* all punctuation, and the expression begins with a capital.

EXAMPLE

The British shows broadcast on American television are not representative of the British public's lust for highbrow social drama. (One of the most popular programs in England is *Kojak*.) They do demonstrate a typically British knack for adding a successful veneer of professional and technical refinement to a crude and ready-made commonplace, in this case the genre of soap opera.

Brackets

18c. Brackets are used to enclose corrections, interpolations, and supplied omissions added to a quotation by the person quoting.

Here is an example from a passage that has already been used (in § 16i) for another purpose.

It was tariff policy which seemed to him [Cordell Hull] "at the very heart of this country's economic dilemma." [The reader would have no idea what person the author was talking about if we had not added the bracketed explanation.]

—ARTHUR M. SCHLESINGER, JR.

429

In this book you will find many examples of conventional use of brackets, like the one just above, where they set off comment about a quoted passage in such a way that the reader may not confuse the comment with the passage itself.

18

EXERCISES

EXERCISE 1, THE COLON AND THE SEMICOLON. *Copy out from any sample of formal modern prose five sentences in which colons are used. In which of these sentences could semicolons be used instead? What effect would such a substitution have on the meaning or the tone of each sentence?*

EXERCISE 2, THE COLON. *Write out three sentences of your own illustrating the use of the colon as a formal introduction, in the manner described in § 17a. Then write out three others in which the colon is used to separate independent clauses (§ 17c).*

EXERCISE 3, PARENTHESES, BRACKETS, DASHES. *From one of your textbooks copy five sentences in which parentheses or brackets are used. Try substituting dashes for the parentheses and brackets. What is the effect on meaning and tone?*

EXERCISE 4, THE DASH. *Try writing a letter in which you use no punctuation at all except dashes and periods. What is the effect on tone: that is, what kind of voice do you hear uttering these words? What kind of person speaks in this way?*

EXERCISE 5, CORRECT PUNCTUATION. *Select the best punctuation for the sentences below. Dashes are appropriate for a sudden, abrupt break in thought; parentheses enclose material that is supplementary or explanatory; and brackets are used to enclose corrections or supplied omissions. Insert punctuation in place of the carets.*

1. Her reasons were simple but compelling: ˄ 1 ˄ he didn't tolerate her friends; ˄ 2 ˄ he never let her have the car; and ˄ 3 ˄ he vacationed alone for three months out of the year.

2. William Carlos Williams ⌄ 1883–1963 ⌄ wrote a poem called "To Waken an Old Lady," which today is widely admired by many critics.
3. Few people realized it was he ⌄ Jesse James ⌄ until the train had completely stopped and men were reaching for their guns.
4. They found the Lincoln the next morning with its engine ⌄ how amazing! ⌄ resting in the back seat.
5. There will probably not be many people eating those mushrooms ⌄ commonly called "toadstools" ⌄ now that the coroner's report is published.

18

12 | *Spelling*

§ 19. THE SPELLING PROBLEM

As everyone knows, many words in English are not spelled the way they are pronounced. That is why spelling our language is so difficult.

Consider the problem of the foreign speaker who runs up against the various pronunciations of just one small group of letters: -*ough* in *cough, dough, rough, bough, through.* The exchange student from France, coming to America to improve his English accent, sees a headline on the front page of a newspaper: EXHIBITION PRONOUNCED SUCCESS. "Ah, this fantastic language!" he exclaims in utter discouragement, but without surprise.

There was a time, several centuries ago, when a writer gave little thought to using the right letters in his words. Some writers, Shakespeare for instance, appear to have spelled their own names in several different ways without a second thought. Our modern attitude toward standardized spelling, however, is very different. Almost everyone— not just your English instructor—takes spelling seriously. One reason is that, unlike most matters of language, spelling is an area where there is usually a Right or Wrong, and it is tempting to make much of someone else's errors when you know they are really errors. There is even an economic importance in trying to learn to spell; employers everywhere assume that poor spelling is a sign of stupidity or illiteracy. They probably reason, rightly or not, that carelessness in spelling is a visible, measurable sign of carelessness in other, more important things. Spelling is something that shows. And because it does show, because

19

it can be easily seen and easily judged, it has become one of the first tests of a person's education and fitness for a job.

What to Do About the Problem. Learning to spell requires memorizing the letters of virtually every word encountered in reading so that it may be reproduced correctly in writing. Most of us, however, have something better to do with our lives, so it is fortunate that there are few systematic approaches to the process and one invaluable resource. The aids do not let us out of the duty to practice words, to memorize a substantial list of essential ones, and to recognize when we need to investigate the spelling of an unfamiliar word rather than just to have a shot at it, but they do give us a method to pursue.

A good beginning is *to learn a basic list of words* that may involve spelling problems. Such a list appears in the next few pages. As memories are fallible, misspellings of even familiar words occur in many writers' first drafts, but if work with the list does not engrave the word on the mind well enough for automatic use, it may yet fix the form in the subconscious so that a misspelling can be recognized after the act of composition. All written work should be proofread, and it is in this process that vague uneasiness at the shape of a word often signals the need for a recheck and correction.

Learn words, then, for two purposes: to spell them correctly and to recognize when they are spelled incorrectly. As for proofreading (best accomplished by having someone read aloud a carbon copy while you check the original), remember that there is no easier way to cite a writer for error than to pick out his or her bad spelling. The instructor who discovers numerous spelling errors in a paper would not be human if the frustration at correcting them did not adversely affect his or her appreciation of the entire work.

Knowing something of the analysis of words helps. To understand prefixes and suffixes and roots and stems increases vocabulary and contributes to the small set of rules applicable to spelling. Realize that *ante-* means "before" and *anti-*

19

"against" and there is less probability that *antecedent* will be spelled as though it meant "something against going" rather than what it does mean, "something that goes before." Many English words are descendants of classical Greek and Latin words, to which they bear a more or less recognizable kinship. Other words have drifted into our usage from French, Italian, German (old and new), Spanish, American Indian, Sanskrit, Hebrew—from, in effect, practically the whole Atlas of languages alive and dead. As the origin language of an English word is likely to follow a reasonably phonetic spelling, a spelling in which letters have consistent sound values, knowing what the original or root word is will suggest the spelling of most of its derivatives. Learning the meaning of a word as well as its derivation can aid the student in making that word part of his or her list of frequently used words.

Learning words in terms of their syllable divisions is another practical tool for mastering spelling. It forces concentration on the letters in the word and breaks down the number of letters to be learned at one time.

There are, too, some mechanical steps toward better spelling. The most effective one is the personal list of the writer. When a spelling error is pointed out, *write down the correction* (there is nothing like coordinating hand, eye, and brain to impress the memory) and compile a list of such corrected errors. Keep the list in rigid alphabetical order, make it out on 3 × 5 cards, or simply jot down additions as they arise, but keep the list active and file it where you can refer to it now and again. Some people treat the list like a parole sheet and note the number of offenses connected with it. The best system is the one *you* find easiest to follow consistently.

We mentioned an invaluable tool. Find a respectable dictionary and use it. Most dictionaries are well made, so don't be afraid of wearing yours out. Look words up in it whenever you are uncertain of their spellings or meanings, and when looking up a word take note of some of the incidental information given. A good desk dictionary gives not only the spelling of a word, its pronunciation and all its standard modern meanings and uses, but its syllabification, its derivation, and its archaic and colloquial (informal) meanings. For some words the dictionary lists synonyms (words that mean almost the same thing) and antonyms (words with an opposite meaning) as well as giving alternative spellings when they are common enough to present a chance of confusion. The greater the detail with which a word is first investigated, the more likely the word and its spelling are to be remembered. Whatever you do, avoid the easy rationalization: "But how can I find the word in my dictionary if I don't know how to spell it?" You can come close enough.

For more on the use of the dictionary, see Section I, Chapter 2.

Finally, there are those spelling rules that seem general to apply. They are introduced after the list of commonly misspelled words.

19a. The following list of words often misspelled by college students is to be used as the instructor thinks necessary.[1]

1. abbreviate	15. acquitted	28. analyze
2. absence	16. across	29. annual
3. absorption	17. additionally	30. answer
4. absurd	18. address	31. apartment
5. accidentally	19. aggravate	32. apology
6. accommodate*	20. all right	33. apparatus
7. accompanying	21. almost	34. apparently*
8. accomplish	22. although	35. appearance
9. accumulate	23. altogether	36. appropriate
10. accustom	24. always	37. arctic
11. achievement*	25. amateur	38. argument*
12. acknowledge		39. arising
13. acquaintance	26. among*	40. arrangement
14. acquire*	27. analysis	41. ascend

[1] Please pay particular attention to the words marked *. Former Vice President Thomas Clark Pollock of New York University has made a study of over 30,000 misspellings in the writing of college students. The words starred here are the words, or belong to the word-groups, that he found misspelled most often. The authors are grateful to Dr. Pollock for permission to use his findings.

19

42. association
43. athlete
44. athletics
45. attendance
46. audience
47. auxiliary
48. awkward
49. bachelor
50. balance

51. barbarous
52. becoming
53. beginning*
54. benefited*
55. biscuit
56. boundaries
57. brilliant
58. bureau
59. business*
60. cafeteria
61. calendar
62. candidate
63. carburetor
64. career
65. category*
66. certain
67. changeable
68. changing
69. characteristic
70. chosen*
71. commission
72. committed
73. committee
74. comparative*
75. competitive

76. compulsory
77. conceivable
78. conference
79. conferred
80. conqueror
81. conscience*

82. conscientious*
83. conscious*
84. continuous
85. convenient
86. courteous
87. criticism*
88. criticize*
89. curiosity
90. cylinder
91. dealt
92. decision
93. definitely*
94. describe*
95. description*
96. despair
97. desperate
98. dictionary
99. dilapidated
100. disagree

101. disappear
102. disappoint
103. disastrous*
104. discipline
105. dissatisfied
106. dissipate
107. doctor
108. dormitory
109. eighth
110. eligible
111. eliminate
112. embarrass
113. eminent
114. enthusiastic
115. environment*
116. equipment
117. equivalent
118. erroneous
119. especially
120. exaggerated
121. exceptionally
122. exhaust

123. exhilarate
124. existence*
125. experience*

126. explanation*
127. extraordinary
128. extremely
129. familiar
130. fascinate*
131. February
132. foreign
133. frantically
134. fraternities
135. generally
136. government
137. grammar*
138. guard
139. guidance
140. height*
141. hindrance
142. humorous
143. illiterate
144. imaginary*
145. imagination*
146. immediately*
147. impromptu
148. incidentally
149. incredible
150. indefinitely

151. indispensable
152. inevitable
153. infinite
154. intellectual
155. intelligence*
156. intentionally
157. interesting*
158. irrelevant
159. irresistible
160. knowledge
161. laboratory
162. legitimate

436

163. lightning
164. literature
165. loneliness*
166. maintenance
167. maneuver
168. marriage
169. mathematics
170. miniature
171. mischievous
172. necessary*
173. nevertheless
174. noticeable*
175. nowadays

176. oblige
177. obstacle
178. occasion
179. occasionally*
180. occurred*
181. occurrence*
182. opportunity
183. optimistic
184. original*
185. outrageous
186. pamphlet
187. parallel
188. particularly
189. pastime
190. permissible
191. perseverance
192. perspiration

193. physically
194. picnicking
195. politics
196. practically
197. precedence
198. preference
199. preferred
200. prejudice*

201. preparation
202. prevalent*
203. privilege*
204. probably*
205. professor*
206. prominent*
207. pronunciation
208. prove
209. quantity
210. recognize
211. recommend
212. reference
213. referred*
214. regard
215. repetition*
216. representative
217. restaurant
218. rhythm*
219. rhythmical
220. ridiculous
221. sandwich

222. schedule
223. secretary
224. separate*
225. siege

226. similar*
227. simultaneous
228. soliloquy
229. sophomore
230. specifically
231. specimen
232. speech
233. strictly
234. surprise*
235. temperament
236. temperature
237. thorough*
238. throughout
239. tragedy
240. tries*
241. truly
242. Tuesday
243. unanimous
244. undoubtedly
245. unnecessarily
246. village
247. villain
248. weird
249. whether*
250. writing*

19

19b. The following spelling rules will help you to remember how certain words are spelled.

1. A word ending in silent -e *generally drops the* -e *before a suffix beginning with a vowel letter . . .*

DROP -e

admire + able = admirable
admire + ation = admiration
amuse + ing = amusing

desire + ous = desirous
dine + ing = dining
explore + ation = exploration

437

arrange + ing	= arranging		fame	+ ous	= famous
arrive + ing	= arriving		imagine	+ able	= imaginable
believe + ing	= believing		imagine	+ ary	= imaginary
care + ing	= caring		love	+ able	= lovable
come + ing	= coming		lose	+ ing	= losing
deplore + able	= deplorable		move	+ able	= movable

but it retains the -e *before a suffix beginning with a consonant letter.* [There are some notable exceptions: judgment, abridgment, acknowledgment.]

RETAIN -*e*

arrange	+ ment	= arrangement
care	+ ful	= careful
force	+ ful	= forceful
hate	+ ful	= hateful
like	+ ness	= likeness
move	+ ment	= movement

But after c *or* g, *of the suffix begins with* a *or* o, *the* -e *is retained to indicate the soft sound of* c *or* g.

RETAIN -*e*

advantage	+ ous	= advantageous
change	+ able	= changeable
courage	+ ous	= courageous
notice	+ able	= noticeable
outrage	+ ous	= outrageous
peace	+ able	= peaceable
service	+ able	= serviceable

2. *In words with* ie *or* ei *when the sound is long ee, use* i *before* e *except after* c.

i BEFORE *e*

achieve	chief	pier	shriek
apiece	field	pierce	siege
belief	fierce	priest	thief
believe	frieze	relieve	wield
besiege	grief	reprieve	yield
brief	niece	retrieve	
cashier	piece	shield	

EXCEPT AFTER *c*

ceiling	conceive	deceive	receipt
conceit	deceit	perceive	receive

Exceptions: either, neither, financier, weird, species, seize, leisure.

These may be remembered by arranging the words in a sentence: "Neither financier seized either species of weird leisure."

The so-called seed words can be easily remembered. For those who cannot memorize, a careful reading of the list will suffice:

1. Only one word ends in *-sede:* supersede

2. Three words end in *-ceed:* exceed
   proceed
   succeed

3. The rest end in *-cede:* accede
   cede
   concede
   intercede
   precede
   recede
   secede

3. Words consisting of one syllable or several syllables accented on the last and which end in a single consonant letter preceded by a single vowel double the final consonant before a suffix beginning with a vowel.

Now this looks like a formidable rule to unravel. Let us see what it involves. In the first place, it applies to short words such as *get, swim, drop, drip.* In the second place, it applies to longer words in which the accent is on the final syllable, such as *refer, begin, equip.* Examine the illustrations below to see what happens:

drop [word of one syllable] + ed [suffix beginning with a vowel] = dropped.
control [accented on the last syllable] + ed [suffix] = controlled.
benefit [not accented on last syllable] + ed [suffix] = benefited.
confer [accented on last syllable] + ed [suffix] = conferred.

439

19

confer [notice the shift in accent] + ence [suffix] = conference.
defer [accented on last syllable] + ed [suffix] = deferred.
defer [notice the shift in accent] + ence [suffix] = deference.

SUFFIX BEGINS WITH A VOWEL
One Syllable

brag	—bragging	man	—mannish
cram	—cramming	plan	—planning
drag	—dragging	snap	—snapped
dun	—dunning	sin	—sinning
drop	—dropped	stop	—stopped
cut	—cutting	quit	—quitting
bid	—bidding	rob	—robbed
flag	—flagged	stab	—stabbed
get	—getting	whip	—whipped
clan	—clannish	sad	—saddest

Accented on Last Syllable

admit'	—admitted	equip'	—equipped
begin'	—beginning	commit'	—committee
commit'	—committed	occur'	—occurrence
concur'	—concurring	submit'	—submitted
confer'	—conferring	compel'	—compelled

Not Accented on Last Syllable

prefer	—preference	benefit	—benefited
refer	—reference	profit	—profitable
happen	—happened	marvel	—marvelous

SUFFIX BEGINS WITH A CONSONANT

sad	—sadness	sin	—sinful
fat	—fatness	equip	—equipment
woman	—womanhood	profit	—profitless

4. *A noun ending in -y preceded by a consonant forms the plural in -ies; a verb ending in -y preceded by a consonant forms its present tense, third person singular, in -ies.*

ENDING IN -y PRECEDED BY A CONSONANT

baby, babies	sky, skies	pygmy, pygmies
marry, marries	copy, copies	fly, flies

440

ENDING IN -*y* PRECEDED BY A VOWEL

attorney, attorneys	valley, valleys	delay, delays
destroy, destroys	enjoy, enjoys	chimney, chimneys

Note: Some other rules for forming plurals are as follows:

5. For most nouns, add -s: boys, girls, houses, ideas, aches, pains.

6. For nouns ending with a sound similar to s, *add* -es: birches, foxes, boxes, classes.

7. For nouns ending in -f, -fe, -ff, *use* -s *or* -ves: chief, chiefs; staff, staffs, staves; wife, wives; sheriff, sheriffs; elf, elves; dwarf, dwarfs.

8. For nouns ending in -o, *add* -s *or* -es: solo, solos; echo, echoes; potato, potatoes; motto, mottos, mottoes; tomato, tomatoes; alto, altos; hero, heroes.

9. Some nouns have irregular plurals: foot, feet; mouse, mice; goose, geese; ox, oxen; woman, women; axis, axes; basis, bases; datum, data; locus, loci; formula, formulas, formulae.

But Mr. and Mrs. Berry are *not* "the Berries," but "the Berrys"; and Mr. and Mrs. Wolf are *not* "the Wolves," but "the Wolfs." Mr. and Mrs. Jones are still "the Joneses."

EXERCISES

Rewrite the following paragraphs, correcting the misspelled words.

EXERCISE 1.

It has often occured to me that any foreign envirement begins to look familiar after sufficient experiance. In the beginning one may believe that a foriegn land is wierd or even barberous. But it is noticable that in the end one usually consedes the virtues of strangeness. What is outragous is to persist in repititions of embarassing criticisms that are definitly eroneous.

EXERCISE 2.

One chilly Febuary day, three sophmores were sitting in their dormitery discussing one of the campuses most prominant prof-

20

fessors. They sprawled on separate bunks in their room, occassionally engaging in arguement about the professor's appearance and achievments.

"I went to see his secretery last Tuesday," one student remarked. "I think she's more intelactual than he is."

"I disagree," said another. "But why is he so predjudiced against fraternities?"

"Anyway," said the third, "I've always prefered a conference with the secretary. It's a priviledge to talk to her."

EXERCISE 3.

The most interesting knowlege is likely to seem irrevalent on its first occurence. Many have benefitted from explanations that at first seemed throughly and unnecessarily ridiculous. I recomend that you sieze consiously every ocasion for learning, even if your committment to grammer may be comparitively unenthusiastic.

EXERCISE 4.

The weather exceded our expectations. After arriveing we got out the bats, balls, and gloves, and began a carful search for our playing feild. The brief search ended when we stoped near an open acre of flatland under clear skys. No one remembers just when the mosquitos struck, but the Terries and the Jones' were the first to run for cover. The biting ended only after every picnicer was completely immersed in water. That was truely an unforgettable Sunday.

§ 20. SIMILAR FORMS

Distinguish between words similar or identical in sound but different in meaning.

The list below is merely a checklist for quick reference. If you need more than this list can give you, refer to your dictionary. You should also look at examples of similar forms in the "Guide to Usage."

accent. Emphasis or stress; to stress. [You accent the wrong syllable.]

442

ascent. Climbing; a way up. [The ascent of the cliff was difficult.]

assent. To agree; agreement. [He finally gave his assent to the plan.]

accept. To take something offered; to agree to; to approve; to believe. [He accepted the gift. I accept your interpretation.]

except. To leave out; to exclude [All except the cook were rescued.]

admittance. Permission to enter a place. [The sign read, "No admittance."]

admission. Admitting to rights and privileges; the price of being allowed to enter. [No admission was charged.]

advice. Counsel given to encourage or dissuade. [He offers advice without charge or invitation.]

advise. To give advice to; to suggest. [I would advise you not to jump.]

affect. To influence; to pretend; to assume. [His threats do not affect me.]

effect. To perform; make happen. [The attorney effected a reconciliation.] *Effect,* not *affect,* is used as a noun. [What *effect* did your words have on him?]

all ready. Everyone is ready. [They were all ready.]

already. By this time. [They had already eaten breakfast.]

allusive. Making a casual but significant reference to. [The poem was highly allusive and hard to follow.]

elusive. Difficult to grasp; tending to slip away. [The idea seems at first elusive. The panther is an elusive prey.]

illusive. Deceptive; unreal or illusory. [His visions of a similar solar system proved illusive.]

altar. Place of worship. [They knelt before the altar.]

alter. To change. [Do not alter any part of my criticism.]

ante. Before. [This song is of ante-Beatle vintage.]

anti. Against; opposed to.[I poured some antifreeze into the radiator.]

breath. Air drawn into lungs. [We need a breath of fresh air.]

breathe. To take a breath. [We cannot breathe in this room.]

capital. Chief; important; leading city; resources. [London is the capital city of England. Invest your capital.]

capitol. The state building. [We will meet on the capitol grounds in Albany.]

censure. Blame; condemn; criticize severely. [They voted to censure the general.]

20

censor. To oversee morals and conduct; to examine and make changes. [Three women will censor all motion pictures.]

charted. Mapped or diagramed. [The Arctic is still not fully charted.]

chartered. Hired; granted certain rights. [We chartered a boat.]

choose. To pick out, select. [Will she choose me again?]

chose. Past tense of *choose*. [They chose a new secretary.]

cite. To quote or use as example. [Did he cite any authorities?]

site. Location. [This is a good site for our church.]

sight. Vision; to see. [His sight was keen. At last we sighted land.]

coarse. Rough; crude. [coarse food; coarse manners; coarse sand]

course. Direction; path; series; order. [a course of study; of course]

complement. That which completes. [a subjective complement]

compliment. Praise; a polite and flattering lie. [He paid her a compliment.]

consul. Government official appointed to look after foreign business interests.

council. A group; an assembly. [We will call a council of the elders.]

counsel. Advice; one who advises; a lawyer. [Give her good counsel. The accused has a right to counsel.]

decent. Proper, respectable; modest; adequate or satisfactory. [His suit was decent for a change. The performance was decent.]

descent. Any downward motion; decline or deterioration; lineage. [rapid and steep descent; descent of morals; of aristocratic descent.]

dissent. To differ in opinion; to withhold approval. [He held it essential to dissent from the popular view.]

detract. Take away. [Her hair detracts from her beauty.]

distract. Draw away; disturb. [The noise distracts me. Do not distract my attention.]

elicit. To draw out, evoke. [She tried to elicit a response to her proposal.]

illicit. Not permitted, unauthorized. [There are laws against illicit gambling in this state.]

eminent. Distinguished. [The eminent statesman spoke briefly.]

imminent. About to happen. [War seems imminent.]

immanent. Existing within. [God's will is immanent.]

444

formally. In formal manner. [He was formally welcomed by the mayor.]

formerly. In the past. [Formerly, no one had greeted him.]

hoards. Stores; collections. [The police found hoards of stolen stereos.]

hordes. Crowds; groups of nomads. [the barbarian hordes; hordes of tourists]

imaginary. Existing in the imagination. [Her life is full of imaginary troubles.]

imaginative. Having imagination; able to imagine. [She is a very imaginative woman.]

implicit. Absolute, implied. [implicit obedience to orders; implicit approval.]

explicit. Distinctly stated; definite. [He gave us explicit directions.]

incredible. Unbelievable. [Your story is incredible.]

incredulous. Unwilling to believe. [He was incredulous when I told my story.]

irrelevant. Not to the point. [His question is irrelevant.]

irreverent. Lacking reverence or respect. [His action was irreverent.]

loose. Not fastened; careless; not confined. [Tie up your loose shoe strings. There is too much loose talk here. Your dog is loose again.]

lose. To mislay; to fail to win; to waste. [She lost her keys again. We may lose this game yet. Put your loose cash away or you will lose it.]

principal. Chief; most important; chief person; chief teacher. [the principal of a school; the principal actor; the principal occupation; paying something on the principal as well as the interest]

principle. A truth; a belief; a scientific rule. [He is a man of high principles.]

prophecy. A prediction made under divine influence (noun).

prophesy. To predict the future under divine influence (verb).

regretful. Feeling full of regret. [He was very regretful about his bad behavior.]

regrettable. Expressing disappointment. [His behavior was regrettable.]

rend. To tear apart; to disturb. [The silence was rent by a frightening roar.]

20

445

20

render. Make; give; represent; play or sing. [You will render a service. The judge rendered his decision.]

respectfully. With respect. [Speak to your teacher respectfully.]

respectively. Each in turn or in order. [His three sons, Igor, Dmitri, and Ivan, were 18, 21, and 25 respectively.]

stationary. Not movable; not changing. [a stationary engine; a stationary enrollment; a stationary income]

stationery. Writing materials. [Please let me have some stationery; I wish to write a few letters.]

straight. Not curved; upright; continuous; direct. [The road is straight. Come straight to the point.]

strait. Narrow; strict; restricting. [a strait jacket; a strait passage; the Straits of Magellan; the Straits of Gibraltar]

undoubtedly. Beyond a doubt. [She was undoubtedly correct.]

undoubtably. No such word.

13 | *Words and*

Phrases

§ 21. DICTION

Use words that convey your meaning exactly and idiomatically.

In the "Words and Phrases" chapter of this book (pages 37–65) we spoke of the *denotation,* or the literal meaning of a word, and of the *connotation,* or associated meaning of a word. If a word in your essay has been marked "D" or "Diction," you should first consult a dictionary to see that its denotation is clear. The solution to a problem of denotation may simply be to choose a different, more accurate word. But if the word is guilty of vague or inappropriate connotation, the only answer is to define its meaning or give examples.

21a. Key words that may be understood in more than one sense should be carefully defined.

Most of the words that you use in writing and speaking will do well enough without being defined. The least tricky words are the names of specific persons or objects, such as *General Grant, laboratory,* the *White House,* a *Polaroid camera,* although each may arouse emotional reactions that color its meaning. More tricky are the words that refer to things or qualities that have been a part of the daily life of many

21

generations, such as *dog, cat, war, generous, honest, selfish,* and so on. Usually the meaning of the word is defined well enough by the *context* (i.e., the sense of the words around it) in which it is used. Nothing of vast importance is lost through a lack of exact communication. But something of vast importance *is* at stake when people use such words as *radicals, reactionaries, liberals, realistic, democratic people, peace-loving, aggression, freedom of speech.* Terms such as these must be defined or qualified.

EXAMPLES

Radicals are taking over local government. [Who are these "radicals"? What is their political persuasion?]

People like John Wayne movies no matter what the subject. [Which "people?" Are they the same people who demand "all power to the people?"]

He is into *aggression* as a means of solving his problems. [Does he simply punch those he doesn't agree with in the nose?]

21b. Words used in an inexact sense should be checked and restudied with the help of a dictionary.

Most of us learn new words as we need them, without much help from vocabulary improvement schemes. All of us depend heavily and very often on the context, on approximations, for meanings. Here and there we miss the point—sometimes by a narrow margin, sometimes by a mile. Here and there someone catches us up. It would be naive to assert that a dictionary can solve all your problems of controlling the meanings of words. But here are a few examples to show how a dictionary can serve you:

The doctor decided to try an *explanatory* operation first. [That sounds reasonable, but is that what he actually decided to try?]

The music served to *diverge* my thoughts to more pleasant things. [Here the writer was trying for a word that sounded like this one, and, in a vague way, meant something like it.]

She was listening *intensely* to the lecture. [The right word here is *intently*.]

448

21c. Vague, blanket words should be replaced with more precise words.

This statement refers primarily to such words as *deal, factor, stance, thrust, line, point of view, angle, proposition, impact, interface.* It refers also to any word that you have used, not because it expresses your idea precisely and cleanly, but because you were in a hurry and it was easier to use a vague word than to think of a more exact one.

INEXACT AND WORDY

Did you *get his deal* about wanting to go into something *along the line* of engineering?

BETTER

Can you understand that he wants to study a branch of engineering?

INEXACT

An exciting *factor* of our summer vacation was a trip to Japan.

BETTER

An exciting event of our summer vacation was a trip to Japan.

INEXACT

I never could decide what his *angle* was from the *point of view* of making high grades.

BETTER

I never could decide what his thoughts (ideas) were about making high grades.

INEXACT

The sphere impacted on the interface between the audience and the green, flat surface.

BETTER

The ball bounced off the wall in left field.

Remember that although you may get away with using

21

blanket words in speaking they are all too noticeable in writing.

21d. A writer should guard against the right word taking an unintended meaning in the context.

A serious writer, that is, should guard against unintentional humor. Bloopers (or malapropisms), either the natural or the synthetic variety, are of course the stock-in-trade of the gag writer or the television comedian. Here are some examples of unintentional slips:

BLOOPER

The writer made the poem more effective by the use of metaphors and illusions.

CORRECTION

The writer made the poem more effective by the use of metaphors and allusions.

BLOOPER

Finally, at midnight, I sat down to learn my history.

CORRECTION

Finally, at midnight, I sat down to study my history assignment.

BLOOPER

Every time he opens his mouth, some fool speaks.

CORRECTION

Every time he starts to speak, some fool interrupts him.

BLOOPER

The book is obscene and difficult to reprehend.

CORRECTION

The book is obscure and difficult to comprehend.

450

EXERCISES

EXERCISE 1, ASSOCIATED MEANINGS. *In the following groups of words, which words suggest an unfavorable attitude and which a favorable attitude?*

1. Teacher, tutor, professor, counselor.
2. Policeman, cop, pig, traffic officer.
3. Dainty, fragile, delicate, weak, flaccid, spineless.
4. Woman, female, chick, broad, girl.
5. Mixture, mess, jumble, patchwork, blend, alloy.

EXERCISE 2, EXACTNESS. *Point out every instance of inexact use of words in the following sentences and suggest a revision.*

1. The long arm of television permeates all of the civilized world.
2. In this poem the author tells about England's downfall from a leading country.
3. Judge Brand ordered the man to disabuse his wife and children.
4. The effect of the poem depends on what the reader divulges from it.
5. In order to solve their curiosity they must read the story to the end.
6. He quickly built a shelter to shed the rain off his precious equipment.
7. He describes in a realistic way about the things he has experienced in the slums.
8. My problems are more of an uncertainty, like being able to place a comma in this place or a semicolon in that place.
9. My hobby includes time, work, and expense.
10. As I am a seldom reader of poetry, I did not enjoy this book.
11. The story centered around life in the White House.
12. He confused Joan for Ellen when he saw her on the street.
13. Harley told us to precede with filling the hot tub.

14. Even George, who's I.Q. is embarrassingly low, could understand the morale of the film.
15. That behavior doesn't conform to passed practice.
16. They played too loosely and ended up loosing the game.
17. With his dyeing words he complained about the color they died his shirt.
18. It was the right devise but it blew up too soon.
19. Her reason for missing the plane was because the cab took her too the train depot.
20. It was an accident irregardless of what you say.

§ 22. APPROPRIATENESS

Use words that are in keeping with the subject of your paper, with the occasion, and with the readers you are addressing.

Many of the papers that you write for your college courses are informal; some are formal. You should always remember that the terms *informal* and *formal* are relative—not absolute. Each covers a wide range. Obviously, you will probably never try to write with the formality of Pope John Paul, or John Kennedy, or Winston Churchill addressing Parliament; you may, however, approach the style of a present-day historian or critic or essayist. Examples of each are to be found in Chapter 1, Section I, of this book.

When you write a serious discussion of a serious subject, you should use language that is dignified but not pretentious or affected. If your occasion is informal, you write in an informal, easy manner—remembering always that as there are degrees of formality so are there degrees of informality. The informality that runs to slang or vague terms has little place in your college work. We have mentioned before the analogy of varieties of writing with manners or dress. Intelligent people have different styles of

452

writing at their command just as they have clothes appropriate for different occasions. A man does not attend a formal dinner in sweater and slacks, or a football game in a tuxedo, unless he is determined to make a spectacular and probably unfavorable impression. There *are* rules and conventions in the use of language, just as there are conventions governing social behavior everywhere else—at a dinner table, at a football game, on a street corner, anywhere. Good sense is the best rule of conduct.

Here are a few examples of failure in appropriateness (in the first two examples, the italicized words do not appear in the originals):

INAPPROPRIATE IN FORMAL WRITING

When Roosevelt took office on March 4, 1933, thousands of American banks *were going broke.* [The original has the more appropriate *verged on insolvency.*]

—WILLIAM MILLER, *A New History of the United States*

There is no doubt that a *whole batch* of new mathematical techniques will have to be *cooked up* before it will be possible to solve satisfactorily *a lot of* scientific problems that today can only be tackled empirically or experimentally. [The original has the more appropriate variety . . . invented . . . innumerable.]

—MARIO G. SALVADORI, "Mathematics, the Language of Science"

The State Department's difficulty was that it had failed to find any device for ensuring that the press would *stay zipped* on the new international agreement. [Say *remain silent.*]

INAPPROPRIATE IN INFORMAL WRITING

I certainly hope you are having a good time at college this year *and realizing your potential for intellectual growth and development.* [Say *and getting a lot out of it.*]

He told me what to do and *I accomplished the operation.* [Say *I did it.*]

She was *informed* that *one did not have to prevaricate* in order to *advance one's cause.* [Say "she was told that she didn't have to lie to get ahead."]

453

22a. In serious writing, inappropriate slang should be avoided.

Slang has often been defined as a kind of made-to-order language, characterized by extravagant or grotesque humor. This is by no means a complete or all-inclusive definition of slang, nor is an all-inclusive definition important in this book. Not even the editors of dictionaries agree on what is slang and what is not. *Webster's Third New International Dictionary* lists the following, among others, as examples of slang: rod [revolver, pistol], rap [to arrest, hold; to converse informally], bread [money], savvy [understanding, to understand], baloney [pretentious nonsense], threads [clothes]. In other dictionaries you may find other words listed as slang, words that the unabridged lists without any usage labels.

Slang is usually inappropriate in serious or formal writing, but some writers use it with telling effects. Writers who strain to avoid slang may still err by using stilted, general, vague, and pompously bookish words under the impression that a simple and direct style is not good enough for important ideas.

In the following example the writer uses an informal expression for a specific effect—irony:

Despite the reverence the Greeks accorded their goddesses, they kept their wives and daughters *pretty well* locked up.
                    —AUDREY C. FOOTE, "Notes
                    on the Distaff Side"

22b. A mixture of the colloquial and the formal styles is usually inappropriate in serious writing.

Most dictionaries—with the notable exception of *Webster's Third New International*—use *colloq.* as a usage label for certain words and phrases. The *New International* uses status labels, such as *slang, substandard, nonstandard,* but not colloquial. *Colloquial* means informal, or characteristic of a conversational style, as opposed to a formal, literary style. In the past, many people believed that *colloq.* implied a condemnation of a word or phrase, in spite of the fact that editors of dictionaries were careful to define the word correctly in the vocabularies and in the explanatory notes. Scholars, lexicographers, and linguists have pointed out that every educated person uses colloquial English, and, what is important to remember, he or she uses it correctly in appropriate situations.

22

EXERCISES

EXERCISE 1, APPROPRIATENESS. *Some of the following italicized expressions are appropriate in serious writing; some are not. With the help of your dictionary, decide which are more appropriate in colloquial than in formal situations.*

1. We are determined to *face up to* this monstrous foe with all our hearts.
2. Finally, after many years of service, the old crate *gave out.*
3. The trusted servant, we discovered, had *made off* with our two cameras.
4. He was to board a plane at ten, but none of his friends was there to *see him off.*
5. The man was instructed to *sing out* if he saw any prowlers.
6. Within a year the young man *had run through* his inheritance.
7. At the end of the year he felt that it was not easy to *take off and leave* his new friends.
8. The principal was trying to find out who had *put him up to it.*
9. His arrogance was something no one was willing to *put up with.*
10. Nobody expected her to *carry on so* when she heard that her daughter had eloped.

23

EXERCISE 2, FORMAL AND INFORMAL EXPRESSIONS.
Give the formal equivalent of each of the italicized expressions.

1. *to back down*
2. He's *into* Zen these days
3. *to go him one better*
4. *How come?*
5. He *got busted* during the raid.
6. You'll *get your cut!*
7. He *fed* his new date *a line.*
8. That music really *moves* me.
9. Give him his *walking papers.*
10. *Stick around* for a while.

§ 23. IDIOMS

23a. Use idiomatic English.

An idiom is an expression peculiar to a given language. It cannot usually be translated word-for-word into another tongue, though its sense can often be rendered by an equivalent idiom native and natural to that tongue. Created out of the day-to-day living of ordinary people, idioms are often irrational, racy, and lively with images. Many of them have originated in someone's clever and original metaphor, which then became "dead" as it was repeated by other people. "You said a mouthful." "He was beside himself with worry." "Who slipped up?" "Water off a duck's back." "I'm getting my act together." As these examples suggest, idioms are often colloquial or slang, though not necessarily so.

Americans have been particularly fertile in producing an idiomatic language, and many volumes have been written on the subject of American word-making. For a useful collection and a guide to recent opinions about usage, see Roy H. Copperud's *American Usage: The Consensus* (New York: Van Nostrand Reinhold, 1970). Students interested in pursuing the history of a particular idiom should consult this work or the *New English Dictionary.* See the further

456

listing under "Dictionaries and Books of Synonyms" in Section I, Chapter 2.

Even more than other elements in the language, idioms change status constantly as they come into or go out of fashion, or as they become respectable in formal English or fall into disrepute. In fact such change has become so rapid and complex in our time that the editors of the latest unabridged *Webster's* have dropped most of their notations of *slang* and *colloq.* Even your desk dictionary, however, can be very useful in listing the various idioms formed from ordinary single words. Many idiomatic phrases have grown up around the verbs of everyday living—*go, do, catch, get, make, take,* and so on.

The student's difficulties in handling idioms are likely to be of two kinds. First, trouble occurs in sensing the status of a particular idiom from a particular purpose. He or she might, for instance, go so far as to write, in a formal essay, and with no humorous intention, "This flipped me!" In this case, of course, the writer has failed to recognize the highly colloquial and ephemeral quality of that expression. Or the student might say, in a serious descriptive essay, "It rained cats and dogs," thus failing to recognize that this particular idiom has long been a very tired cliché. (Clichés are treated more fully in §25.) The best guard against errors of this kind is constant reading, writing, and listening, with an awareness of how different kinds of expressions are acceptable in different situations.

A second source of student difficulty with idioms might be called a failing of the ear—that is, the student may forget just how an idiom is said in English, and that there is seldom much justification for the phrasing of idioms. The problem is most severe in the case of prepositions, as the subsection immediately following will show.

23b. Observe the idiomatic use of prepositions after certain verbs, participles, adjectives, and nouns.

The following list will not take the place of an unabridged dictionary. It will serve merely as a check list

23

to put you on your guard. Consult the dictionary for more complete information.

abstain from	distaste for
accede to	empty of
acquiesce in	envious of
acquit of	expert in
addicted to	foreign to
adept in	guard against
adhere to	hint at
agree to (a thing)	identical with
agree with (a person)	independent of
agreeable to	infer from
angry at (a thing)	initiate into
angry with (a person)	inseparable from
averse to	jealous of
capable of	obedient to
characteristic of	oblivious of
compare to (for illustration)	preparatory to
compare with (to examine qualities)	prerequisite to
	prior to
concern in (interest in)	proficient in
concerned for (troubled)	profit by
concerned with (involved)	prohibit from
concur in (an opinion)	protest against
concur with (a person)	reason with
desire for	regret for
desist from	repugnant to
devoid of	sensitive to
differ about	separate from
differ from (things)	substitute for
differ with (a person)	superior to
different from	sympathize with
disagree with	tamper with
disdain for	unmindful of
dissent from	vie with

It is characteristic of English that an idiom may have several meanings, and that it may shift into a new part of speech.

23. IDIOMS

The professor *makes up* a roster of students, and the *makeup* of the class displeases him. A lady *makes up* her face, which is to say she applies *makeup*. I *make up* a funny story, which then appears *made-up*. Idioms such as these, composed originally of a verb and an adverb, quickly become nouns in our language, as the following short list will suggest:

blowup	run-in
carryover	runaround
cookout	runaway
countdown	turnover
drive-in	upkeep

This process of word formation is one of several such shifts taking place as you read this book. Many nouns so formed are obviously of recent origin: *cookout, countdown, drive-in.* The student should not hesitate to make use of such new terms, in spite of their predominantly informal quality. In the list above, for example, almost every term is at least conceivably appropriate in almost any context.

On the other hand, the temptation to transform certain nouns into verbs should be resisted, especially when the nouns are not concrete. "He wanted to know whether or not to *prioritize* the items" is a sentence that sounds unnecessarily pretentious. *Impact, interface, input, author, craft* are examples of words that work best as nouns.

EXERCISES

EXERCISE 1, IDIOMS. *In your dictionary find the idioms listed under several of the following words. You will find idiomatic phrases printed in boldface type, usually after the synonyms. Bring to class a number of these for discussion. Try to decide why some are marked* colloq. *and some are without a label.*

eat	go	head	mouth	stand
foot	hand	heart	pick	take
get	have	horse	run	word

24

EXERCISE 2, MISUSE OF IDIOMS. *Rewrite the following paragraph, correcting the misuses of idiom.*

He was superior than all of us, or so he thought, but his bragging was no substitute of ability. He felt himself independent from the rest of us, though he was usually agreeable with going along with the majority. I was often angry at him, since he differed from me so often. When he left he showed no concern with the way others felt. He was entirely oblivious to public opinion. We were all very surprised and jealous of him when he was elected President.

EXERCISE 3, IDIOMATIC PREPOSITIONS. *Supply the idiomatic prepositions as required in the following sentences.*

1. Since I was so concerned (   ) my business at that time, she was concerned (   ) my health.
2. At that period we differed (   ) almost everything.
3. She especially differed (   ) me about money matters.
4. Finally we separated (   ) one another.
5. Neither of us, however, proved to be capable (   ) living alone.

§ 24. CONCISENESS

Avoid using more words than are necessary for the adequate expression of your thought.

The stylistic fault of *wordiness* has been the concern of writers and speakers for many centuries. Wordiness has been called by many names—verbosity, prolixity, diffuseness, circumlocution, periphrasis. By any name, wordiness simply means the use of more words than you need in a particular situation. To achieve conciseness, you must ask whether every word you write is doing its work, carrying its proper load of meaning, and helping its fellow workers with their loads.

Do not mistake brevity for conciseness. A sentence is not concise if it lacks the words necessary to adequate expression. Cutting out words in a good essay might also cut out of it those qualities that make it good—strength, variety, maturity, grace, wit, even accuracy.

Study the following sets of sentences. Do you see what is meant by conciseness?

24

1. Whenever anyone called for someone to help him do some certain thing, Jim was always the first to volunteer and lend his help for the cause.
2. Whenever anyone called for help, Jim was always the first to volunteer.
1. This spirit of cooperation is essential and necessary for anyone to have in order to get along with other people, and this is a quality that Jim had.
2. Jim had the spirit of cooperation which is necessary if one wishes to get along with people.
1. Jim was one of those people of whom there are few in this world like him.
2. There are few people like Jim.
1. Lumbering is placed in the upper ten industries in the United States from the standpoint of importance.
2. Lumbering is one of the ten most important industries in the United States.
1. To consider self-perpetuation or to consider its alternative, these are the fundamental parameters of the interface.
2. "To be or not to be, that is the question."
—WILLIAM SHAKESPEARE, *Hamlet*

This section will concern itself with several kinds of wordiness to be avoided by the writer who hopes to be concise, direct, and to the point.

24a. Avoid careless repetition of the same word.

Careless repetition of a word weakens the effectiveness of a sentence and is often a symptom of wordiness. The fault may be corrected by using synonyms, by using pronouns, or by completely rewriting the sentence.

461

24

POOR

I have been asked to write on a controversial subject that has been the subject of controversy among historians for years. That subject, as you have probably guessed, is none other than how to account for the rise of Hitler's Germany. The rise of Hitler's Germany has fascinated me for a longer time than I can remember.

BETTER

I will try to account for the rise of Hitler's Germany, a controversial subject that has fascinated me for some time.

POOR

He felt that the remark about his reputation would do great damage to his reputation.

BETTER

He felt that the remark would do great damage to his reputation.

The importance of avoiding awkward repetition must not distract the writer from the possibilities of *repetition for emphasis*—a valuable device for securing certain kinds of attention from the reader.

In the following excerpt E. B. White repeats the word *owners* (and its variants *own* and *ownership*) to emphasize the inherent value of an independent free press. Note that White does not try for stilted variety by substituting synonyms like *possess* or *proprietorship* for the key word.

The press in our free country is reliable and useful not because of its good character but because of its great diversity. As long as there are many *owners,* each pursuing his *own* brand of truth, we the people have the opportunity to arrive at the truth and to dwell in the light. The multiplicity of *ownership* is crucial. It's only when there are few *owners,* or, as in a government-controlled press, one *owner,* that the truth becomes elusive and the light fails.

—E. B. WHITE, *Letters of E. B. White*

The speech-making style in this selection suggests that repetition is a characteristic device of oratory. (Notice White's ingenious use of the phrase "we the people," echoing the Declaration of Independence.) For serious defenses of concepts like free speech or freedom of religion, such a style is obviously indispensable.

Repetition can also prove effective in establishing an ironic tone, as illustrated in this example:

> The columnist described Lawson's performance as "adequate." Indeed, his victories in twenty-seven primaries could be termed "adequate," and there is little doubt that the thirty million dollars he received in contributions will prove "adequate" in future campaigning. One wonders whether when Lawson is elected to the Senate his achievement will be found "adequate" or "surprising" by the press.

Quotation marks are required to achieve the desired effect, which can be especially appealing to your reader. By saving such ammunition for just the right battle, however, you avoid the danger of wasting it in sniperlike exchanges.

24b. Avoid repetition of words with the same meaning (tautology).

WORDY

The analysis was *thoroughly and wholly complete.*

All the requirements of *frank* and *honest candor* made his speech popular.

The *basic fundamental essentials* of a college education are *simply* and *briefly* these.

He woke up at six *a.m. this morning.*

There is no need to change pilots *at this point in time.*

Many clichés, particularly those picked up from legal jargon, are tautologies: *Null and void, cease and desist, swear and affirm.*

24c. Avoid the double *that* before a clause (pleonasm, a grammatical tautology).

I was very glad that when I came into the house that I found everything in order. [Omit the second *that*.]

463

Mailer feels that it is only *The Naked and the Dead* that many critics regard as his sole great work. [Revision: Mailer feels that many critics regard *The Naked and the Dead* as his sole great work.]

24

24d. Avoid roundabout expressions (circumlocution or periphrasis).

WORDY

The reason why I was so upset was because she seemed so angry with me. [reason—why—because] [*Revise:* I was upset because she seemed so angry with me.]

24e. Avoid wordy use of intensives and other modifiers.

It is wise to question critically all modifiers (adjectives and adverbs), because it is often through these words that wordiness gets a foothold. The so-called intensives—*very, much,* and so on—are likely to weaken a sentence.

WORDY

They were absolutely so much astonished to find so very much still to do that they were absolutely speechless. [They were speechless with astonishment to find so much still to be done.]

She was completely and totally pleased by the very fine report that the children gave her. [She was pleased by the children's fine report.]

Officials were really very pleased to find the missile-launcher that they thought had been stolen. [Officials were pleased to find the missile-launcher. . . .]

24f. Avoid repetition of similar sounds.

The awkward repetition of similar sounds in prose may seriously distract your reader from what you are trying to communicate. Consider the following examples:

The *loss* of the *toss* meant that the *Packers* could not be *attackers.* (Revision: Because they were losers of the toss, the Packers began the game on defense.)

464

To *relent* to the *extent* that you lose your *rent* deposit is unwise. (Revision: Giving in at this point may mean the loss of your rent deposit.)

The stock of refrigerated Snickers bars was ve*ry* near*ly* complete*ly* dep*le*ted. (Revision: The stock of refrigerated Snickers bars was almost gone.)

It is *common* for the *nom*inating *comm*ittee to res*pon*d the next day. (Revision: The nominating committee usually reports the next day.)

24

24g. Avoid officialese (also called "gobbledygook").

The language of official life, government and the military, is seldom concise. You will find there many examples of wordiness such as we have been illustrating. Note especially, in such writing, the overuse of passive verbs (see §6c) and a fondness for abstract nouns. A similar kind of stuffiness infects the report writing of committees—writing created, that is, by more than one author. And extracurricular student writing is not always free from the wordiness of hot air. See your own campus newspaper.

For an example of official style—by no means an extreme one—study this passage from the "Regulations and Information" section of the University of Missouri-Kansas City *Bulletin.*

Students enrolling in the University assume an obligation and are expected by the University to conduct themselves in a manner compatible with the University's functions and missions as an educational institution. For that purpose students are required to observe generally accepted standards of conduct. Obstruction of University teaching, research, administration, or other activities, indecent conduct or speech, failure to comply with requests of University officials in the performance of their duties, and violation of the laws of the city, state, or nation are examples of conduct which would contravene this standard.

It would not be too facetious to assert that a rendering of this paragraph in concise English might read:

Students at the University are expected to behave themselves.

465

24h. Avoid "fine writing."

"Fine writing" is not, as the phrase seems to indicate, good writing. It is flowery, artificial, overblown writing. In an effort to be literary, the writer loads his style with too many adjectives and adverbs, with big words, awkward repetitions of high-sounding phrases, foreign language phrases, and trite figures of speech. (See also §25c.) "Fine writing" is often the result of an overcomplicated sentence structure. Its effect is that of a voice that sounds pompous and stuffy, and no sensitive reader will listen to such a voice for very long.

EXAMPLES

Heller's style is marked by a certain dementia praecox that lends sparkle to the demimondes he creates.

Her *Weltanschauung* could be described in no other way than by pointing to the *Weltschmerz* expressed by her heroines.

Below is a parody of the prose style of Henry James, which illustrates many of the faults of "fine writing."

Author Winner sat serenely contemplating his novel. His legs, not ill-formed for his years, yet concealing the faint cyanic marbling of incipient varicosity under grey socks of the finest lisle, were crossed. He was settled in the fine, solidly-built, cannily (yet never parsimoniously, never niggardly) bargained-for chair that had been his father's, a chair that Author Winner himself was only beginning to think that, in the fullness of time, hope he reasonably might that he would be able (be possessed of the breadth and the depth) to fill. Hitching up the trousers that had been made for his father (tailored from a fabric woven to endure, with a hundred and sixty threads to the inch), he felt a twinge of the sciatica that had been his father's and had come down to him through the jeans. Author Winner was grateful for any resemblance; his father had been a man of unusual qualities: loyal, helpful, friendly, courteous, kind, obedient, cheerful, thrifty, brave, clean and reverent; in the simplest of terms: a man of *dharma*.

—FELICIA LAMPORT, "By Henry James Cozened"

24

EXERCISES

EXERCISE 1, AWKWARD REPETITIONS. *In the following sentences, underline the awkward repetitions and examples of wordiness. Then rewrite the sentences, making them more concise by cutting or other revision.*

1. The several features of the situation were complex, and altogether the situation was complicated because of the many elementary elements involved.
2. It was perfectly clear that if she had come along with you as your companion that she would have been welcome.
3. I need hardly say to you all at this time and place that the very great economic loss is a serious source of loss to us all.
4. The chief significant reason why the economy failed was on account of an economic imbalance in the balance of trade.
5. I told him about the courses we were taking, French and history and so on and so forth, so he would get a good idea of the curriculum in which we take courses.
6. He had an arbitrary, set, inflexible rule for everything that he did, and for anything on which he had made up his mind it was very difficult to persuade him otherwise.
7. I really mean it, I certainly was relieved to make that discovery, to my real relief.
8. Unless a person is thoroughly and completely prepared, both mentally and psychologically, the chances of success in marriage are dim, doubtful, and obscure.
9. In regard to this matter of your new insurance policy, please be advised that your new policy is being taken up in a matter of approximately a week or thereabouts.
10. Without any doubt it is very true and unarguable that

25

this great nation of ours is very ready to prepare to defend itself to the very last gas station.

EXERCISE 2, OFFICIALESE. *Here is an example of officialese, not much exaggerated. Rewrite in plain English.*

It is desired by the administration at this particular time that students refrain and desist from the excessive noise and jostling that has characterized their behavior in halls and corridors during recent occasions that I have observed. The magnitude of the noise involved has reached a degree where, in some cases of particularly recalcitrant offenders, the awarding of the degree in June may be jeopardized. All faculty personnel are enjoined to be alert to transmit to this office any flagrant discrepancies of this sort that may come to their attention from time to time.

§ 25. VIVIDNESS AND METAPHOR

25a. Try to use words and phrases that give life and freshness to your style.

There are many ways to make a style vivid. Some of them were discussed in previous sections under the headings of "concreteness" and "conciseness." In this section we consider a few other devices available to the writer who wishes to create fresher, livelier language. First, you should be aware of the possibilities for freshness in the various parts of speech—nouns, modifiers, verbs. Second, you should see the possibilities in figurative language, or metaphor. Then you must beware the dangers of metaphor, particularly since so much figurative language has been used before and has lost its freshness. Finally, you must recognize the related problem of overused language generally: the problem of triteness and clichés.

1. *Specific rather than general nouns will help to produce a vivid style.* (Go back to §24 to find out what is meant by *specific* and *general*.) When you write, "I heard a bird singing," your words may call up a definite sense image in

the mind of your reader—or they may not—but you do not know what that image is. If instead of "bird" you say "canary" or "robin," your reader will at least make an effort to recall or imagine the song of a canary or a robin. Whenever you use a specific noun, you make it easy for your reader's mind to create a specific image. Word images direct the picture-making that goes on in your reader's brain.

2. *Try to use strong, picture-making adjectives and adverbs.* (See also §21.) No part of speech is more likely to turn blue and rot than a flat, uninspired adjective or adverb. You say, "That was a good lecture," when you mean that it was witty, or stimulating, or instructive, or entertaining. You say "She is a nice person," when you mean that she is friendly, or sympathetic, or generous, or loyal, or modest, or conventional. You can find many adjectives that are more accurate and more vivid than *nice, cool, heavy, big, easy, hard.* A book of synonyms will help you find them.

It is a good idea to be on guard against all weak, overused adverbs, such as *very, pretty, rather, little.* Often a weak verb-adverb group can be replaced more effectively by a single strong verb. Note the following examples:

He ran quickly. [He fled, sprinted, jogged, rushed, surged, dashed.]

He was breathing rapidly. [He was panting, blowing, wheezing, puffing, gasping.]

She cut through it. [She pierced it, sliced it, tore it, split it, ripped it.]

He threw it down violently. [He hurled it, flung it, heaved it, pitched it.]

3. *Try replacing general or colorless verbs with more specific and descriptive verbs. Here are some examples.*

He moved toward the door. [He crept, sneaked, crawled, strolled, sidled, inched, drifted toward the door.]

He spoke several words. [He whispered, roared, shouted, hissed, mumbled, muttered several words.]

469

25

We put it on the truck. [We tossed, lifted, pitched, threw it on the truck.]

She got on the horse. [She scrambled, leaped, jumped, vaulted on the horse.]

25b. Figurative language can be used to add freshness to your style.

Some college freshmen feel that figurative language is a bit insincere, a little phony perhaps, good enough for poetry but out of place in honest prose. The truth is that all writing, from the deeply serious or reverent to the lightest, is often metaphorical. Our daily talk is salted with figures of speech. We meet metaphors in our reading and take them as they come, hardly realizing what they are.

Although all figurative language is usually called metaphorical, some elementary distinctions are useful. A *metaphor* is a figure that likens one thing to another by saying that one thing *is* another, not literally of course: "Life's but a walking shadow, a poor player" . . . "all the world's a stage" . . . "a critic is a legless man who teaches running" . . . "a camel is a greyhound designed by a committee" . . . "an Edsel is a lemon"—these are metaphors. When the likeness is actually expressed by the use of *as* or *like,* the metaphor becomes a *simile* "All the world is *like* a stage" . . . "insubstantial *as* a dream" . . . "the water lay gray and wrinkled *like* an elephant's skin"—these are similes. Figurative language, it is true, can be overdone, especially by a writer striving for a flashy style.

Figures of speech are best observed in context, where they look at home, as in the following selections. Seen alone as specimens they too often remind us of brightly colored butterflies pinned to a board. In the following, note also the vivid nouns, verbs, and adjectives:

Many of us, if we have happy childhoods, are tempted to believe that life is a pony, beribboned and curried, which has been given to us as a present. With the passing of years we, sooner or later, come to learn that, instead of being a pony, life is a mule

470

which unfortunately has more than four legs. To the best of my knowledge, no one who lives long enough fails to be kicked, usually again and again, by that mule. Why this should surprise us or unnerve us, I as an older person have long since ceased to understand.

> —JOHN MASON BROWN, "Prize Day Address," at Groton School for Boys

Then the creeping murderer, the octopus, steals out, slowly, softly, moving like a gray mist, pretending now to be a bit of weed, now a rock, now a lump of decaying meat while its evil goat eyes watch coldly. It oozes and flows toward a feeding crab, and as it comes close its yellow eyes burn and its body turns rosy with the pulsing color of anticipation and rage. Then suddenly it runs lightly on the tips of its arms, as ferociously as a charging cat. It leaps savagely on the crab, there is a puff of black fluid, and the struggling mass is obscured in the sepia cloud while the octopus murders the crab. On the exposed rocks out of water, the barnacles bubble behind their closed doors and the limpets dry out.

> —JOHN STEINBECK, *Cannery Row*

He gave his speech out of that bolt of cloth he had been weaving for all his life, that springless rhetoric so suited to the organ pipes of his sweet voice, for it enabled him to hold any note on any word, and he could cut from the sorrows of a sigh to the injunctions of a wheeze. He was a holy Harry Truman. Let us not quote him except where we must, for the ideas in his speech have already entered the boundless deep of yesterday's Fourth of July, and ". . . once again we give our testament to America . . . each and every one of us in our own way should once again reaffirm to ourselves and our posterity that we love this nation, we love America!"

> —NORMAN MAILER, *Miami and the Siege of Chicago*

25c. Metaphors and other phrases that have become trite should be avoided.

Trite expressions, whether they were once metaphors or not, are also called *hackneyed phrases* or *clichés*. At one time they may have been apt or witty and appropriate, but now, because they have been used so often, they are

471

25

stale and flat. They put off the reader. The following list may help to put you on your guard:

acid test
after all has been said
all in all
all work and no play
among those present
ardent admirers
as luck would have it
at a loss for words
at one fell swoop
avoid like the plague
beat a hasty retreat
beggars description
better half
better late than never
blissfully ignorant
bolt from the blue
breathless silence
budding genius
busy as a bee
by leaps and bounds
caught like rats in a trap
checkered career
conspicuous by his absence
course of true love
discreet silence
doomed to disappointment
drastic action
dull, sickening thud
dyed in the wool
each and every one
easier said than done
equal to the occasion
face the music
fair sex
familiar landmark
favor with a selection
festive occasion
few and far between
goes without saying
gridiron warriors

grim reaper
holy bonds of matrimony
in all its glory
in the last (or final) analysis
irony of fate
justice to the occasion
last but not least
leaves speechless
long-felt need
meets the eye
method in his madness
monarch of all he surveys
mother nature
motley crowd
needless to say
nipped in the bud
none the worse for wear
no sooner said than done
partake of refreshments
play with fire
pleasing prospect
pot luck
powers that be
presided at the piano
proud possessor
psychological moment
reigns supreme
rendered a selection
riot of color
ripe old age
sadder but wiser
shadow of the goal posts
silence reigned supreme
specimen of humanity
sumptuous repast
sweat of his brow
sweet girl graduate
table groaned
tempest in a teapot
tired but happy

472

troubled waters
untold wealth
vale of tears
venture a suggestion
[make a] virtue of necessity
water over the dam or under
  the bridge
wee small hours

wends his way
where ignorance is bliss
with a vengeance
with bated breath
words fail to express
worked like a horse
wrought havoc

EXERCISES

EXERCISE 1, WRITING FOR VIVIDNESS. *Rewrite the following paragraph. Pay special attention to the verbs, adjectives, and adverbs, and try to make use of metaphors or similes where they can be made appropriate.*

The boy walked home from school very slowly. It was April, and he observed as he went the various signs of the spring season. As he approached his own house, he paused to speak to his neighbor, who was working on his lawn. Finally he turned and walked indoors, for he was hungry.

EXERCISE 2, CLICHÉS AND TRITE PHRASES. *Now rewrite this passage again, this time using as many clichés and trite phrases as you can.*

§ 26. REFERENCE OF PRONOUNS

26a. The antecedent of a pronoun in a sentence should be immediately clear to the reader.

As a rule, pronouns should have definite antecedents and should be placed as near their antecedents as possible. The hedging in this last sentence, represented by the phrase "as a rule," refers to two or three special situations. First, there are a number of idiomatic phrases in which a pronoun has no visible antecedent, such as *it rained last night; it's the climate; it is time to go home.* There is no lack

473

of clearness in these sentences. Second, the pronoun *you,* in the sense of *one,* or a *person,* has wide currency in informal written and spoken English, and occasionally in good formal writing. Third, the pronouns *which, this, that* may refer to an idea or fact expressed by a whole clause or a sentence, or by a part of a clause, if the reference is unmistakably clear. These last, however, present a greater risk than the previous two idioms. Even when the reference *is* unmistakably clear, *which, this,* or *that* may be weaker than some more specific noun.

In good writing, the meaning of a sentence should be clear on the first reading. If the reader has to hesitate, if he has to search for the substantive (i.e., a noun or anything that functions as a noun) to which the pronoun refers, or if he has to puzzle over which of two possible antecedents it does refer to, the sentence is inept.

INDEFINITE

She saw a play at the awesome new Plymouth Theatre, but later she was not able to remember it very well. [What could she not remember, the play or the theatre?]

CLEAR

At the awesome new Plymouth Theatre she saw a play that she later was not able to remember very well.

OR

She saw a play at the awesome new Plymouth Theatre, but later she was not able to remember the building very well.

INDEFINITE

Since my grandfather was a doctor, it is not surprising that I have chosen *that* for a career. [The antecedent of *that* is only vaguely implied.]

CLEAR

Since my grandfather was a doctor, it is not surprising that I have chosen medicine for my career.

It is usually awkward to have a pronoun refer to an antecedent in a subordinate position, such as the object of a preposition. The reader will instinctively associate a pronoun with the most prominent substantive in the clause he or she has just read. The result is confusion—possibly a momentary confusion but still an undesirable one.

CONFUSING

Conscientious doctors do attempt to quiet the fears of their patients; they are often better able to face their symptoms as a result. [The reader will hesitate at "they are," because "Doctors" still appears to be the subject of the sentence.]

CLEAR

Conscientious doctors do attempt to quiet the fears of their patients, who are often better able to face their symptoms as a result.

As long as they occur close together in the same sentence, a pronoun and its antecedent may change places, the pronoun coming first.

EXAMPLE

Although she was an attractive woman who could have made herself beautiful, Maria refused to wear makeup or have her hair styled.

26b. The reference of a pronoun should not be ambiguous.

AMBIGUOUS

The title of the book was so dramatic that *it* was a great help in remembering *it*. [Does the first *it* refer to the title, or to the drama of the title? Does the second *it* refer to the book, or to the title of the book?]

CLEAR

I remembered that book easily because of its dramatic title.

AMBIGUOUS

The players and umpires know one another well and sometimes they call them by their first names.

CLEAR

Players who know umpires well sometimes call them by their first names.

AMBIGUOUS

Leonard told his brother that he did not yet know the game thoroughly.

CLEAR

As Leonard admitted to his brother, he did not yet know the game thoroughly.

OR

Leonard charged his brother with not knowing the game thoroughly.

It is clumsy to resort to a parenthetic repetition of the antecedent after a pronoun. When you find yourself painted into this corner, revise the sentence according to one of the models listed here.

AWKWARD

Leonard told his brother that he (Leonard) did not yet know the game thoroughly.

26c. In formal writing, the indefinite reference is less common than in informal writing and in speech.

We are here referring to two particular situations: (1) the use of the indefinite *you* to mean *one, a person* and the indefinite *they* to mean *people,* and (2) the use of *this, that,* and *which* to refer to a clause, sentence, or a general idea.

1. The indefinite *you* and *they* are common in speech and in many forms of informal writing; they are less appropriate in formal writing. Guard against making their use a habit, especially in papers of explanation.

FORMAL

First the seed is scattered evenly over the ground; then the soil is raked lightly and firmed with a roller. [Note the passive voice here.]

476

26. REFERENCE OF PRONOUNS

INFORMAL

First you scatter the seed; then you rake it in and firm the soil with a roller. [Or "First scatter the seed; then rake it in and firm the soil with a roller." *You* is understood.]

FORMAL

When a player hits the forehand, he should bend his knees and follow through on his stroke.

INFORMAL

When hitting a forehand, you should bend your knees and follow through on your stroke.

FORMAL

In the army, a soldier does not ask; he obeys.

INFORMAL

In the army, you do not ask; you do what you are told.

2. A pronoun may have a clause or a sentence for its antecedent; it may even refer to a thought expressed by a part of the preceding sentence. As long as the reference is unmistakable, the sentence is clear. But the careless writer may fall into the habit of stringing together a series of *this-*, *that,-* and *which-* clauses without worrying about either clearness or exactness. When the writer suspects the clearness or definiteness of an antecedent, he or she can sometimes summarize the idea of the clause referred to by an expression such as *this truth, this condition, a circumstance which,* and so forth. The sentence should be rewritten if the result is still unsatisfactory.

Notice that the references are clear in the following sentences.

CLEAR

I have finished my work at last. That should satisfy the boss.

He recommended that I write to the secretary, which I did without delay.

If you have decided to speak out on this issue, it should be done quickly.

477

Now notice the vague references in the following sentences.

VAGUE

The antismoking campaign in England, which had such little effect, has cost a good deal of money and energy, and this leads to pessimism about our own campaign.

CLEAR

The expensive and energetic antismoking campaign in England has had little effect, a result that leads to pessimism about our own campaign.

VAGUE

The fish are kept alive and fresh in glass tanks, and it also attracts people which helps the business considerably. [What do *it* and *which* refer to?]

CLEAR

The fish are kept alive and fresh in glass tanks. The display of live fish helps business by attracting people to the place.

VAGUE

No one knew what the President would do about this, but it was clear that it had to be settled by an executive decision.

CLEAR

No one knew what the President would do about this strike, but some form of executive decision was needed to settle it.

26d. The careless use of *same, such, above,* **and** *said* **as reference words often produces an awkward sentence.**

These words are used as reference words in legal or technical writing; in ordinary writing they should be avoided, not because they are incorrect but because they usually lead to awkwardness of expression. Use one of the common pronouns (*it, them, this*) or the name of the thing to which you refer.

478

POOR

I stood there holding the monkey wrench and oil can in my hands. The foreman ordered me to return the same to the engine room.

BETTER

I stood there holding the monkey wrench and oil can in my hands. The foreman ordered me to return the tools to the engine room.

POOR

The significance of said decision is not yet fully comprehended.

BETTER

The significance of this decision is not yet fully comprehended.

POOR

Please return same to me by bearer.

BETTER

Please return it [or name the object] to me by the bearer of this note.

POOR

The above is a complete refutation of their arguments.

BETTER

The facts mentioned completely refute their arguments.

26e. A pronoun should agree with its antecedent in number, gender, and person.

For a discussion of the agreement of pronouns, see § 4i.

POOR

Every student is required to bring their books.

BETTER

Every student is required to bring his (or her) books.

479

POOR

A team that loses most of its games may owe its failure to the fact that they do not have a good coach. [You must be consistent. If you begin by considering *team* as singular, you must continue to refer to it as one unit.]

26

BETTER

A team that loses most of its games may owe its failure to its lack of a good coach. [Or, more simply, "may owe its failure to poor coaching."]

26f. It is usually considered awkward to begin an essay with a reference to the title.

It is better to repeat the words of your title in your first sentence than it is to refer to your title with a pronoun. For example, if your title is "Coming About in a Smaller Boat," do not begin your paper, "This is difficult for the beginning sailor to learn." Say instead, "The beginning sailor will have some difficulty learning how to come about in a small boat." (The writer would do well, in fact, to lead up to a reference to his subject with a more intriguing opening altogether. This one is flat. When taking an essay test, however, in which the question must be incorporated in the answer, and where there is little time for stylistic nicety, the first sentence of the response might well rephrase the question as a beginning for the argument.)

EXERCISE

EXERCISE, FAULTY REFERENCE. *In each of the following sentences underline the pronoun or pronouns with faulty reference. Rewrite each sentence so as to correct the error.*

1. The baggage was loaded onto a small handcart which was the only way to get it through the crowded airport.
2. I worked for the college physics department last year, washing equipment for them and cleaning their laboratories.

3. He told me all about it, and very well too. It was something I would like to have done myself.
4. The history of this community goes back to the seventeenth century which makes a visit well worth while.
5. The obligations of an army sergeant are that of any leader in a small group.
6. While a person would suppose that she wanted nothing else in life, you could be very wrong about this.
7. The wealth of the country is controlled by a few who live in the city, which is usual in such societies.
8. Every player must learn his signals which will make an efficient and coordinated team.
9. He laughed at what I had said. This was amazing.
10. Everybody knows the reason why the economy is in such poor shape. It is a source of dismay to us all.
11. In *Being There*, the gang that threatened Chance did not understand how silly their threats sounded.
12. There seems to be no general agreement on this, but attitudes are changing.
13. Between you and me, Charles doesn't know the first thing about good music.
14. Anybody can stand up and state their views on abortion.
15. This is the decision that led to the defeat, and that ended the war.

26

§ 27. PROPER ARRANGEMENT

The parts of a sentence should be so arranged that the meaning of the sentence is clear at the first reading.

Since English is not a highly inflected language (i.e., not one in which words change form to reflect grammatical relations), the meaning of an English sentence depends largely on the arrangement of the words in it. The reader naturally assumes that the parts of a sentence that are placed next to each other are logically related to each other. You must therefore be careful to arrange words

27

in a sentence in such a way that its meaning will be clear on the first reading. The rule that will guide you may be stated in two parts: (1) place all modifiers, whether words, phrases, or clauses, as close as possible to the words they modify; (2) avoid placing these elements near other words they might be taken to modify.

27a. In formal writing, place adverbs logically.

Let us use *only* as an illustration of what happens when idiom contradicts logic. Logically, an adverb should be placed near the word it modifies; idiomatically, it is often placed elsewhere. For instance, would you say, "We have room for only two more," or, "We only have room for two more"? The person with a logical mind says that "only" modifies "two"; the person who prefers the second form answers that idiom does not pay much attention to logic. Both forms are used. The second is used generally in speech, in a great deal of informal writing, and often in formal writing. The first is used by writers and speakers who are disturbed by the logic of the second. In order to avoid confusion, use the first form in writing essays.

COMMON IN SPEECH

He *only* worked half a day.

Everyone is *not* honest.

The child *hardly* ate any food.

She *just* took one apple.

He *almost* weeded the whole garden.

MORE LOGICAL IN WRITING

He worked *only* half a day.

Not everyone is honest.

The child ate *hardly* any food.

She took *just* one apple.

He weeded *almost* the whole garden.

482

27b. Avoid ambiguous placement of phrases.

There is no exact position in a sentence that phrases must always occupy; the best rule to follow is to keep them away from words they must *not* be understood to modify. The result of such misplacement is often unintentionally humorous.

27

MISPLACED

He began to lose his desire to reach the summit *after a time.*

BETTER

After a time he began to lose his desire to reach the summit.

MISPLACED

I was dressed and ready to start climbing *within an hour.* [Does the phrase refer to *being dressed* or to *starting to climb?*]

BETTER

Within an hour I was dressed and ready to start climbing. [*Or*] I was dressed *within an hour* and ready to start climbing.

MISPLACED

Economic sanctions would work against Iran *without doubt.*

BETTER

Without doubt economic sanctions would work against Iran.

27c. Avoid ambiguous placement of clauses.

Clauses, like phrases, may be placed wherever they seem to fit in a sentence—except near words they can be mistaken to modify.

AMBIGUOUS OR LUDICROUS

I hid the ring in my pocket *that I intended to give to her.*

BETTER

The ring *that I intended to give to her* I hid in my pocket. [*Or*] I hid in my pocket the ring *that I intended to give to her.*

483

27d. Avoid squinting modifiers.

27

Modifiers so placed in a sentence that they may be understood with either the preceding or the following words are called *squinting modifiers.* As a rule, it is better not to try to cure the fault by means of punctuation.

SQUINTING

I firmly decided *the next day* to start studying.

CLEAR

I firmly decided to start studying *the next day.*

SQUINTING

After we had stopped at a service station *with the help of the attendant* we found our position on the map.

CLEAR

After we had stopped at a service station, the attendant helped us to locate our position on the map.

SQUINTING

The girl who had sat down *quickly* opened her textbook.

CLEAR

The girl who had sat down opened her textbook *quickly.*

27e. Use the split infinitive only to avoid awkwardness.

Placing an adverbial modifier between the sign *to* and the verb of an infinitive results in what is traditionally known as a "split infinitive" ("to quickly walk" *splits* the infinitive *to walk;* "to walk quickly" is a better arrangement). The split infinitive is no longer considered one of the capital crimes of composition—if it ever was. It is not true that the parts of an infinitive are inseparable. But since a split infinitive still causes many persons (especially compo-

484

sition instructors) discomfort, it is better not to split infinitives too rashly or frequently. A good rule to follow is this: place the adverbial modifier between *to* and the verb of an infinitive only when such an arrangement is necessary to avoid an awkward phrase. Here are some examples: "to even wish," "to seriously cripple," "to further confirm," "to utterly forget," "to further complicate," "to first consider." Remember that these are exceptions to the rule.

27

27f. Avoid the awkward separation of any words that normally belong near each other.

Words that usually belong near each other are subject and verb, verb and object, the parts of a verb phrase, noun and adjective modifier, and noun and appositive.

AWKWARD

Justice Holmes, in a brilliantly written interpretation of the Fourteenth Amendment, dissented. [Subject and verb split by long phrase]

BETTER

Justice Holmes dissented in a brilliantly written interpretation of the Fourteenth Amendment.

AWKWARD

Finally, we caught, after sitting in our rowboat for four hours, a small salmon. [Verb and object split]

BETTER

Finally, after sitting in our rowboat for four hours, we caught a small salmon.

AWKWARD

After it got dark, the girls bedded down beside a stream, wet, tired, and discouraged.

485

27

BETTER

After it got dark, the wet, tired, and discouraged girls bedded down beside a stream. [*Or*] After it got dark, the girls—wet, tired, and discouraged—bedded down beside a stream.

EXERCISES

EXERCISE 1, ELIMINATING SPLIT INFINITIVES. *Improve each of the following sentences by eliminating an awkward split infinitive.*

1. I hope to some day in the near future visit Paris again.
2. You should now begin to methodically and carefully budget your time for study.
3. If you care to remain in college, you must plan to quickly change your habits.
4. Your first concern should be to not carelessly waste your time.
5. If you really care to materially improve your grades, you should promise to immediately give up your trips to the bar.

EXERCISE 2, CORRECTING MISPLACED ELEMENTS. *Point out the misplaced element in each of the following sentences. Then show how the sentence can be improved. Do not use punctuation as a means of correcting an error in arrangement.*

1. We decided at nine o'clock to call him at his home.
2. Taking too many vitamin pills frequently causes excessive smiling.
3. Her dropped packages were collected before any had been stepped on by the bus driver.
4. The fullback returned to the team after two days' absence on Friday.
5. Paul, not wishing to prolong the argument far into the night, agreed to wash my car.
6. To be misunderstood often is the fate of an original lover.
7. The departing train brought thoughts of distant friends to the poor girl rumbling over the high bridge.

8. Our teacher has many theories about things that are different.
9. The sheriff was stabbed while sleeping by an unknown person.
10. He needs someone to show him how to put his affairs in order badly.

28

§ 28. DANGLING OR MISRELATED MODIFIERS

28a. Awkward dangling modifiers should be avoided.

There is considerable difference of opinion among educated people over the use of what is traditionally known as the "dangling modifier." Some say that it should be called the "misrelated modifier," for instead of dangling it actually attaches itself too easily to the wrong word. When it does, especially when it results in confusion or in unintentional humor, it is bad. When it calls attention to itself and away from the intended meaning of the sentence, it is bad. One might add that it is wrong because so many educated persons have been taught to regard it as a careless way of writing.

Here are some examples of dangling participles, the most common error in this category. Notice that the phrasing often results in unintentionally ludicrous meanings.

Walking along the quiet street, the houses looked old and comfortable.

While waiting for the coffee to warm, the cereal boiled away.

Strewn on the floor in large piles, he glanced idly through the remains of his books.

I had a summer job that year, thereby enabling me to return to school. [This is more awkward than plain wrong. Who or what enabled me to return to school?]

28

In addition to participles, infinitives are sometimes left dangling. The problem here is that there is no visible subject of the infinitive in the sentence.

To see this view properly, the sun must be shining. [Does the sun see the view?]

To succeed as a businessman, the basic facts of economics are apparently not always necessary.

In each of these sentences, it does not matter whether the phrase dangles because it is not attached where it should be or is misrelated because it attaches itself where it should not be. Each sentence is awkward or misleading.

A dangler may be corrected in three ways: (1) by changing the phrase to a clause, (2) by providing a noun or pronoun to which the dangler can properly attach itself, or (3) by reordering the sentence.

EXAMPLES

As I walked along the quiet street, the houses looked old and comfortable.

While I waited for the coffee to warm, the cereal boiled away.

He glanced idly through the remains of his books, which were strewn on the floor in large piles.

The money I made on a summer job that year enabled me to return to school.

To appreciate this view properly, one should see it when the sun is shining.

In order to succeed as a businessman, it is apparently not always necessary to know the basic facts of economics.

Note that the absolute phrase does not dangle. In the absolute phrase the word that the participle attaches itself to is in the phrase itself.

EXAMPLES

The day's work being over, we returned to town.

The guests having arrived, the dog headed downstairs.

488

Three more girls, their wet hair plastered down over their eyes, stumbled into the classroom.

It may be helpful to think of the participle as a kind of preposition in such sentences as these:

Considering the size of the house, it seemed remarkably cheap.
Judging by his voting record, he is a responsible congressman.

A slight shift in phraseology, however, produces a dangler, even though the meaning is essentially unchanged:

Viewing his voting record, he is a responsible congressman. [The sentence suggests that the congressman is responsible, and he is viewing his voting record.]

Certain idiomatic phrases, especially those that express a general action and those that serve as directive and transitional links, are always acceptable in either formal or informal situations. These are phrases like *generally speaking, looking at it from another point of view, taking everything into consideration, provided that, failing,* and others that are similar.

EXAMPLES
Failing agreement, the meeting was adjourned.
Generally speaking, the worse a pun is, the better it is.

28b. A sentence with any sort of expression, such as a phrase or an appositive, that is not easily understood with the rest of the sentence is awkward and usually misleading.

ILLOGICAL
A gentleman farmer, his wardrobe ranges from faultlessly tailored suits to four-buckle rubber boots. [The expression *a gentleman farmer* seems to be in apposition with *wardrobe*.]

REVISED
As he is a gentleman farmer, his wardrobe ranges from faultlessly tailored suits to four-buckle rubber boots.

28

489

ILLOGICAL

After five years in a city school, a country school presents many problems in adjustment. [One naturally associates the opening phrase with *a country school*.]

REVISED

A person who has spent five years in a city school encounters many problems in adjustment when he goes to a country school.

28

ILLOGICAL

When only a few years old, Yakland's president was indicted for bribery and extortion.

REVISED

When Yakland was only a few years old, its president was indicted for bribery and extortion.

The dangling or misrelated modifier, it can be seen from the examples offered, is a stylistic mistake. If it causes confusion, even momentary confusion, or if it is associated with an unintentionally humorous image, it is undesirable.

EXERCISE

EXERCISE, CORRECTING DANGLERS. *Some of the following sentences are correct, while some contain objectionable danglers. Pick out the faulty sentences and correct them.*

1. Buying her ticket at the box office, she walked into the opera house.
2. While waiting to be seated, the usher approached her.
3. He delayed taking her ticket, thus causing a small traffic jam.
4. Seated at last, she glanced through her program.
5. The opera, based vaguely on Shakespeare, was the famous *Falstaff*.
6. One of Italy's most beloved composers, the music was by Verdi.
7. The curtain having gone up at last, she sat back in her seat feeling thoroughly relaxed.

8. While sitting there quietly, the stage exploded with excitement.
9. To see an opera at its best, the scenery too must be appreciated.
10. Rising at the intermission, she strolled into the outer lobby.
11. She heard a familiar voice, thereby meeting an old friend.
12. Being an old opera lover, they got along famously.
13. When young, the opera had seemed too complicated.
14. Now, however, having matured, she enjoyed almost all performances.
15. Returning home in a taxi, the music of Verdi still seemed to sing in her ears.

§ 29. EMPHASIS IN THE SENTENCE

The relative importance of ideas in a sentence may be shown by various devices of structure. The principle used is known as *emphasis.*

Emphasis is a word that may be understood in more than one sense. A speaker may emphasize his words by shouting or screaming them; a writer may emphasize words by indicating that they be printed in italics or capitals. Some writers and speakers have used these methods. But that is not the sense in which we use the word here. By *emphasis* we mean using rhetorical devices that show the relative importance or prominence of ideas and details in a sentence or paragraph. Some of these devices we have discussed elsewhere in connection with other qualities of good writing—clarity, directness, order, coherence, conciseness, directness. Two or three others will be pointed out here and in the following sections.

It may be useful to restate the various devices by which the relative importance of ideas can be shown:

1. By placing the important idea by itself in a short sentence. [Empire policies bred rebellion.]

29

2. By placing the idea in a main clause of a complex sentence. [The Empire depended too heavily on military force, which it could not generate after losing its weapons.]

3. By changing the normal order of a sentence. [Such unrest the rulers could not tolerate. Order they must have.]

4. By using parallel structure. [No one could have predicted the extent or the destructiveness of the rebellion. *See §31.*]

5. By using the order of climax. [The rebel leaders were intelligent, bold, and successful. Their tactics were simple, their weapons portable, and their victories stunning.]

6. By repeating key words. [Their spoils were money and influence: money to hire more mercenaries, influence to gain political advantage. *See §24a.*]

7. By using the active instead of the passive voice. [Darth Vader fired the laser gun; *not*, The laser gun was fired by Darth Vader. *See §29c.*]

8. By giving an important idea fuller treatment. [Without the help of warp thrust, a system that aided the ship in achieving star speed, the rebels could not have escaped.]

9. By placing important words in prominent positions. [*Firepower* was what gave the Empire a crucial advantage. No one could deny that one quality gave the rebels the final edge: *determination. See §29a.*]

10. By using periodic structure. [To continue to fight against all odds is of course impractical but brave; *not*, It is of course impractical but brave to continue to fight against all odds. *See §29b.*]

29a. Placing important words in the important positions in the sentence will help to show the relative importance of ideas.

The most conspicuous positions in a sentence of some length are the beginning and the end. These are the posi-

492

tions that should be used for ideas that deserve attention and emphasis. The less important details, the modifiers, the qualifying comments, should be tucked away inside the sentence.

WEAK

Students who cheat in an examination are cheating only themselves ultimately.

BETTER

Students who cheat in an examination are ultimately cheating only themselves.

WEAK

Public speaking should be taught in freshman English, I think.

BETTER

Public speaking, I think, should be taught in freshman English.

No writer can consistently rearrange his sentences to begin and end them with important ideas. Many sentences are so short that the reader's mind comprehends them as units. In many others the word order is determined by the nature of the English language. A writer may occasionally construct a sentence such as this—as Stephen Leacock once did—"Him they elected president," but in sentences such as the following no problems of emphasis can arise: "He is a good person." "Her son was killed in Vietnam." "The day's work is done." "The President saluted the flag."

29b. Occasionally you may express a thought more effectively by changing a sentence from the loose to the periodic form.

A *periodic sentence* is one in which the main idea is held until the end; a *loose sentence* is one in which the main idea is followed by details and modifiers. The effect of a periodic sentence is one of suspense—that is, the reader is asked

29

to wait for the main idea until he has comprehended the details upon which the main idea is based or by which it is limited or changed. Not all sentences in English are periodic; many of them, in fact, are loose. It is precisely for this reason that an occasional periodic sentence is emphatic.

LOOSE

In recent years many factories were established in the city, especially plants engaged in the manufacture of rubber ducks.

PERIODIC

In recent years many factories, especially plants engaged in the manufacture of rubber ducks, were established in the city.

LOOSE

Stop writing if you have nothing more to say.

PERIODIC

If you have nothing more to say, stop writing.

LOOSE

It is of course impractical to legislate for those who will behave themselves while completely ignoring those who will not.

PERIODIC

To legislate for those who will behave themselves while completely ignoring those who will not is, of course, impractical.

The periodic effect, one of suspense, of waiting, is not limited to sentences in which the dependent clauses all come before the main clause. Note the following two sentences:

Metaphors are so vital a part of our speech, so common and used so unconsciously, that they become, as William Empson has indicated, the normal mode of development of a language. And it is the incalculable reach of the image—the establishment of a kinship between unrelated objects, the combination of exactness and ambiguity—which is its charm and power.
— LOUIS UNTERMEYER, "Play in Poetry"

29

Then note the way a writer creates suspense by using a summarizing main clause with *all* or *such:*

To transfer admiration from the thing possessed to its possessor; to conceive that the mere possession of material wealth makes of its possessor a proper object of worship; to feel abject before another who is wealthier—such emotions do not so much as enter the American mind.

—HILAIRE BELLOC

29c. Use the active instead of the passive voice where the active is more direct and natural.

The use of the passive voice is not in itself a grammatical or stylistic fault; it is the *overuse* of it that is a fault. The passive voice has several proper and necessary uses: (1) when the object or receiver of the action of the verb is more important than the doer; (2) when the doer of the action is not known; (3) when the writer wishes to place the emphasis on the receiver instead of on the doer.

To the satisfaction of everyone, Grabowski was chosen best player of the tournament.

Several priceless old manuscripts were destroyed.

The wounded hostage was dragged into the building.

Then note the difference in the following sentences when the active voice replaces the passive:

PASSIVE

A good time was had by everyone.

Then a driver's test was taken by me.

A feeling of nausea is experienced by the passengers.

ACTIVE

Everyone had a good time.

Then I took a driver's test.

The passengers experienced a feeling of nausea.

495

29

EXERCISES

EXERCISE 1, EMPHASIS. *Using the principle of emphasis by position, improve the following sentences.*

1. A fool can ask more questions than a wise man can answer, according to the Italian proverb.
2. Long sentences in a short theme are like large rooms in a small house, the professor explained.
3. Generally speaking it is well not to speak generally, as someone has said.
4. Generally speaking, one good teacher is worth a dozen good books.
5. When in danger or in doubt, run in circles, scream and shout, the sergeant advised.

EXERCISE 2, LOOSE AND PERIODIC SENTENCES. *Change the following loose sentences to periodic sentences.*

1. Stress has a harmful effect on our ability to learn, it was discovered by these experiments.
2. For this experiment two control groups were selected who had the same ability to memorize.
3. One group was told that its scores were poor after they had completed about half the test.
4. Their performance at once deteriorated when the testing was resumed.
5. But their ability improved considerably after they had been praised for their improved performance.

EXERCISE 3, ACTIVE OR PASSIVE VERBS. *Improve the following sentences by changing the verb from the passive to the active.*

1. The skidding car was brought safely to a stop by the alert driver.
2. The policeman's warning was accepted by her with humility.
3. I thought that she would be nervous and tearful, but a very different reaction was observed by me.

4. As she informed me, a set of new tires had been bought by her husband a few days ago.
5. But the need for new tires, she said, was vetoed by her.
6. Instead, the new tires were returned to the dealer and a new guitar was purchased with the money by her.
7. "Do you think now that a new guitar is worth your life?" was asked by the officer.
8. The workings of a careless person's mind cannot be understood by more cautious people.
9. After a few minutes the trip to our destination was resumed by us.
10. Glancing up at the rear-view mirror, it was observed that the woman's car was now following us.

30

§ 30. SHIFT IN POINT OF VIEW

Any unnecessary and illogical shift in point of view should be avoided.

Three common grammatical shifts in point of view are (1) from active to passive voice, (2) from past to present tense, and (3) from *one* to *you* and similar shifts of person. These and other shifts are described below. Writing is both clearer and more pleasing if you maintain your point of view.

30a. Unnecessary shifts from active to passive voice are undesirable.

SHIFT

You wrap the gift carefully in paper; it is then tied securely.

We were acquainted with his brother, and his eighty-year-old father was also well known to us.

Paul drove the car into a ditch, but later it was pushed out by him.

497

BETTER

You wrap the gift carefully in paper and tie it securely.

We knew both his brother and his eighty-year-old father.

Paul drove the car into a ditch, but later he pushed it out.

30b. Needless shifts in tense—from past to present or from present to past—are usually objectionable.

See also §6.

SHIFT

I *go* right on into the room and then *looked* around me to see what he *would be doing* with all that furniture. [Such shifts in tense must be watched for especially in narrative accounts.]

BETTER

I *went* right on into the room and then *looked* around me to see what he *might be doing* with all that furniture. [Or *might have done* with all that furniture]

SHIFT

After *planning* the trip I *had thought* I *deserved* a little credit for its success.

BETTER

After *having planned* the trip, I *thought* I *deserved* a little credit for its success. [All verbs in past tense]

SHIFT

Styron's hero Stingo *drank* heavily while he *writes* his first novel.

BETTER

Styron's hero Stingo *drinks* heavily while he *tries to write* his first novel. [It is customary to use the present tense, called the "historical present," in discussing literary situations.]

30c. Needless shifts in number or person should be avoided.

498

SHIFT

If one really wishes to sample fine cooking, try that restaurant on the corner.

CORRECT IN FORMAL CONTEXT

If one really wishes to sample superior cooking, he [or *he or she*] should try the restaurant on the corner.

CORRECT IN INFORMAL STYLE

If you really want to enjoy some good eating, try that restaurant on the corner.

See also §26e for a discussion of number in pronouns.

30d. A writer should guard against mixing two distinctly separate constructions in a sentence.

A *mixed construction* is usually the result of hasty and careless writing. The writer begins one construction, and immediately, without troubling to look back on what has been written, continues with another construction.

MIXED

In our basement we found a small wood stove, which upon removing the front, made it resemble a fireplace. [*Which* refers to *stove*. The stove cannot remove its own front, nor can the stove make itself resemble anything.]

CLEAR

In our basement we found a small wood stove, which we made into a fireplace by removing its front.

In our basement we found a small wood stove. By removing its front, we made it resemble a fireplace.

MIXED

She did not say a word, but took me to the back yard in what seemed to me a bit hurriedly. [The writer has forgotten his original intention. He could say either *took me in what seemed a hurried manner* or *took me a bit hurriedly.*]

Occasionally a writer will run an independent clause into a sentence in such a way that it appears to stand as the subject of a verb.

MIXED

We were tired of traveling is the main reason we came here.

I was all alone was what truly frightened me.

The loss of good pilots was what destroyed their strategic advantage.

CLEAR

We came here mainly because we were tired of traveling.

What truly frightened me was that I was all alone.

The loss of good pilots destroyed their strategic advantage.

30e. Mixed figures of speech are inappropriate in serious writing.

In the teaching of writing, warnings against scrambled metaphors may have been given an undeserved and an unfortunate prominence. A *mixed metaphor* is often a sign of mental vitality. Even Shakespeare spoke of taking up arms against a sea of troubles. The danger is that in scrambling two incongruous images your phrase or sentence may become unintentionally comic. Speaking of Shakespeare, consider this blooper from a student theme: "Shakespeare, not leaving a screw unturned, ties up the first scene in a neat bundle."

Another danger is that in attempting to use metaphors students often either misunderstand them or lapse into cliché. An example comes from a term paper in which the writer talked of the college experience as "a tough road to hoe." The expression is trite to begin with, but the city-dwelling student also did not know that "rows," not "roads," are hoed.

The following samples illustrate more clearly what is meant by "mixed imagery."

500

Many high-school athletes think they can ride on their high-school laurels right into a position on the college team. [How can one ride on a laurel?]

The future of jazz was at its lowest ebb. [Even were the future not transported to the past, a rare feat in itself, how could a future ebb?]

A college education enables the graduate to meet the snares and pitfalls of life with a broader point of view.

30

EXERCISES

EXERCISE 1, ILLOGICAL SHIFTS. *In each of the following sentences specify the type or types of illogical shift that you find—in tense, voice, number, or person. Then make the necessary corrections.*

1. The submarine *Seashark* goes down in April of 1978, and many scientists participated in the investigation that followed.
2. They conducted research from several ships; also a survey of the ocean bottom was made.
3. One would suppose the task would have been easy, since all you have to do is find the hull on the ocean floor.
4. The scientific group had its hands full, however, for they could discover no trace of the missing craft.
5. The Navy called off its search in September; they had done all they could.
6. New efforts have been undertaken by private scientific organizations and universities have continued research into the mishap.
7. Until late 1979, no one knows just where the ship is lying—you would have been amazed to learn how the discovery was finally made.
8. A bathysphere is ordered; it has been at work for some time on the scene.
9. No doubt many scientists on the project would prefer to return to shore as a laboratory researcher.
10. In the process, however, the ocean floor in the area

501

30

has been fully investigated, which had been useful for future oceanographers.

EXERCISE 2, MIXED CONSTRUCTIONS. *Here are ten badly confused sentences. Rewrite them. Do not be afraid to break them up if they can be improved in that manner.*

1. You could view that painting as a complex pattern of colors or as an amateur who knows very little about art.
2. They had a big wedding which I regret to say they never asked me to come.
3. The table was made of inlaid wood and a source of admiration to all who saw it.
4. Everybody considered her a beauty that she was an asset to the community.
5. The dean said he believed in a straightforward, middle-of-the-road, thoroughly well-rounded plan of education which everyone ought to have the opportunity.
6. Hard work has always been a bad point with me due to my time has always been so preoccupied with fun.
7. He looked bravely into the eye of the future with a fast and unfaltering step.
8. The reason things are at such a low ebb is because of the inevitable swing of the economic pendulum.
9. Sometimes you see a student reading comfortably in the library and looks as if he has fallen asleep as indeed he has.
10. Anyone who writes sentences like these that thinks he can write English ought to know better.

§ 31. PARALLEL STRUCTURE

31a. Parallel structure expresses similar ideas in the same grammatical and rhetorical patterns.

Parallel structure is primarily a rhetorical device that writers use to give their sentences force, clearness, grace, and rhythm. In its more elementary uses it gives sentences

502

greater clarity and smoothness. For a more complete discussion of rhetorical uses of parallelism and balance, turn to Chapter 3. Here are two examples from the works of writers to whom style is important:

In football what fans prize most is the interaction of grace and brutality—

> how a halfback's marvelous sense of balance enables him to gain yardage while being buffeted by 270-pound monsters, or
> how a wide receiver can leap, grab, and hold a pass while a linebacker is knocking his feet from under him.
> —THOMAS GRIFFITH

> The study of fortification caught up with the destructive power of cannon, so that wars became a matter of long, costly sieges interspersed with raids and skirmishes, rather than pitched battles, and the whole craft of war from supply to assault had to be rethought to suit these conditions.
> —JOHN R. HALE, *The Art of War and Renaissance England*

In its simpler and more elementary form, parallel structure is a balancing of noun with noun, an infinitive with another infinitive, a phrase with another phrase, and a clause with another clause. Used at this level, the device will cure many a deformed or wandering sentence:

AWKWARD

Sororities teach a young woman to be a friend and courteous. [Noun paralleled with adjective]

PARALLEL IN FORM

Sororities teach a young woman to be *friendly* and *courteous.*
[Adjective | | adjective]

503

31

AWKWARD

Our English instructor asked us to close our books, to take pen and paper, and that we were to write a short theme. [Two infinitives and a clause]

PARALLEL IN FORM

Our English instructor asked us | | | *to close our books,*
to take pen and paper, and
to write a short theme.
[Infinitive | | infinitive
| | infinitive]

AWKWARD

Few of the leaders anticipated the bitterness of the strike or how long it would last. [A noun and a clause]

PARALLEL IN FORM

Few of the leaders anticipated | | | *the bitterness* or
the duration of the strike.
[Noun | | noun]

31b. Avoid the *and who* and the *and which* constructions.

The "and who" or "and which" fault, as it is called, consists of using *and who* or *and which* in a sentence that does not have a preceding *who* or *which* clause.

FAULTY

He is a man of wide experience *and who* is also very popular with the farmers.

PARALLEL

He is a man of | | | wide experience and
great popularity among the farmers.

FAULTY

I am interested in electronics, because it is a new field *and which* offers interesting opportunities to one who knows science.

504

31. PARALLEL STRUCTURE

PARALLEL

I am interested in electronics, | which is a new field and which offers interesting opportunities . . .

31c. Avoid the false parallel.

Straining for parallelism where it is not natural is a fault that occurs rarely in college writing. The false parallel, however, is not the result of too much care for form; it is purely accidental.

ILLOGICAL

I finally realized that my new personality was not making me happy, intelligent, or friends. [The three words seem to depend on *making me,* but two of them are adjectives and one is a noun. They are not logically parallel.]

REVISED

I finally realized that my new personality was not making me happy and intelligent or bringing me friends.

Parallel forms may be used with the correlative conjunctions *both—and, either—or, neither—nor, not only—but also.* Care should be taken in placing these correlatives so that the intended meaning of the sentence is not obscured.

EXERCISES

EXERCISE 1, PARALLEL FORM. *In the following sentences underline the parts that should be expressed in parallel form. Then revise each sentence.*

1. Professor Macy is a middle-aged woman, short, stocky, blue eyes, and partly gray-haired.
2. Her lectures are witty, interesting and she outlines them carefully.
3. She told us that we should read our text and to write a short review of it.

505

31

4. The book is interesting and I can learn from it.
5. Ms. Macy said she would give us a quiz on the first chapter and for us to review it carefully.

EXERCISE 2, FALSE PARALLELS. *In the following sentences correct the faulty use of correlatives.*

1. My summer's work proved not only interesting but I also learned much from it.
2. I wondered whether I should continue with it or should I return to college.
3. My boss was not only pleasant but she was also generous.
4. A college education was both necessary and I could afford it.
5. Not only was I getting older fast, but I also planned to be married soon.

§ 32. COMPARISONS

32a. In standard formal English, comparisons should be logical and complete.

Written English, especially formal written English, requires a logic and a precision in expressing comparisons that is often lacking in loose, informal speech. In informal speech certain illogical comparisons have become accepted as idioms. Some of these shortened comparisons, or illogical comparisons, are becoming more and more common in *both formal and informal* writing; as in other cases of divided usage, the choice made by the student should be based on an understanding of the facts of usage and a desire for clarity.

1. In informal writing do not omit than *or* as *in a double comparison.*

USUALLY INAPPROPRIATE IN FORMAL USAGE

The bus is about as fast if not faster than the train.

Football coaches earn as much if not more than college presidents.

506

California is now as populous, if not more populous than New York.

LOGICAL BUT AWKWARD

The bus is about as fast as, if not faster than, the train.

Football coaches earn as much as, if not more than, college presidents.

California is now as populous as, if not more populous than, New York.

The last three examples illustrate what is often called the *suspended construction*. Some writers use it; others object to it because of its awkwardness. It can be easily avoided.

LOGICAL AND SMOOTH

The bus is about as fast as the train, if not faster.

Football coaches earn as much as college presidents, if not more.

California is now as populous as New York, if not more so.

2. *Avoid ambiguity in making comparisons.*

AMBIGUOUS

I saw more of him than Clark ["more than Clark did" or "more than I saw of Clark"?]

CLEAR

I saw more of him than I saw of Clark. [Or *more of him than Clark did*]

AMBIGUOUS

Our country helped France more than England.

CLEAR

Our country helped France more than England did. [Or *more than our country helped England*]

3. *Do not omit* other *after* than *or as* in comparing two members of the same group or class.

507

MISLEADING

Ms. Jenkins is more literate than any woman in the class. [If Ms. Jenkins is not a member of the class, the sentence is clear. If she *is* in the class, she cannot be more literate than herself.]

CLEAR

Ms. Jenkins is more literate than any other woman in the class.

BETTER

Ms. Jenkins is the most literate woman in the class.

   4. Finish your comparisons so that you will not seem to be comparing something that you do not intend to compare.

MISLEADING

The salary of an English professor is lower than a lawyer. [Are you comparing salaries, or are you comparing salary and lawyer?]

CLEAR

The salary of an English professor is lower than that of a lawyer. [The *that* here completes the comparison and also avoids needless repetition of *salary.*]

MISLEADING

The opening of *The Searchers* is more intriguing than *Final Entries.*

CLEAR

The opening of *The Searchers* is more intriguing than that of *Final Entries.*

MISLEADING

The duties and responsibilities of a traffic officer are more complex than a cabin attendant.

CLEAR

The duties and responsibilities of a traffic officer are more complex than those of a cabin attendant. [Name the second term of the comparison.]

508

32. COMPARISONS

32b. In standard English, comparisons are completed except when the missing term of the comparison can be easily supplied by the reader.

NOT CLEAR

It is easier to remain silent when attacks are made upon the people one loves. [Easier than what?]

CLEAR

It is easier to remain silent when attacks are made upon the people one loves than to risk criticism by defending them.

NOT CLEAR

Students who live in a dormitory do better work. [Better than students who live where?]

CLEAR

Students who live in dormitories do better work than those who room in apartments. [Or *who live in fraternity houses*].

There are, however, many idiomatic expressions in which an unfinished comparison is easily understood, such as "It is always better to tell the truth"; "we thought it wiser to agree." No misunderstanding is possible in statements like these. The uncompleted superlative is also used, especially in speech, and its sense is not that of a comparison but of an intensive, as in: "She is the *most* unselfish woman," "he is a *most* appealing man."

EXERCISE

EXERCISE, COMPARISONS. *Revise the comparisons in the following sentences. Use the forms appropriate in standard written English.*

1. The snails of South America known as apple snails are as interesting if not more interesting than the allied *Pila* of the Old World.

509

33

2. Their shells are like apples, greener and rounder than other snails.
3. They are one of, if not the most amphibious kind of snail known to science.
4. Equipped with both gills and lungs, they are better swimmers than any snails.
5. When one compares the two types, the apple snail is clearly the best adapted to its environment.
6. The English periwinkle is as common if not more common than most other snails.
7. The lungs of the periwinkle are more developed than most other such sea animals.
8. Here the development of the lungs has reached a point higher than any place on earth.
9. Some snails can live as long if not longer than six months out of water.
10. Snails are the most fascinating animals; they are so attractive and varied in appearance.

§ 33. WORDS LEFT OUT

Words necessary for clearness should not be left out.

Two kinds of omissions need to be considered here. One is the result of carelessness. Its cure is careful proofreading. The second results from carrying speech habits into writing. We often speak in a more clipped or telegraphic manner than is acceptable in writing, especially in serious writing on serious subjects.

The following are some of the omissions that need to be guarded against.

33a. Do not omit *that.*

MISLEADING

I soon observed nearly all the women, especially the young and pretty ones, were carrying strange little baskets. [Did he "observe the women, especially the young and pretty ones," or did he observe *that* the women were carrying baskets?]

510

He told me his story in its original version had been rejected by thirteen publishers. [Supply *that.* "He told me *that* his story . . ." The confusion is undesirable even if it is momentary.]

(Be careful, however, about needless repetition of *that,* as in: "He told me that there were numerous obscene magazines in that store, and that that troubled him." A useful correction would be: "He told me that there were numerous obscene magazines in Weston's [name the store], a situation which troubled him.")

33b. Do not omit part of a verb or of a verb phrase.

MISLEADING

The patient was given an anesthetic and the instruments made ready. [It is better to say *were made ready,* because *patient* is singular, and the verb *was,* which follows it, cannot be understood with *instruments made ready.* We need a plural verb.]

His ideas were progressive and adopted without debate. [Repeat *were.* The two verbs are not parallel. The first *were* is used as a main verb—*ideas were*—but the second *were* is an auxiliary verb—*were adopted. Progressive* is not part of the verb phrase.]

33c. Do not omit words required by the use of a noun or a verb in a double capacity.

AWKWARD

He never has and never will deceive a customer. [Supply *deceived* after *never has.* Although this sort of construction is common in speech, many people object to it in written English.]

This young man is one of the best, if not the best fullback I have ever watched. [Say *one of the best fullbacks.*]

33d. Do not omit necessary prepositions in idiomatic expressions.

INCOMPLETE

Spring term the course will be repeated for all new students. [Say *During the spring term. . . .*]

We must show our faith and devotion to our country. [Say *faith in*. *Faith to* is not idiomatic.]

Customers have neither respect nor faith in a merchant who cheats. [Say *respect for*. *Respect in* is not idiomatic.]

33e. Do not omit function words that indicate balanced and parallel constructions.

WEAK

He said that Communism had never had many adherents in the United States and there were fewer party members today than at any time since the Russian revolution.

STRENGTHENED

He said *that* Communism had never had many adherents in the United States and *that* there were fewer party members today than at any time since the Russian revolution.

WEAK

We thanked her for her kindness, which we had not always reciprocated, the stimulation we found in her classroom, and the long hours she had spent helping us with extracurricular activities.

STRENGTHENED

We thanked her *for* her kindness, which we had not always reciprocated, *for* the stimulation we found in her classroom, and *for* the long hours she had spent helping us with extracurricular activities.

EXERCISE

EXERCISE, MISSING WORDS. *Supply the missing words in the following sentences. Rearrange the wording wherever necessary.*

1. This student, I feel sure, never has and never will write a passing theme.
2. We visited one of the oldest, if not the oldest church in Vermont.

3. We noticed many churches were almost surrounded by graveyards.
4. He needed better evidence to prove his demands were justified.
5. Sundays more men studied their newspapers than women.
6. Critics noticed that Hope did not have funny material and the skits were too long.
7. Winter the economy will begin to slow again.
8. In order to behave in a humane way countries should show a sympathy and understanding of other countries' beliefs.
9. Her gifts were beautiful and accepted with favorable comments.
10. The team was given a rousing pep talk and their equipment repaired.

34

§ 34. VARIETY

Variety in the length and the structure of sentences usually makes writing more effective.

A writer may avoid monotony of sentence structure by avoiding the following:
1. Beginning a series of sentences with the same word or the same subject.
2. Beginning a series of sentences with participial phrases.
3. Using the same sentence pattern in a group of sentences.
4. Beginning each of a series of sentences with the same kind of subordinate clause.

Here are some elementary examples of monotony. Notice the consistent shortness of the sentences, the unvaried vocabulary, and the needless repetition of sentence structure.

SHORT SENTENCES, ALL BEGINNING WITH THE SUBJECT

Mrs. Helmer is a fine woman. She has always been kind to me. I have appreciated her efforts in my behalf. She helped

513

me find a summer job. I met a number of interesting people through her. She has always been a good friend of mine.

SHORT SENTENCES BEGINNING WITH A PARTICIPIAL PHRASE

34

Waking up in the morning, I dressed quickly. Hurrying into the kitchen, I saw my mother at the stove. Pouring me a cup of coffee, she advised me not to delay. Gulping my coffee quickly, I began to collect my thoughts for the day ahead.

Few students should be guilty of such monotonous writing; the examples cited make for monotonous reading. Some common techniques for introducing variety include the following:

1. Mixing simple sentences with complex or compound sentences.
2. Putting a short sentence in the midst of several long ones.
3. Occasionally beginning a sentence with modifiers instead of with the subject. ["Disappointed by this response, I . . . ;" "At other times, he . . ."]
4. Occasionally beginning with a conjunction instead of with the subject. ["But this decision was wrong;" "And no one accepted the plan."]

In the selection that follows, note how richness and variety are achieved by weaving various details, in phrases, clauses, and appositives, into the sentences themselves.

The week before, at home, some academic friends had been over and as we talked and drank we looked at a television showing of Tod Browning's 1931 version of *Dracula.* Dwight Frye's appearance on the screen had us suddenly squealing and shrieking, and it was obvious that old vampire movies were part of our common experience. We talked about the famous ones, Murnau's *Nosferatu* and Dreyer's *Vampyr,* and we began to get fairly involved in the lore of the genre—the strategy of the bite, the special earth for the coffins, the stake through the heart versus the rays of the sun as disposal methods, the cross as vampire repellent, et al. We had begun to surprise each other by the affectionate, nostalgic tone of our mock erudition when the youngest person present, an instructor in English, said, in a

514 .

clear, firm tone, "*The Beast with Five Fingers* is the greatest horror picture I've ever seen." Stunned that so bright a young man could display such shocking taste, preferring a Warner Brothers forties mediocrity to the classics, I gasped, "But why?" And he answered, "Because it's completely irrational. It doesn't make any sense, and that's the true terror."

—PAULINE KAEL, *Zeitgeist and Poltergeist; Or, Are Movies Going to Pieces?*

35

§35. AWKWARDNESS AND OBSCURITY

Sentences that are confused, awkward, illogical, or obscure should be rewritten.

An awkward and confused sentence may occasionally be a sign of slovenly thinking, but it is probably more often a result of haste and carelessness in writing and revision. A confused sentence may have several faults:

1. The central thought may be lost in a tangle of modifiers.
2. The thoughts may not be arranged properly.
3. The words used may be inexact, ambiguous, or inappropriate.
4. Several constructions may be telescoped into one. See also §30.

CONFUSED

If more emphasis was stressed in college on extemporary speaking, the graduating student would be better prepared to face people of social prominence and college professors.

REVISED

Colleges should stress courses in extemporary speaking in order to give their graduates more confidence and social ease.

CONFUSED

The word *laureate* comes from the Greeks when they used laurels to crown certain people.

REVISED

The word *laureate* comes from the language of the ancient Greeks, who used a laurel crown as a mark of special honor.

CONFUSED

Hamlet wishes to act morally in the right way.

REVISED

Hamlet wishes to act morally.

CONFUSED

Iago is discovered at the end of the play, but that hardly makes things better.

REVISED

Iago's villainy is discovered at the end of the play, but the discovery comes too late.

EXERCISE

EXERCISE, AWKWARD AND OBSCURE SENTENCES. *Revise the following sentences.*

1. Some allergic people live in pollen-proof rooms created by air-conditioning, not including air-cooling, to escape paroxysms of sneezing caused by chilling.
2. The hay fever patient should be wary of spraying insecticides about the yard or house, for spraying pyrethrum, the ground-up flower of the chrysanthemum, which is a member of the composite family, also is contained in these.
3. A student spends two or three terms in college to become accustomed with the rules needed for comprehensive learning.
4. Proper use of the English language is very essential in any type of work, whether a business woman or a profession.
5. Many people have sacrificed wonderful professions because of simple misconceptions of their judgment.

6. There are some girls who really cannot afford to live in a sorority house but who would rather have it known that she belongs to a sorority and do without other things like food and clothes.
7. Having never attended college before gives me the opportunity to develop to the fullest extent my study habits and idle time.
8. Still half asleep and unconscious of what I was doing, I applied the makeup on the left-hand side of the table, which happened to be the kind used for formal occasions.
9. Privacy hindered my studying while in high school because living in a house where there are many children it is very hard to secure privacy.
10. The subject of classifying what I think is an ideal roommate should be written to an unlimited length if one was to take every point in doing so.

36

§ 36. COHERENCE AND DEVELOPMENT IN PARAGRAPHS

36a. A skillful arrangement of details helps to produce an effective paragraph.

A discussion of coherence in an *opening* paragraph appears in Chapter 4 under "Kinds of Introductory Paragraphs." In that section three common ways of beginning an essay with an effective paragraph are analyzed:

1. A statement of the thesis to be argued.
2. Narration of an anecdote related to the argument to follow.
3. Definition of a key term important to the thesis.

Paragraphs in the body of a paper must maintain coherence too, and a few suggestions for their development are worth consideration.

1. Try presenting your material in "deductive order," that is, "from the general to the particular." Most paragraphs of exposition follow this order. State your general

36

idea first in a topic sentence, and then present the reasons, details, examples, illustrations, and so on, that make your general statement understandable and convincing.

2. Try the "order of enumeration." In your topic sentence state that your idea may be seen from two points of view, that it has three important aspects, that you are going to use four illustrations, that you have two excellent reasons for believing it, and so on. There are numerous uses for this method, and its declaration of an order contributes to a clear, compact, and well-organized paragraph.

The following topic sentences from the works of professional writers demonstrate how this method is used:

All social organization is of two forms.

There were also three less desirable results of the Peace Conference.

There are two uses of knowledge.

Among the leading purposes of law today we may list three.

Remember, however, that this sort of beginning gives a formal tone to your writing. Use the device occasionally, when the material of your paragraph is adapted to classification and enumeration.

3. Try the "time order." If details can be arranged in the order of their occurrence, there is no particular advantage to be gained by trying any other arrangement. The order of time (often called the "chronological" order) or occurrence produces a clear and orderly paragraph. It is inherently simple, perhaps elementary—but it has the unquestioned virtue of being almost foolproof. It may be used with material that at first glance does not arrange itself in the order of time.

4. Try using the "inductive order." It may be that your paragraph idea should not be stated bluntly in the first sentence. The reader may not be ready for it. Prepare him for it by using your details, your examples and instances, to guide his thoughts, so that when you are ready to use your summarizing topic sentence he will also be ready to accept it. This process is the reverse of "the gen-

eral to the particular," for the generalization concludes the paragraph.

If the problem of coherence is in your concluding paragraph, especially in its relation to your beginning, review the section on "Beginnings and Endings" in Chapter 6. In that section, eight possible beginning-and-ending combinations are listed, with examples.

36

36b. Paragraphs should be fully developed and of suitable length.

If your instructor writes "No ¶" next to what you believe *is* a paragraph, your response will probably be one of surprise and confusion. The correction simply asks, however, that you *add details or examples* or *reveal the process of reasoning by which you reached the conclusion.* Often this problem is caused by a so-called paragraph that is in fact made up of one or two generalizations or abstractions: "Rome fell because of immoral behavior"; "The war was caused by economic conditions." To develop and support such statements, start asking specific questions: What instances of immoral behavior do I have in mind? Where did they occur? Who was involved? What led me to the conclusions that economic conditions caused the war? What specific conditions do I want the reader to notice? These questions will add more than just padding—i.e., needless repetition of words and phrases, circumlocution—to your underdressed paragraph.

A handy guide: If each page of your essay consists of four or more paragraphs, your instructor is likely to reach for his or her red-ink pen to write "No ¶" or "Add details" or "Lacks dev."

36c. Paragraphs are made more effective by the skillful use of connectives and transitions.

Chapter 4 ("Problems of Internal Organization"), lists four main ways of linking ideas—by using conjunctions and transitional words and phrases, by using pronouns, by repeating key words, and by expressing related ideas in parallel structure.

1. Transitional Expressions. The following is a brief list of transitional words and phrases. You must not think that this list is complete. The natural, spontaneous phrases of transition that occur to you as you write are by no means necessarily incorrect or unliterary.

on the other hand	conversely	finally
in the second place	of course	after all
on the contrary	in conclusion	indeed
at the same time	to sum up	next
in particular	moreover	similarly
in spite of this	in addition	again
in like manner	for example	and truly
and so again	for instance	meanwhile
as I have said	furthermore	
in contrast to this	accordingly	

EXAMPLES OF TRANSITIONS

In like manner, all kinds of deficient and impolitic usages are referred to the national love of trade; though, *oddly enough,* it would be a weighty charge against a foreigner that he regarded the Americans as a trading people.

—CHARLES DICKENS

I am not blaming or excusing anyone here. . . . I find, *for instance,* that prejudice, essentially, is worse on the prejudiced than on their targets.

—LOUIS ADAMIC

There were then very few regular troops in the kingdom. A town, *therefore,* which could send forth, at an hour's notice, twenty thousand men. . . .

—THOMAS BABINGTON MACAULAY

Their [the immigrants'] children, *however,* follow the general increase which is found in the American population. *Furthermore,* the form of the body of immigrants' children undergoes certain changes. . . .

—FRANZ BOAS

520

2. Pronouns Referring to Antecedents in the Preceding Sentences. The technique of using pronouns for transition is a standard practice, but often runs the risk of vagueness of reference. See § 26 for illustrations of vagueness.

EXAMPLES

In the summer, Jonas had his usual two or three weeks of vacation. *These* were spent usually at our cabin in the mountains.

I know a writer of newspaper editorials. *Himself* a liberal, *he* has to grind out a thousand words daily which reflect the ultra conservative policy of the paper for which *he* works. *He* keeps a record like a batting chart. . . .

—STUART CHASE

If the use of a pronoun in one sentence that refers to an antecedent in a preceding sentence is risky, the use of a pronoun in one paragraph with its antecedent in the preceding paragraph is even more likely to involve dangerous confusion. The wisest course is to rely on the use of pronouns from paragraph to paragraph only when the antecedent is emphatically central to both paragraphs—as in a discussion of the work of one author, who may be referred to as he or she after one identification.

3. Key Words Repeated. In the two following passages, the words *civilization* and *understanding* are repeated to hold the arguments together.

EXAMPLES

Nothing in the way of civilization is inborn, as are the forms and workings of our body. Everything that goes to make up civilization must be acquired anew in infancy and childhood, by each and all of us.

—JAMES HARVEY ROBINSON

In some of my early writings I spoke of the twofold problem of understanding—there was the problem of understanding the world around us, and there was the problem of understanding the process of understanding, that is, the problem of understanding the nature of the intellectual tools with which we attempt to understand the world around us.

—P. W. BRIDGMAN

36

37

4. Parallel Structure. In the example, the repeated subject-verb phrasing relates each clause to all the others.

EXAMPLE

While I talk and the flies buzz, a sea gull catches a fish at the mouth of the Amazon, a tree falls in the Adirondack wilderness, a man sneezes in Germany, a horse dies in Tartary, and twins are born in France.

—WILLIAM JAMES

§ 37. GLOSSARY: A GUIDE TO USAGE

This section is to be consulted for information about current usage.

Correctness and incorrectness in English usage are relative terms. We usually prefer to speak of the appropriateness of an expression in a given context, rather than of its correctness. An expression is appropriate in a certain situation, on a certain occasion, in a certain locality, among certain people; it may be inappropriate in another situation, on another occasion, in another locality, among other people.

But saying this much hardly solves your difficulties in deciding what is or is not appropriate in various situations. You have a right to expect some firm assistance on such questions from an English handbook, in spite of the relativity in usage that we all recognize. Your questions will no doubt arise in a number of cases where the current status of an expression is debatable, and the list that follows is intended to help you respond intelligently to some of these cases, as well as to those many other cases of confusing or troublesome usage where no argument exists.

In considering this matter of status, important in perhaps half the items in our guide, we will speak of three classifications of language, conscious as we do so of the artificial nature of such constructions. First, there are all those words and expressions that are part of Standard Literary

English, and as a matter of fact these account for most of the words in the language. Very many words in Standard English are appropriate on any occasion, formal or informal, anywhere. Second, we label certain expressions Colloquial or Informal, which simply means that these expressions are perfectly natural in most conversations, and perhaps in some informal writing, but are usually not appropriate in formal expository writing. An example is the expression *I guess:* "I guess his analysis was correct." Most problems of usage arise from a failure to recognize and avoid the Colloquial-Informal in the writing of serious essays. (The fact remains, of course, that many fine writers of serious prose are able to modify their formality of style by the deliberate, occasional use of informal language. Their skill depends, naturally, on a high sensitivity to the current status of words, so that just the right mixture can be concocted.) Finally, there is a small body of language that simply has to be called Illiterate. For example, to use the phrase *could of* for *could have* ("I could of come if I'd wanted to") is conceivable in writing only if you are quoting someone who uses language of that sort.

As we have said, there are some expressions whose current status is a matter of argument, and their number is probably increasing in our fast-changing society. For example, no one can tell just when it will become widely acceptable to use such words as *put-down* or *hassle* in formal prose—if it ever will. Similar fluid and unpredictable conditions in words have reached a point where, as noted earlier, the editors of *Webster's Third New International Dictionary* (1971) have simply omitted such labels as *colloq.* in many of their dubious entries. This does not of course mean that these editors believe the status of all language is the same, but simply that the status of current English words has become so complicated and various that strict labels would be misleading.

You can learn much that is both useful and entertaining by following some of these controversies, or by examining the recent history of some fast-changing expressions. The books listed below, arranged in chronological order, will

37

help you pursue a study of any doubtful expressions you choose. (Our own guide contains only a small fraction of the words included in a full dictionary of usage.) It is important to recognize, however, that popular usage, in conversation or in informal writing, is *not* the same as usage in formal expository prose. For our purposes in this handbook, the differences matter. Although colloquial expressions may often be included in serious formal writing, they are usually effective only when the writer is clearly aware of the shifts in tone that he or she is introducing. The books below, and our guide to usage, should help you become aware of the available choices, so that you can be genuinely discriminating in your acts of composition. (For further examples, see §20, "Similar Forms.")

BERGEN EVANS and CORNELIA EVANS, *A Dictionary of Contemporary American Usage.* New York: Random House, 1957.

MARGARET M. BRYANT, *Current American Usage.* New York: Funk & Wagnalls, 1962.

H. W. FOWLER, *A Dictionary of Modern English Usage.* 2nd ed., revised by Sir Ernest Gowers. New York: Oxford University Press, 1965.

WILSON FOLLETT et al., *Modern American Usage: A Guide.* New York: Hill and Wang, 1966.

ROY H. COPPERUD, *American Usage: The Consensus.* New York: Van Nostrand Reinhold, 1970.

EDWIN NEWMAN, *Strictly Speaking: Will America Be the Death of English?* Indianapolis: Bobbs-Merrill, 1974.

a, an. Use *a* before a word beginning with any consonant sound except silent *h*. EXAMPLES: *a book, a tree, a European, a union, a house.* Use *an* before a word beginning with a vowel sound. EXAMPLES: *an American, an onion, an hour, an honorable man.*

above. Used awkwardly as a transition: "As we pointed out *above.* . . ." A better transition would be *Therefore* or *Consequently.*

accelerate, exhilarate. Sometimes confused because of resemblance in sound. To *accelerate* is to quicken or speed up. To *exhilarate* is to arouse joy, to give pleasure. EXAMPLE: *An exhilarating experience can accelerate the heartbeat.*

accept, except. Often confused because of resemblance in

524

sound. *Accept* means to receive, to agree to; *except* means to exclude or make an exception. EXAMPLES: *He accepted the invitation. She was excepted from the list of guests.*

acquiesce. Use *acquiesce in; to* and *with* are vague.

A.D., B.C. Should be placed *before* the date: "A.D. 1540," B.C. *follows* the date: "85 B.C."

ad. This clipped form and others like it (such as *math, exam, bike*) are appropriate in informal speech, but in formal writing the words usually appear in full.

adapt, adept, adopt. To *adapt* is to change something for a purpose. *Adept* (adjective or noun) means skillful, or one skilled. To *adopt* is to take possession of. EXAMPLES: *He adapted the motor to another current. He was adept at fixing electric appliances. She was an adopted child.*

adverse, averse. *Adverse* means antagonistic or unfavorable; *averse* means disinclined. EXAMPLES: *He was a victim of adverse fortune. The company president was averse to his suggestion.*

advice, advise. *Advice* is a noun, *advise* a verb. EXAMPLES: *She refused to heed his advice about swimming there. We asked Paul to advise us about home loans.*

affect, effect. A famliar confusion. To *affect* is to influence. To *effect* means to bring about. *Effect* as a noun means result, what has been brought about. EXAMPLES: *The strike will affect the industry. The effect of the strike will be severe. The labor board will try to effect a settlement.*

aggravate. *Aggravate* means to intensify, to increase. Colloquially it means to irritate, to annoy. COLLOQUIAL: *The speaker's mannerisms aggravated everyone.* FORMAL: *The speaker's mannerisms annoyed everyone.*

agree to, agree with. You *agree that* something is true. You *agree to* a proposal. You *agree with* a person. One thing *agrees with* (corresponds with) another.

aggression. Use the singular *aggression*. Avoid the plural as a general statement of your feelings: "I got rid of my *aggression* by kicking the chair." *Hostility* or *frustration* would be more precise in this context.

ain't. Colloquial. Avoid its use in your writing.

all right. See *alright.*

allude, refer. *Allude* means to refer to a person or thing indirectly or by suggestion. EXAMPLE: *When the teacher spoke of "budding Swifts," every student wondered to whom he was alluding.* To *refer* to something means to mention it specifically. EXAMPLE: *I shall now take time to refer to the question of smoking on the campus.*

37

37

allusion, illusion. An *allusion* is an indirect reference. (See *allude.*) An *illusion* is a deceptive appearance or false notion. The two words have nothing in common except a resemblance in sound.

a lot. Should not be written as "alot."

already, all ready. *Already,* an adverb, means by this time, before this time. *All ready,* two words, means entirely ready or that everyone is ready. EXAMPLES: *The war had already started. The men were all ready to go.*

alright. The correct spelling is *all right. Alright* is a colloquial expression.

alternately, alternatively. *Alternately* means to follow one another by turns; *alternatively* means to choose between two things. EXAMPLES: *The contestants answered questions alternately. She decided alternatively not to go with him.*

altogether, all together. *Altogether* (one word) is an adverb meaning entirely, completely, on the whole. *All together* means in a group. EXAMPLES: *He was altogether too generous. They were all together again at last.*

alumnus, alumna, alumni, alumnae. A male graduate is an *alumnus,* a female an *alumna;* male graduates are *alumni,* females *alumnae.* In current usage *alumni* frequently serves to describe graduates of coeducational colleges.

A.M., P.M., a.m., p.m. Should not be used for *in the morning, in the afternoon.* Correct only with the name of the hour.

among, between. *Among* is used with three or more things or persons, as: "They divided the property *among* six relatives"; "talk this over *among* yourselves." *Between* usually refers to two things or persons, as: "Let nothing stand *between* you and me"; "much must be done *between* sunrise and breakfast." *Between* can sometimes refer to more than two things in such expressions as: "*between* the leaves of a book"; or "the agreement *between* France, West Germany, and England."

amoral, immoral. *Amoral* describes acts not subject to moral or ethical judgments; *immoral* means consciously violating moral principles. EXAMPLES: *Because he lacks a sense of right and wrong, his actions must be considered amoral. The sadistic games of the camp guards were immoral.*

amount, number. *Amount* refers to quantity; *number* refers to things that can be counted. EXAMPLES: *the number of pages, the amount of steel.*

526

37

analyzation. No such word. The writer means *analysis*.

and etc. *Etc.,* for *et cetera,* means "and so forth." *And etc.* is obviously redundant. In any case it is better for most purposes not to use the abbreviation.

angry at, angry with. *Angry at* is used when a thing or situation is concerned; *angry with* when a person is involved.

ante-, anti-. Both are prefixes, but *ante-* means before, *anti-,* against.

any place, anyplace. These are colloquial forms for *anywhere,* like *no place* for *nowhere,* *every place* for *everywhere,* and *some place* for *somewhere.*

anyways, anywheres. Colloquial forms of *anyway* and *anywhere,* to be avoided in formal prose.

a piece, apiece. *A piece* is a noun; *apiece* is an adverb. EXAMPLE: *All those present are to have a piece of pie apiece.*

apprehend, comprehend. To *apprehend* something is to perceive its *meaning;* to *comprehend* a system or a theory is to understand it completely. EXAMPLES: *I think I apprehend the sense of that word. I don't think I will ever comprehend the meaning of love.*

apt, likely, liable. *Apt* suggests a habitual or inherent tendency. *likely* suggests a probability. *Liable* suggests a chance, a risk of some sort, or a danger. But in American speech all three are often used to mean a probability and nothing more. EXAMPLES: *She is apt to be irritable because she is not well. A cheerful boy is likely to succeed. You are liable to break your neck if you climb that rock.*

as. (1) Highly colloquial when used in place of *that* or *whether.* EXAMPLE: *I cannot say as I care much for that.* (2) *As* in the sense of *because* is frowned upon by some writers, but is widely current in speech and writing nevertheless, especially in clauses at the beginnings of sentences. EXAMPLE: *As I was free that day, I went along with him.*

as—as, so—as. In negative statements some careful writers prefer *so—as* to *as—as.* At present, *as—as* seems to be established in both speech and writing for both positive and negative statements. For negative statements in a very formal style, *so—as* is probably preferable. EXAMPLES: *Your promise is as good as your bond.* FORMAL: *A vast army is not so important as a well-equipped air force.* INFORMAL: *A vast army is not as important as a well-equipped air force.*

aspect. A clichéd word with no concrete basis when used as

527

37

a synonym for *consideration,* as in: "There are many *aspects* of this problem." Use more precise words, such as *parts* or *sides.* (*Facet,* like *aspect,* has been overused without any hint of its literal meaning.)

assume, presume. *Assume* connotes taking something for granted, while *presume* implies a more forceful or defensive attitude. EXAMPLES: *Let us assume that the statement is true. You presume too much in your claim.*

at. Redundant, in both speech and writing, in such sentences as: "Where are we *at* now?" "Where does he live *at?*"

at this point in time, at the present moment. The writer means *now.* Testimony in Congressional hearings has engendered such silly redundancies as "within this time frame" and "time bracket." Be sure that these redundancies do not creep into *your* prose.

avocation, vocation. A *vocation* is one's principal life work. An *avocation* is not. EXAMPLE: *His vocation was medicine; his avocation was collecting stamps.*

awake, wake, waken. For the most part these verbs are interchangeable. *Awake* is widely favored for *becoming awake:* "I *awoke* at noon." *Wake* is better suited for transitive constructions: "I *waked* him at noon." For passive constructions, *waken* is probably best: "I was *wakened* at noon."

award, reward. You are given an *award* in a formal and specific sense, while *reward,* though it may be a specific amount of money or a gift, may also be used in an unofficial or general context. EXAMPLES: *Elizabeth Taylor won the acting award. Faye Dunaway didn't win the award, but her reward was the consolation of her friends.*

awful, awfully. Colloquially these words, and others like *frightful, terribly, shocking, disgusting,* are used as mild intensives. Often they mean little more than *very.* In formal writing, *awful* and *awfully* should be saved for their precise meaning, to describe something truly awe inspiring. EXAMPLE: *He accepted the awful responsibility of carrying on the war.*

bad, badly. In formal and informal writing *bad* should not be used as an adverb meaning severely ("My feet hurt *bad*"), or as a predicate adjective meaning impressive or well-dressed ("In his new suit he looked *bad*"). *Badly* may be used to mean "very much" only in the negative sense: "Her face was *badly* burned."

528

balance. When used for the *remainder, the rest,* it is usually considered colloquial, COLLOQUIAL USES: *The balance of the crew will be released. We listened to records the balance of the evening.* FORMAL: *The rest of the crew will be released.*

basically, essential. These adverbs should be avoided in such sentences as: "*Basically,* the Administration has a plan to end the war." "This is *essentially* what the president means." They add nothing to the meaning of the sentence.

because. Often used in informal speech, and sometimes in literary English, as a substitute for *that* in constructions like "the reason was *because.* . . ." *That* is still preferable in formal written prose.

being. This participle is frequently used redundantly in student writing: "The players were unhappy, with the better ones *being* ready to quit the team." Notice that *being* provides a too easy means of adding afterthoughts to the main clause. It can be dropped without any loss of coherence.

being as, being that. Dialectal for *since, because.* EXAMPLE: *Since* (not *being as*) *it is long past midnight, we should abandon the search.*

beside, besides. According to present usage, *beside* is used as a preposition meaning at the side of, as in: "Please sit down *beside* me." *Besides* is ordinarily used as an adverb, meaning in addition to, as in: "There were no casualties *besides* the one reported earlier."

between. See *among.*

between you and I. The writer means *between you and me. Between,* a preposition, requires the objective pronoun *me.*

broke. Colloquial when used as an adjective to mean poverty-stricken or short of cash.

bunch. Colloquial when used to mean several, a group. EXAMPLES: *We saw a group* (not *a bunch*) *of men near the gate. Several* (not *a bunch*) *of them belonged to another union.*

but however, but yet. These expressions are redundant. *However, yet, nevertheless, probably* should stand alone.

but what, but that. Formerly considered colloquial. *But that* now appears to be standard literary English in sentences like: "I don't doubt *but that* he is disappointed." *But what* should not be used to refer to persons. Most careful writers still prefer a simple *that* to both these expressions. EXAMPLE: *There is no doubt that* (not *but what* or *but that*) *the president wishes to avoid war.*

37

can, may. In formal usage, *may* implies permission or possibility, *can* implies ability. In informal usage, *can* is very often used in the sense of *may*. INFORMAL: *Mother, can I go now? Can't we stay up until midnight? No, you can't.* FORMAL: *Sir, may I go now? The delegate can speak three languages.*

cannot help but, can't help but. These forms are widely used in speech and by some writers in formal prose.

can't hardly. A double negative, objectionable in conversation, unacceptable in formal writing.

case, instance. *In the case, instance of* is a circumlocution. Note that *for* can be substituted for *in the case of* in the following sentence: "Who is to blame *in the case of* John's failure?"

cause and reason. *Cause* is what produces an effect; *reason* is what man produces to account for the effect, or to justify it. EXAMPLES: *His reasons for going were excellent. The cause of his departure remained a mystery.*

cause of. To say that the *cause of* something was *on account of* is a muddled construction. EXAMPLES: *The cause of my late theme was my having* (not *on accout of I had*) *too much work to do. The cause of my late theme was the fact that I had too much work to do.* Both of these sentences, however, are awkward. It may be better to avoid the *cause-of* construction entirely and simply say, "My theme is late because I had too much to do."

censor, censure. A *censor* (who is censorious) is one who supervises public morals, expurgates literature, and so on. *Censure* is adverse judgment, condemnation.

center around. *Center* means a point, not a circle. *Center on* makes more sense, but even this expression is a circumlocution: "The question *centers on* a failure of communication." ("The question *is. . . .*")

climactic, climatic. *Climactic* has to do with climax, as: "The play had reached a *climactic* moment." *Climatic* has to do with climate, as: "*Climatic* conditions in Bermuda are ideal."

close proximity. Redundant.

compare to, compare with, contrast. *Compare to* means to represent as similar. *Compare with* means to examine the differences and similarities of two things. To *contrast* two things is to examine the differences between them. EXAMPLES: *One may compare some men to wolves. One may compare the novels of Dreiser with those of Zola. The novels of Dreiser can be contrasted to those of James.*

complementary, complimentary. *Complementary* means completing or making up what is lacking; *complimentary* means paying a compliment or giving something as a courtesy. EXAMPLES: *His personality and hers are complementary. The note about John's performance was highly complimentary.*

comprise, compose. *Comprise* means include; *compose* means make up. *Comprise* is used mistakenly in: "The university is *comprised* of faculty, staff, and administrators." The sentence should read: "The faculty, staff, and administrators *compose* (or *constitute*) the university."

concept, idea. *Concept* means a generalized or abstract notion which characterizes elements of a class. *Idea* is a broader term and generally more suitable than *concept* or *conception*. Note that *concept* would be too narrow a word in the following sentence: "My *idea* received little comment from the manager."

contact. Widely used in the sense of *communicate with, meet, interview,* but it should be used sparingly, if at all, in preference to the more exact expressions.

contemptible, contemptuous. *Contemptible* is used to describe something or someone deserving contempt, while *contemptuous* means expressing contempt. EXAMPLES: *She told him his behavior was contemptible. He was contemptuous of my argument.*

continual, continuous. Any event that recurs at intervals is *continual; continuous* means uninterrupted. EXAMPLES: *We were bothered by the continual dripping of the faucet. When I tried to repair the faucet, I was greeted by a continuous stream of water.*

contractions. Less appropriate in formal writing, where they are occasionally found, than in speech and informal writing, where they are entirely at home. EXAMPLES: *I'd like to go, but I'm tired. Can't he explain it to you, or doesn't he care?*

convince, persuade. The following sentences illustrate the differing connotations of these two words: "I *convinced* her that she was wrong." "I *persuaded* her to join our group." *Convince* means winning agreement; *persuade* means moving to action.

could of. Illiterate for *could have.*

couple. Colloquial for *two, a few, several.* COLLOQUIAL: *A couple of men left the theater.* FORMAL: *Two (or several) men left the theater.* Standard for a man and woman married, betrothed, or otherwise appearing as partners.

credible, credulous. An event, fact, argument is *credible* when it is believable; you are said to be *credulous* if you are easily convinced, or gullible.

criteria. The plural form of *criterion.*

37

cute. A colloquialism to describe attractive children and small animals. Not to be used in formal writing.

data, strata, phenomena. These are the plurals of *datum, stratum,* and *phenomenon.* At present these words seem to be in a transitional stage, inasmuch as some good writers and speakers use them as singular forms while others believe strongly that only the correct Latin forms should be used. There is no doubt, however, that a mixture of forms is undesirable, as: "Although the *data* collected at the laboratory are vouched for by several scientists, much of it has to be restudied."

date. Inappropriately colloquial when referring to an appointment with the dean, but perfectly acceptable when referring to Saturday night at the movies.

deal. Used figuratively in phrases like "square *deal*," "new *deal*." Informal in the sense of a commercial transaction or political bargain. COLLOQUIAL: *Good deal!* But with the indefinite article it is literary English, as: "a good *deal* of trouble."

decimate. To reduce by one tenth, not to destroy entirely.

deduce, deduct. *Deduce* is used to mean infer; *deduct* means to take away. EXAMPLES: *We deduced a certain dislike in his actions. The company deducted ten dollars from her pay.*

denotation, connotation. Use *denotation* when referring to a word's specific meaning; use *connotation* when speaking of a word's implications.

deprecate, depreciate. *Deprecate* means to express regret over, or disapproval of, while *depreciate* means to lessen the value of.

device, devise. A *device* is an instrument for performing some action. To *devise* something is to invent it, to contrive or plan it.

dichotomy. A splitting into parts or pairs. The word is now overused, especially in contexts where *difference* or *split* is more appropriate.

differ from, differ with. One thing *differs from* another. One person *differs with* another when he disputes or quarrels with him. One may also *differ from* a person when he disagrees with him.

different from, different than. Both forms have been used by good writers. At present, *different from* seems to be preferred when a single word follows it, as in: "His suggestion is *different from* mine." When a clause follows, many speakers and writers use *than* to avoid a round-about construction, as in: "This group of engineers will use a very *different* method of extracting the ore *than* the old Quebec miners used."

discreet, discrete.   A *discreet* person is tactful or judicious; a *discrete* matter is distinct or separate from another.

dissociate, disassociate.   These words mean the same thing, but *dissociate* is more common in modern usage.

double negative.   An expression in which two or more negatives are used to make the negative more emphatic is of course illiterate. EXAMPLES: *Nobody never tells me nothing. We ain't seen nobody.* Another type of concealed double negative appears in a very small number of expressions like *can't hardly, didn't hardly, wouldn't scarcely.* These expressions are not appropriate in writing, though they are widely heard in speech. A third type of deliberate double negative is entirely correct, and common in formal writing. EXAMPLES: *The brief rest was not unwelcome. These people were not uneducated.* (Notice that these expressions are more cautious and moderate than the corollary affirmative statements: *The brief rest was welcome. These people were educated.*)

dove.   The most generally used form is *dived,* though *dove* has been widely used in speech and occasionally in writing.

dubious, doubtful.   The result of an action or the truth of a statement may be *dubious,* while the person who questions either is *doubtful.*

due to, owing to.   *Due to* was originally an adjective, and no one questions its use in sentences like these: "His lameness was *due to* an accident." "The spring floods, *due to* prolonged rains, did much damage to the stockyards." The adverbial use of *due to* is also common, as: *"Due to* an accident, we arrived late." If a more formal tone is desired, the expression *owing to* may be substituted for *due to. Due to the fact that* is a common, and deplorable, substitute for a simple *because.*

each other, one another.   The first refers to two people only, at least in formal discourse. The second refers to more than two. EXAMPLES: *The two senators started hitting each other. The whole senate started hitting one another.*

effect.   See *affect.*

e.g., i.e.   Although these abbreviations are often used interchangeably, *e.g.* means "for example" and *i.e.* means "that is." They should be used only in parenthetical expressions and in footnotes.

533

37

elicit, illicit. You *elicit* a *reaction* or *response* from someone; a person may commit an *illicit act*. EXAMPLES: *His proposal elicited support. Society labels certain acts illicit.*

emigrate, immigrate. Use of these words depends on point of view. You *emigrate* when you leave America for Canada; from Canada's standpoint you have *immigrated* there, and are called an *immigrant.*

eminent, imminent, immanent. *Eminent* means outstanding, noteworthy; *imminent* means impending, threatening; *immanent* means inherent or operating within. EXAMPLES: *Senator Danforth is an eminent statesman. Scientists have predicted the imminent eruption of Mount Douglas. God's power has been described as immanent.*

end up. Unacceptable colloquialism for *end* or *conclude.*

enthuse. U.S. colloquial for "to be enthusiastic" or "to show enthusiasm." Many people dislike it thoroughly. FORMAL: *She never showed any enthusiasm* (not *enthused*) *about grand opera.*

equally as good. This may be wordy, but many educated people use the expression. It means "equally good," or "just as good." EXAMPLE: *My composition was just as good* (not *equally as good*) *as his.*

escalate. A currently attractive but inaccurate substitute for *increase. Escalate* means specifically to increase in intensity or size by calculated stages.

et al. Proper in footnotes and bibliographical lists, *et al.* means "and other people."

etc. See *and etc. Etc.* is to be avoided at the end of a series when the reader cannot grasp the reference. EXAMPLE: *All his friends—John, Al, Len, etc.—were invited.*

euphemism, euphuism. A *euphemism* is a mild or roundabout word which is substituted for another word thought to be too harsh or blunt ("passed away" for "died"). *Euphuism* is an artificially elegant style of writing that was popular in Renaissance England.

everyone, every one. EXAMPLES: *Everyone has arrived by now. Every one of those dishes must be washed thoroughly.*

exam. See *ad.*

except. See *accept.*

exception that proves the rule. A confusing cliché that should be avoided in formal and informal writing.

exhilarate. See *accelerate.*

expect. Colloquial in the sense of *suppose.*

facet. See *aspect.*

37

fact that. This expression can be easily deleted, thereby achieving economy and directness. "I was shocked by *the fact that* you behaved so childishly" should be rewritten: "I was shocked by your childish behavior."

fallacy. The word has a specific meaning in logic: a formal mistake in reasoning or in the conclusion of an argument. It should not be used when *mistake* or *error* is meant in the general sense.

farther, further. The fine distinction between these two words, and between the superlative forms, *farthest, furthest,* is that both can be used to speak of distance, but that *further* and *furthest* have an additional meaning of "additional." STANDARD USAGE: *They could go no farther. The Johansen party penetrated furthest into the jungle. The senator promised further revelations soon.*

faze. American slang or colloquial for *disconcert, worry, disturb, bother, daunt.* It has no connection with *phase.* COLLOQUIAL: *He wasn't fazed by the amount of work he had to do.*

feel. A spineless substitute for *think* or *believe,* in such examples as "I *feel* that the United Nations is doing more harm than good." Don't feel it—just say it.

fewer, less. Use *fewer* when referring to numbers. Use *less* when referring to quantity or degree. (See also *amount, number.*) EXAMPLES: *There will be fewer* (not *less*) *men on the campus next year. Most women are earning less than they did last year.*

finalize. Many are irritated by this and other recent coinages from business and officialese: *optionalize, prioritize.* Avoid these verbs in your writing. Also see *contact.*

fine. See *nice.* A vague word of approval, entirely proper in conversation, but in exact writing a more exact word should be used.

first and foremost. A cliché—avoid it like the plague (another cliché).

fix. Colloquial in the sense of *predicament,* as: "The headmaster was in a predicament (not *fix*)." Also colloquial in the sense of *arrange* or *prepare.* COLLOQUIAL: *Give me a few minutes more to fix my hair.*

flaunt, flout. You may *flaunt* your intelligence or your sexual prowess, but you *flout* rules and conventions when you *ignore* them.

flunk. Colloquial for *fail.*

folks. Colloquial for *relatives, family.*

former, latter. Use only when referring to two items which

535

37

your reader will clearly recognize. To avoid needless confusion, simply repeat the items. EXAMPLE: *Doctors and lawyers are fighting vigorously over malpractice insurance rates; lawyers* (not *the latter*) *have an advantage because of their expert knowledge.*

formulate. Use only when you mean *state systematically.* EXAMPLE: *She formulated a new approach to teaching preschool children.* Otherwise, use *form.*

fun. Not to be used as an adjective: "a *fun* thing to do." This is a transitory colloquialism.

funny. Colloquial for *strange, queer, odd.*

gap. Such expressions as *generation gap* or *credibility gap* are clichés—avoid them.

get. *Get* has a large number of uses, both formal and informal. In formal or literary contexts, it means obtain, receive, procure, acquire. In informal and conversational usage, it has a large number of meanings, figurative, idiomatic, and otherwise. In speech *have got* in the sense of *have* is very common. The form *have got* in the sense of *must* or *have to* is felt to be more emphatic. *Got* and *gotten* are both past participles found in speech and in writing.

graduate. The passive *was graduated* is no longer required in formal usage. "She *graduated* from Wisconsin" is proper in formal and informal writing.

guess. The expression *I guess* is too colloquial for most formal prose. Write *I suppose,* or *I presume,* or *I assume.*

guys. Colloquial for *friends* or *companions.*

had better, had best, had rather. Correct idiomatic forms, as are *would better, would best, would rather.*

had ought, hadn't ought. Colloquial. It is easy to substitute *ought, should, should have, shouldn't have,* all forms appropriate in both speech and writing.

hanged, hung. People are *hanged;* objects are *hung.* EXAMPLES: *The murderer was hanged. The clothes were hung on the line.*

hangup. Colloquial for *problem, inhibition, perversion.* Precisely because it is too often used to mean any one or all of these states, *hangup* should be avoided in your writing.

hardly, scarcely. See *double negative.*

hassle. Colloquial for *problem, conflict, annoyance, fuss.*

have got. See *get.*

healthy, healthful. Strictly, *healthy* means being in a state of health; *healthful* means serving to promote health. People are healthy, but good food is healthful.

536

hear, listen. *Hear* means auditing any sound; *listen* means focusing your hearing. EXAMPLE: *She listened for his voice but heard only the birds' song.*

hopefully. When used in the sense of *it is hoped* (i.e., "Hopefully we can agree on a price"), the word is inappropriate.

humaneness, humanity. Both words may be used to mean possessing compassion or sympathy, but *humanity* is also used to describe human kind. There is no such word as *humanness.*

identify, relate. These words should not be used without the reflexive pronoun. EXAMPLES: *I identify myself with Othello's fate. He cannot relate himself to any institution.* In most cases other constructions are more exact: "I feel a strong identity with Othello's fate."

if, whether. Both *if* and *whether* are used to introduce a noun clause in indirect questions after verbs like *doubt, ask, wonder. Whether* is more likely to be used if an alternative introduced by *or* is stated. There is still some feeling among teachers and writers that *whether* is more formal, but both words are used and have been used for many years to introduce noun clauses. EXAMPLES: *I doubt if they can come. He wondered whether or not he should warn the settlers. Ask him if he has any food left.*

ignorant, stupid. *Ignorant* means lacking knowledge of, while *stupid* means unable to comprehend. EXAMPLES: *She was ignorant of the facts in the case. Running into other cars is a stupid habit.*

illusion. See *allusion.*

imply, infer. *Imply* means to indicate or suggest without stating; *infer* means to derive or conclude a meaning. EXAMPLES: *The professor implied that her answer was wrong. She inferred a different meaning from his words.*

important. *More important,* not *importantly,* is the correct adverbial usage of the word.

in, into. In theory, the distinction between these words is that *in* denotes location inside something, whereas *into* denotes motion from outside to inside something. In practice, however, *in* is also used in the sense of *into.* EXAMPLES: *Throw that in the waste basket. Please jump in the lake.* "Are you *into* painting?" is a colloquialism.

in back of, back of. Both forms, still considered by many to belong to informal speech, have been used in writing for some time. The more formal word is *behind.*

in conclusion, in summary. Use of such expressions as introductions to the final paragraph of your essay is awkward and

537

37

mechanical. Simply state your conclusion (your reader can *see* that you have reached your last paragraph) without this rhetorical throat-clearing.

in terms of, in connection with. Officialese. These phrases should be avoided, as they add nothing to the import of sentences. EXAMPLE: *(In terms of sheer power,) Hank Aaron is the best home run hitter in baseball.*

in this day and age. Cliché. Use *now*.

ingenious, ingenuous. An *ingenious* person is inventive, or clever; an *ingenuous* person is unaffected, or artless. EXAMPLES: *The general's plan showed ingenious thinking. Tom is so ingenuous he didn't realize that he was being tricked.*

insightful. A recently invented adjective, which has quickly become overworked: "an *insightful* person," "an *insightful* comment." It is probably better to declare that "She *showed insight*" or that hers was "a *perceptive* remark."

irony, ironic. Use *irony* or *ironic* only when there is a *dramatic* discrepancy between what is said and what is meant, or between what is supposed to happen and what does happen. It is a *coincidence* if two people with the same car models have an accident. It is *ironic* if both are members of the National Safety Council.

irregardless. The writer means *regardless*.

is when, is where. These expressions when used in definitions appear awkward and juvenile.

its, it's. *Its* is the possessive form of *it*. *It's* is the contraction of *it is*. The two forms should not be confused.

kind, sort. In colloquial usage, these words are often felt to be plural in constructions like this: "These *kind* of dogs are usually hard to train." In more formal situations, both in speech and in writing, most people prefer the singular, as: "I do not like this *sort* of entertainment." "That *kind* of man is not to be trusted."

kind of, sort of. Colloquial when used to modify a verb or an adjective. Use *somewhat, somehow, a little, in some degree, rather, for some reason* in formal contexts.

lay, lie. The principal parts of *lay* are as follows: "Now I *lay* it down"; "I *laid* it down"; "I have *laid* it down." The principal parts of *lie* are these: "I *lie* down"; "I *lay* down yesterday morning"; "the dog *had lain* in the shade all day." The participles of *lie* and *lay* are *lying* and *laying*. STANDARD: *He had laid* (not

37

lain) his bundle on the table. It had lain (not *laid*) *there all morning. The dog was lying* (not *laying*) *in the road.*

lead, led. The past tense of *lead* (pronounced *leed*) is *led* (pronounced like the metal *lead*).

leave, let. It is just as correct to say *leave him alone* as *let him alone*. But *leave* cannot be used for *allow* in such a sentence as "I begged my mother to *leave* me do it."

lend, loan. Generally speaking, *lend* should be used as a verb, *loan* as a noun. EXAMPLES: *I lent him ten dollars. We signed many forms to get the loan.*

less. Often used in place of *fewer* with collective nouns: "*less* clothes, *less* people." But say *fewer hats, fewer persons.*

liable, likely. See *apt.*

lie. See *lay.*

like, as, as if. In written English, *as* and *as if* introduce clauses; *like* generally governs a noun or pronoun. In speech the substitution of *like* for *as* is widespread. It is probable that the use of *like* as a conjunction will eventually gain acceptance in formal writing. It has not done so yet. INFORMAL: *I wish you would do it like I said you should.* FORMAL: *The war, just as he had predicted, lasted more than five years. Few men could sway an audience as he did.*

line. Often vague and redundant, as: "Have you anything interesting in the *line* of fiction?" "He wrote epics and other works along that *line.*" BETTER: *Have you any interesting novels? He wrote epics and other narrative poems.*

locate. In the sense of *settle,* it is appropriate only in informal use.

lose, loose. These two words are often confused. Careless writers sometimes write *loose* when they mean *lose.* You may *lose* a game or your keys. When screws are *loose* they should be tightened.

lots, lots of. Widely used colloquially for *many, much, a large number, a large amount, a great deal.* COLLOQUIAL: *He has a lot to learn. There are lots of exceptions to this rule.*

mad. Colloquially *mad* is used in the sense of *angry.* In formal usage it means *insane.*

majority. Inaccurate when used with measures of quantity, time, distance. The appropriate word is *most.* EXAMPLE: *Most of the day* (not *the majority of the day*) *we stood in line and waited. Most people* (not *the vast majority*) support some form of gun control.

material, materiel. *Material* means any kind of substance, while *materiel* refers specifically to arms or other military equipment.

may be, maybe. Don't confuse the two. EXAMPLES: *The plane may be late. Maybe the pilot had trouble with the weather.*

media. The plural of *medium.* This word is now overworked as a shorthand label for newspapers, radio, and television. Be specific; write "the newspaper reporter," not "the *media* representative."

might of. Illiterate for *might have.*

mighty. Colloquial for *very.* Unacceptable in most writing.

militate, mitigate. *Militate* means to have influence (used with *against); mitigate* means to make less severe. EXAMPLES: *Conditions militate against a peaceful solution. The extra pay mitigates the tedium of the work.*

most, almost. *Most,* in formal written English, is the superlative form of *much* or *many.* EXAMPLES: *Much food, more food, most food, many men, more men, most men. Almost* is an adverb meaning nearly. In colloquial use *most* is often substituted for *almost.* FORMAL: *Almost* (not *Most*) *all of our friends have returned from college.* In conversational usage, *most* is frequently used to qualify *all, everyone, everybody, anyone, anybody, always.*

much, many. *Much* should not be used in place of *many* with most plural nouns. EXAMPLES: *There was too much food. There were too many courses.*

nauseous, nauseated. Something that causes nausea is *nauseous;* a person experiencing nausea is *nauseated.* EXAMPLES: *The fish had a nauseous odor. He became nauseated after eating it.*

neat. When used as a general honorific ("That's *neat!*"), it is another overused and transitory colloquialism, like *the greatest,* or *fun* (adjective). To be avoided in writing.

neither, nor; either, or. *Neither* should be followed by *nor* and *either* by *or.* Both *neither* and *either* may be used with more than two alternatives, as: "*Either* past, present, *or* future. . . ."

nice. Strictly used, *nice* means discriminating. When used as a vague word of mild approval, it is to be avoided in serious writing.

no good, no-good. Colloquial when used for *worthless, useless, of no value.*

no one. Not *noone.*

now. An adverb, not an adjective, as in "This is the *now* generation." Be on guard against letting such jargon creep into your writing.

37

nowhere near, nowheres near. The first is common in both speech and writing; the second is common in colloquial speech. In formal writing it is better to use *not nearly.* EXAMPLE: *That was not nearly* (not *nowhere near*) *as much as he had expected.*

O, oh. *O* is used with another word, a substantive, usually in direct address, often in poetry. It is always capitalized and is not followed by any mark of punctuation. *Oh* is an exclamation, not capitalized except when it begins a sentence, and is followed by either a comma or an exclamation point.

obviate. *Obviate* means to dispose of or provide for, as in "The arms agreement *obviated* the risk of war." It does not mean to make obvious.

occur, take place. *Occur* is a broader term than *take place,* which is properly used to refer to planned activities. EXAMPLES: *The accident occurred on the corner. The trial will take place on June 10th.*

of, have. never use "would *of*" or "should *of*" for "would *have*" or "should *have*."

off of. The *of* is unnecessary. EXAMPLE: *He took the book off* (not *off of*) *the shelf.*

O.K. Colloquial.

on account of. The writer means *because of.*

one another. See *each other.*

oral, verbal. *Oral* refers to spoken language; *verbal* refers to all words, spoken or written.

orient, orientate. Modern usage generally prefers *orient* to *orientate,* as in: "We waited until we became *oriented* to the campus rules."

out loud. Somewhat less formal than aloud, loudly, audibly.

outside of. Colloquial for *except, besides.* EXAMPLE: *There was no witness to the robbery except* (not *outside of*) *the mailman.*

over with. Colloquial in the sense of *finished, ended.*

party. Except in legal and telephone usage, *party* is colloquial and semihumorous when it means a person.

past history. *Past* is redundant here.

percent. Used after numbers. The sign % is not used except after figures in tabulations or in technical writing. *Percent* is not an exact synonym for *percentage.*

persecute, prosecute. To *persecute* is to harass or treat oppressively; to *prosecute* is to bring suit against, with a legal connotation.

personal, personally. Students are understandably disposed to hedge their bets, with expressions like *in my personal opinion,* *personally I believe, my view is,* and so on. In essays on literary interpretation, expressions such as *I get the feeling that . . .* are common. In many cases such qualification weakens the force of what is being said. If you are wrong in what you say, then you are wrong, whether you say it's your personal opinion or not.

plenty. Colloquial when used as an adverb in such expressions as *plenty good, plenty good enough, plenty rich,* and so on, or as an adjective before a noun. COLLOQUIAL: *He was plenty rich. The room is plenty large. There is plenty wood for another fire.* FORMAL: *He was very rich. The room is large enough. There is plenty of wood for another fire. Ten dollars is plenty.*

plus. *Plus* should not be used in place of *moreover* or *in addition.* "I worked overtime; moreover (not *plus*), I had to wait weeks for my paycheck."

P.M. See *A.M., a.m.*

poorly. Colloquial for *in poor health, not well, unwell.*

practicable, practical. *Practicable* means something possible, feasible, usable. *Practical* means useful, not theoretical, experienced. *Practical* may apply to persons, things, ideas; *practicable* may not apply to persons.

predominate, predominant. *Predominate* is a verb, *predominant* an adjective. Be sure to keep these words distinct in your writing. EXAMPLES: *Threatening weather conditions predominate today. He has the predominant army on his side.*

prescribe, proscribe. *Prescribe* means to set down or give directions; *proscribe* means to prohibit.

principal, principle. *Principal* is an adjective or noun meaning chief or first in rank. *Principle* is a noun meaning fundamental law or truth. EXAMPLES: *The principal reason we failed was poor organization. His belief in the principle of fair play guides his behavior.*

proceed, precede. *Proceed* means to go on with; *precede* means to go before. EXAMPLES: *After a short interruption, she proceeded with her analysis. His wife preceded him to the stage.*

prophecy, prophesy. Don't confuse these words. *Prophecy* is a noun ("The *prophecy* came true"), *prophesy* a verb ("He claimed he could *prophesy* the outcome").

proposition, proposal. *Proposal* implies a direct and explicit act of proposing; *proposition* implies a statement or principle for discussion. The loose use of *proposition* to mean an idea, a thing, a task, a business enterprise, a problem is disliked by many people. EXAMPLES: *It is a poor practice* (not proposition) to study until three in the morning. Moving the settlers out of the district was an impractical plan (not *proposition*).

quiet, quite. Two words carelessly confused. *Quiet* has to do with stillness or calmness. In formal standard usage, *quite* means entirely, completely. "You are *quite* right." In informal usage it may also be used to mean very, to a considerable degree. "The dog seems *quite* friendly."

quite a few, quite a bit. Overused in student writing.

raise, rise. Two verbs often confused. The principal parts of *raise:* "I *raise* my hand"; "he *raised* the window"; "they *have raised* the flag." The principal parts of *rise:* "I *rise* in the morning"; "they *rose* before I did"; "they *had risen* at sunset."

rap. Colloquial for *sentence* or *judgment*, as in "a bum *rap*." Recently the word has been used as a verb and noun to mean discuss or debate: "We *rapped* about drug abuse." It is colloquial in this use too.

ravage, ravish. These words are often confused but they mean different things. EXAMPLES: *The city was ravaged (destroyed) by fire. She was ravished (raped) by her abductor. Ravish* also means to carry away or transport with joy or pleasure.

real. *Real* as an adverb, in the sense of *very* ("It was a *real* exciting game") is colloquial. Its formal equivalent is *really*. Both, however, are vague and weak intensifiers, of little use in promoting meaning. See *awful, so, such*.

reason is because. See *because*.

refer. See *allude*.

relation, relationship. These words are used synonymously, though *relationship* means specifically the state of being related. EXAMPLE: *Something has changed in the relationship* (not *relation* or *relations*) *between John and his father*.

relevant. This word should be used with *to*, then a noun: "*relevant to* her beliefs"; "*relevant to* the funds available." Such sentences as "This book is not *relevant*" are vague and misleading. The book is *certainly* relevant to someone's interests, if only to the author's.

same, such. Appropriate in legal documents. In ordinary speech and writing it is better to use *it, this, that*. EXAMPLE: *When you have repaired the watch, please ship it* (not *same*) *to me*.

scene. Colloquial when used in such sentences as "This is a bad *scene*."

see where. For *see that*, as: "I *see* where the team lost another game." Permissible only in colloquial speech.

37

sensibility, sensitivity *Sensibility* means the ability to perceive or feel; *sensitivity* means ready susceptibility to outside influences. EXAMPLES: *The music critic possesses a mature sensibility. The plant's reaction revealed its sensitivity to light.*

sensual, sensuous. *Sensual* usually means lewd or unchaste; *sensuous* means pertaining to the senses. A *sensuous* person is one who puts value in experiences of the senses, but he or she need not be *sensual* in the process.

set, sit. Two verbs often confused. Learn the principal parts: "I *set* it down"; I *have set* it down"; "now he *sits* down"; "I *sat* down"; "they *have sat* down." But of course one may speak of "a *setting* hen," and the sun *sets,* not *sits.* "You may *set* the cup on the shelf and then *sit* down." "I *sat* on the stool after I had *set* the cup down."

shape. Colloquial for *condition.* COLLOQUIAL: *The athlete was in excellent shape.* FORMAL: *The equipment was in very good condition* (not *shape*).

situation, position. Both words are abused in officialese: "Regarding the present *situation . . .*"; "With respect to the president's *position on. . . .*" If you must use these words, try to restrict their connotations as much as possible. EXAMPLE: *Her position on the team was right field.*

so. As a conjunction between main clauses, *so* is much overused in student writing. Usually the primary fault is too little subordination instead of too much use of *so.* EXAMPLES: *The bridge was blown up during the night, and so the attack was delayed. The attack was delayed because the bridge had been blown up during the night. The Russians were not ready, so they waited until August to declare war on Japan. Since the Russians were not ready, they waited until August to declare war on Japan.*

In clauses of purpose, the standard subordinating conjunction is *so that,* as in: "They flew low *so that* they could observe the results of the bombing." But *so* is also used, especially in spoken English.

So as an intensive can be easily overworked in speech and it often is. EXAMPLES: *She is so kind and so charming. The work is so hard.*

social, societal. Social describes society or its organization, persons living in it, or the public. *Societal* should be reserved for describing large social groups, their customs and activities. EXAMPLES: *Excessive drinking is a major social problem. Doctors and lawyers hold opposing societal views.*

544

sort of.   See *kind of.*

state.   Used frequently when *say* is more precise. *State* is appropriate when you mean an official declaration.

strata.   See *data.*

such.   As an intensive, it is used like *awful* or *so.* Also see *real.* *Such* introducing a clause of result is followed by *that.* EXAMPLE: *There was such an explosion that it could be felt for miles.* When introducing a relative clause, *such* is followed by *as.* EXAMPLE: *Such improvements as are necessary will be made immediately.*

sure.   Colloquial for *certainly, surely, indeed.*

tactics, strategy.   *Tactics* means specific actions, while *strategy* means an overall plan. EXAMPLES: *Her tactics included holding long meetings and evading questions. Her strategy was to avoid confrontation.*

temerity, timorousness.   *Temerity* means rashness; *timorousness* means fearfulness. Be sure not to confuse these two words.

that there, this here.   Illiterate forms.

their, they're.   *Their* is a possessive pronoun. *They're* means "they are." EXAMPLE: *They're happy because their team won.*

theirself, theirselves.   Nonstandard for *themselves.*

thorough, through.   An elementary spelling problem.

to, too, two.   Another elementary spelling problem. EXAMPLE: *He too should make two trips to the dictionary to learn how to spell. It's not too hard.* Do not use *too* as a substitute for *very.*

try and.   The writer means *try to.*

type of.   The phrase is excess baggage and should be avoided. EXAMPLES: *He is a moody type of person (a moody person). It is a racing-type bicycle (a racing bicycle).*

use, utilize.   In most cases *utilize* is officialese for *use. Utilize* means specifically to put to use. Note the awkwardness in the following sentence: "To these natives the *utilization* of knives and forks is foreign."

verbal.   See *oral.*

very, very much.   Many educated persons object to *very* instead of *very much* or *very greatly* as a modifier of a verb or a participle in a verb phrase. Other persons point out examples of its use in the works of reputable writers. See the note under *very* in *Webster's Third New International.* EXAMPLES: *They were very pleased. They were very much pleased. They seemed very disturbed. They seemed very greatly disturbed.*

viable.   Now overworked in officialese: "a *viable* alternative." Use *workable* or *practicable* in its place.

37

545

37

vocation. See *avocation*.

wait on. Regional for wait for, stay for. Standard in the sense of attend, perform services for, as: "It was the other girl who waited on me."

want in, want out, want off, etc. Dialectal forms of *want to come in, want to go out, want to get off,* and so forth.

way, ways. *Way* is colloquial for *condition*. *Ways* is dialectal for *distance, way*. FORMAL: *When we saw him, he was in bad health* (not *in a bad way*). *We walked a long distance* (not *ways*) *before we rested*.

where at. The *at* is unnecessary. EXAMPLE: *Where is he now?* (not *Where is he at now?*) A sentence such as "I don't know *where* you're *at* intellectually" is both colloquial and redundant. You may get away with it in speaking but not in writing.

which and that, who and that. *Which* refers to things; *who* refers to people. *That* can refer to either things or people, usually in restrictive clauses. EXAMPLES: *The pictures, which were gaudy and overdecorated, made me wince. The pictures that I bought yesterday were genuine; the others were fake. Who* can also be used in a restrictive clause, as: "I want to see all the people *who* care to see me." With *that,* the same clause is still restrictive: "I want to see all the people *that* care to see me."

while. Frequently overused as a conjunction. Usually *but, and,* or *whereas* would be more precise. It is standard in the sense of *at the same time as* or *although*. It is colloquial in the sense of *whereas*.

who, whom. *Who* should be used for subjects, *whom* for objects of prepositions, direct or indirect objects, subjects and objects of infinitives.

-wise. This suffix has been so absurdly overused that it has become largely a joke. "He is a competent administrator *economy-wise,* but *politics-wise* he is a failure." Avoid.

The Letter

THE FORMAL LETTER AND ITS PARTS

Every letter is a composition. Each is in some degree governed by the considerations that govern other kinds of writing. But when you dash off a note to the deliveryman, you need not worry very much about your grammar and punctuation. Your first draft is probably adequate. On the other hand, a letter to a prospective employer may be the most important document you ever write, one in which every detail may count. The variety of letters is enormous. In every letter you write, however, even the one to the deliveryman, you are explicitly expressing yourself to one other individual. *A letter is not an essay intended for general interest; it is, usually, a private communication between you and another person.* In no other writing, therefore, is the emphasis so heavily on the character of your reader, what you know and expect of that person.

Your letter to the deliveryman probably needs no improvement; the test of it is whether you get the package left next door. Furthermore no one, not even an English teacher, should presume to tell you how to write your most personal correspondence. You know best what ought to go into it. (The history of literature, however, provides many a love letter composed with grace and style, even if true love never did run smooth.)

What a teacher *can* help you to write, and what this chapter is concerned with, are all those relatively formal letters, letters addressed to individuals you don't know intimately or otherwise composed under circumstances inappropriate to a casual style. These include not only letters of application and business letters, but all those letters you have to write to people, especially older people, with whom you are not on easy terms.

Formal letters, then, are governed by considerations similar to those you must have in mind for all compositions. You should be clear, well organized, coherent. You should be careful about spelling, grammar, and punctuation. But in addition to these familiar injunctions, there are certain other laws, or conventions, of usage that the letter writer cannot ignore.

These are the parts of a letter:
1. The heading
2. The inside address.
3. The salutation or greeting.
4. The body of the letter.
5. The complimentary close.
6. The signature.

For each of these parts usage has prescribed certain set forms. These forms should not be ignored or altered, especially in business letters. Conformity, not originality, is a virtue here.

The Heading

The parts of a heading, written in the following order, are *the street address, the name of city or town, the name of the state, the date.* A printed letterhead takes the place of a typed address. On paper with letterheads, the writer types the date either directly under the letterhead or flush with the right-hand margin of the letter.

[Letterhead]

September 23, 1980 [or] September 23, 1980

A growing number of letter writers, influenced possibly by European practice, or by the military services, are writing dates with the number of the day first, the month next, then the year—all without punctuation—for example, 23 September 1980. There is a logic and simplicity to this form that may in time win universal acceptance.

548

On paper that does not have a letterhead, the writer types the heading at the right according to one of the following forms:

Block form with open punctuation—that is, end punctuation is omitted. This form is rapidly becoming almost universal.

```
                    327 East Walnut Street
                    Springdale, Wisconsin 54875
                    September 23, 1980
```

Indented form, with closed punctuation. Final punctuation is usually omitted.

```
                    76 Belmont Street,
                      Canton, Iowa 52542
                        September 23, 1980
```

Whichever form is used, the writer should be consistent throughout the letter—in the heading, in the inside address, and in the address on the envelope.

The Inside Address

In a business letter *the inside address is the address of the person written to.* The envelope of a business letter is often discarded before the letter reaches the intended recipient. Repeating the address ensures that the addressee's identity is not accidentally lost and that it remains on any copy of the letter kept in the sender's files.

In a personal letter the inside address is usually omitted, though it may be added at the bottom of a fairly formal personal letter, in the lower left-hand corner. The first line of the inside address should be flush with the left-hand margin of the letter. Either the block form or the indented form may be used.

```
Mr. H. G. Warren
Warren & Stacey, Builders
132 First Avenue
Ogden, Maine 03907
```

```
Dear Mr. Warren:
```

or

549

```
Parr Oil Company,
  20 Main Street,
    Helena, Illinois  61537
```

Gentlemen:

The block form, illustrated first, is preferred by a majority of letter writers for business purposes.

The name of the person addressed in a business letter should be accompanied by a personal title. The use of a personal title is correct even when a business title follows the name. Common personal titles are *Mr., Mrs., Miss* (or *Ms.*), *Dr., Professor, Messrs.* A business title designating the office or function of an individual should not precede the person's name but should either follow the name immediately if the title is short or, if it is long, appear on the line below.

```
Mr. T. C. Howard
Secretary                 Mr. William R. Jones
Pueblo Rose Society       Personnel Manager

Dr. James L. Pendleton    Ms. Laura Jackson
Director of Admissions    Treasurer, City Action
                          Club
```

The inclusion of a business title usually implies that the writer is addressing the reader in his or her capacity as holder of a particular office or authority. In such cases, answers may properly be made by an assistant who speaks for his or her superior, or by a successor, should the original addressee have left office for some reason.

The Salutation or Greeting

The following forms are correct for business and professional letters:

```
Gentlemen:               Ladies:
Dear Sir:/Dear Sirs:     Dear Madam:
Dear Mr. Jackson:        Dear Miss (or Ms.) White:
```

In personal letters the range of greetings is unlimited, but somewhere between the inappropriately formal *Sirs* or *Madam* at one extreme, and an inappropriately affable *Hi Swinger* at the other, we may mention the following as usually appropriate:

```
Dear Jack,    Dear Mr. Howard,    Dear Miss (or Ms.) Brown,
```

We also ought to be aware that a great deal of modern business is transacted on a first-name basis, even when the relations between the parties are entirely professional.

Correct usage in addressing government officials and other dignitaries will be found in a good desk dictionary such as *Webster's New World Dictionary,* the *American College Dictionary,* or *Webster's Eighth New Collegiate Dictionary.* Local newspapers will also provide titles and addresses of government officials.

A colon is used after the salutation in a business letter; either a colon or a comma may be used in a personal letter. A comma is considered less formal. A dash—appropriate enough for a letter to an intimate friend—should be avoided in formal letters.

The Body of the Letter

The composition of business letters is a subject much too complex to be discussed here except in a very introductory way. A good letter, again, obeys the principles of any good writing. It should be clear, direct, coherent, and courteous. A student who can write a good class paper ought to be able to write a good business letter. But there are whole college courses devoted to the subject, and the interested student should either enroll in such a course or consult one of the numerous special guidebooks available.

At its best, the efficient and graceful composition of a business letter is a genuine art. Much more flexibility is required than is generally understood. There are times when a letter must speak very formally, as if in the abstract voice of its letterhead, a large and impersonal corporation. There are other times when warmth and genial good fellowship are appropriate. The executive who can say no

551

without hurting a reader's feelings is a valuable person to the company. But these skills, however interesting and important, are beyond the range of this handbook.

The Complimentary Close

Correct forms for the complimentary close of business letters are as follows:

```
Yours truly,              Faithfully yours,
Yours very truly,         Sincerely yours,
Very truly yours,         Yours sincerely,
Respectfully yours,       Cordially yours,
```

It is now considered bad taste to use a participial phrase in closing a letter, such as *Hoping you are well.* A comma is the usual punctuation after the complimentary close; only the first letter is capitalized. In ordinary formal business letters, *Yours truly* or *Yours very truly* is the accepted form. In business letters between persons who know each other well, *Yours sincerely* and *Cordially yours* are used, or even, more informally, *Sincerely* and simply *Yours.*

The Signature

For the ordinary person it is correct to sign a business letter as he or she would sign a check. If possible, you should write your name legibly. But just to make sure, it is desirable to type the name under the signature.

Some of the conventions that govern the form of a signature are the following:

1. Neither professional titles, such as *Professor, Dr., Rev.,* nor academic degrees, such as *Ph.D., LL.D., M.A.,* should be used with a signature.
2. An unmarried woman should not sign herself as Miss Laura Blank, but she may place *Miss* (or *Ms.*) in parentheses before her name if she feels that it is necessary for proper identification.
3. A married woman or a widow who elects to adopt her husband's last name signs her own name, not her married name. For example, *Diana Holoday Brown*

552

is her own name; *Mrs. George Brown* is her married name. She may place *Mrs.* in parentheses before her signature, or her married name in parentheses under it.

4. When a secretary signs her employer's name to a letter, she may add her own initials below the signature.

The following is an example of a business letter, of the type that might be written to a business organization from a private individual:

37 North Cove Road
Los Gatos, California 95030
June 18, 1980

Acme Camera Shop
876 Fifth Street
Palo Alto, California 94302

Gentlemen:

I am returning to you a lens which you sent me, on my order, on June 16. The lens is a 35-mm F 2.5 (wide angle) P. Angenieux Retrofocus, with a bayonet mount to fit the Exacta camera. The number of the lens is 463513.

You will notice by holding the lens against a bright light that there is a distinct scratch on the front element. As the lens is guaranteed to be free from imperfections, I am returning it to you for a replacement.

Will you kindly send me a new lens as soon as you can? I must have it by June 25, as I am leaving then on a camera trip to Utah.

You have my check for $120, dated June 12, in payment.

Yours very truly,

Martin H. Hanson

Martin H. Hanson

LETTERS OF APPLICATION

One of the most difficult and probably most important letters that you will have to write is the letter of application for a job. Of course it is impossible to say what will appeal to every employer, but there are certain general guides.

In applying for work you usually have to fill out a printed application form. So will five hundred others applying for the same job. The letter you write will help you stand apart from the crowd.

A letter of application should be direct, sincere, and informative. It must not be vague; it must not grovel in undue modesty or boastfully promise what cannot be delivered. It should not include irrelevant personal information. Something is to be gained, as it often is in other types of writing, by putting yourself in the place of the person you are addressing. Suppose *you* were a busy personnel manager, shuffling through dozens of letters of application. What would attract you favorably? Obviously, long-windedness would not.

An effective letter of application contains the following components:

1. An introductory statement in which the writer indicates that he or she has heard of a possible vacancy.
2. Personal data.
3. Record of education.
4. Personal experience in the job area.
5. References.
6. Request for an interview.

Probably the most important section is the one in which you outline how your experience or education has a vital bearing on the job for which you are applying. This is difficult to write, but it can also be decisive.

37 Twenty-third Street
Corvallis, Oregon 97330
April 10, 1980

Mr. F. C. McVey
Personnel Officer
Department of Parks and Recreation
City of Portland, Oregon
Portland, Oregon 97208

Dear Mr. McVey:

Ms. Jane Ryan, one of the counsellors on your staff, has informed me that you will need several guides for your residence camps this summer. I wish to apply for a job as a camp guide.

554

I am twenty years old and in excellent health.

Two years ago, when I was eighteen, I graduated from Central High School, where I took the college preparatory course with emphasis on botany and geology. With this background, I am trained to point out many interesting natural phenomena to the children.

When I was in high school, I spent my weekends and vacations working for Bert's Camping Equipment, where I learned a great deal about the operation and maintenance of various types of outdoor equipment. Mr. Bert Jenkins will write you about my work there.

Since then I have worked at various jobs to earn money for my college education. I am now finishing my first year in the division of arts and sciences at Oregon State College. After graduation from high school I spent a year working for the Ochoco Ranch, near Knappa, Oregon, where I taught hiking and horesback riding to beginners. Then last summer I entered the Yosemite Mountainclimbing Club, an experience that taught me a good deal about organizing outings of various kinds. Here I also learned to conduct nature trips. I believe that my experience should qualify me for this job.

The following employers have given me permission to use their names as references:

Mr. H. D. Winslow
Ochoco Ranch
Knappa, Oregon 97601

Mr. Karl Swensen
Yosemite Mountainclimbing Club
Yosemite National Park, California 95389

I would appreciate the opportunity to come to your office for an interview at any time that you designate. My telephone number is 749/753-5948.

Yours very truly,

Jane Williamson

Jane Williamson

Sometimes a shorter letter of application, though for a more permanent position, may be used as a supplement to other records—college grades, statements of recommendation—that are forwarded to an employer by a placement service. Here is an example of such a letter, in which it is wise not to repeat much of the information that the employer already possesses in the official dossier.

555

1401 Ridge Avenue
Columbus, Ohio 43215
May 10, 1980

Dr. Leroy Faust
Superintendent of Schools
Shaker Heights, Ohio 44120

   I understand from our local placement office that a position as third grade teacher is open for next fall in your school system. I believe I am qualified for that position. My record of training at the University School of Ohio State University is being forwarded to you, and as you will see, I maintained a "B" average at the University and completed all necessary requirements in teacher training. I hold a temporary teacher's certificate for the state of Ohio. This letter is meant to convey, in addition, my great enthusiasm for teaching and my personal interest in becoming a part of your system.

   Though I have done no classroom teaching beyond that provided by my university courses, I believe my devotion to young people may in part compensate for inexperience. My enthusiasm for teaching those younger than I began early in my life, and was increased by my years as a leader in Boy Scout work. Summer jobs as a camp counselor, involving instruction in outdoor activities for young children, improved my confidence in handling the eight-to-ten age group. Considerable testimony from parents and from the children themselves convinced me that I have been successful in reaching these young people.

   Naturally I am eager to become a part of a school system so well thought of as yours at Shaker Heights. I am available on short notice for interview, at your convenience.

                Sincerely yours,

                James A. Clark

                James A. Clark

SOME FAMILIAR FAULTS TO AVOID

   Do not omit pronouns, prepositions, and articles where they are grammatically necessary. If your letter should begin with *I* or *we,* begin with *I* or *we.*

OLD FASHIONED

Received your letter yesterday.

Am writing to you in reply. . . .

Have not heard from you. . . .

556

BETTER

I received your letter yesterday.

I am writing to you. . . .

I have not heard from you. . . .

Do not close a letter with a sentence or a phrase introduced by a participle.

INDIRECT

Hoping to hear from you soon. . . .

Hoping for an early answer. . . .

Thanking you again for your past favors. . . .

Trusting to hear from you by return mail. . . .

Do not write *yours, your favor,* or *your esteemed favor* for *letter.*

AFFECTED

In reply to yours of the 20th. . . .

Your esteemed favor at hand, and in reply. . . .

And avoid certain other trite and stilted expressions frequently used in business letters.

In reply would say. . . .

Yours of the 10th inst. received. . . .

And contents thereof noted. . . .

Your valued favor. . . .

And oblige, Yours truly. . . .

Enclosed please find. . . .

PUBLIC LETTERS

We have spoken of letters as, usually, private communications from one individual to another. The exception is the public letter in which the writer, while ostensibly addressing a single person, is in fact addressing a larger audi-

557

ence. An obvious example is the letter to the editor, in which the greeting *Dear Sir* might more accurately read *Dear Everybody* or *Dear World.* Many business letters, without being directed to the world, are intended for more than one reader—a committee, a sales force, a staff of officers. Modern duplicating methods are so cheap and efficient that any member of an organization may expect to find his semipublic report to a superior photocopied and spread all over the office. When this happens, of course, his errors of expression, his misspellings, and his vague logic are photocopied too.

The composition of a public, or semipublic, letter requires a special kind of skill. When addressing a group of individuals—a committee, for example—one must often be aware of the likes and dislikes of particular individuals among one's readers. Sometimes these likes and dislikes conflict. How can one persuade some of one's readers without offending others? What modified expression of one's own view might win a majority approval, or at least acquiescence? Astute corporate and bureaucratic officials often report that every word they write is chosen for its suitability to a variety of possible responses from readers whose prejudices may be, or are known to be, in conflict. If there is any excuse for the astounding circumlocutions of *officialese* (see §24g. in the "Handbook"), it is the need to perform verbal high-wire acts to the detriment of precise, vigorous prose.

EXERCISES

EXERCISE 1, A LETTER OFFERING SUGGESTIONS. *Write a letter to the principal of your high school in which you suggest two or three specific ways students might be better prepared for your particular college.*

EXERCISE 2, A LETTER OF CORRECTION. *Write a letter to your college newspaper in which you correct a wrong impression produced by a news story that has just appeared in the paper. Make your letter courteous, dignified, and logical.*

EXERCISE 3, A LETTER REQUESTING A SPECIAL PRIVILEGE. *Write a letter to your dean or instructor in which you request permission to take your final examinations several days before the scheduled period. Give your reason clearly and convincingly.*

EXERCISE 4, A LETTER URGING ACTION. *As secretary of a student organization, write a letter to the members urging them to pay their dues.*

EXERCISE 5, A LETTER OF PROTEST. *As a member of the same organization, write a letter to its secretary protesting his undue anxiety about the members' dues.*

EXERCISE 6, A LETTER OF APPLICATION. *You plan to work at one of the national parks during the summer. Write a letter of application. Apply for some position that you could fill. Give adequate information about yourself and your qualifications.*

EXERCISE 7, A LETTER TO A CONGRESSMAN. *Write to your congressman requesting an interview with him when you visit Washington in a month's time.*

EXERCISE 8, A LETTER REQUESTING PAYMENT. *A man for whom you worked last summer owes you thirty dollars. Write him a letter that will induce him to pay you what he owes you.*

EXERCISE 9, A LETTER TO THE EDITOR. *Write to your local newspaper complaining about the ear-splitting noise made by motorcycles zooming past your house late at night. Use humor to address the problem and in such a way as to make even motorcyclists want to support you.*

THE RÉSUMÉ

Anyone applying for a job should know how to compose an effective résumé or detailing of information sought by an employer. Although the format for such listings may vary, most résumés contain personal data, education and work experience, and names and addresses of references.

559

This formal introduction to a prospective employer works best if short and readable. It is probably wise therefore to boil down your experience to essentials that can be listed on a single typed page.

Form

The following order is suggested for listing information on the résumé.

1. *Personal data.* Name, address, and telephone number. Details about age, health, and marital status may also be added here.
2. *Education.* Use a separate heading as shown in the sample below. Starting with the most recent degree, list your educational experience back through high school. Information about scholastic honors should be included here.
3. *Experience.* Begin with the most recent jobs and work backward. Try to include details about the nature of your work, in addition to any title given the job. Even if you were unemployed for a period of time, be sure to cite that interlude.
4. *References.* Give the names, addresses, and telephone numbers of at least three people who have agreed to write strong supporting letters. College instructors and professors are usually willing to write such letters, but do not forget the names of people who have supervised you in job situations. Whenever possible, let these references know the kind of position for which you are applying.

The following is a sample résumé that might be used as a model.

```
Paul E. Green, Jr.
730 West Garden Street
Kansas City,
Missouri 64112
Telephone: 816/555-8766

Age: 22
Marital Status: Mar-
  ried, no children
Health: Excellent
```

THE RÉSUMÉ

Education
Sept. 1979–May 1981	University of Missouri-Kansas City Will receive B.A. in English, May 1981
Sept. 1977–May 1979	Penn Valley Community College, Kansas City A.A., May 1979
Sept. 1973–June 1977	Center High School, Kansas City Graduated with distinction
Honors	Barbara Storck Poetry Award University of Missouri-Kansas City, May 1979 Paul A. Samith Scholarship Award University of Missouri-Kansas City, Sept. 1980

Experience
Sept. 1979–present	The U-News, University of Missouri-KC Write sports and movie reviews
May–Sept. 1979	Pizza O Restaurant, Kansas City Full-time waiter and cashier
May–Sept. 1978/ May–Sept. 1977	Radio Station WDAF, Kansas City Full-time mail clerk; some work in radio sales

References

Mr. Paul Taylor, Manager Pizza O Restaurant 5422 Small Ave. Kansas City Mo 64110 Telephone: 816/555-2092	Dr. Charles Ruggles Professor of English University of Missouri-Kansas City Mo. 64110 Telephone: 816/555-4000

Mr. Tony Smith
Business Manager
WDAF Radio
1800 Signal Hill St.
Kansas City MO 64122
Telephone: 816/555-8800

Index

569

573

575